MEDICAL AND PSYCHOSOCIAL ASPECTS OF CHRONIC ILLNESS AND DISABILITY

Donna R. Falvo, RN, PhD

Professor
Rehabilitation Institute and
School of Medicine
Former Director of Behavioral Science
Southern Illinois University at Carbondale
Carbondale, Illinois

AN ASPEN PUBLICATION®
Aspen Publishers, Inc.
Gaithersburg, Maryland
1991

Library of Congress Cataloging-in-Publication Data

Falvo, Donna R.
Medical and psychosocial aspects of chronic illness and disability /
Donna R. Falvo.
p. cm.
Includes bibliographical references and index.
ISBN: 0-8342-0238-7
1. Chronic diseases—Patients—Rehabilitation. 2. Chronic diseases—Social
aspects. 3. Chronic diseases—Psychological aspects. I. Title.
[DNLM: 1. Chronic diseases. 2. Chronic Diseases.
3. Handicapped. WT 500 F197m]
RC108.F35 1991
616—dc20
DNLM/DLC
for Library of Congress
91-13953
CIP

The authors have made every effort to ensure the accuracy of the information herein,
particularly with regard to drug selection and dose. However, appropriate information
sources should be consulted, especially for new or unfamiliar drugs or procedures.
It is the responsibility of every practitioner to evaluate the appropriateness of a
particular opinion in the context of actual clinical situations and with due consideration to new developments. Authors, editors, and the publisher cannot be held
responsible for any typographical or other errors found in this book.

Editorial Services: Ruth Bloom

Library of Congress Catalog Card Number: 91-13953
ISBN: 0-8342-0238-7

Printed in the United States of America

2 3 4 5

To Richard
without whose love and support
this book would not have been possible

To Michael
whose understanding and patience
have been greatly appreciated

To Harry, Christina, Ernest, and Armida
whose own experiences served
as an inspiration for this book

Table of Contents

Foreword

Disability impacts an individual's functioning in all aspects of life. In the decade of the 1990s, with the passage of the Americans with Disabilities Act and other relevant legislative initiatives, persons with disabilities will be integrating into community services in increasing numbers. In order to successfully work with persons with disabilities, it is essential that all nonmedical practitioners understand the medical and psychosocial aspects of chronic illness and disability.

The goal of rehabilitation is to assist persons with disabilities to achieve functional independence and effective adjustment. The rehabilitation concept is based on the fundamental concept of the dignity and worth of each person. Rehabilitation represents the philosophy that, whenever possible, persons with a disability are to be integrated into the least restrictive environment. Thus, rehabilitation is a comprehensive individualized process, prescriptive in nature and directed toward the development or restoration of functional independence. Regardless of the setting and specific clientele, the nonmedical practitioner must be able to work with the whole person from a multifaceted and integrated service standpoint.

As a person who has taught medical and psychosocial aspects of disabilities for the past twelve years, I am familiar with the range of textbooks and other literature in the area of medical and psychosocial aspects of disability. This book is the first nonedited, comprehensive, integrative text that has been written for the nonmedical rehabilitation practitioner. Dr. Falvo's experiences as a practitioner and educator provide her with a unique perspective from which to write this book. I believe this text will provide an essential reference for education programs, for service delivery agencies, and ultimately, for the nonmedical practitioner who is responsible for providing for the rehabilitation needs of persons with disabilities.

Medical diagnosis and treatment of disability is the entry point to rehabilitation services. From a rehabilitation perspective, it is the individual's residual capacities, functional limitations, and transferable skills that operationalize the impact of disability for persons with disabilities when adapting to their various and unique environments. For the nonmedical practitioner responsible for the translation of medical aspects to the behavioral and social aspects of chronic illness and disability, language and terminology are essential. First, it is the fundamental component of transdisciplinary communication. From this base, the translation of medical aspects to the individual's psychological, social, and vocational functioning provides the basis for service planning and delivery. This text presents the language and terminology necessary for the nonmedical practitioner to understand and effectively translate essential medical and psychosocial aspects of chronic illness and disability into the functional domains of living.

Essential psychosocial and functional aspects of disability provide a conceptual beginning for this text, which subsequently considers each of the major body systems in a framework from normal structure and function, to major disorders, diagnostic procedures, treatment, and completes the analysis with functional implications. This continuity of structure provides comprehensive coverage of the major chronic illnesses and disabling conditions encountered in contemporary rehabilitation practice. Each chapter is presented in clear, concise terms highlighting fundamental medical terminology. In clearly understandable language, the focus of each chapter, and subsequently the entire text, is on the essential medical, psychosocial, and functional aspects of disability necessary to the work of the practitioner. Through blending medical information with the implications for all aspects of the individual's life, this text demands that the reader never lose sight of the uniqueness and wholeness of each individual.

Medical and Psychosocial Aspects of Chronic Illness and Disability provides essential knowledge of disabling conditions and their functional aspects that will permit the reader to go beyond general knowledge and efficiently work at the individual's level in the development of comprehensive, individualized rehabilitation services. This text provides an excellent resource for the nonmedical professional as well as others in understanding the medical and psychosocial aspects of chronic illness and disability.

Dennis R. Maki, PhD
Coordinator, Rehabilitation Counselor
Education Program
The University of Iowa
Iowa City, Iowa

Preface

The consequences of chronic illness and disability are varied and far reaching. In addition to impacting on physical function and activities of daily living, chronic illness and disability can affect psychological, social, and vocational functioning as well. A major goal of rehabilitation is to assist individuals to return to their optimal level of function and independence. In order to achieve this goal, professionals working with individuals with chronic illness and disability must have knowledge not only of the medical aspects of the condition, but also how symptoms, treatments, or residuals from the condition affect the individual psychologically, socially, and vocationally.

Rehabilitation is a multidisciplinary effort, requiring the expertise of a number of medical as well as nonmedical professionals. *Medical and Psychosocial Aspects of Chronic Illness and Disability* is directed toward those professionals who have little or no formal medical training, but who are involved in the counseling, care, and rehabilitation of persons with chronic illness or disability. The book is written for rehabilitation counselors, vocational evaluators, and other nonmedical professionals, as well as university students who are in training. It provides basic descriptions of common chronic illnesses and disabilities including physical manifestations, common diagnostic tests, and associated treatments. The book avoids highly technical terms, attempting to acquaint the reader with concepts and medical terminology without cumbersome medical jargon. In addition to basic medical information, the book specifically addresses the functional impact of medical conditions on psychological, social, life style, and vocational aspects of daily life.

The introductory chapter of the book presents a brief overview of psychosocial aspects of disability. In addition to emotional reactions to illness and disability, coping strategies, stages of adaptation, and life cycle and family issues, the chapter also presents a foundation for viewing the impact of chronic illness and disability on functional aspects of individuals' lives.

Each of the following chapters is organized around a specific body system, giving a brief description of common medical conditions, common diagnostic procedures and treatments, and ending with a discussion of the potential functional impact of the medical condition psychologically, socially, and vocationally, as well as on general life style.

The necessity of looking beyond the medical condition and taking a more complete view of how chronic illness or disability affects the individuals' functioning within their environment is crucial to the rehabilitation process. This book strives to help nonmedical professionals increase their understanding of medical aspects of chronic illness and disability so that the information can be utilized to assist individuals to attain maximum function and independence.

Donna R. Falvo

Acknowledgments

Special thanks to the following people who have generously volunteered their time to read various segments of the book and offer their comments, suggestions, and critique.

Reviewers

Southern Illinois University School of Medicine
Chandra Banerjee, MD, PhD, Professor
Peggy Brown, MD, Clinical Associate Professor
Donald Darling, MD, Clinical Associate Professor
Kevin Dorsey, MD, Clinical Associate Professor
Martha Ellert, PhD, Associate Professor
Richard Falvo, PhD, Professor
Bert Fasnacht, MD, Clinical Associate Professor
Robert Holmes, MD, Adjunct Instructor
Robert Lehr, PhD, Professor
Stacey Leithliter, RN, BS
Brian McElheny, MD, Clinical Assistant Professor
Parvis Sanjabi, MD, Clinical Associate Professor
Sandra Shea, PhD, Assistant Professor
David Spencer, MD, Professor
Lelan Stallings, MD, Clinical Assistant Professor
Kathy Swafford, MD, Clinical Associate Professor
Penny Tippy, MD, Associate Professor
David Wade, PhD, Associate Professor

Southern Illinois University Rehabilitation Institute
Gary Austin, PhD, Professor
Richard Beck, PhD, Assistant Professor

Bill Crimando, PhD, Professor
Stanford Rubin, PhD, Professor
Brockman Schumacher, PhD, Professor
Patrick Taricone, PhD, Assistant Professor

Southern Illinois University Department of Communication Disorders and Sciences
Martin Schultz, PhD, Professor

Illinois Division of Rehabilitation Services
Beverly Harnett, MS, CRC
Cathy Overturf, MS, CRC

University of Louisville School of Nursing
Beverley Holland, RN, MSN, RhD, Assistant Professor

Case Western Reserve School of Medicine
Robert Kelly, MD, Associate Professor

Northern Illinois University College of Professional Studies
Jim Lankford, PhD, Professor

Cape Girardeau Prosthetic Lab, Cape Girardeau, MO
Lee Cobb, Certified Prosthetist
Pat Cobb

Biomedical Application Dialysis Center, Carbondale, IL
Beverly Danhof, MSW, and Dialysis Center Staff

University of South Carolina Department of Educational Psychology
Robert Chubon, PhD

Central Missouri State University
Brian McClerran, PhD, Assistant Professor

Others
Frank Bleyer, MD, Internal Medicine, Carbondale, Illinois
Michael Altoff, PhD, Psychologist, Carbondale, Illinois
Randy Allnatt, MS, Doctoral Student, Rehabilitation Institute, Southern
   Illinois University
Jerry Brenner, MS, Doctoral Student, Rehabilitation Institute, Southern
   Illinois University

Paul Hanson, BS, Master's Student, Rehabilitation Institute, Southern
   Illinois University
Rehabilitation students enrolled in the class "Medical and Psychosocial
   Aspects of Disability," Rehabilitation Institute, Southern Illinois University

Illustrations
   Michael Falvo
   Karen Fioriono

Thanks is also offered to the Research Photography and Illustration Facility at
Southern Illinois University for its excellent technical support.

Clerical Support

Thanks and appreciation are also offered to Linda Patrick and the staff of the
Southern Illinois University College of Education Operational Support Center
for their excellent work. The patience, efficiency, and professionalism of the
staff contributed greatly to this book's development.

chapter 1

Psychosocial and Functional Aspects of Chronic Illness and Disability

Chronic illness and disability have a major impact on the psychological, familial, social, and vocational aspects of the lives of the individuals who are experiencing them. Although several factors influence the extent of the impact, every chronic illness or disability requires some alteration and adjustment in daily life. The type of impact is dependent on the nature of the condition, the individual's pre–illness/disability personality, the meaning of the illness or disability to the individual, the current life circumstances of the individual, and the degree of family and social support within the individual's environment.

A medical condition must be considered in the context of the effect of its diagnosis, symptoms, and treatment on all aspects of the individual's life, specifically on the individual's capacity to function within his or her environment. Functional capacity goes beyond specific tasks and activities. It also includes significant events and relationships in the individual's life, such as relationships with family, friends, employers, and casual acquaintances. No relationship exists in isolation. Just as the individual's reaction to the illness or disability influences the reaction of others, the reactions of others affect the individual's self-concept and perception of his or her own strengths and abilities.

Participation in family, social, and work activities assumes interaction and the capacity to perform a variety of activities. As interactions or capacities change, or as they become limited or restricted, alterations in roles and relationships also occur. Although some changes and adjustments may be made with relative ease, other changes can have repercussions in a variety of areas of daily life. The meaning and importance that the individual and family attribute to these changes can affect the individual's ability to accept the condition and to make necessary adjustments. These factors, together with the medical condition itself, determine ability to function effectively.

STRESS IN CHRONIC ILLNESS AND DISABILITY

Change is an unavoidable part of life. Change of job, change of home, change of family composition, or changes brought about through the normal aging process are all events that everyone experiences. Depending on the perception of the individual involved, change may be positive or negative; in either instance, however, change requires some adjustment or adaptation that produces a certain degree of stress. This stress is less pronounced when individuals are able to maintain confidence in their ability to maintain some control over their destiny and believe that changes, although inevitable, are manageable.

Chronic illness or disability requires a number of changes that cause stress by potentially threatening the individual's accustomed role and level of functioning. Potential threats include

- threats to life and physical well-being
- threats to body integrity and comfort as a result of the illness or disability itself, diagnostic procedures, or treatment
- threats to independence, privacy, autonomy, and control
- threats to self-concept and fulfillment of customary roles
- threat to life goals and future plans
- threats to relationships with family, friends, and colleagues
- threats to the ability to remain in familiar surroundings
- threats to economic well-being

An individual's response to the stresses imposed by these threats depends on the perception of the impact of illness or disability on various areas of life, as well as on the individual's capacity to cope. Stress cannot be easily quantified. Individuals in the same situation do not necessarily experience the same degree of stress, nor is the amount of change or adjustment required necessarily an indicator of the amount of stress perceived.

Quality of Life

Perceptions of the same condition and its impact vary from individual to individual. People with similar conditions, symptoms, and limitations may respond in totally different manners. The perception of illness or disability depends partly on the condition's perceived impact on the quality of life. Quality of life is subjective in nature with no universal meaning. Although it may be viewed in general as optimal functioning at the highest level of independence, only the individual can determine the personal meaning of the quality of life. Individual value systems, cultural backgrounds, spiritual perspectives, and the attitudes and reactions of those within the environment influence the interpretation of the quality of life. Assessment of the impact of chronic disease or disability on the overall quality of life often determines daily choices and day-to-day management of the condition itself. Some individuals assess the impact of their condition on their quality of life in terms of the degree to which they feel control over their life circumstances or destiny. Accurate knowledge about their condition and treatment, together with active participation in decision making about the management of the condition, can reduce associated stress by increasing their sense of control. As a result, perception of quality of life may also be enhanced.

Self-Concept and Body Image

Defined as an individual's perceptions and beliefs about his or her own strengths and weaknesses, as well as others' perceptions of them, self-concept is tied to self-esteem and personal identity. An individual's self-concept also influences the perceptions of others. A negative **self-concept** can produce negative responses, just as a positive self-concept can increase the likelihood that others will react in a positive manner. Consequently, self-concept has a significant impact on interactions with others.

Body image, an important part of self-concept, involves an individual's perception of his or her own physical appearance and physical function. Body image changes throughout life with aging and is influenced by sensations, cultural and societal expectations, and by reactions of and experiences with others. Changes in appearance, capabilities, or functional status can contribute to an altered body image and, thus, to an altered self-concept. Illness or disability requires an alteration of self-view in order to accommodate the associated changes. The degree to which this alteration is perceived in a negative way can greatly influence interpersonal interactions as well as functional capacity.

Physical disfigurement or other visible body changes may cause significant alterations of body image, depending on the meaning of the changes to the individual. The degree of physical change or deformity is not always proportional to the reaction that it provokes. Change that one person considers minimal may be considered catastrophic by another. Moreover, changes do not always have to be readily observable in order to alter body image and self-concept. The type of reaction is determined to some degree by the importance placed on the change or the extent to which change affects the ability to participate in cherished activities. An important part of the adjustment process is the integration of associated changes into a restructured body image and self-concept that can be assimilated and incorporated into the activities of daily living.

Uncertainty

Some chronic illnesses and disabilities have an immediate and permanent impact on levels of functional capacity. In other instances the course of the illness or disability is more variable, with deterioration occurring slowly over the span of several years. In some cases the same condition may progress at different rates for different individuals. For some, the condition may progress rapidly while for others progression of the condition may be slow. Some conditions have periods of remission when symptoms become less noticeable or almost nonexistent only to be followed by periods of unpredictable exacerbations when symptoms become worse. At times it is difficult to determine the point at which, or if, severe disability will occur or whether a dramatic change of functional capacity will take place. Such uncertainty of prognosis or progression of the condition can make planning and prediction of the future difficult.

The unpredictability of the condition can be extremely frustrating for individuals as well as for those around them. There may be reluctance to plan for the future at all, so that the inability to predict the future becomes more disabling than the actual physical consequences of the condition itself. In other instances, given the unpredictability of their condition, individuals may elect to follow a different life course than they would have otherwise chosen. For those conditions in which symptoms or residual effects are unapparent to others, such decisions may be met with misunderstanding or criticism. Decisions not to have children, to cut down on the number of hours spent in the work environment, or to suddenly relocate to a different part of the country may be misinterpreted by those who are unaware of the individual's condition or its associated unpredictability. Criticisms of such decisions may be particularly distressing to individuals who do not wish to disclose or share intimate details of their condition with the casual observer. Insecurity about the course of the condition may also be reflected by the attitude of those closest to the individual who, in an attempt to protect themselves from potential future loss, withdraw emotional interactions or support.

Uncertainty of progression of a condition imposes particular challenges for individuals and their families and can be a source of stress. Viewing the importance of living in the present rather than dwelling on events that may or may not occur in the future can help to reduce stress and anxiety experienced as well as enhance the quality of life currently experienced.

Stigma

By creating a heightened awareness of the negative impact of prejudice and stereotypes, social change and public policy have helped to reduce the stigma that has been associated with chronic illness or disability. Fear of stigma, however, still exists for many individuals with chronic or disabling conditions.

Societal expectations define, by general standards, the appearance, activities, and roles that are acceptable. Individuals who deviate from expectations in any of these areas are labeled as different from the majority and, thus, may be stigmatized. The degree of stigma may vary from setting to setting, from disability to disability, and from person to person. Conditions that are particularly anxiety-provoking or threatening are likely to have more stigma attached.

Stigma often results in discrimination, social isolation, disregard, depreciation, devaluation, and, in some instances, even threats to safety and well-being. Factors such as gender and/or race can be additional sources of prejudice and subsequent stigma, causing additional stress and creating additional barriers to effective functioning.

Stigma can have a profound impact on the ability to regain and maintain functional capacity and on the acceptance of illness or disability. Not only can stigma affect self-concept and self-esteem, but also it can produce barriers that prohibit individuals from reaching their full potential. In an effort to avoid stigma associated with their condition, individuals may deny, minimize, or ignore the condition and/or treatment recommendations, even though such actions prove detrimental to their welfare.

Although efforts to reduce or obliterate stigma in society should continue, stigma is most likely to be overcome through individuals. It is possible to reduce the negative impact of societal stigma by helping individuals to establish a sense of their own intrinsic worth, despite the characteristics of their medical condition.

EMOTIONAL REACTIONS TO CHRONIC DISEASE OR DISABILITY

Sudden, unexpected, or life-threatening chronic illness or disability engenders a variety of reactions in the individuals affected. The emotional experiences of those encountering chronic illness or disability vary, but the following reactions are commonly experienced to some degree.

Grief

A normal reaction to loss is grief. Individuals with chronic illness and disability may also experience grief as a reaction to the loss of function, role, or position, or other perceived losses associated with the medical condition. Although the grieving process and the progression through the stages of grief may vary from individual to individual, a common initial reaction to chronic illness or disability is shock, disbelief, or numbness in which the diagnosis or its seriousness may be denied or disputed. As the reality of the situation becomes evident, individuals experience the pain of grief as they attempt to accept the loss that they have experienced. After repeated confrontations with elements of the loss, there is a gradual change in emphasis and focus that enables individuals to accept the loss emotionally and to make the adjustments and adaptations that are necessary to reestablish their place within the everyday world.

Fear and Anxiety

A threat normally causes anxiety. In the presence of chronic illness or disability, anxiety can stem from the threat of loss of function, loss of love, loss of independence, or loss of financial security. For some individuals, the fear of the unknown or the unpredictability of the condition provokes anxiety. For others, hospitalizations that immerse them in a strange and unfamiliar environment away from home, family, and the security of routine produce anxiety. In some conditions, fear and anxiety may be associated not only with loss of function, but also with loss of life. Fear and anxiety associated with chronic illness or disability can place individuals in a state of panic that renders them unable to act. Helping individuals regain a sense of control over their situation can be an important step in reducing anxiety and in facilitating the rehabilitative process.

Anger

Individuals with chronic illness or disability may experience anger at themselves or others for perceived injustices or loss associated with their condition. If they perceive themselves as victims, they may direct their anger toward the persons or circumstances that they blame for the condition or situation. If they believe that their own actions were partly to blame for the illness or disability, they may direct their anger inward.

Anger can also result from frustration with the situation. Individuals may vent frustration and anger by displacing hostility toward others who have no relationship to the development of the illness or disability and no influence over its outcome. Anger may also be an expression of the realization that the situation is serious and associated feelings of helplessness. At times, anger may be hidden in the struggle to stay in control through quarreling, arguing, complaining, or being excessively demanding.

Depression

With the realization of the reality, seriousness, and implications of the chronic illness or disability, individuals may experience feelings of depression, helplessness and hopelessness, apathy, and/or feelings of dejection and discouragement. Signs of depression include sleep disturbances, changes in appetite, difficulty concentrating, and withdrawal from activity. Not all individuals experience prolonged depression with chronic illness and disability; the extent of depression varies from individual to individual. When depression is unresolved, however, it can result in self-destructive behaviors, such as substance abuse or attempted suicide.

Guilt

Even if no one's actions contributed in any way to the illness or disability, the need to blame may be compelling in the individuals with the condition or in those around them. They may view the illness or disability as punishment for previous transgressions. Guilt may also be experienced if the individual or others believe that the illness or disability results from real or perceived negligence or that avoidable circumstances contributed to or caused the condition.

Guilt may be expressed or unexpressed and can occur in varying dimensions. It can be an obstacle to the successful adjustment to the condition and limitations. Self-blame or blame ascribed by others is detrimental not only to the individual's self-concept, but to rehabilitative efforts as a whole.

COPING STRATEGIES

Individuals attempt to survive emotionally after a perceived catastrophic and overwhelmingly stressful event as best they can. Survival behavior is manifest in a number of coping mechanisms that help individuals deal with stress so that they can begin to make necessary adjustments and preserve their psychological integrity.

Coping is a constellation of many acts rather than a single act and is constantly changing. Coping mechanisms are learned and developed over time. Individuals use them to manage, tolerate, or reduce the stress associated with significant life events. Everyone has a variety of such mechanisms developed through life experiences, although each individual has a predominant coping style to reduce anxiety and to restore equilibrium when confronted with a stressful situation. The behavior is effective and adaptive when it helps individuals reduce stress and enhances the attainment of their fullest potential, despite their limitations. It is ineffective and maladaptive, however, if it inhibits growth and potential or contributes to physical or mental deterioration.

Chronic illness and disability produce significant stress and are often associated with both physical imbalance and psychological turmoil as individuals must deal with a change of customary life style; loss of control; disruption of physiological processes; pain or discomfort; and potential loss of role, status, independence, and financial stability. Coping may be required not only for dealing with the initial diagnosis, but also for subsequent events. If the condition is slowly progressive or necessitates ongoing treatment and/or changes that must be incorporated into daily life, continued, long-term coping strategies may be essential.

Individuals cope with illness and disability in different ways. Some may actively confront the condition by learning new skills or by engaging in treatment to control or manage the condition. Others may defend themselves from the stress and realities of the diagnosis by denying its seriousness, ignoring treatment recommendations, or refusing to learn new skills or behaviors associated with the condition. Still others may cope by engaging in self-destructive behavior, actively continuing behavior that has detrimental effects on their physical condition. Effective coping must be viewed in the context of each individual's personal background and experiences, life situation, and perception of the circumstance. Individuals tend to use coping strategies that have worked successfully for them in the past. When old strategies are no longer effective or are not appropriate to the new situation, new coping strategies must be implemented to neutralize events surrounding the chronic illness or disability and to adjust to any associated limitations. Effective coping enables individuals to attain emotional equilibrium, to achieve a positive mental outlook, and to avoid incapacitation from fear, anxiety, anger, or depression.

Coping, however, does not occur in a vacuum. The social milieu in which individuals find themselves can facilitate or discourage effective coping. In general, an environment that helps individuals gain a sense of control through active participation in decision making and in responsibility for their own destiny as much as possible best equips them to cope effectively with chronic illness and disability.

Denial

The implications of chronic illness or disability can be devastating. Denial is a coping mechanism that individuals use to negate the reality of a situation. One of the most common reactions to illness or chronic disability is the nonacceptance of the condition and its implications. In the early stages of adjustment, denial may be beneficial; it allows individuals to adjust to the painful reality at their own pace, thus preventing excessive anxiety. If denial continues, however, it can prevent these individuals from following health care advice or from learning new skills that would be helpful in the rehabilitative process.

Denial of the condition can have far-reaching effects on others if such denial imperils the welfare or safety of others. For example, the spread of contagious diseases, such as tuberculosis or acquired immunodeficiency syndrome (AIDS), can be greatly reduced with proper precautions. An individual in active denial may neglect to take proper precautions, putting others in jeopardy. Individuals who have been prohibited from driving because of their medical condition, but who continue to do so because they do not recognize their limitations, also put others at risk.

Avoidance

Although often confused with denial, avoidance differs in that the individual accepts the situation and the associated implications as real, but, because of the anxiety that this realization produces, actively attempts to ignore the ramifications. As a result, he or she may not seek appropriate medical care, thus reducing the chance of effective interventions, or may fail to follow recommended treatment.

Regression

Individuals may react to illness or disability by becoming more dependent, behaving more passively, and exhibiting more emotionality than may normally be expected at their developmental level. Returning to a state of dependency that was experienced in an earlier stage of development can be therapeutic in the early stages of illness or disability if the treatment of the condition requires rest and inactivity. Continued regression, however, can interfere with the adjustment and the attainment of a level of independence that allows the individual to reach maximum functional capacity.

Compensation

Some individuals learn to counteract limitations in one area by becoming stronger or more proficient in other areas. When function is lost in one area individuals may find ways to excel in another. Compensatory behavior is generally highly constructive when new behaviors are directed toward positive goals and outcomes. It can be detrimental, however, when the new behaviors used in compensating for limitations are self-destructive or socially unacceptable.

Rationalization

As a coping mechanism, rationalization enables individuals to excuse themselves for not reaching goals or not accomplishing tasks. Although this coping mechanism can soften the disappointment of dreams unrealized, it can also produce negative effects if it becomes a barrier to adjustment or effective management of the medical condition itself.

Diversion of Feelings

One of the most positive and constructive of all coping styles can be the diversion of unacceptable feelings or ideas into socially acceptable behaviors. Individuals with chronic illness or disability may have particularly strong feelings of anger or hostility about their diagnosis or the circumstances surrounding their condition. If their emotional energy can be redefined and diverted into positive activity, the result can be quite beneficial, making virtue out of necessity, and transforming deficit into gain.

STAGES OF ADAPTATION AND ADJUSTMENT

The adjustment process includes a search for meaning in the experience and an attempt to regain control and self-determination over events that affect one's life. Most individuals with chronic illness and disability experience some loss, either a direct physical loss or a more indirect loss of the ability to participate in some previously performed activity. Regardless of the nature of the loss, a variety of reactions may take place while individuals attempt to make the necessary adaptations and changes.

The stages of adjustment are individual and varied. The shock of diagnosis and its consequent implications may have a numbing effect, so there may be little emotional reaction initially. As the reality of the situation becomes clear, some individuals may experience a sense of hopelessness and despair, mourning for a self, a role, or a function that is lost. Feelings of anger may alternate with depression. Many individuals go through a period of mourning and bereavement similar to that experienced when a loved one is lost. Mourning is a natural reaction to loss and allows time for reflection and reestablishment of emotional equilibrium.

As individuals begin to appraise their condition realistically, examine the limitations that it imposes, and adjust to the associated losses, they may gradually seek alternatives and adaptations to achieve their integration into a broader world. The ultimate outcome of adjustment is an acceptance of the condition and its associated limitations, along with a realistic appraisal and implementation of strengths. As individuals accept their condition, they attain their maximal functional capacity. The amount of time that an individual needs to reach acceptance is dependent on personality, reaction of family and significant others, life circumstances, available resources, and the types of challenges that confront the individual.

Some individuals never reach acceptance. Maladjustment and nonacceptance are characterized by immobility, marked dependency, continued anger and hostility, prolonged mourning, or participation in detrimental or self-destructive activities. Just as coping mechanisms are a vital part of human nature, serving to protect against stress, reduce anxiety, and facilitate the adjustment process, overuse or maladaptive use of coping mechanisms can postpone or inhibit adjustment.

CHRONIC ILLNESS AND DISABILITY THROUGHOUT THE LIFE CYCLE

Reactions to chronic illness or disability may differ among individuals in different stages of development. Each stage of life has its own particular stresses or demands, apart from those experienced as a result of illness or disability. For example, the needs, responsibilities, and resources of adults differ from those of children. Illness and disability can create barriers to the activities considered normal at a certain life stage and can impede the development of certain qualities and life skills associated with a particular stage of life.

Development is not static or finite. It is a continual process from infancy to old age and death. Each stage of life is associated with certain age-appropriate behaviors and skills. Family members and others generally adjust their behavior to accommodate and to interact appropriately with individuals as they pass from one life stage to the next. When an individual becomes ill or disabled, however, others may modify their expectations of the individual's age-appropriate behavior, and these modified expectations may interfere with the individual's mastery of the normal skills required to meet the challenges of future stages of life.

All aspects of development are related. Each life stage must be understood within the context of the individual's past and current experience. Each individual with an illness or disability must be considered in the context of his or her particular point in life and the way in which the changes and limitations associated with the medical condition influence attitudes, perceptions, actions, and behaviors characteristic of the individual's life stage. The stage of life serves not only as a guideline in assessing the individual's functional capacity, but also as a guideline to determine potential stressors and reactions.

Individuals with an illness or disability and those without such conditions have similar age-related problems and stresses as they progress from one life stage to the other. Ideally, those with an illness or disability should be encouraged to progress through each stage of development as normally as possible, despite the illness or disability. Individuals whose emotional, social, educational, or occupational development has been thwarted may be more handicapped by their inability to cope with the subsequent challenges of life than by any limitations experienced because of illness or disability per se.

Although there are no clear lines of demarcation between life stages and all individuals develop at different rates, there are some commonalities associated with different life stages.

Infancy and Early Childhood

In early life, children develop a sense of trust in others, a sense of autonomy, and an awareness and mastery of their environment. During these years, they begin to learn the communication skills and social skills that enable them to interact effectively with others. They also learn that limits are set on their explorations, expressions of autonomy, and behaviors. Important to their development is a balance between encouraging initiative and setting limits consistently.

Illness or disability can impede attainment of the normal developmental goals characteristic of this life stage. Repeated or prolonged hospitalizations may deprive the child of nurturing by a consistent and loving caregiver. The physical limitations of the condition or treatment may prevent normal activities, socialization, and exploration of the environment. In some cases, overly protective family members may restrict the child's activities or prohibit the child from displaying normal emotional expression. In other instances, overly sympathetic parents may condone inappropriate behaviors rather than correct them. Conditions that affect the development of communication skills may also affect the child's interaction with the environment, as well as future development.

Those conditions that are present at birth or occur in childhood require adjustments throughout the individual's development. Limitations imposed by the condition must be confronted and compensated for with every new aspect of the normal developmental process. The professional's and parents' awareness of a child's normal developmental needs and the facilitation of experiences that foster normal development can greatly enhance the child's ability to reach his or her full potential.

The School-Aged Child

For most children, entering school expands their world beyond the scope of their family. Before children attend school, the values, rules, and expectations that they experience are, for the most part, largely those expressed within the family. As they enter school, however, they are exposed to a larger social environment. Not only do they learn social relationships and cooperative interactions, but also, at the same time, they begin to develop a sense of initiative and industry. Children gradually become aware of their special strengths. As new skills begin to develop, school-aged children gain the capacity for sustained effort that eventually results in their ability to follow through with tasks to their completion. The approval and encouragement of others and the acceptance of their peers help children to build self-confidence, further enhancing development.

When the physical or cognitive limitations imposed by chronic illness or disability result in a school-aged child's loss or deficiency of skills normally valued at this stage, peers may not accept the child. The need for repeated absences or the inability to interact on a consistent basis within the peer group may also diminish social interactions with peers. In an attempt to shield the child from hurt and emotional pain, family members may further isolate the child from social interactions, creating the potential for reduced self-confidence. The reluctance of sympathetic family members to allow the child to participate in activities in which there may be failure may interfere with the child's ability to evaluate accurately his or her potential. The encouragement of social interactions and activities to the degree possible allows the child the opportunity to develop the skills and abilities that are needed for later integration into the larger world.

Adolescence

The perceptions of and interactions with peers become increasingly important as adolescents further define their identity apart from membership in their family. With the need to establish independence, adolescents begin to emancipate themselves from their parents and may rebel against the authority of parents or others. The physical maturation of adolescence may bring about a strong preoccupation with body and appearance, and the adolescent's identity as a person attractive to others often becomes paramount. The awareness of and experimentation with sexual feelings present a new dimension with which the adolescent must learn to cope.

Illness or disability during adolescence can disrupt relationships with peers. Limitations imposed by the condition, its treatment, or the sympathetic and protective reactions by family members may become barriers to the adolescent's attainment of independence and individual identity. Any alteration in physical appearance caused by the condition can influence the adolescent's perception of body image and self-concept, thwarting the expression of sexual feelings. In some instances, the characteristics of normal adolescent development, such as rebellion against authority or the need to be accepted by a peer group, can inter-fere with the treatment necessitated by the illness or disability, thus having further detrimental effects on physical and functional capacity.

Young Adulthood

During their young adulthood, individuals establish themselves as productive members of society, integrating vocational goals, developing the capacity for intimate relationships, and accepting social responsibility. The limitations imposed by an illness or disability, rather than the interests or abilities of the individuals themselves, may define vocational and occupational goals, however. Physical limitations may also inhibit individuals' efforts to build intimate rela-tionships or to maintain such relationships that they have already established. In this age group, established relationships are likely to be recent, and the level of commitment and willingness to make necessary sacrifices may be variable. Procreation may be difficult or impossible, or, if the individual already has young children, child care issues may be the source of additional concerns in light of the functional limitations inherent in the individual's illness or disability. For young adults who had not yet fully gained independence or left their family of origin by the onset of the illness or disability, gaining independence may become more difficult; the family's overprotectiveness may prevent these indi-viduals from having experiences appropriate to their own age group.

Middle Age

Individuals in middle age are generally established in their career, have a committed relationship, and are often providing guidance to their own children as they leave the family to establish their own careers and families. At the same time, middle-aged individuals may be assuming greater responsibility for their own elderly parents, who may be becoming increasingly fragile and dependent. During middle age, individuals may begin to reassess their goals and relationships as they begin to recognize their own mortality and limited remain-ing time.

Illness or disability during middle age can interfere with further occupational development and may even result in early retirement. Such changes can have a significant impact not only on the economic well-being of individuals and their families, but also on their identity, self-concept, and self-esteem. It may be nec-essary to alter established roles and associated responsibilities within the family, for example. The partner in an intimate relationship, even a long-term relation-ship, may be reevaluating his or her own life goals, may perceive the illness or disability as a violation of his or her own-well being, and may choose to leave the relationship. Responsibilities for children and aging parents can provide additional financial and emotional stress to that experienced as a result of illness or disability.

Older Adulthood

Ideally, older adults have adapted to the triumphs and disappointments of life and have accepted their own life and imminent death. Although physical limitations associated with the normal aging process are variable, older adults often experience diminished physical strength and stamina, as well as losses of visual and hearing acuity. Illness or disability during older adulthood can pose physical or cognitive limitations in addition to those due to the aging process. The spouse or significant others of the same age group may also have decreased physical stamina, making the physical care of the ill or disabled individual more difficult. When older ill or disabled adults are unable to attend to their own needs or when care in the home is unmanageable, they may find it necessary to surrender their own life style and move to another environment for care and supervision. Many individuals in the older age group live on a fixed retirement income, and the additional expenses associated with illness or disability place significant strain on an already tight budget. Not all older individuals, of course, have retirement benefits, savings, or other resources to draw on in time of financial need.

OTHER ISSUES IN CHRONIC ILLNESS AND DISABILITY

Invisible Disabilities

Although some chronic illnesses or disabilities have associated physical changes or functional limitations that necessitate the use of adaptive devices, others (e.g., diabetes or cardiac conditions) have no outward signs that alert casual observers to the individual's condition. The term *invisible disability* refers to these latter conditions. Because there is no atypical appearance or other cues to indicate the limitations associated with the illness or disability, those who interact with the individual have no basis on which to alter their expectations with regard to the individual and his or her functional capacity. Although this lack of reaction can be positive in the sense that it prevents actions by others that are based on prejudice or stereotypes, it can also be negative in that the lack of feedback from casual observers gives the individual an opportunity to deny or avoid acceptance of the condition and its associated implications.

The degree to which a condition remains invisible may be a function of the closeness of the observer's association with the individual. Although casual acquaintances may not notice the limitations, those more closely involved with the individual in day-to-day activities may more readily observe them. Other conditions under normal circumstances may offer no visible signs or cues, however, no matter how close the association with the individual.

The unapparentness of limitation in invisible disability may be a unique element related to an individual's adjustment and acceptance of the limitation. Without environmental feedback to create a tangible reality of the condition, individuals with invisible disability may postpone the adaptation process or ignore medical treatment or recommendations necessary for control of the condition and prevention of further disability.

Sexuality

More than genital acts or sexual function, sexuality is a normal and fundamental part of life. Sexuality encompasses the whole person and is reflected in all that he or she says and does. It is an important part of identity, self-image, and self-concept. Each person is a sexual being with a need for intimacy, physical contact, and love. Although chronic illness and disability may change individuals' perceptions of themselves as sexual beings or may change the perceptions of others, it does not change the inherent need for closeness.

The expression of sexual urges is one form of sexuality. Chronic illness or disability can affect sexual expression through physical limitations, depression, lack of energy, pain, alterations in self-image, or the reactions of others. With some conditions, the main barrier to sexual expression may be problems with self-concept and self-image; with other conditions, physical changes may affect sexual function directly.

Regardless of the type of limitations associated with illness or disability, sexual expression continues to be an important part of function that should be addressed. In some instances, it may be necessary to help individuals overcome their own misperceptions and fears in order to establish a means for sexual expression. In other instances, individuals may need assistance to overcome barriers or to learn methods of sexual expression different from those used previously. In any case, sexual adjustment is a significant element in the restoration of an individual's maximal functional capacity.

Family Adaptation to Chronic Illness and Disability

The family is the social network from which the individual derives identity and with which he or she has strong psychological bonds. Family has different meanings for different people; its members are not always related by blood or law. A family provides protection, socialization, physical care, support, and love. Each individual within the family structure plays some role that is incorporated into everyday family function.

Chronic illness or disability has emotional and economic impact on the family, as well as on the individual. Family reactions to chronic illness and disability may be similar to those experienced by the individual and may include shock, denial, anger, guilt, anxiety, and depression. The family must make adaptations, adjustments, and role changes both as a unit and as individual family members. The way in which the family reacts and adapts to the situation can have a major impact on the individual's subsequent adjustment. Whether the family fosters independence or dependence, accepts or rejects the individual and his or her limitations, or encourages or sabotages compliance with restrictions and recommended treatments has a profound effect on the individual's ultimate functional capacity.

Families, like individuals, have differing resources, depending on life circumstances, previous experiences, and the personalities involved. Individual family members may be called upon to provide not only emotional support, but also physical care, supervision, transportation, or a variety of other services necessitated by the individual's condition. In addition, changes of roles or financial circumstances due to chronic illness or disability may alter the goals and plans of other family members. The amount of care and attention required by the individual with an illness or disability may create considerable emotional strain among family members, which can result in feelings of resentment, antagonism, and frustration. Role change and ambiguity may make it necessary to redefine family relationships as new and unaccustomed duties and responsibilities arise.

Adherence with Prescribed Treatment and Recommendations

Most chronic illnesses or disabling conditions require ongoing treatment, medical supervision, or restrictions on activity in order to control the condition or to prevent complications. Some individuals with chronic illness or disability fail to follow the recommendations prescribed, however, thus imperiling their own well-being. Neglecting to take medications as prescribed, resisting restriction of activities, or engaging in behaviors that are likely to cause complications of the illness or disability can significantly influence the individual's medical prognosis and functional capacity. The best rehabilitation plan is of little value if individuals do not follow the treatments designed to control their symptoms or disease or to prevent complications or progression of the disease.

Although individuals who purposely behave in a way that makes their condition worse seem irrational, there are a number of explanations for nonadherent behavior. Illness or disability elicits many responses from individuals and their families. Different reactions, experiences, and motives direct behavior and can help or hinder adherence with treatment recommendations.

Individuals' lives are guided by a set of norms and values—expressed or unexpressed. Each individual has a personal, unique perspective on health, illness, and medical care itself. There is a remarkable difference in perceptions of and reactions to apparently similar medical conditions. The meaning of illness and the consequences ascribed to adherence to recommendations are based mainly on an individual's perception of the condition and its associated limitations, as well as of treatment recommendations and their implications. While some individuals react mildly to a condition that may devastate another, others display considerable emotional and physical discomfort with conditions that most people consider minor. Obviously, various psychosocial factors determine individuals' reactions to illness and, consequently, their reactions to the recommendations and advice given.

Chronic illness or disability disrupts the way individuals view themselves and the world, and it can produce distortions in thinking. Most individuals initially experience a feeling of vulnerability, a shattering of the magical belief that they are immune from illness, injury, or even death. With this realization, they may lose their sense of security and cohesiveness. Life may seem a maze of inconveniences, hazards, and restrictions. Nonadherence to recommendations may be an attempt to exert self-determination, to regain a sense of autonomy and control, and to claim some mastery over individual destiny. In other instances, resistance to treatment recommendations may be a denial of the condition itself.

Nonadherence can also be a reflection of the individual's feelings about his or her life circumstances. For some individuals, being an ill or disabled person is not a positive role; for others, it may be far preferable to the social role that they held previously. Some may vacillate between the wish to be independent and the wish to remain dependent. The illness or disability can be a means of legitimizing dependency, as well as a means of increasing the amount of attention received. Subsequently, these individuals may be reluctant to return to their former roles and obligations. The motivation to retain the sick role is at times greater than the motivation to gain optimal function. As a result, ultimate rehabilitation is hampered.

The failure to adhere to recommendations can be a response to guilt that has been incorporated into the reaction to or beliefs about illness or disability. If health and well-being are perceived as rewards for a life well lived, illness or disability may be viewed as punishment for real or imagined transgressions. Adherence to medical advice may be perceived as interference with a punishment believed to be deserved. In other instances, individuals may feel guilty because they believe that the illness or disability is a direct result of their own negligence or overt actions. Guilt or shame at being different may also hinder adherence to treatment recommendations. Some individuals may attempt to hide their condition from others and, thus, fail to follow recommendations that they fear may call attention to their condition.

The impact of illness or disability on an individual's general economic well-being can also affect the individual's ability and willingness to follow treatment recommendations. While many occupations offer fringe benefits, such as paid sick days or even time off with pay in which to seek medical care, other occupations provide no such benefits. In the latter instances, days taken off from work because of illness or medical appointments can decrease income. The economic consequences of illness or disability may also cause a reverse reaction. If an individual is receiving disability benefits and has little opportunity for satisfactory employment, he or she may not follow recommendations that increase capacity to return to work, thereby decreasing or eliminating benefits.

Finally, the quality of life is a relative concept, uniquely defined by each individual. If the treatment recommendations result in pain, discomfort, or inconvenience greater than the benefit perceived by the individual in terms of his or her own subjective definition of the quality of life, compliance with the prescribed recommendations may not be perceived as worth the psychological, social, or physical cost. Treatment can sometimes, but not always, be adjusted to make following recommendations more palatable. The individual's right to self-determination must be carefully balanced with assurance that the choice of non-adherence is based on information and full understanding of the consequences.

Some individuals readily adjust to the challenges, limitations, and associated behavioral changes necessitated by an illness or disability. Many individuals, however, actively sabotage treatment and recommendations—to their own detriment. In such instances, professionals' goals should attempt to understand the underlying problems and motivations of individuals and to help them make necessary adjustments and adaptations in order to maximize functional outcomes. Rather than criticizing those who are ill or disabled for disinterest, a lack of motivation, or failure to follow recommendations, it is important to identify the barriers that prohibit adherence and to recognize that such reactions may indicate difficulty in accepting the condition or adapting recommendations into the individual's own unique way of life.

Patient (Client and Family) Education

Although medical care, support, and auxiliary services are important aspects of helping individuals reach their maximum potential, the successful management of chronic disease or disability requires considerable individual and family effort. Regardless of the complexity of the condition, many individuals are now expected to carry out treatments in their home rather than to depend on medical personnel in health care settings. Individuals' understanding of their condition and treatment is one of the basic components of self-determination and responsible care. Not only must they understand how to integrate regimens into daily routines and how to carry out daily care activities, but also they must understand preventive health care measures to retain function and prevent further disability or health problems. Because of the increasing public awareness of the need for individuals to accept this greater role of responsibility and self-determination, a number of programs and counseling services have been established to help clients and their families reach this goal.

FUNCTIONAL ASPECTS OF CHRONIC ILLNESS
AND DISABILITY

The functional effects of illness or disability are many and varied. Each individual has different needs, abilities, and circumstances that determine how illness or disability affects his or her functional capacity. The extent to which the condition is handicapping depends to a great extent on the individual's perception of the condition; the environment; and the reactions of family, friends, and society in general. The severity of the condition as measured by diagnostic tests does not always indicate the severity of the functional impairment, nor is the individual's ability to function always directly correlated with the severity of the condition itself. Individual reactions may differ to a similar illness or disability. Professionals who work with chronically ill and disabled individuals need an understanding of the potential limitations or restrictions associated with a specific condition or treatment, however, in order to help individuals and their families make appropriate changes to gain maximal functional capacity.

The effects of chronic illness and disability are far-reaching. Effects include psychological, social, and vocational effects, changes and adjustments in both general life style and activities of daily living. The medical diagnosis per se is not as important as the degree of impairment that the condition imposes on interactions in each area of an individual's life. The interactive nature of function between each of the areas determines the extent to which individuals reach their maximal potential. A focus on any one area without full consideration of the impact of the illness or disability on all other areas can dilute the effectiveness of total rehabilitative efforts. Understanding and working effectively with individuals who have a chronic illness or disability require a broad outlook that goes beyond medical diagnosis. The most important factor is the individual's ability to function with the condition within the environment and all areas of life.

Psychological Implications

Individuals react both cognitively and emotionally to events that involve them. These reactions, in turn, affect the further course of those events. Psychological factors are ever-present in all aspects of illness and disability. Psychological factors influence an individual's response to the illness or disability, and sometimes psychological factors are part of the symptoms of the condition itself. They affect not only the individual's adjustment and subsequent functional capacity, but also the outcome and the prognosis.

Life Style Implications

Life style comprises the daily tasks and the activities of daily living within the individual's environment. It includes the ability to perform tasks related to grooming, housekeeping, and preparing meals. Also included are activities related to transportation, daily schedules, need for rest or activity, recreation, sexuality, and privacy. At times, limitations in performing the activities of daily living result from environmental considerations that serve as barriers to effective functioning. Modifications such as widening doorways to permit the passage of a wheelchair, placing handrails in a bathroom, or installing more effective lighting may be required to increase functional capacity.

Other life style modifications may be necessary because of the additional tasks and time commitments related to medical treatment of a specific condition. In some instances, restrictions of diet or activity may require considerable life style change. Continued treatments, medical appointments, and related activities may require significant alteration of daily schedule.

Social Implications

The social environment can be defined as the individual's perceived involvement in personal, family, group, and community relationships and activities. Social well-being is based on emotionally satisfying experiences in social activities with those within the individual's social group. Chronic illness and disability often lead to changes in social status. Ill or disabled individuals may find themselves in a socially devalued role, experience changes in social relationships or interactions, or limit the number of social activities, any of which can result in social isolation. Even when these individuals attempt to remain socially active, they may have difficulty entering community facilities because of environmental barriers or because of prejudice or stereotyping.

Many factors contribute to an individual's adaptation or adjustment to any social limitations associated with a particular medical condition. The individual's perception or misperception of the reactions of others in social groups may determine the level of acceptance that he or she receives. The degree to which individuals are able to adapt, accept, and adjust to their functional limitations may be determined in part by their interactions with others in their environment, as well as by their interpretation of the reactions of others.

Vocational Implications

Work involves more than remuneration for services rendered and does not necessarily include only activity related to financial incentives. Work provides a sense of contribution, accomplishment, and meaning to life. Consequently, the loss of the ability to work extends beyond financial considerations to social and psychological well-being. The loss of the ability to work means more than the loss of income, it also means the loss of a socially valued role. For many individuals, work is not only a major part of their identity, but also a source of social interaction, structure, and purpose in life.

The degree to which chronic illness and disability affect an individual's ability and willingness to work depends on a variety of factors in addition to the limitations imposed by the illness or disability itself. Other factors include the nature of the work, the physical environment of the work setting, and the attitudes of employers and co-workers. Psychosocial variables may also complicate functional capacity and, thus, the rehabilitation process.

At times, individuals with chronic illness or disability may continue to perform the same work that they performed before the onset of the condition. At other times, certain work tasks, environmental conditions, or work schedules must be modified to accommodate the limitations imposed by the illness or disability. If modifications cannot be made in these cases, the individual must change employment. Some individuals must assume disability status because appropriate modifications cannot be made or because their limitations are severe.

Job stress or the attitudes of employers or co-workers can significantly interfere with an ill or disabled individual's ability to return to the work force. Problems with transportation to and from work because of limitations associated with the illness or disability may also make a return to the work more difficult. In other instances, the time required to carry out treatment recommendations related to the condition may make completing a full day at work virtually impossible.

The individual's capacity to function at a job can depend on cognitive, psychomotor, and attitudinal factors, as well as on the physical aspects of illness or disability. An accurate assessment of an individual's capacity to return to work consists of more than evaluation of physical factors alone. Success or failure at work is often determined by factors other than physical skill or ability.

The individual's fear of re-injury, vocational dissatisfaction, or legal issues can hamper the return to work. The individual's ability to relate to and interact with others within the work environment must also be considered. Interests, aptitudes, and abilities are always pivotal factors in determining vocational success, regardless of limitations. Effective rehabilitation that enables individuals to function effectively in their job often involves the interdisciplinary efforts of many types of medical and nonmedical professionals to conduct assessment, evaluation, therapy, and vocational guidance.

BIBLIOGRAPHY

Backman, M.E. *The Psychology of the Physically Ill Patient: A Clinician's Guide.* New York: Plenum Press, 1989.

Balis, G.U.; Wurmser, L.; McDaniel, E.; and Grenell, R.G. *The Behavior and Social Sciences and the Practice of Medicine.* Boston: Butterworth Publishers, 1978.

Bordieri, J.E.; Comniel, M.E.; and Drehmer, D.E. "Client Attributions for Disability: Perceived Accuracy, Adjustment, and Coping." *Rehabilitation Psychology* 34(1989):271–278.

Caplan, B. *Rehabilitation Psychology Desk Reference.* Gaithersburg, Md.: Aspen Publishers, 1987.

DiMatteo, M.R., and DiNicola, D.D. *Achieving Patient Compliance: The Psychology of the Medical Practitioner's Role.* New York: Pergamon Press, 1982.

Eisenberg, M.G.; Sutkin, L.C.; and Jansen, M.A., eds. *Chronic Illness and Disability Throughout the Life Span: Effects on Self and Family.* New York: Springer Publishing Co., 1984.

Falvo, D.R. *Effective Patient Education: A Guide to Increased Compliance.* Gaithersburg, Md.: Aspen Publishers, 1985.

Falvo, D.R.; Allen, H.; and Maki, D.R. "Psychosocial Aspects of Invisible Disability." *Rehabilitation Literature* 43(1982):2–6.

Gerber, K.E., and Nehemkis, A.M., eds. *Compliance: The Dilemma of the Chronically Ill.* New York: Springer Publishing Co., 1986.

Hafen, B.Q., and Frandsen, K.J. *Psychological Emergencies and Crisis Intervention.* Englewood, Colo.: Morton Publishing Co., 1985.

Henker, F.O. "Body-Image Conflict Following Trauma and Surgery." *Psychosomatics* 20(1979): 812–820.

Kent, G., and Dalgleish, M. *Psychology and Medical Care.* Berkshire, England: Van Nostrand Reinhold (UK) Co., 1983.

Lewis, K. "Grief in Chronic Illness and Disability." *Journal of Rehabilitation* 49(1983):8–11.

Lubkin, I.M. *Chronic Illness: Impact and Interventions.* Boston: Jones and Bartlett Publishers, 1986.

Marinelli, R.P., and Dell Orto, A.E. *The Psychology and Social Impact of Physical Disability.* New York: Springer Publishing Co., 1977.

McDowell, W.A.; Coven, A.B.; and Eash, V.C. "The Handicapped: Special Needs and Strategies for Counseling." *Personnel and Guidance Journal* 58(1979):228–232.

McKay, D.A.; Blake, R.L.; Colwill, J.M.; Brent, E.E.; McCauley, J.; Umlauf, R.; Stearman, G.; and Kivlahan, D. "Social Supports and Stress as Predictors of Illness." *Journal of Family Practice* 20(1985):575–581.

Neff, W.S., and Weiss, S.A. "Psychological Aspects of Disability." In *Handbook of Clinical Psychology*, edited by B.B. Walman, 785–825. New York: McGraw-Hill Book Co., 1965.

Nichols, K.A. *Psychological Care in Physical Illness.* Philadelphia: The Charles Press, 1984.

Rando, T.A. *Grief, Dying and Death.* Champaign, Ill.: Research Press Co., 1984.

Reading, A. "Illness and Disease." *Medical Clinics of North America* 61(1977):703–710.

Roessler, R., and Bolton, B. *Psychological Adjustment to Disability.* Baltimore: University Park Press, 1978.

Scheer, S.J., ed. *Medical Perspectives in Vocational Assessment of Impaired Workers.* Gaithersburg, Md.: Aspen Publishers, 1991.

Sigelman, C.K.; Vengroff, L.P.; and Spanhel, C.L. "Disability and the Concept of Life Functions." *Rehabilitation Counseling Bulletin* 23(1979):103–113.

Simons, R.C., and Pardes, H., eds. *Understanding Human Behavior in Health and Illness.* Baltimore: Williams & Wilkins Co., 1978.

Stolov, W.C., and Clowers, M.R. *Handbook of Severe Disability.* Washington, D.C.: U.S. Department of Education, Rehabilitation Services Administration, 1981.

Stone, G.C.; Cohen, F.; and Alder, N.E. *Health Psychology.* San Francisco: Jossey-Bass, Publishers, 1980.

Stubbins, J., ed. *Social and Psychological Aspects of Disability: A Handbook for Practitioners.* Baltimore: University Park Press, 1977.

Szasz, T.S. "Illness and Indignity." *Journal of the American Medical Association* 227(1974): 543–545.

Tuck, M. "Psychological and Sociological Aspects of Industrial Injury." *Journal of Rehabilitation* 49(1983):20–25.

Van Dyke, C.; Temoshok, L.; and Zegans, L. *Emotions in Health and Illness: Applications to Clinical Practice.* Orlando, Fla.: Grune & Stratton, 1989.

Weinberg-Asher, N. "The Effect of Physical Disability on Self-Perception." *Rehabilitation Counseling Bulletin* 20(1976):15–20.

Worden, J.W. *Grief Counseling and Grief Therapy: A Handbook for the Mental Health Practitioner.* New York: Springer Publishing Co., 1982.

Wright, B.A. *Physical Disability—A Psychosocial Approach.* New York: Harper & Row, 1983.

Wright, G.M. *Total Rehabilitation.* Boston: Little, Brown & Co., 1980.

chapter 2

Cardiovascular System

NORMAL STRUCTURE AND FUNCTION

The heart, located somewhat to the left of the center of the chest, acts as a pump circulating blood throughout the body (Figure 2-1). It is enclosed in an outer covering consisting of the two layers. This covering is called the **pericardium**. The space between the two layers of the pericardium contains a small amount of fluid to lessen friction between the two surfaces as the heart beats. The lining of the inner surface of the heart is called the **endocardium**.

The **myocardium,** or heart muscle, is composed of a special type of muscle that has the ability to work continuously with only brief periods of rest between contractions. Like all muscles of the body, the myocardium requires oxygen and nutrients to survive. The vessels that carry the blood with oxygen and nutrients to the myocardial muscle are called the **coronary arteries.**

The heart contains four chambers. The two upper chambers are called **atria;** the two lower chambers, **ventricles**. The right atrium receives unoxygenated blood from the general circulation through a large vein called the **vena cava**. Both atria contract simultaneously. As the atria of the heart contract, blood is pumped from the right atrium to the right ventricle through a valve called the **tricuspid valve**. As the two ventricles contract, blood is pumped from the right ventricle through the **pulmonary semilunar valve** into the **pulmonary artery**. The pulmonary artery carries blood to the lungs, where it takes up oxygen and gives off carbon dioxide. Oxygenated blood from the lung is then returned to the left atrium through the pulmonary vein. As the atria contract, blood is pumped through the **mitral**, or **bicuspid, valve** to the left ventricle of the heart. With contraction of the left ventricle, the blood is pumped through the **aortic semilunar valve** into the largest artery in the body, the **aorta**, to the general circulation. The valves of the heart permit the blood to flow in only one direction;

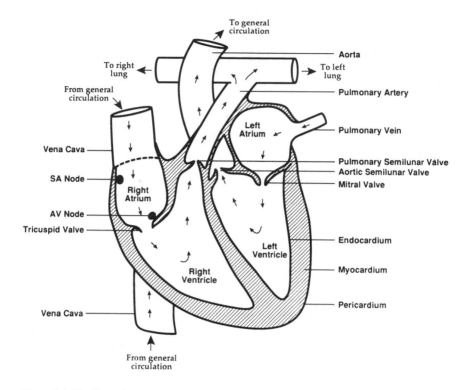

Figure 2-1 The Heart. SA, sinoatrial; AV, atrioventricular.

the mitral and tricuspid valves, for example, prohibit the backflow of blood from the ventricles to the atria.

Blood carries oxygen and nutrients to all parts of the body through the peripheral vessels. A network of arteries that diminish in size to small vessels called **capillaries** carries blood from the heart. In the capillaries, blood delivers oxygen and nutrients to the tissues, then picks up waste products; after passing through small veins that increase in size, blood returns to the heart through a large vein called the **vena cava** to begin the process again.

Contractions of the atria and the ventricles are coordinated through a special nerve conduction system within the **heart**. Special cells located within the right **atrium, called the sinoatrial node,** initiate the contractions. Impulses from the sinoatrial node spread over both atria, causing them to contract. Other special cells in the **atrioventricular node,** located in the lower portion of the right atrium, receive the impulses and transfer them to muscle fibers in the ventricles, enabling the ventricles to contract. At this point, the cycle starts over. The conduction of these electrical impulses is beyond conscious control. Because of the stimulation by these involuntary nerve impulses, however, the heart is able to adjust to the changing needs of the body, speeding or slowing the heart rate as needed.

The contraction phase of the heart's work is called **systole**. The time when the heart is relaxed and the chambers are filling is called **diastole**. These two phases produce different pressure gradients. The ratio of these two pressures is called the **blood pressure**. The amount of pressure produced is dependent on the force with which the heart pumps and the degree to which the blood vessels resist blood flow.

CARDIOVASCULAR DISORDERS

Hypertension

Individuals with hypertension, or high blood pressure, have a sustained elevation of pressure in the arteries. Both the systolic and diastolic pressure may be elevated. This prolonged elevation of pressure can eventually damage other organs, such as the heart, kidneys, brain, or vessels behind the eye.

Blood pressure normally fluctuates with physical activity, becoming lower at rest and higher with changes in posture, exercise, or emotion. Consequently, hypertension is most accurately diagnosed when blood pressure is measured under similar conditions over a period of time.

The most common type of hypertension is **primary** or **essential hypertension**. Its onset is gradual, and it is usually discovered for the first time during a routine physical examination. A less common, but more severe, type of hypertension is **malignant hypertension**, which has an abrupt onset, more severe symptoms, and more associated complications.

The symptoms of hypertension are often vague or even nonexistent. The symptoms that do occur are often due to complications. Treatment of hypertension is directed toward lowering blood pressure and preventing complications. It may involve improving general health habits, such as maintaining a proper body weight, getting sufficient rest and relaxation, ceasing to smoke, eating a well-balanced diet, and limiting salt intake. A variety of medications, called **antihypertensives**, are also used to control high blood pressure.

Arteriosclerosis (Atherosclerosis)

Conditions in which the walls of the arteries become thickened or less elastic, obstructing circulation and diminishing blood flow to various parts of the body, are grouped under the general term *arteriosclerosis*. Plaques may build up along the interior vessel wall, causing **stenosis** (narrowing of the vessel) and further impeding blood flow. Plaque can also contribute to **thrombus** (blood clot) formation within the narrowed vessel, blocking blood flow even more. Occasionally, the thrombus may be dislodged from the vessel wall and travel in the bloodstream until it lodges in a blood vessel too small to allow its passage. In this instance, the blood clot is called an **embolus**. Arteriosclerosis may also lead to an **aneurysm** (ballooning out of a weakened blood vessel).

Symptoms of arteriosclerosis develop slowly and are generally nonexistent until the decreased blood flow severely hampers the oxygen supply to a body part. Symptoms vary with the location of the impeded blood flow. For example, a decreased blood flow to the brain may cause cognitive changes, a decreased blood flow to the kidneys may contribute to kidney damage, and a decreased blood flow to the heart may cause **angina pectoris** (chest pain). Treatment is directed at the complications of arteriosclerosis, such as angina pectoris, arrhythmias, myocardial infarction, stroke, kidney failure, and peripheral vascular disease.

Aneurysm

The local dilation or ballooning out of a blood vessel, usually an artery, is called an aneurysm. Although often associated with arteriosclerosis and hypertension, an aneurysm may also result from a congenital abnormality. The weakened wall of the artery, if under increased pressure (e.g., because of hypertension), may burst and lead to hemorrhage. A **dissecting aneurysm** is a weakness of the vessel wall in which blood leaks between the layers of the wall of the vessel, moving longitudinally to separate the layers along the length of the vessel rather than rupturing into a body cavity.

The symptoms of an aneurysm vary according to its location. In some instances, there are no symptoms until the aneurysm becomes large enough to create pressure, causing pain at the site. In other instances, there are no symptoms until the aneurysm ruptures. Rupture of aneurysms of the aorta or of vessels in the brain may be fatal.

When detected before rupture, aneurysms may be corrected surgically. If hypertension is present, treatment is directed toward controlling the hypertension. This is an important aspect of continuing treatment after surgery.

Congestive Heart Failure

When the heart muscle is weakened or damaged and cannot pump out an adequate amount of blood, congestive heart failure occurs. The causes of congestive heart failure include **myocardial infarction** (heart attack); damage to the heart muscle from poisonous substances, as may result from chronic alcohol abuse; and hypertension, arteriosclerosis, and valvular dysfunction, all of which cause the heart to work harder. When the heart must work harder to pump, it may become enlarged and even more ineffective in its pumping action. Fluid backs up into the lungs, causing congestion, **dyspnea** (difficulty breathing), and difficulty breathing when lying down at night (**nocturnal dyspnea**).

Because of the decreased amount of blood pumped and, consequently, the lack of sufficient oxygen throughout the body, symptoms of congestive heart failure may also include fatigue and physical weakness. There may be cognitive changes if the oxygen supply to the brain is inadequate. The backing up of blood and subsequent congestion may also lead to swelling or **edema** of the extremities.

Treatment of congestive heart failure depends on the type and causes of the condition. It is usually directed toward controlling or correcting the cause of heart failure and toward alleviating the symptoms. Often, medications to lower blood pressure (**antihypertensives**) are prescribed. These medications decrease the vascular resistance, thus decreasing the amount of work that the heart must perform to circulate blood. Medications to help the heart muscle work more efficiently by increasing its pumping action (e.g., **digitalis preparations**) may also be prescribed. **Diuretics** (medications that help rid the body of excess fluid) and a low salt diet to eliminate some of the excess fluid may also be part of the treatment plan.

Cardiac Arrhythmias

An **arrhythmia** is an abnormality of the heart rate or rhythm. Arrhythmias may decrease the heart's ability to work effectively and to supply adequate amounts of blood to any of the body's organs. A dysfunction in the heart's conduction system causes irregularities in its rhythm and/or rate. The heart may beat too fast (**tachycardia**), too slow (**bradycardia**), or irregularly. There are many different types of arrhythmias, which are usually named for the type of disorder or the part of the electrical impulse system that is affected. For example, a **sinus bradycardia** would indicate that there is an abnormally slow rhythm arising in the SA node of the heart, whereas an **atrioventricular (AV) block** would be used to describe an arrhythmia in which electrical impulses are blocked at the atrioventricular junction. Some arrhythmias may be life-threatening, while others may be relatively minor and require little or no treatment.

The symptoms of an arrhythmia reflect the inadequate blood supply to a body part. For example, an inadequate blood supply to the brain may cause symptoms such as **syncope** (fainting), or visual or speech difficulties. In other instances, individuals may complain of feeling **palpitations** (being able to feel their heart beat).

Treatment, which depends on the underlying condition, is directed toward correcting or controlling the factors causing the arrhythmia. Medications called **antiarrhythmics** regulate the heart beat and are often a central part of treatment. In more severe disorders, therapy in the form of electric shock may be instituted to return the heart to its normal rhythm. **Pacemaker** therapy may also be used.

Coronary Artery Disease

Arteriosclerotic changes may narrow the coronary arteries to the extent that insufficient blood passes through the arteries to meet the oxygen demands of the heart muscle. In this situation, myocardial **ischemia** (inadequate blood supply to the heart muscle) may result, causing **angina pectoris**. Because the heart muscle's need for oxygen is greatest when demands are placed on the heart, angina is often experienced during activity. Stopping the activity and, thus, decreasing the workload of the heart may relieve the chest pain. **Nitroglycerin**, a medication that dilates the coronary arteries and enables the heart muscle to receive more oxygen, may also be taken to relieve the pain.

The myocardium, like all other muscles, cannot live without oxygen. When the cardiac muscle is receiving no oxygen (**anoxia**), **necrosis** (tissue death) of part of the heart muscle occurs. This is called a **myocardial infarction** (heart attack). Myocardial infarction may occur any time the blood supply to the heart muscle is insufficient. Not only arteriosclerosis, but also a clot, a particle of vegetation from a diseased valve, or other foreign material that has traveled through the bloodstream to lodge in the vessel may occlude a coronary artery and reduce the heart muscle's blood supply.

In the initial stages of myocardial infarction, pain may be experienced and treated with narcotics. In addition, **anticoagulants** may be given to decrease the likelihood of further clot formation and to decrease the size of the clot that may already be obstructing a coronary artery.

The heart muscle cannot regenerate once a portion of it has been destroyed. The ability of the heart to continue functioning as a pump is directly related to the amount of heart muscle damage. Consequently, myocardial infarction may affect the function of the heart, resulting in arrhythmias or congestive heart failure.

Valvular Heart Disease

Damage to the valves of the heart is most often the result of **rheumatic fever** or **endocarditis**, although valvular abnormalities may also be congenital. Two types of problems generally occur. Valves may become weakened or floppy, permitting a backflow (**regurgitation**) of blood from the ventricle to the atria, or valves may become scarred, narrowing the valvular opening (**stenosis**) and causing an obstruction of blood flow from a chamber of the heart.

Valvular conditions are classified according to the nature of the abnormality and the valve affected. For example, **mitral prolapse** refers to the bulging of all or part of the mitral valve into the left atrium during ventricular contraction. **Mitral regurgitation, mitral insufficiency,** or **mitral incompetence** refers to the inadequate closing of the mitral valve, which allows blood to flow backward into the atria. **Mitral stenosis** refers to narrowing of the mitral valve, which obstructs the blood flow from the left atrium to the left ventricle. **Tricuspid regurgitation,** or **tricuspid stenosis,** is a similar condition, but it occurs on the right instead of the left side of the heart. The same process may affect the pulmonary or aortic valves. Valvular defects of the aortic valve, such as **aortic stenosis** and **aortic regurgitation,** place additional loads on the left ventricle of the heart, possibly resulting in **left ventricular heart failure**.

Symptoms of valvular disease vary in severity, but often include fatigue, dyspnea, and palpitations. Specific treatment depends on the severity of the problem. Some individuals may need to avoid strenuous activity. Others need not undergo any treatment or take any precautions. Prophylactic antibiotics may be given to prevent **endocarditis** when there is the chance for a generalized bacterial infection, such as after a dental extraction. Severe damage to the valve may require surgery to open or replace the valve.

Endocarditis (Acute Bacterial Endocarditis, Subacute Bacterial Endocarditis)

Most people have isolated incidents in which bacteria enter the bloodstream. In most instances, the body's own defenses overcome the organism with no untoward results. At times, however, because of the strength of the organism or the reduced effectiveness of the body's defenses, the organism settles on the inner lining of the heart. **Endocarditis** (inflammation of the membrane that covers the heart valves and chambers of the heart) is caused by this type of infection. Damage to the valves can result.

There is a marked relationship between rheumatic heart disease and endocarditis. Endocarditis is also associated with intravenous drug abuse. Moreover, it may be a complication of invasive medical procedures.

Individuals with damaged heart valves are more vulnerable to endocarditis. Complications include **embolism**, in which some of the vegetation from the affected valve breaks away and occludes a blood vessel in another part of the body. Such embolic phenomena can affect any organ or part of the body, depending on the vessel occluded.

The condition may have an insidious onset with early symptoms mimicking the flu. As the disease progresses, symptoms such as high fever, weight loss, and extreme fatigue become more pronounced. Treatment consists of the administration of appropriate antibiotics to eradicate the infection before serious complications develop.

Pericarditis

Any organism can cause pericarditis, or inflammation of the **pericardium**. When inflamed, the pericardial layers can adhere to each other creating friction as their surfaces rub together during cardiac contraction. A common sign of pericarditis is chest pain, which is aggravated by moving and breathing because of the rubbing together of the two inflamed surfaces. Treatment of pericarditis is directed toward alleviating the pain caused by the inflammation and fighting the infective organism with antibiotics.

Severe inflammation or excessive fluid within the pericardial sac may constrict the heart. If constriction of the heart is severe because of increasing amounts of fluid, a condition called cardial **tamponade**, **pericardiocentesis** may be performed. During this procedure, the physician inserts a needle into the pericardial sac and drains the fluid, thus relieving the constriction. Constrictive pericarditis may also be treated surgically by the removal of a portion of the pericardium.

Rheumatic Heart Disease

Rheumatic heart disease is a type of heart disease brought about by a condition called rheumatic fever. **Rheumatic fever** is a condition in which the body undergoes a type of allergic reaction in response to an organism called **streptococcus**. Since not everyone develops rheumatic fever after a streptococcal infection, the reason for the allergic type of reactions in some individuals is unknown. Although recovery from rheumatic fever can be complete with no residual effects, some individuals experience permanent cardiac damage as a result. Valves of the heart are most frequently affected resulting in stenosis, insufficiency, or regurgitation as described earlier in the discussion of valvular disease.

PERIPHERAL VASCULAR CONDITIONS

Disorders of the peripheral blood vessels (i.e., those in the extremities) can lead to damage of the tissues supplied by those vessels. When the oxygen supply is inadequate because of the diminished blood flow, extremities feel cold and appear pale or cyanotic (blue). Pain is also characteristic when the oxygen supply is diminished.

Peripheral Atherosclerotic Disease (Arteriosclerosis Obliterans)

When arteriosclerotic changes have narrowed or occluded the larger peripheral vessels, an adequate blood supply cannot reach tissues in the extremities. Symptoms depend on how extensive the obstruction is, which vessels are involved, and whether alternate blood supply routes, called **collateral circulation**, have formed.

Because of the increased demand for oxygen by muscles during exercise, a deficient blood supply to the muscles, such as in peripheral vascular disease, may cause aching, cramping, or fatigue of the muscles in the legs (**intermittent claudication**) when walking. Pain is relieved quickly by rest, which decreases the muscles' need for oxygen. If the condition progresses, however, pain in the extremity may occur even at rest. In severe cases, the feet may become numb and cold, and ulcerations of the foot may appear. Surgical procedures, such as a bypass graft of the severely affected vessel, may restore vascularization to the extremity in selected cases.

Owing to the diminished blood supply in peripheral atherosclerotic disease, even tiny injuries in the extremities may become infected and may not heal properly. If circulation becomes so severely impaired that **necrosis** results, amputation of the extremity may be necessary to prevent complications, such as the spread of infection throughout the body.

Thromboangitis Obliterans (Burger's Disease)

A rare condition of the small and medium-sized arteries and, often, superficial veins of the extremities, **thromboangitis obliterans** diminishes the blood flow to the affected part. In contrast to peripheral atherosclerotic disease, thromboangitis obliterans occurs predominantly in individuals between the ages of 20 and 40 who do not have significant atherosclerosis. Symptoms include numbness, tingling, and pain in the upper or lower extremities. Although the exact cause is unknown, thromboangitis obliterans occurs almost exclusively in individuals who smoke. Consequently, the major treatment of the condition is cessation of smoking. If the individual continues to smoke, the disease continues to progress and can ultimately require the amputation of the affected extremities.

Raynaud's Phenomenon and Disease

In **Raynaud's phenomenon** or disease, spasms of the vessels in the fingers or toes impair the blood flow to those areas. Occasionally, the condition also affects the nose and the tongue. In most instances, the cause of the condition is unknown; however, it may be associated with other conditions, such as rheumatoid arthritis or arteriosclerosis obliterans. Attacks of vasospasm may last from minutes to hours, but they rarely last long enough to cause the loss of large amounts of tissue. Attacks result in color changes in fingers or toes, either blanching or cyanosis, and are precipitated by cold or emotional upsets.

If Raynaud's phenomenon is secondary to another condition, treatment is directed toward the underlying disorder. In the majority of cases, in which the cause is unknown, treatment is designed to ensure protection from the cold and to avoid emotional upsets. Because smoking constricts the blood vessels, tobacco use should be avoided. Treatment with biofeedback or the use of relaxation techniques may sometimes be helpful.

Venous Thrombosis (Thrombophlebitis, Phlebitis)

Phlebitis is the inflammation of a vein; **thrombophlebitis** is the inflammation of a vein with associated clot formation. Although phlebitis and thrombophlebitis can occur in any vein, they frequently occur in the veins of the lower extremities. Symptoms may be minor, or there may be pain, redness, or swelling over the affected vein. If thrombophlebitis is unrecognized or inadequately treated, clots can break off; travel to the heart, lungs, or other parts of the body; and lodge in a vessel. Massive damage to the part can result from the occlusion of the blood supply.

Treatment of phlebitis and thrombophlebitis is directed toward decreasing inflammation and preventing or dissolving clots. Bed rest is usually prescribed during therapy, along with medications that decrease clotting (**antithrombotic agents**).

Varicose Veins

When blood cannot be returned efficiently to the heart, the backup of blood causes distention and congestion of the veins—**varicose veins**. Anything causing stricture or pressure on the veins can aggravate the condition. For example, prolonged standing, obesity, or constriction of the leg by circular garters are aggravating factors. Symptoms include a feeling of heaviness in the legs, fatigue, and, at times, pain.

Treatment may consist of the application of lightweight compression hosiery in mild cases and heavier support hosiery for more involved cases. Surgery to tie and strip the veins may be indicated when the condition involves severe pain or recurrent phlebitis.

DIAGNOSTIC PROCEDURES

In addition to a physical examination and medical history, a variety of tests are used to diagnose cardiovascular conditions. These tests may also provide information that is used to make treatment determinations or to evaluate treatment effectiveness.

Chest Roentgenography (X-Ray)

A noninvasive radiographic procedure, roentgenography makes it possible to visualize the organs of the chest cavity on x-ray film. The film may show evidence of congestion or fluid in the lungs, **hypertrophy** (enlargement) of any of the heart's chambers, or other abnormalities in the chest cavity.

Electrocardiography

A graphic representation of electrical currents within the heart muscle, an **electrocardiogram** (ECG) is helpful in identifying abnormalities of the heart's rhythm, assessing the amount and location of damage to the cardiac muscle, determining whether the cardiac muscle is receiving an adequate supply of oxygen, and obtaining information about the effects of certain medications. In a painless, noninvasive procedure, electrodes are placed externally on the skin and then connected to a special machine that transforms the electrical impulses from the heart to the graphic printout that records the heart's activity. The ECG is usually performed in the physician's office, hospital, or other medical setting.

Holter Monitor

The **Holter Monitor** is a form of ECG in which several electrodes attached externally to the chest are connected to a small portable device that records the heart's activity. The device is worn on the shoulder or waist so that the individual can go about regular activities at home or work. The advantage of the Holter Monitor is that the graphic reading of the heart's electrical impulses is continuous rather than a one-time reading in a laboratory situation. Readings from the

Holter Monitor enable a physician to assess the heart's functioning during various normal activities throughout a 24-hour period or longer.

Cardiac Stress Test

A noninvasive exercise test that provides a graphic record of the heart's activity during forced exertion, the cardiac stress test may be used diagnostically to determine the extent of cardiac disease. It can be used as a basis for recommending either medical or surgical treatment, as well as for counseling individuals with cardiac disease about the type and amount of physical activity in which they may safely engage. The stress test is performed in a cardiology unit or clinic with a physician present.

Electrodes are placed externally on the chest and connected to an ECG monitor. The individual is then asked to step on a motor-driven treadmill or to sit on a stationary bicycle with an ergometer. Activity is begun slowly, with a gradual increase of pace. During this time, the physician monitors the individual's ECG reading, pulse, and blood pressure. The test is stopped if the individual is no longer able to keep up the pace or develops chest pain, or if the physician determines that blood pressure, pulse, or ECG readings indicate excessive strain on the heart.

The stress test is performed in a controlled, laboratory environment, but consideration must also be given to any additional stress that the heart may endure in the individual's natural environment. For example, emotional stress, extremes in temperature, and the physical terrain (such as steps or ramps) can all increase the heart's workload beyond that experienced in the laboratory situation.

Angiography

When it is necessary to study one or more blood vessels, an invasive procedure called angiography is used. An angiogram enables the physician to identify abnormalities in the size or the shape of the vessels, the extent of narrowing or occlusion, and the sequence and time in which the vessel fills with blood. Angiograms are named for the specific area of the body being studied. If arteries are being studied, the test is called an **arteriogram**. If veins are being studied, the test is called a **venogram**. If vessels of the heart are being studied, the test is called a **cardiac angiogram**.

A **radiologist**, a physician who specializes in x-ray procedures, performs an angiogram. The procedure is usually performed in the radiology department. During the procedure, a special catheter is placed into a vein in the arm or leg and dye injected. At this time, a rapid series of roentgenograms are taken, enabling the physician to visualize the vessels.

Echocardiography

Like the ECG, the echocardiogram is obtained by means of a noninvasive procedure. Ultrasound is used to record the size, motion, and composition of the heart and large vessels on an echocardiogram. A transducer converts sound waves to electrical signals, which are then recorded as visual images and displayed on a type of television screen called an oscilloscope. Images can be photographed for further evaluation by a radiologist or cardiologist. Echocardiograms are helpful for identifying and evaluating valvular defects or other structural abnormalities of the heart.

Radionuclide Imaging

The procedure for radionuclide imaging begins with the intravenous injection of a radioactive substance that localizes in heart tissue. Multiple views of the heart are taken with a special camera; additional views are repeated for comparison hours later. The procedure is most useful in evaluating the myocardium or damage to the myocardial tissue. It may also be used to evaluate coronary artery disease or valvular disease. It can be performed with the individual either at rest or during exercise.

Cardiac Catheterization

An invasive procedure, cardiac catheterization is performed to study the chambers, valves, and blood supply to the heart. A catheter is passed into a vessel in an arm or a leg and then threaded into the heart. A special x-ray machine called a **fluoroscope** enables the physician to watch as the catheter advances into the heart. When the catheter is in place, internal pressures in the heart are measured. Dye is then injected into the catheter, allowing the physician to visualize the pumping action of the heart and the blood flow through the coronary arteries.

Cardiac catheterization may be performed to determine the extent of coronary artery disease, valvular disease, congenital heart disease, or damage to the heart muscle. The information gained from this procedure may be used to determine whether cardiac surgery is indicated or to assess the function of the heart after cardiac surgery.

The procedure may be performed in the radiology department, operating room, or special rooms within cardiac clinics.

TREATMENT

For those with cardiovascular conditions, treatment may be medical, surgical, or a combination of the two. In any case, treatment requires regular medical follow-up in order to monitor the success of the treatment and the progression of the disease.

Medical Treatment

Although it varies with the type of disorder, medical treatment of cardiovascular conditions generally consists of medication and/or life style changes. In many instances, hypertension is associated with other cardiovascular disorders; consequently, **antihypertensives** or medications that rid the body of excess fluid, called **diuretics**, are often prescribed. If there are associated arrhythmias, **anti-arrhythmics** may also be prescribed. **Nitroglycerin** may be taken to dilate the coronary vessels when there is chest pain from inadequate oxygen supply to heart muscle. Nitroglycerin may also be taken prophylactically before any activity that may increase the heart's workload. **Anticoagulants** may be prescribed to reduce the coagulability of the blood and, thus, the risk of clot formation. **Cardiotonic** medications, such as **digitalis** preparations, may be prescribed to change heart rhythm or rate and generally to strengthen the heart. In all instances, medications are taken under the direction of a physician.

The physician should prescribe the degree and type of activity permissible for individuals with cardiovascular disease. Because the heart responds to different types of muscular activity in different ways, the physician takes into account the nature of the condition and the ability of the heart to function under various types of muscle action in prescribing activity. Exercise may also be prescribed as a part of the treatment regimen in order to increase tolerance to activity.

Factors that contribute to cardiovascular disease or place additional burdens on the heart, such as obesity, smoking, and undue stress, are also considered in treatment goals. Obesity can increase strain on the heart; consequently, individuals with cardiac disease are often placed on low-calorie diets. Sodium, which contributes to water retention that increases the heart's workload, may also be restricted. Because cholesterol levels have also been associated with cardiovascular disease, individuals with such disease may be placed on a diet that restricts the intake of cholesterol. Smoking is associated with an increased pulse rate, blood pressure changes, and blood vessel constriction. Consequently, individuals with cardiovascular conditions should avoid tobacco use.

Surgical Treatment

Surgery may be indicated to correct structural abnormalities that are responsible for the cardiac symptoms. One procedure that may be used to enlarge a narrowed coronary artery is **coronary angioplasty**. In this procedure, a long catheter with a balloon on its tip is guided into the coronary artery. The balloon is then inflated, which compresses the occluding material against the vessel wall. The vessel is dilated as the inflated catheter tip is withdrawn, thus increasing the blood flow to the myocardium. Although helpful for some, the procedure may not be appropriate for all individuals.

Coronary bypass is another surgical procedure used to relieve narrowing or constriction of the coronary arteries. A graft, usually a vein from the individual's leg, is used to bypass an obstructed coronary artery. Often, several coronary arteries are constricted, and more than one graft is needed. The bypass increases the myocardium's blood supply, thus potentially increasing the individual's ability to engage in activity. Although this surgery relieves the restriction of blood flow to the heart muscle, the disease process that caused the initial constriction of the coronary arteries is still present. Consequently, additional bypass procedures may be necessary at a later date.

Surgical interventions for valvular abnormalities are intended either to widen a valve that is narrowed or constricted or, in the case of valvular insufficiency or regurgitation, to replace a diseased valve with an artificial valve. Artificial valves may be mechanical, or they may be made of tissue. Mechanical valves are made entirely from synthetic materials, while tissue valves may be made from a combination of synthetic and biological tissue. Mechanical valves require long-term anticoagulant therapy to prevent thrombus formation. Although tissue valves decrease the risk of clot development, they may not have the long-term durability of mechanical valves. Because prosthetic valves are more vulnerable to infection, individuals may need to take antibiotics before procedures in which infection is a risk (e.g., dental work) are performed.

Aneurysms may also be treated surgically if they are diagnosed early or if surgery is not contraindicated because of associated medical problems. In surgical procedures to correct aneurysms, the surgeon removes the weakened area of the artery and then connects the two remaining ends. If a large portion of the vessel has been removed, the two remaining ends of the artery may be joined by a graft.

Pacemakers

When the heart's ability to maintain an effective rate or rhythm is altered, an artificial cardiac pacemaker may be used to stimulate the electrical activity of the heart and to maintain function. The pacemaker consists of a battery-operated pulse generator and a lead wire with an electrode tip. One end of the lead wire is inserted into a vessel and advanced into the individual's heart; the other end is connected to the generator. The generator then sends out an electrical stimulus to the heart muscle. The generator may be external if the need for pacing is only temporary. If the pacemaker is to be permanent, a small battery-operated generator is placed under the skin and fatty tissue of the upper chest or lower thoracic area.

There are various types of pacemakers. Pacemakers are usually classified according to the chamber of the heart that is being stimulated, the chamber of the heart that is being monitored, and the response that the pacemaker is expected to deliver. The classification system uses a three-letter code to describe pacemaker function. The first letter of the code signifies the chamber being stimulated, the second letter indicates the chamber being monitored, and the third letter indicates the pacemaker response. For example, a code VVI would indicate that a ventricle is being both stimulated and monitored. The I stands for "inhibited response," indicating that the pacemaker will not allow impulses from the atria to stimulate the ventricle.

There are several modes of pacing that pacemakers are designed to deliver. The oldest type of pacing, **fixed rate**, is rarely used today. In this type of pacing the pacemaker is set to fire at a fixed rate, usually about 70 beats per minute, and is unaffected by the heart's own rhythm. Another type of pacing, **demand or standby**, is accomplished with a pacemaker that has a special sensing circuit that is set at a specific rate. When the individual's own conduction system in the heart falls below that specific rate, the artificial pacemaker fires accordingly. Other types of pacing, namely **synchronous** and **bifocal**, use pacemakers that are programmed in similar ways to monitor and deliver specific types of impulses. The physician determines the type of pacemaker to be used and the amplitude of the stimulus based on the individual's condition.

For most individuals, even permanent pacemakers may be inserted under local anesthesia with mild sedation. The potential complications of pacemaker insertion include inflammation or infection of the surrounding area.

The level of activity permitted to individuals who wear a pacemaker depends on the underlying disease process, age, and the degree of cardiac functional capacity. Normal daily activities can usually be resumed 6 weeks after the implantation of the pacemaker. Activities that could expose the internal pacemaker to a blow, such as contact sports, should be avoided. Although driving may be restricted for a short time after the pacemaker insertion, most individuals can begin driving in approximately a month if the pacemaker is functioning well. Individuals who wear a pacemaker should at all times wear identification, such as Medic Alert, or carry a card that contains information about the type of pacemaker, the date of implant, and the pacemaker's programming.

Because the pacemaker's generator is battery-operated, failure of the battery means that the heart returns to beat at its previously abnormal rate or rhythm. Individuals with pacemakers should be aware of the signs of battery depletion such as a change in the cardiac rate or the appearance of symptoms similar to those experienced before the pacemaker was inserted. The length of time that a battery lasts depends on the model and can vary from one to several years. A physician should evaluate the pacemaker's function regularly. Periodic evaluations may be conducted with special telephone monitoring in which information about the pacemaker's function is transmitted over regular telephone lines to a special device in the physician's office.

Although the shielding around battery-operated generators has been improved significantly, individuals who wear these devices should be aware of possible interference from a variety of external electrical signals in the environment. Microwave ovens, radar installations, arc welding devices, antitheft devices, and other sources of electrical signals may interfere with pacemaker signals. The pacemaker may also set off metal detection devices installed at airports.

Cardiac Transplantation

Now an accepted, established form of therapy when heart disease is so advanced (end-stage heart disease) that standard therapy is no longer effective and survival is severely threatened, cardiac transplantation involves removing the diseased heart and replacing it with the heart of a donor. Not all individuals with heart disease are candidates for cardiac transplantation. Selection is based on factors such as general physical condition, absence of other systemic disease that would in itself limit survival, the ability to return to normal function after surgery, and the ability to comply with the complex medical regimen that necessarily follows transplantation. Individuals who undergo successful transplantation not only increase their chance for survival, but also are frequently able to return to a normal, productive life.

Individuals who undergo cardiac transplantation must follow a complex medical regimen in order to prevent rejection of the donor organ and other complications. Because the body never really ceases its efforts to reject the donor heart, medications (**immunosuppressants**) that block the body's natural response to foreign objects must be taken indefinitely. These medications are a necessary part of treatment, but they have serious side-effects that must be monitored on a continuing basis. Potential complications of immunosuppression include an increased susceptibility to infection and an increased rate of malignancy.

In order to identify early signs of rejection, cardiac biopsies are performed frequently at first, but less often over time. Cardiac biopsies can be performed under local anesthesia as an outpatient procedure. If there are signs of rejection, additional medications are prescribed to augment immunosuppression.

FUNCTIONAL IMPLICATIONS

Psychological Issues

Fear and anxiety are common reactions to cardiac conditions. Although any chronic illness can trigger these reactions, many people consider the heart the most vital organ and associate any malfunction of the heart with sudden death. Most individuals come to accept their condition and the associated restrictions or treatment. In other instances, however, individuals' responses seriously affect treatment and rehabilitation. Reactions of anger, anxiety, and depression can be the most debilitating factors in cardiac disease. Such reactions can contribute to inactivity, social isolation, or withdrawal from the activities that were previously enjoyed. Consequently, it is necessary to consider the impact of emotional reactions on the ability to return to a comfortable, productive life.

Individuals with cardiovascular disease may be immobilized by fear, subsequently restricting their activities more than needed. Excessive concern that additional stress or exertion may lead to cardiac failure may cause individuals to alter their job, recreational, and family activities severely. Depression may result from concerns about work, family activities, sexual activities, and the life style changes that abound. If the cardiovascular condition requires significant modifications in life style or employment, changes may be associated with a sense of loss and bereavement.

Denial is part of a normal psychological defense that can be used to cope with a severe threat. Although denial can be an effective mechanism for reducing anxiety levels, it can also have a detrimental effect on treatment. Symptoms may be ignored or trivialized, physical incapacity denied, or recommendations for treatment or life style change ignored. As a result, care and treatment may be inadequate, leading to complications or hastening the progression of the condition itself.

Although the way in which individuals respond to cardiovascular conditions is dependent to some extent on their personality, the magnitude of the response may be due to their personal situation at the time. Financial, work, and family concerns, in addition to the diagnosis of a cardiac condition and its implications, can intensify the response expressed.

Life Style Issues

Although not all cardiovascular conditions require significant life style changes, some changes are generally recommended. Modifications in diet, a decrease in or the elimination of the use of alcohol and tobacco, or changes in levels of activity may be required. Because smoking constricts blood vessels, persons with cardiovascular disease, particularly peripheral vascular disease, should not smoke in order to avoid diminishing blood flow to the heart or extremities further. The physician may prescribe exercise, such as daily walks, as a therapeutic tool. Even when recommended changes are minimal, individuals may perceive the changes as having a negative effect on the quality of life; depression or anger may result.

The degree and the way in which stress contributes to the development of cardiovascular disease is unknown. Even if stress itself does not directly cause pathological changes in the cardiovascular system, the behaviors used to cope with stress may do so. For example, the overuse of tobacco and alcohol can have adverse effects on cardiovascular function. Those who have used smoking and alcohol to cope with stress in the past may need to learn different coping strategies. At times, significantly cutting down on activity and involvement can be more stressful than continuing the activity itself. Therefore, helping individuals to learn new ways to cope with stress may be more beneficial than insisting that potentially stress-producing activities be avoided.

Many cardiovascular diseases require long-term treatment with medication. Often individuals' successful rehabilitation and subsequent progress depend on their willingness and ability to take medications accurately. Potential barriers to effective treatment with medication may be financial, attitudinal, or logistical. Appropriate strategies must be developed to maximize an individual's ability to comply with treatment as prescribed.

After the diagnosis of a cardiac condition, sexual activity may be a special source of anxiety for individuals, as well as for their partners. In most instances, sexual activity can be resumed; however, associated fear and anxiety can hamper both enjoyment and performance, altering self-esteem and contributing to depression. Often, the lack of information contributes to fear and misperceptions. The physician should discuss specific recommendations regarding the resumption of sexual activity, as well as any restrictions or modifications.

Social Issues

To some degree, the reactions of those in the environment influence the success with which an individual copes with any chronic condition. Family members may be a source of support and consolation. They may also, however, contribute to the individual's fear and anxiety by being overprotective or showing anxiety out of proportion to the medical condition. Qualified professionals should discuss such reactions and their potential impact on the individual's return to function with family members.

Although those with cardiovascular disease may continue most forms of recreation, they must sometimes curtail their activities. If an individual must give up a recreational activity that was a major social outlet, social isolation and depression may result unless another recreational activity can be substituted.

Cardiac conditions often have few visible signs of disability. Although this may seem advantageous at first glance, the lack of visible cues may contribute to a misunderstanding of the activity restrictions that are part of the treatment protocol. As a result, individuals with such conditions may be pressured into participating in activities that are more strenuous than are those at the prescribed level of activity. The absence of outward signs of disability may also foster an individual's denial of the condition and subsequent noncompliance with the medical treatment plan.

Vocational Issues

For most individuals, work is a source of pride, as well as a financial necessity. The degree to which the cardiovascular condition inhibits the return to regular employment can influence an individual's reactions to the condition. In some instances, the attitudes of employers are barriers to the successful return to work. Employers may be reluctant to employ or re-employ individuals with cardiovascular disease because of the fear of liability or responsibility for medical costs if the condition should worsen.

Each job must be viewed in relation to the individual's physical and emotional abilities, and the effect that the job has on the individual's health status. In some instances, a job change may be necessary. Such a change can be an additional source of stress. In other instances, the individual can return to the former job with little or no modification.

Physicians generally prescribe the degree and type of activity in which individuals with cardiovascular disease may safely engage. Most individuals with heart conditions are able to engage in light to moderate activity. Because of their effect on the cardiovascular system, environmental conditions such as excessive heat or cold should be avoided. Isometric exercise elevates blood pressure and places an extra burden on the heart; consequently, any exertion that involves muscular activity against a fixed, unmoving resistance is usually to be avoided. Individuals with pacemakers should be aware that certain types of equipment may interfere with pacemaker function.

The ability of individuals with peripheral vascular conditions to walk without pain should be evaluated before they return to work. Factors that reduce the blood supply to the extremities, such as cold temperatures, should be avoided. Because of the potential for infection in the lower extremities associated with their inadequate blood supply, work environments that contain hazards for trauma to the feet or legs should also be avoided.

In most instances, once cardiovascular conditions are stabilized and appropriate treatment is instituted, functional decline is slow or minimal. The greatest barrier to productive vocational activity may be the individual's unwillingness or inability to make recommended life style changes or noncompliance with the medical treatment prescribed.

BIBLIOGRAPHY

Barber, T.C., and Langfitt, D.E. *Teaching the Medical/Surgical Patient—Diagnostics and Procedures*. Bowie, Md.: Robert J. Brady Co., 1983.

Berkow, R., and Fletcher, A.J., eds. *The Merck Manual of Diagnosis and Therapy*. Rahway, N.J.: Merck Sharpe and Dohme Research Laboratories, 1987.

Brunner, L.S.; Emerson, C.P.; Ferguson, L.K.; and Suddarth, D.S. *Textbook of Medical-Surgical Nursing*. Philadelphia: W.B. Saunders Co., 1970.

Corbett, J.V. *Diagnostic Procedures in Nursing Practice*. Norwalk, Conn.: Appleton-Century-Crofts, 1982.

Corbett, J.V. *Laboratory Tests in Nursing Practice*. Norwalk, Conn.: Appleton-Century-Crofts, 1983.

Fowles, R. F. "Acute Myocardial Infarction." *Postgraduate Medicine* 84(1988):89–110.

Grauer, K.; Curry, W.; Kosch, S.G.; Kravitz, L.; Moore, W.; and Stewart, W.L. "Exercise Testing and Coronary Artery Disease." *Journal of Family Practice* 16(1983):241–257.

Gray, R.M.; Reinhardt, A.M.; and Ward, J.R. "Psychosocial Factors Involved in the Rehabilitation of Persons with Cardiovascular Disease." *Rehabilitation Literature* 30(1969):354–362.

Griffith, J.L., and Griffith, M.E. "Structural Family Therapy in Chronic Illness." *Psychosomatics* 28(1987):202–205.

Grisanti, J.M. "Raynaud's Phenomenon." *American Family Physician* 41(1990):134–141.

Guyton, A.C. *Human Physiology and Mechanisms of Disease*. Philadelphia: W.B. Saunders Co., 1982.

Hunt, S.A., and Schroeder, J.A. "Managing Patients after Cardiac Transplantation." *Hospital Practice* (October 1989):83–100.

Katz, A. "Changing Strategies in the Diagnosis and Treatment of Congestive Heart Failure." *Modern Medicine* 57(1989):54–60.

Keele, C.A.; Neil, E.; and Joels, N. *Samson Wright's Applied Physiology*. New York: Oxford University Press, 1982.

Luckman, J., and Sorensen, K.C. *Medical-Surgical Nursing: A Psychophysiologic Approach*. Philadelphia: W.B. Saunders Co., 1987.

McLane, M.; Krop, H.; and Mehta, J. "Psychosexual Adjustment and Counseling after Myocardial Infarction." *Annals of Internal Medicine* 92(1980):514–519.

Messerli, F.H. "Essential Hypertension." *Postgraduate Medicine* 81(1987):165–180.

Nursing 87 Books. *Patient Teaching*. Springhouse, Pa.: Springhouse Corporation Book Division, 1987.

Patterson, R.E.; Pitt, B.; and Schelbert, H.R. "Cardiac Imaging: Thallium and Beyond." *Patient Care* 24(1990):24–43.

Popma, J.J., and Dehmer, G.J. "Management of Patients after Coronary Angioplasty." *American Family Physician* 41(1990):121–128.

Rakel, R.E. *Conn's Current Therapy 1990*. Philadelphia: W.B. Saunders Co., 1990.

Renshaw, D.C. "Sexuality and Heart Disease." *Cardiovascular Research and Rehabilitation* 9(1988):24–26.

Scheer, S.J., ed. *Medical Perspectives in Vocational Assessment of Impaired Workers*. Gaithersburg, Md.: Aspen Publishers, 1991.

Smith, D.W., and Hanley-Germain, C.P. *Care of the Adult Patient*. Philadelphia: J.B. Lippincott Co., 1975.

Steinhart, M.J. *Emotional Aspects of Coronary Heart Disease*. Kalamazoo: The Upjohn Company, 1984.

Stolov, W.C., and Clowers, M.R. *Handbook of Severe Disability*. Washington, D.C.: U.S. Department of Education, Rehabilitation Services Administration, 1981.

Thoreson, R.W., and Ackerman, M. "Cardiac Rehabilitation: Basic Principles and Psychosocial Factors." *Rehabilitation Counseling* 24(1981):223–259.

Thurer, S. "Sexual Adjustment Following Coronary Bypass Surgery." *Rehabilitation Counseling Bulletin* 24(1981):319–322.

Vander, A.J.; Sherman, J.H.; and Luciano, D.S. *Human Physiology: The Mechanisms of Body Function*. New York: McGraw-Hill Book Co., 1985.

Wehrmacher, W.H. "Angioplasty versus Bypass Surgery." *Postgraduate Medicine* 84(1988):62–68.

Wenger, N.K. "Rehabilitation of the Patient with Coronary Heart Disease." *Postgraduate Medicine* 85(1989):369–378.

Wilson, D.B., and Vacek, J.L. "Angina and Coronary Artery Disease." *Postgraduate Medicine* 84(1988):77–85.

Wyngaarden, J.B., and Smith, J.H. *Cecil Textbook of Medicine*. Philadelphia: W.B. Saunders Co., 1988.

chapter 3

Respiratory Conditions

NORMAL STRUCTURE AND FUNCTION

The functions of the respiratory system are to deliver oxygen to the blood and to remove carbon dioxide, a waste product of tissue metabolism. Abnormal functioning of the respiratory system can affect every system of the body if it diminishes the oxygen supply

Respiration consists of taking air into the lungs (**inspiration**) and expelling air from the lungs (**expiration**). It is under the control of a respiratory center located in the brain. Normally, an increased concentration of carbon dioxide stimulates the respiratory center, which subsequently increases the rate and the depth of breathing.

The lungs are contained within the **thoracic cavity** (Figure 3-1). The **thorax** (chest cavity), which is surrounded by ribs, is separated from the abdominal cavity by a muscular wall called the **diaphragm**. The left lung contains two lobes, the upper and lower lobes. The right lung contains three lobes, the upper, middle, and lower lobes. The heart is located between the two lungs. The chest cavity is lined by a thin membrane called the **pleura**, which secretes a thin layer of fluid to help minimize friction as the lungs expand and contract against the chest wall during respiration. Pressure within the lungs and the thorax must be less than the pressure in the atmosphere in order for inspiration to occur. As air is taken into the lungs, intrathoracic pressure increases, consequently moving air out of the lungs. In addition to changes of pressure within the thoracic cavity, other muscles in the thoracic area, as well as the diaphragm, assist in respiration.

Air first enters the respiratory system through the nose during inspiration. The air entering the nostrils comes in contact with a mucous membrane that warms and moistens it. Tiny hairs within the nostrils help to trap dust particles and organisms before they reach the pharynx. The **pharynx** (throat) serves as a pas-

47

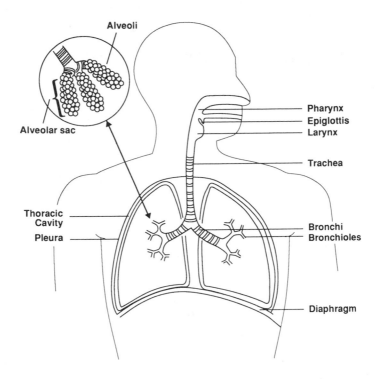

Figure 3-1 Respiratory System

sageway for both air and food. At the bottom of the pharynx are two openings, one into the esophagus for the passage of food and the other into the larynx for the passage of air. The **larynx** (voice box) contains the vocal cords. A flap called the **epiglottis**, located on top of the larynx, closes over the larynx when food is ingested to prevent food from entering the respiratory system.

As air is taken in, it passes through the larynx into the **trachea** (wind pipe). The trachea is a cartilaginous tube lined with special hairlike projections called **cilia**. These cilia are part of the body's defense against foreign objects, such as bacteria, or other particles that have not been filtered out by the upper part of the respiratory system. With a rhythmic motion, the cilia project mucus or other particles up toward the pharynx where they can be expectorated. The trachea divides into two branches after it enters the chest cavity; these branches are called the right and left **bronchi**.

Each bronchus, which also contains cilia, enters a lung and continues to branch into smaller segments called **bronchioles**. These bronchioles terminate in tiny sacs called **alveolar sacs**. Within the alveolar sacs are small pockets called

alveoli, which make up most of the lung's substance. It is within the alveoli that the exchange of oxygen and carbon dioxide takes place.

After delivering oxygen to the body tissues, blood returns to the heart from the general circulation; at this point, it carries an excess of carbon dioxide. The blood is pumped from the right ventricle of the heart into the lungs. Here, the thin walls of the alveoli come in contact with the thin walls of tiny blood vessels called **capillaries**. Carbon dioxide passes from the capillaries across the alveolar wall to be expelled through expiration of the lungs. In turn, the oxygen that has been taken into the alveoli through inspiration, passes across the alveolar wall into the capillaries. The red blood cells take up oxygen, and the blood returns to the heart, where it is pumped into the general circulation to supply body tissues with oxygen.

RESPIRATORY DISORDERS

Upper Respiratory Tract Disorders (Pharyngitis, Laryngitis, Sleep Apnea)

The upper respiratory tract consists of the nose, the pharynx, and the larynx. Many conditions of the upper respiratory tract, such as **pharyngitis** (sore throat) or **laryngitis** (inflammation of the larynx that causes hoarseness), are relatively minor and self-limiting. Some conditions of the upper airway are more serious and debilitating, however. One of these is **sleep apnea**, the cessation of breathing during sleep.

There are several types of sleep apnea. The least common type is **central sleep apnea**, which is caused by a disruption of the signals from the central nervous system that stimulate respiration. This condition may be due to a variety of disease conditions of the central nervous system.

Peripheral sleep apnea, the most common type, is a cessation of breathing for 10 seconds or more because of an upper airway obstruction. An abnormality of the upper airway itself or enlarged structures, such as the tongue or tonsils, may be responsible for the obstruction. Individuals with sleep apnea may be unaware that they stop breathing during sleep, but may experience excessive daytime drowsiness or difficulty with attention or concentration. Family members may observe loud snoring or sudden body movements while the individual is sleeping. **Mixed** type sleep apnea is a combination of central and peripheral sleep apnea.

The evaluation of sleep apnea often takes place in a sleep laboratory where breathing during sleep is monitored. The treatment of peripheral sleep apnea may consist of surgical intervention to remove the obstruction or to correct the structural abnormality. Central sleep apnea is often not correctable and may require the use of mechanical devices, such as ventilators, during sleep.

Bronchial Asthma

In **bronchial asthma**, there is a reversible narrowing or constriction of the bronchi in response to a variety of stimuli. The narrowing of the airways obstructs the airflow, resulting in wheezing, coughing, and **dyspnea** (difficulty in breathing). Asthma may be allergic or nonallergic. Exposure to a substance that triggers an allergic response, such as dusts and molds, pollen, and animal dander, may precipitate allergic asthma. A combination of allergic factors may trigger an attack. A variety of factors, such as exercise, emotional upset, inhalation of cold air, or exposure to irritants (e.g., fumes from paint or gasoline, or cigarette smoke), may precipitate nonallergic asthma.

The severity of symptoms and frequency of asthma attacks vary with individuals. Some individuals may have a slight cough and shortness of breath during an attack, while others may be so restricted by cough and shortness of breath that they are unable to speak more than a few words at a time.

The treatment of asthma is directed toward the identification and avoidance of precipitating factors, the symptomatic relief of attacks, and the prevention of future attacks. Medications called **bronchodilators** are commonly used in the treatment of asthma attacks. These medications dilate the bronchioles by relaxing the muscles of their walls, thus creating a larger opening for the passage of air. Bronchodilators may be used orally, or as inhalers or nebulizers. A **nebulizer** converts the liquid medication into tiny droplets that the individual then inhales. Nebulizers and inhalers deliver the medication directly to the lungs so that it begins to act immediately. Individuals with asthma may use special instruments, such as the Wright Peak Flow Meter, to assess the effect of inhaled bronchodilators or to assess their respiratory status. If asthma is traced to allergic factors, the precipitating factors should be eliminated.

Atelectasis (collapse of the lung) is a possible complication of asthma. Another is a severe, prolonged attack (**status asthmaticus**). This condition is potentially life-threatening and requires emergency medical treatment.

Chronic Obstructive Pulmonary Disease

The term *chronic obstructive pulmonary disease* (**COPD**) is used to describe a generalized obstruction of the airways that causes dyspnea. In most instances, an oversecretion of mucus and/or constriction of the airways with loss of the lungs' elasticity cause the airflow obstruction. A number of conditions may be considered COPD. The most common are chronic bronchitis and emphysema. These two conditions are not always linked, but they do frequently occur together.

Bronchitis is considered chronic when symptoms have occurred for at least 2 consecutive years. Symptoms consist of a persistent cough, often in the early morning, accompanied by an excessive volume of mucus and expectoration. The lining of the air passages becomes irritated, swollen, and clogged with mucus. Mucus obstructs airflow in and out of the **alveoli**. Sometimes, the small muscles around the air passages tighten. This is called **bronchospasm** and makes breathing even more difficult. Chronic bronchitis often leads to emphysema.

Emphysema is defined as a permanent enlargement of the alveoli owing to the overinflation of and destructive change in the alveolar walls. Consequently, the alveoli have less surface available for the exchange of oxygen and carbon dioxide, and the bronchioles close before exhalation is complete. As more and more alveoli are affected, the lungs lose some of their natural ability to stretch and relax, thus diminishing the efficiency of expiration. Airways become obstructed, and stale air, which is high in carbon dioxide and low in oxygen, is trapped in the alveoli. The lungs become overinflated because all the air cannot be expelled. Bronchitis often predisposes individuals to the development of emphysema, but emphysema can also result from other conditions of the lung, such as occupational lung diseases and cystic fibrosis.

The most important risk factor for the development of COPD is cigarette smoking, even though COPD may develop in those who have had chronic asthma for years and do not smoke. Smoking and air pollution in combination may facilitate the development of COPD. The course of COPD varies. In most cases, the condition develops slowly; respiratory function may remain relatively stable for years. In other cases, however, respiratory function deteriorates rapidly. Many people have COPD for years before it is diagnosed. Individuals usually seek medical advice when they note shortness of breath with exercise or at rest. At this point, more than 50 percent of their lung function may already have been lost.

Because of the airway obstruction, **hypoxemia** (decreased oxygen in the blood) may occur. As COPD becomes more advanced and hypoxemia increases, the oxygen supply to the brain may be inadequate, resulting in impaired judgment, confusion, or motor incoordination. A buildup of carbon dioxide (**hypercapnia**) may also occur because of the inadequate gas exchange in the lungs, resulting in drowsiness or apathy.

In order to counteract the low concentration of oxygen, the body's production of red blood cells increases, resulting in a condition called **polycythemia**. The increased number of red cells in the blood increases blood viscosity, which, in turn, can interfere with blood flow. When polycythemia is severe, periodic **phle-**

botomy (removal of blood) may be performed to reduce the number of red blood cells and, thus, to decrease the viscosity of the blood.

As COPD advances, there may be increased difficulty expectorating secretions; increased shortness of breath, especially upon exertion; and increased vulnerability to respiratory infections. For individuals with COPD, respiratory infections can be life-threatening, because they further compromise an already diminished gas exchange.

Right ventricular failure (**cor pulmonale**) may develop as a complication of COPD. As a result of the obstruction of airflow in the lungs and the subsequent breakdown of the alveolar walls, many capillaries in the lungs are destroyed. The surrounding capillaries become constricted, as a compensatory mechanism in response to lower concentrations of oxygen. Constriction of the capillaries channels additional blood flow to those areas of the lungs that are better oxygenated; however, constriction of capillaries also creates a resistance to the blood being pumped into the lungs by the right ventricle of the heart. Therefore, the right ventricle must pump against resistance and becomes **hypertrophied** (enlarged), losing the ability to pump effectively (see Chapter 2). Because of the inefficient pumping action of the enlarged right ventricle, blood returning to the right side of the heart from the general circulation begins to back up, causing **edema** in other parts of the body. The organs of the digestive system may become engorged with fluid, causing nausea and vomiting. There may also be edema of the lower extremities, predisposing the individual to skin ulcerations.

In general, COPD is irreversible. Most treatment is designed to provide symptomatic relief, control or prevent complications, and improve the quality of life. In addition to medication, specific forms of therapy may include postural drainage, chest physiotherapy, or the use of resistive breathing devices. The avoidance of pulmonary irritants, especially smoking, is of primary importance.

Bronchiectasis

Chronic inflammation caused by conditions such as bronchopneumonia and chronic sinusitis may lead to **bronchiectasis**, the dilation of bronchi or bronchioles. **Purulent** (pus-containing) material collects in these dilated areas. Individuals often cough and expectorate foul sputum. They may also complain of fatigue, weight loss, or loss of appetite.

Treatment includes the administration of antibiotics to control the infection, maintenance of general health through rest and nutrition, and avoidance of further infections. Individuals may also learn special techniques or receive treatment (e.g., percussion and postural drainage) to help drain the purulent discharge. Damaged bronchi do not return to normal. If the inflammatory and destructive process continues, surgical removal of the diseased part of the lung may be necessary.

Occupational Lung Diseases (Pneumoconiosis, Asbestosis, Berylliosis, Byssinosis, Occupational Asthma)

Some lung disorders are directly related to matter inhaled from the occupational environment. Although disabling, occupational lung diseases are preventable. They are classified by the type of material particles inhaled.

Silicosis may occur in those with occupations such as metal mining, foundry work, pottery making, or sandblasting in which there is exposure to silica. When particles of silica enter the alveoli, special cells within the lungs engulf the foreign material and then die. In response, a special substance is released in the lung, and **fibrosis** (fibrous tissue within the lung) results. There may be no respiratory impairment initially, although damage in the form of nodules may be identified by roentgenogram. As the damage continues, there is a progressive restriction of lung function with associated **hypoxemia**. There may later be severe shortness of breath, cough, and sputum production. If the condition progresses further, complications such as right ventricular failure may result. There is no effective treatment. Persons with airway obstruction as a result of silicosis are treated similarly to those individuals with COPD, as described previously.

Coal miners' pneumoconiosis, or **black lung disease**, is characterized by a wide distribution of coal dust throughout the lungs, leading to a mild dilation of the bronchioles and the development of abnormalities surrounding the bronchioles. Although not all cases of pneumoconiosis progress, a small percentage of individuals develop progressive scarring of the lung that, in turn, interferes with air exchange. There is no specific treatment for pneumoconiosis; treatment is similar to that for COPD.

Asbestosis results from the long-term inhalation of asbestos fibers. Exposure may be through the mining, milling, or manufacturing processes involved in the production of items such as cement, shingles, or siding, or through asbestos products such as insulation. The inhalation of asbestos fibers can cause fibrinous changes within the lung. Individuals usually notice **dyspnea** on exertion. The treatment of asbestosis is symptomatic. Because asbestosis increases the risk of lung cancer, it is recommended that individuals with the condition abstain from smoking.

The inhalation of dust or fumes that contain beryllium compounds may cause **berylliosis**. Exposure to beryllium is common in many chemical plants, in factories (e.g., those that manufacture fluorescent light bulbs), and in the aerospace industry. Symptoms of the condition may not appear for as long as 10 to 20 years after the exposure. Inhaled beryllium creates an inflammatory process in the lungs that alters the lung tissue. Symptoms may include progressive difficulty with breathing on exertion, with progressive loss of respiratory function. The treatment of berylliosis is largely symptomatic.

Byssinosis occurs primarily in textile workers. It is caused by the inhalation of dusts from fibers such as cotton, flax, and hemp. The resulting bronchoconstriction causes chest tightness. Unlike those with other occupational lung diseases, which become worse with increased exposure, individuals with byssinosis experience symptoms after they return to work from days off, but as the week goes on, symptoms gradually lessen. With prolonged exposure over a number of years, chest tightness may extend for longer periods.

Asthma may be induced by exposure to sensitizing agents in the work environment. The term *occupational asthma* is not used to describe instances in which environmental factors provoke an attack in someone who already has asthma. Rather, it applies to an individual who became asthmatic because of exposure to environmental agents in the work place, a process that may take from days to years. The list of agents considered potential causes of occupational asthma is growing daily. If asthma is proved to be occupational, exposure must be reduced or avoided completely, depending upon the severity of the disease. The treatment and management of occupational asthma are individual. In some instances, even those who leave the work environment continue to have symptoms for a number of years.

Tuberculosis

An infectious disease caused by an organism called the tubercle bacillus, tuberculosis is an inflammatory acute or chronic disease that may occur in almost any part of the body, although it occurs most frequently in the lungs. Tuberculosis of the lung is called **pulmonary tuberculosis**. Infection occurs primarily through the inhalation of infectious droplets that an infected individual has released through coughing. Nodules form in the lung as a result of the infection.

Exposure to the tubercle bacillus may or may not lead to active disease. Whether active tuberculosis develops depends on an individual's general physical condition and the intensity of the exposure. Ordinarily, tuberculosis is not contracted from brief exposure to the infectious agent. Many factors predispose an individual to the development of tuberculosis. A lowered body resistance because of inadequate rest and poor nutrition may be one predisposing factor. Persons with other disabling conditions, such as diabetes, alcoholism, and conditions that affect the lungs (e.g., silicosis), are more vulnerable if they should come in contact with the infectious agent.

Individuals infected with tuberculosis for the first time are said to have a primary infection. Primary infections may or may not become active. The infection may be dormant for years until physical resistance is lowered. The most common form of tuberculosis is re-infection, or secondary tuberculosis.

Individuals with active pulmonary tuberculosis may have few symptoms until the nodules in the lung are large enough to be seen on a roentgenogram. Initial symptoms may be weight loss, **anorexia** (loss of appetite), and a slight elevation of temperature. Symptoms may then progress to cough, overproduction of sputum, and **hemoptysis** (blood-streaked sputum).

Infection with the tubercle bacillus is diagnosed through cultures of sputum, chest roentgenograms, and tuberculin skin tests. A positive reaction to a skin test indicates that the individual has been infected, but it does not indicate whether the disease is active. Although it reveals nodular changes in the lungs, a chest roentgenogram may not make it possible to distinguish between active and inactive disease. Active tuberculosis is confirmed mainly through the identification of the tubercle bacillus in cultures of sputum or other body secretions.

Individuals with active tuberculosis should undergo prompt treatment, not only for their own well-being, but also for the protection of others. Treatment consists of taking medication from 6 to 24 months. The average length of treatment with medication is from 9 to 12 months. It is of the utmost importance that individuals being treated for tuberculosis take the prescribed medication accurately and consistently if treatment is to be effective. Usually, after 2 to 4 weeks of intensive treatment with medication, the individual is no longer a public health threat and can return to normal activities.

Tuberculosis that occurs outside the lungs is called **extrapulmonary tuberculosis**. Possible disease sites include the lining of the brain and spinal cord, the kidney, bones, or the abdomen. Tuberculosis that is widespread throughout the body is called **miliary tuberculosis**. The treatment of extrapulmonary tuberculosis is similar to that of pulmonary tuberculosis, although treatment may continue for a longer period.

Cystic Fibrosis

The hereditary disorder cystic fibrosis involves several body systems, including the pulmonary system. Although often perceived as a disease of childhood, recent improvements in the management of complications enable many individuals with cystic fibrosis to live into adulthood.

One manifestation of the disorder is the formation of thick mucus in the small bronchi, which can lead to severe bronchitis and emphysema. Pulmonary symptoms require the administration of antibiotics to prevent or treat infection, the use of humidity aerosols to liquefy secretions, and special mechanical techniques to help drain mucus. Individuals with cystic fibrosis should be particularly careful to avoid respiratory infections and adverse environmental conditions.

Chest Injuries

Fractured ribs are a common chest injury. Although painful, they are usually relatively easily treated by wrapping a strap or binder around the chest for support. In some instances, however, a fractured rib punctures other organs, such as the lungs or heart, and the consequences are more serious.

An open wound to the chest may allow air to enter the thoracic cavity. This condition, called **pneumothorax**, may cause the lung on the affected side to collapse. If air escaped into the thoracic cavity because of a tear or rupture of the alveoli or bronchus, the condition is called a **closed**, or **spontaneous, pneumothorax**. The escape of blood into the thoracic cavity because of an injury to the chest that damaged vessels in the thoracic cavity is called **hemothorax** that may also cause collapse of a lung. In the case of pneumothorax or hemothorax, the lung is compressed, hampering breathing. A large pneumothorax or hemothorax requires emergency treatment to remove air or blood and repair the injury. The removal of fluid from the thoracic cavity is called **thoracocentesis**.

DIAGNOSTIC PROCEDURES

Chest Roentgenography (X-Ray)

Roentgenography of the chest is a radiographic procedure that allows bony structures (e.g., the ribs), the lungs, and other organs in the thoracic cavity to be viewed as a still image on x-ray film. It may be useful in diagnosing tuberculosis, in noting changes in the lungs due to COPD, or identifying structural abnormalities or tumors.

Bronchoscopy

The visual examination of the bronchial tubes through a long hollow tube inserted through the mouth and into the bronchus is called **bronchoscopy**. With the bronchoscope, the physician can view the walls of the bronchus and note any abnormalities. A **pulmonologist** (a physician who specializes in diseases of the lung) usually performs the procedure, although other physicians who have had special training in the procedure may do so. Individuals who are undergoing bronchoscopy are usually given a sedative, but they remain awake during the procedure.

Laryngoscopy

Like bronchoscopy, **laryngoscopy** is a procedure performed with a hollow tube. A **laryngoscope** inserted into the larynx enables the physician to inspect the structures of the larynx visually and to assess the function of the vocal cords. The procedure is usually done under a local anesthetic, although the individual may be sedated for the procedure.

Skin Tests

After being infected by the tubercle bacilli, the body develops an allergic response over time, resulting in tissue sensitivity. A skin test consists of an injection of a small amount of filtrate from dead tubercle bacilli under the skin. If an individual has been exposed to the tubercle bacilli, there will be a local skin reaction at the injection site. Skin tests are interpreted for reaction at 24 hours and at 48 to 72 hours after injection.

Pulmonary Angiography

In a procedure called **pulmonary angiography**, a catheter is inserted into a vessel, and a contrast agent (special dye) is injected into the catheter to enable the physician to visualize the pulmonary vessels. X-ray films are then taken and the circulation of the lungs studied. Pulmonary angiography may be used to assess the extent to which emphysema has destroyed lung tissue or may be used prior to surgery for lung cancer to assess the potential benefits of surgery.

Pulmonary Function Tests

Physicians use **pulmonary function tests** to assess the volume of air that an individual can take in and expel from the lungs, as well as the individual's ability to move air in and out of the lungs. Pulmonary function tests may be used to determine the cause of dyspnea, the extent of lung disease, or the effectiveness of treatment for lung disease. Generally done in a pulmonary laboratory, the tests involve breathing into a special machine called a **spirometer**. The results are then printed out in a graphic representation called a **spirogram**. The spirogram measures several types of pulmonary function.

- **vital capacity**: the maximum volume of air that can be inspired and expired.

- **forced expiratory volume (FEV)**: the volume of air that the individual can forcibly exhale at 1-, 2-, and 3- second intervals. Readings of the FEV are reported as FEV_1, FEV_2, and FEV_3.
- **residual lung volume**: the amount of air left in the lungs after maximum expiration.
- **maximum voluntary ventilation (MVV)**: the maximum volume that an individual can breathe in 12 seconds, breathing in and out as rapidly and forcefully as possible.
- **tidal volume**: the amount of air breathed in and out at rest.
- **inspiratory capacity**: the volume of air taken in by maximal inspiration after normal expiration.
- **functional residual capacity**: the volume of air remaining in the lungs after normal expiration.

Ventilation/Perfusion Scan (Lung Scan)

Ventilation is the process by which gases are transported between the atmosphere and the alveoli. **Perfusion** is the process by which blood or other fluid passes to a body part through a vascular bed. The **ventilation/perfusion scan** is a radiographic procedure that makes it possible to measure the ventilation and/or perfusion of the lung. The test may be done to determine whether a blood clot has traveled to the lung and lodged there or to diagnose other disease conditions, such as emphysema. For the ventilation scan, the individual inhales radioactive gas; the image taken shows where ventilation is occurring in the lung. For a perfusion scan, a radioactive dye is injected intravenously, enabling the radiologist to visualize blood flow to the lung.

TREATMENT

Because many diseases of the pulmonary system are irreversible, treatment may be directed toward the control of symptoms and the prevention of complications or further deterioration. Pollutants and other irritants, especially cigarette smoke, should be avoided, as they can aggravate respiratory conditions. In areas where pollution is severe or if allergies complicate the condition, special air filters or purifiers may be needed.

Persons with respiratory disorders in which mucus production is increased may have difficulty clearing secretions. The clearance of secretions is important because it deprives infectious organisms of an environment in which they can grow and thrive. In order to help clear secretions, individuals may be taught specific procedures to assist coughing, or they may be encouraged to increase fluid intake in order to liquefy secretions. Individuals may also be instructed in various forms of postural drainage to be used at home to drain mucus. For example, they may be instructed to lie over the side of the bed with the head in a downward position; placing the head lower than the rest of the body several times a day facilitates the drainage of mucus. Other measures include breathing warm humidified air or inhaling steam several times a day.

In some instances, individuals with increased mucus production may be referred for chest physiotherapy. **Percussion** is a form of massage in which the chest is repeatedly tapped or vibrated in order to loosen mucus and allow it to drain. This procedure may be done by a physical therapist, or it may be done at home, either with an electric percussor or manually by another individual. Even when special exercise therapies are not prescribed, the physician often advises individuals with this condition to engage in a daily walking and exercise program to keep in shape and build strength and endurance.

Many individuals with COPD benefit from learning new breathing techniques that stress abdominal breathing. Others find it helpful to use a simple resistive breathing device in the home daily in order to "exercise" their muscles of respiration. Like those with excessive mucus production, those with COPD may be advised to engage in a daily walking or exercise program to keep in shape, to build strength and endurance, and to maintain good physical condition.

The physician may recommend that individuals with severe breathing problems have a series of small meals throughout the day rather than a few large meals because a distended stomach or abdomen can push against the lungs and further interfere with breathing. Foods that cause gas and bloating should also be avoided.

A number of medications may be used for respiratory conditions, depending on the nature of the respiratory dysfunction.

- **Bronchodilators** help to open the airways so that more air can move in and out. Bronchodilators come in several forms, including pills, liquids, and sprays.
- **Antibiotics** may be taken for infections. They may be taken by mouth or injected.
- **Diuretics**, sometimes called water pills, rid the body of extra fluid, such as fluid buildup because of right ventricular failure.
- **Expectorants** are oral medications that make mucus thinner and easier to clear.
- **Steroids** are hormonal preparations that help reduce swelling in the airways, consequently easing breathing. Steroids are usually taken orally, but may also be injected. Because of their serious side-effects, they are usually prescribed only for temporary relief of severe symptoms rather than for long-term use. Additional information about steroids can be found in Chapter 7.

A variety of breathing aids may be used in the treatment of respiratory disorders. Many devices are designed to help put medicines, oxygen, or moist air deep into the lungs and to help individuals clear their lungs of mucus. An **intermittent positive pressure breathing (IPPB) machine**, for example, delivers air under pressure to the lungs. It may have a nebulizer attached so that it delivers medication and humidity to the lungs as well.

Small portable devices are also available to deliver oxygen to the lungs. Because the body's ability to respond to different concentrations of oxygen diminishes in some respiratory conditions, oxygen should be used only as prescribed, and the use should be carefully monitored. Oxygen should never be used near an open flame because of the danger of combustion.

The physician may prescribe home oxygen therapy for individuals with advanced COPD. Often these individuals have right ventricular failure, an elevated level of red blood cells, severe dyspnea, and sleep-associated hypoxemia. The prescription for oxygen therapy usually depends on the degree of hypoxemia experienced at rest or during exercise. Oxygen may be supplied from a stationary source, such as an oxygen tank mounted near the bed that is used at night during sleep, or from a portable machine that is used throughout the day. Portable systems generally consist of canisters weighing 6 to 9 pounds that are carried by the individual. Larger units are also available, but the difficulty of carrying these devices may make it necessary for them to be wheeled. Therefore, the larger device may limit mobility; in addition, there is the possibility of tripping over the device or becoming entangled in the tubing.

Individuals with cancer or severe chest injuries may require surgery. At times, the removal of the lung (**pneumonectomy**) or a portion of the lung is indicated. Most people are able to function normally even with a portion of the lung removed.

FUNCTIONAL IMPLICATIONS

Psychological Issues

Difficulty in breathing can be a frightening and distressing experience. The associated fear and anxiety may lead to inactivity, which, in turn, may result in a variety of additional physical problems. Prolonged breathing difficulty often causes feelings of helplessness and despair. For those individuals who have been active and self-sufficient, the inability to engage in even simple activities without breathing difficulty can be devastating. Depression is common. Individuals may focus on the activities in which they can no longer participate, at least not as vigorously, rather than attempt to attain their highest level of functional capacity.

If the respiratory disorder reduces the oxygen concentration in the blood and the oxygen available to the brain is insufficient, there may be associated cognitive changes. Clouding of consciousness or changes in cognitive function can be frightening for the individual who is experiencing these changes, as well as for family members who observe the changes. Close monitoring of the oxygen and carbon dioxide concentrations is important in the care of individuals with respiratory disorders so that low oxygen or high carbon dioxide concentrations can be identified and appropriate measures can be instituted to reestablish normal concentrations.

Emotional factors may compound the physical symptoms of respiratory conditions. Anxiety or emotional upsets may increase the difficulty in breathing, causing more anxiety and leading to more difficulty in breathing. When it is possible to identify the situations that increase anxiety or stress, it is important to institute interventions to decrease anxiety so that the difficulty in breathing does not escalate.

The response of family and friends to respiratory disorders may affect an individual's ability to cope with the condition. Family members may unintentionally place an individual with a respiratory condition in an invalid role, reducing their expectations of the individual in the family structure or removing responsibility from the individual, even though he or she may be capable of engaging in a number of activities. The individual may respond to these reactions by using the breathing difficulty to escape from life's demands, to receive emotional rewards, or to manipulate or control the behavior of others. In other instances, family members may overestimate the individual's abilities, not fully understanding the seriousness of the condition and its implications for function. Such reactions may push the individual to go beyond his or her functional capacity or to ignore the physician's specific recommendations for control of the condition.

The circumstances that surround the development of the respiratory condition may elicit guilt on the part of the individual or anger on the part of family members. Because smoking has been linked to a variety of respiratory conditions, individuals who have smoked heavily may feel guilty for their actions that contributed to the disease. Family members may express anger, blaming the individual for smoking and possibly contributing to the development of the disease. When the respiratory disorder is related to occupational factors, both the individual and the family may be angry because of the exposure to unrecognized hazards or, if hazards were identified, the failure to take proper precautions.

Unless the individuals have severe respiratory distress or use some type of breathing aid, their conditions are not usually as easily recognizable as are conditions in which there are visual cues, such as crutches or a wheelchair. Consequently, the expectations of employers, co-workers, or casual acquaintances regarding these individuals' activity may not be consistent with their functional capacity. The lack of visual cues may also enable these individuals to deny the condition and potentially avoid treatment, which can prove hazardous not only for the individual, but also, in the case of infectious disease (e.g., tuberculosis), for others with whom the individual has contact.

Today, tuberculosis may be considered no different from a variety of other respiratory conditions, but in years past, tuberculosis was associated with poverty and uncleanliness. Individuals with tuberculosis who remember the social stigma once associated with the condition may feel ashamed and embarrassed. They may try to hide their diagnosis from others, ignore the physician's recommendations, or discontinue treatment. Such reactions have serious consequences for both individuals with tuberculosis and those in close contact with them.

Individuals who use a portable oxygen therapy device may become psychologically dependent on it and may be reluctant to venture out without the oxygen source, even when they do not need it. Some insist on using oxygen, even though their difficulty in breathing is not the result of a lowered oxygen content of the blood. In such instances, the psychological dependency on the oxygen may be more debilitating than the respiratory condition itself.

Life Style Issues

As with other chronic conditions, the life style changes required by a respiratory disorder depend on the seriousness of the condition and the individual's previous state of health and functional capacity. In general, it is important to maintain a good nutritional status and a normal weight. Because of the increased load that obesity or overeating can place on breathing capacity, individuals with respiratory conditions should be urged to avoid both.

Cessation of smoking is a necessary component of treatment, regardless of the type of respiratory condition. Many individuals consider this task the most difficult part of their treatment regimen. Even when they are aware that smoking exacerbates their respiratory condition, they may find it difficult to alter their behavior. Enrollment in specially designed smoking cessation programs may be necessary to help these individuals stop smoking. Some individuals resist participation even in these interventions, however.

Although exertion may cause difficulty in breathing, individuals with respiratory conditions are generally able to maintain activity unless they have associated cardiac complications. An exercise regimen can both improve self-esteem and reduce symptoms somewhat. If the dyspnea experienced results partly from ineffective breathing patterns and partly from lack of conditioning, it is crucial that the individual practice daily breathing or conditioning exercises, as well as other exercise routines, to increase exercise tolerance.

Unless the cause of dyspnea can be corrected, it may be necessary for individuals with respiratory disorders to become accustomed to feeling short of breath and to adapt to the sensation so that they can maintain their maximum level of activity without undue fear or anxiety. They may need extra time to accomplish tasks so that they can take rest periods. They may need to divide some activities into smaller tasks rather than trying to accomplish the complete task at one time.

Although an environment near sea level with a mild climate and minimal air pollution is ideal for individuals with chronic respiratory disorders, it is not always possible to live in this type of environment. Individuals living in less moderate climates should avoid extremes in temperatures. Home and work temperatures should be kept cool. Radiant or baseboard heaters may be better than forced-air heating systems, as the latter have filters that need to be cleaned or changed regularly. If a humidifier is used, it should be cleaned regularly to forestall mold growth. Fireplaces and wood-burning or coal-burning stoves should be avoided as potential sources of air pollution in the home.

Maintaining adequate hydration is important in respiratory conditions in which there is an overproduction of mucus. The environment should be well humidified, and a nebulizer or aerosol may be used periodically throughout the day to deliver humidity directly to the lungs. High levels of humidity may make breathing more difficult, however. Therefore, individuals living in hot, humid environments should have air conditioning to maintain the temperature and the humidity at acceptable levels. Filters on air conditioners should be changed on a regular basis.

If factors in the home are contributing to the respiratory disease, environmental modifications, such as removing the cause of the allergic reaction, may be required. This is especially distressing if the offending factor is a pet. The environment should also be kept dust-free. It may be necessary to install special filters in order to cut down on molds and household dusts.

Individuals with respiratory disorders may become very anxious about participating in any type of physical activity that increases respiratory difficulty. Because both the rate and the depth of respiration are increased during sexual excitement, the fear of suffocation may cause these individuals to be reluctant or restrained when engaging in sexual activity. Although dyspnea may be uncomfortable, those who have a respiratory disorder with no complications can generally maintain sexual activity. They can often increase their tolerance to sexual activity through conditioning, or their partners may assume a more active role.

Social Issues

Individuals with respiratory disorders may avoid social contacts and social situations that they once enjoyed if dyspnea, especially on exertion, is pronounced. The resulting social isolation can contribute to depression and lowered self-esteem. As much as possible, they should continue to participate in social activity, modifying the circumstances as necessary. For example, the use of a golf cart may reduce the exertion required in golf to the extent that those with respiratory disorders can still enjoy the game as a form of recreation and time to be spent with friends. Outdoor activities should be avoided, of course, when temperatures are very hot or very cold, or if pollution levels are especially high.

Even though crowded, polluted environments aggravate respiratory conditions, individuals with such a disorder need not refrain from participating in activities in urban areas. It may be necessary to plan travel time to and from the events so that traveling does not take place during the time of heaviest traffic. Arriving early at events can help to cut down on the crowding and the potentially anxiety-provoking rush. Establishments that do not prohibit smoking altogether usually provide nonsmoking areas; individuals should check on smoking rules at the facility ahead of time and request seating in the no smoking section.

Pronounced coughing or the excessive, foul-smelling mucus production that may accompany the cough in some respiratory conditions can be embarrassing and interfere with communication and social interactions. Individuals with a respiratory disorder should be open and honest about the condition with others, not making excuses or excessive apologies. Frequent mouth care can help to alleviate foul-smelling breath.

Because of the potential seriousness of respiratory infections in individuals with lung disease, those with respiratory disorders should avoid contact with persons who have upper respiratory infections or flu as much as possible. Although this is not always possible without severely limiting social contacts, exposure to large groups of people in confined environments at the height of the flu season, for example, should be discouraged.

Vocational Issues

The extent to which individuals with respiratory disorders can continue their regular employment depends on the type of work, the work environment, and the severity of the respiratory disease. If factors in the work environment have contributed to or aggravated the respiratory condition, a change may be needed. In some instances, individuals may transfer to another location in the facility where the offending factors are not present.

The extent of activity that the individuals with a respiratory disorder can tolerate should be evaluated. If, for example, they can walk the length of the hall, but cannot walk up one flight of stairs without severe dyspnea, it may be possible to use an elevator or to change floors. The degree to which upper body movements are used in work and the impact of these movements on dyspnea should be considered. If the work demands lifting and carrying that increase dyspnea, alternate strategies may be devised so that the work can be performed with less exertion. These individuals, their employers, and their co-workers should be helped to understand that moderate dyspnea, although uncomfortable, is not in itself life-threatening.

Because cough and sputum production can be cosmetically displeasing, they may interfere with the individual's effectiveness in jobs that require close personal contact or continued conversation. The degree to which the work place demands this type of interaction and the impact of these symptoms on job effectiveness should be assessed.

If any type of breathing device or aid is used, the extent to which the aid will be a hazard in the work environment must be considered. The tubing in some portable devices may be caught in machinery, for example, or cause falls. Oxygen, because of the danger of fire or explosion, should not be used in close proximity to open flame.

In addition to the stress in the work setting that could increase anxiety and subsequently add to breathing difficulty, stressors such as those involved in transportation to and from work should also be noted. If commuting necessitates travel in polluted, congested areas, it may be possible to modify the work schedule to allow travel at less busy times. Flexibility of the work schedule may also be important if specific treatments or rest periods are required during the day.

The legal implications of many lung disorders, especially if they are occupationally related, may be barriers to continued employment. For individuals eligible for workers' compensation or other benefits, financial considerations may affect their motivation and cooperation with treatment. In other instances, the employer's fear of liability may limit job opportunities for individuals with respiratory disorders.

BIBLIOGRAPHY

Andrews, J.L. "Pulmonary Disease: Improving the Prognosis." *Modern Medicine* 55(1987):88–103.

Ayres, S.M. "Chronic Bronchitis: A Clinical Guide." *Hospital Medicine* (May 1984):213–241.

Banks, D.E., and Barkman, H.W. "Common Occupational Lung Disorders." *Hospital Medicine* (June 1983):93–110.

Barber, T.C., and Langfitt, D.E. *Teaching the Medical/Surgical Patient—Diagnostics and Procedures.* Bowie, Md.: Robert J. Brady Co., 1983.

Berkow, R., and Fletcher, A.J., eds. *The Merck Manual of Diagnosis and Therapy.* Merck Sharpe and Dohme Research Laboratories, 1987.

Brunner, L.S.; Emerson, C.P.; Ferguson, L.K.; and Suddarth, D.S. *Textbook of Medical-Surgical Nursing.* Philadelphia: W.B. Saunders Co., 1970.

Burns, M. "Outpatient Pulmonary Rehabilitation." *Postgraduate Medicine* 86(1989):129–137.

Carroll, P.F. "What You Can Learn from Pulmonary Function Tests." *RN* (July 1986):24–27.

Connolly, M.J., and Hendrick, D.J. "Occupational Asthma." *Postgraduate Medicine* 76(1984):179–189.

Corbett, J.V. *Diagnostic Procedures in Nursing Practice*. Norwalk, Conn.: Appleton-Century-Crofts, 1982.

Corbett, J.V. *Laboratory Tests in Nursing Practice*. Norwalk, Conn.: Appleton-Century-Crofts, 1983.

Creer, T.L. "Asthma." *Journal of Counseling and Clinical Psychology* 50(1982):912–921.

Digregoria, G.J., and Kodtyuk, B.L. "Toxicology of Asbestos." *American Family Physician* 32(1985):201–204.

Francis, P.B.; Petty, T.L.; and Winterbauer, R.H. "Helping the COPD Patient Help Himself." *Patient Care* 18(1984):177–184.

Francis, P.B.; Petty, T.L.; and Winterbauer, R.H. "COPD: Making an Earlier Diagnosis." *Patient Care* 22(1988):102–114.

Gottlieb, L.S. "Decline and Rise of Tuberculosis." *Medical Times* (September 1990):9–14.

Guyton, A.C. *Human Physiology and Mechanisms of Disease*. Philadephia: W.B. Saunders Co., 1982.

Heimlich, H.J. "Oxygen Delivery for Ambulatory Patients." *Postgraduate Medicine* 84(1988):68–79.

Hoffman, L.A.; Berg, J.; and Rogers, R.M. "Daily Living with COPD." *Postgraduate Medicine* 86(1989):153–166.

Jones, M.D., and Yeager, H. "Inhaler and Spacer Use in Obstructive Airway Diseases." *American Family Physician* 42(1990):1007–1013.

Kaliner, M.S. "Inhaled Corticosteroids for Chronic Asthma." *American Family Physician* 41(1990):1609–1615.

Keele, C.A.; Neil, E.; and Joels, N. *Samson Wright's Applied Physiology*. New York: Oxford University Press, 1982.

Kutty, K., and Varkey, B. "Chronic Obstructive Pulmonary Disease." *Postgraduate Medicine* 84(1988):60–80.

Luckman, J., and Sorensen, K.C. *Medical-Surgical Nursing: A Psychophysiologic Approach*. Philadelphia: W.B. Saunders Co., 1987.

Nursing 87 Books. *Patient Teaching*. Springhouse, Pa.: Springhouse Corporation Book Division, 1987.

Parsons, E.J. "Coping and Well-Being Strategies in Individuals with COPD." *Health Values* 14(1990):17–23.

Petty, T.L. "New Developments in Home Oxygen Therapy." *Consultant* 27(1987):53–63.

Petty, T.L. "Practical Tips on Prescribing Home Oxygen Therapy." *Postgraduate Medicine* 84(1988):83–90.

Petty, T.L. "Primary Care Treatment of Chronic Obstructive Pulmonary Disease." *Modern Medicine* 56(1988):82–91.

Petty, T.L. "Prevention of Emphysema." *Postgraduate Medicine* 86(1989):115–123.

Rakel, R.E. *Conn's Current Therapy 1990*. Philadelphia: W.B. Saunders Co., 1990.

Scheer, S.J., ed. *Medical Perspectives in Vocational Assessment of Impaired Workers*. Gaithersburg, Md.: Aspen Publishers, 1991.

Smith, D.W., and Hanley-Germain, C.P. *Care of the Adult Patient*. Philadelphia: J.B. Lippincott Co., 1975.

Stafford, C.T. "New Concepts in Chronic Asthma." *Postgraduate Medicine* 84(1988):85–98.

Stolov, W.C., and Clowers, M.R. *Handbook of Severe Disability.* Washington, D.C.: U.S. Department of Education, Rehabilitation Services Administration, 1981.

Tiep, B.L. "Inpatient Pulmonary Rehabilitation." *Postgraduate Medicine* 86(1989):141–150.

Valiante, D.J., and Rosenman, K.D. "Does Silicosis Still Occur?" *Journal of the American Medical Association* 262(1989):3003–3007.

Vander, A.J.; Sherman, J.H.; and Luciano, D.S. *Human Physiology: The Mechanisms of Body Function.* New York: McGraw-Hill Book Co., 1985.

Wyngaarden, J.B., and Smith, J.H. *Cecil Textbook of Medicine.* Philadelphia: W.B. Saunders Co., 1988.

chapter 4

Renal and Urinary Tract Disorders

NORMAL STRUCTURE AND FUNCTION

The term **renal** refers to the kidney, while the term **urinary tract** refers to the collecting system for urine (i.e., the ureters, bladder, and urethra). The kidney is one of several organs in the body that dispose of wastes generated by metabolism. There are two kidneys, bean-shaped organs that lie on the **posterior** (back portion) of the abdominal cavity (Figure 4-1). Two tubes (**ureters**), one leading from each kidney, drain into the bladder, a hollow reservoir that holds urine until it is eliminated. A single tube (**urethra**) leads from the bladder to the outside opening (**urinary meatus**) through which urine is eliminated.

The outer layer of the kidney is called the **cortex**; the inner portion, the **medulla**. The medulla contains 10 to 15 triangular structures called **renal pyramids,** which serve as a portion of the drainage system. Within the cortex and medulla lie units called **nephrons**, which are the functional units of the kidney. There are approximately 1 million nephrons in each kidney. Nephrons contain many clusters of capillaries, called **glomerular capillaries**, that are surrounded by **Bowman's capsule**. The capillaries and Bowman's capsule are called the **glomerulus**.

The kidney filters a large volume of blood each day. Approximately one-quarter of the body's blood flow passes to the kidney through the **renal arteries** at a rate averaging about one liter of arterial blood per minute. The remaining three-quarters of blood goes to the general body circulation. Within the kidney, the blood flows first to the glomerular capillaries, where it is filtered, and then to a second capillary bed (**peritubular capillaries**), which surrounds the nephrons. Blood leaves the kidney through the **renal veins** and returns to the general circulation.

The process by which the kidney removes waste products from the blood is called **glomerular filtration**. The initial filtration, which occurs as the blood

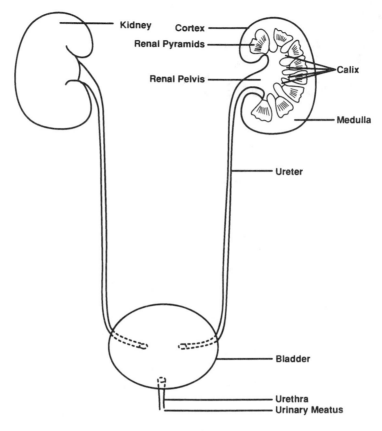

Figure 4-1 Kidneys and Urinary Tract

enters the glomerulus, removes some waste products. As the filtrate continues to move through the tubules of the nephrons, substances are either reabsorbed into the bloodstream or continue through the tubules. As the filtrate moves into the collecting system, it eventually drains into the calix at the mouth of each pyramid and empties into the renal pelvis as urine. From the renal pelvis, urine drains into the ureters to the bladder, where it is stored until ready to be excreted through the urethra and urinary meatus. Although waste products (e.g., **urea**, **creatinine**, and **uric acid**) are either filtered from the blood or only partly reabsorbed, many substances (e.g., sugar and **amino acids**, the building blocks of protein and the end products of protein digestion) are totally reabsorbed into the bloodstream under normal circumstances. **Electrolytes**, which are electrically charged particles of substances that are important to many of the body's internal functions (e.g., **sodium** and **potassium**), are filtered and returned to the bloodstream along with 99 percent of the water in the filtrate. The amounts of water and electrolytes reabsorbed are variable, regulated according to the body's specific needs. The filtrate finally moves into the renal tubule and then into the central portion of the kidney, called the **renal pelvis**. The filtrate (**urine**) moves from the renal pelvis down the ureters and into the bladder, where it is stored until eliminated through the urethra and urinary meatus.

In addition to ridding the body of wastes, the kidneys have many other important functions.

- filtering and reabsorbing valuable nutrients, such as **glucose** (sugar) and vitamins
- maintaining the balance (**homeostasis**) of the body's chemistry by regulating the water content and electrolyte concentrations
- producing substances that regulate blood pressure, the synthesis of red blood cells, and calcium absorption from the intestine

Because of the kidneys' many functions, disorders of the kidney can affect many body systems.

RENAL AND URINARY TRACT DISORDERS

Cystitis (Lower Urinary Tract Infection)

The bladder and urine are usually sterile. When bacteria invade the bladder, **cystitis** (inflammation of the bladder) occurs. The invasion of bacteria can take place through the external urinary meatus, or it can be secondary to an infection in another location of the urinary tract. Because the urethra is shorter in females than in males, external contamination is more likely to be responsible for cystitis in women. Cystitis is more commonly secondary to other causes in men.

The symptoms of cystitis may include frequent urination, even though the bladder may not be full; **dysuria** (painful urination), pain in the lower abdomen or lower back; and, at times, **hematuria** (blood in the urine). If the bacteria have also entered the blood, causing **bacteremia**, the individual may also experience fever and chills.

Cystitis is diagnosed by the symptoms reported and by an examination of the urine for evidence of bacteria, white blood cells, or other indication of infection or inflammation. The treatment of uncomplicated infections includes the administration of medications, such as antibiotics. If cystitis is recurrent, the treatment may include identifying and removing or correcting factors that contribute to the development of urinary tract infections. For example, structural conditions such as stricture or narrowing of part of the lower urinary tract can prevent adequate emptying of the bladder, predisposing the individual to infection.

Although uncomfortable, cystitis itself is generally not debilitating. Of greater concern is recurrent or inadequately treated cystitis in which the infection may travel up the urinary tract and invade the kidneys.

Pyelonephritis

Sometimes a complication of cystitis in which bacteria have progressed to the kidneys from the lower urinary tract, **pyelonephritis** (infection of the kidney) may also be caused by the obstruction or stricture of a portion of the urinary tract. Obstruction or stricture leads to **stasis** (stagnation) of urine, which enhances the growth of bacteria and predisposes the individual to infection.

The symptoms of pyelonephritis include fever, chills, flank or abdominal pain, and, possibly, nausea and vomiting. The diagnosis is based on the symptoms and an examination of the urine for the presence of bacteria and white blood cells. The most important therapeutic measures are the elimination of any obstruction and the eradication of the bacteria by means of appropriate antibiotics. The removal of the obstruction or stricture may require surgical intervention.

Pyelonephritis may be acute or chronic. No long-term debilitation is usually associated with acute pyelonephritis. Chronic pyelonephritis, however, can cause a deterioration of the kidney structure and function, and can lead to renal failure.

Urinary or Renal Calculi (Kidney Stones, Nephrolithiasis, Urolithiasis)

Ranging in size from a stone as tiny as a grain of sand to a stone large enough to fill the inner portion of the kidney, urinary **calculi** (stones) may occur anywhere in the urinary tract. They frequently cause pain, obstruction, and secondary infection. Some individuals appear more prone to develop calculi than others. In addition to structural or metabolic abnormalities, prolonged immobility or bed rest may predispose an individual to the formation of calculi.

Individuals with urinary calculi may have no symptoms, or they may experience excruciating pain in the flank or kidney area, nausea and vomiting, **hematuria**, or frequency of urination. The diagnosis is based on the symptoms, together with an examination of the urine for hematuria or bacteria. A radiologic examination called an **intravenous** or **retrograde pyelogram** may also be performed to detect the presence of stones and, if they are present, to evaluate the extent of the obstruction. If a stone severely obstructs its flow, urine may back up to the kidney, causing kidney damage.

Most calculi are passed through the urinary meatus spontaneously. If a stone does not pass spontaneously, it may have to be removed surgically. The type of surgery depends on the size and the location of the stone. Where available, a procedure called **extracorporeal shock wave lithotripsy** may be used to break up the stone through the use of ultrasound.

Hydronephrosis

An obstruction can occur anywhere in the urinary tract for a variety of reasons: a stone or a stricture caused by an infection, an injury, a congenital abnormality, or a tumor. The obstruction prevents urine from flowing through the urinary tract, and the urine backs up into the kidneys. Because the kidney continues to produce urine during the backflow, the kidney pelvis eventually becomes swollen and distended. This distension is called **hydronephrosis**. The obstruction of the urinary tract and the backflow of urine also predispose the individual to infection of the kidney.

Individuals with hydronephrosis may experience pain or may feel little discomfort. The diagnosis of hydronephrosis is usually made through a roentgenogram. In order to prevent permanent damage to renal function, the kidney must be drained and the obstruction removed. The degree of disability experienced because of hydronephrosis depends on whether the damage has been severe enough to cause kidney failure.

Acute Glomerulonephritis (Acute Nephritic Syndrome)

Nephritis is an inflammation of the kidney. **Glomerulonephritis** is a type of nephritis that is characterized by an inflammation of the glomeruli of the kidney. Glomerulonephritis occurs as an immunological response to bacteria, viruses, or systemic disease; it does not result from an invasion of the glomeruli themselves by a disease agent. The immunological response often follows an infection elsewhere in the body by the streptococcal organism, such as **streptococcal pharyngitis** ("strep throat") or bacterial endocarditis (see Chapter 2).

Initially, the symptoms may be mild, going undetected. They commonly include **hematuria; proteinuria** (protein in the urine); and some impairment in kidney function with the retention of salt and water, possibly leading to elevated blood pressure (**hypertension**) and **edema,** especially in the face and hands. Generalized edema (**anasarca**) may be accompanied by other symptoms, such as **dyspnea** on exertion, visual disturbances, and headache. Glomerulonephritis can result in irreversible structural changes in the kidney. The extent of kidney damage depends on the speed and the effectiveness with which the process can be stopped.

The treatment of glomerulonephritis focuses on the symptoms and the underlying cause. Although many individuals with glomerulonephritis recover completely, some develop **chronic glomerulonephritis**, which can be a forerunner to **end-stage renal disease**. Often, individuals with chronic glomerulonephritis are asymptomatic, and it is not uncommon for them to have no history of acute glomerulonephritis.

Nephrosis (Nephrotic Syndrome)

A general term used to describe conditions in which a kidney has been damaged by conditions other than direct infection of the kidney itself, nephrosis is a collection of signs and symptoms that can be caused by a variety of kidney conditions. It may be the result of hypertension (see Chapter 2), diabetes, glomerulonephritis, or the **hyperproliferation** (overgrowth) of renal cells because of a tumor. It may also be mediated by the immune system and appear secondary to systemic disease, such as rheumatoid arthritis.

The collection of symptoms experienced in nephrosis is termed the **nephrotic syndrome**. This syndrome may include a variety of symptoms (e.g., edema), but **proteinuria** is its hallmark. When the kidneys are damaged, certain substances that would normally be reabsorbed into the bloodstream during the filtering process are passed through the membranes of the glomerular capillaries and excreted in the urine. Protein is one of these substances. Thus, an important complication of nephrotic syndrome is severe protein malnutrition, which may require nutritional supplementation. Although the kidneys may sometimes repair themselves, renal failure may also result from nephrosis.

Polycystic Kidney Disease

A hereditary disease, **polycystic kidney disease** is characterized by the presence of many cysts in the kidneys. The cysts enlarge, compressing and exerting pressure on the functioning kidney tissue. As the disease progresses slowly over many years, individuals may be unaware that they have the disease. A physician may discover it by accident during a routine examination, or as cysts enlarge, these individuals may develop low back pain, **hematuria**, or frequent urinary tract infections.

The condition eventually progresses to end-stage renal disease, but the progression sometimes takes as long as 20 years. The treatment of end-stage renal disease may include dialysis and/or kidney transplantation. Although transplantation is feasible for those with polycystic kidney disease, close family members may not be appropriate donors because of the hereditary nature of the condition.

Renal Failure (End-Stage Renal Disease)

When kidney function is insufficient to meet the body's demands, renal failure has occured. It can be acute or chronic, temporary or permanent. Kidney damage can eventually progress to **end-stage renal disease** in which the kidneys essentially cease to function.

Acute renal failure is sudden and can occur for several reasons. For example, kidney function may be disrupted if blood flow to the kidney is inadequate, such as during shock, or if the renal artery is occluded, such as by a blood clot (**thrombus**). Toxic doses of medications or other chemicals, or a transfusion of blood from an incompatible blood group can also cause acute renal failure.

If the causative factor can be corrected before irreversible structural changes occur in the kidney, acute renal failure may be temporary. In order to prevent permanent kidney damage, treatment must begin immediately. Dialysis may be instituted to take over kidney function temporarily until the cause of the kidney failure can be corrected. Dialysis may also be used to remove toxic substances from the blood before they cause permanent kidney damage.

Chronic renal failure can result from acute renal failure in which irreversible damage occurs before the cause of the acute failure can be corrected, or it can result from disease of the kidney itself, such as glomerulonephritis. Chronic renal failure can also result from systemic disease, such as hypertension and diabetes, or arteriosclerosis in which the arteries of the kidney become thickened (**nephrosclerosis**). Whereas acute renal failure occurs rapidly, chronic renal failure may gradually progress over many years.

The signs and symptoms of renal failure, whether acute or chronic, depend on the cause, the degree of dysfunction, and the rate of renal failure. The symptoms experienced by individuals whose kidneys have failed depend on the stage of the condition. Both acute and chronic renal failure diminish the kidneys' ability to filter blood adequately and remove water and wastes (**glomerular filtration**). This decreased function affects the body's delicate internal balance and has an impact on all other organ systems.

The first sign of renal failure may be **oliguria** (decreased production of urine). Because of the kidneys' reduced function, the body is unable to maintain a normal balance of water and electrolytes. As a result, individuals may experience generalized symptoms, such as muscle weakness or muscle cramps, nausea, vomiting, appetite loss, or dysfunction of other organs (e.g., the heart). Electrolyte imbalances can cause numbness and tingling in the extremities. Activity intolerance or fatigue may result from the anemia associated with impaired kidney function. Many individuals experience dry skin and itching (**pruritus**).

As the kidney becomes less efficient in producing urine and ridding the body of excess water, individuals may experience generalized **edema** with subsequent weight gain. The waste products of protein metabolism, such as **urea** and **creatinine**, may accumulate in the blood, causing a toxic condition called **uremia**. The buildup of waste products in the blood may lead to mental cloudiness or confusion. The kidneys may eventually be unable to excrete urine (**anuria**). Without medical intervention to correct these imbalances and the impaired production of urine, death results.

The treatment of acute renal failure is directed toward removing the cause of the kidney failure when possible, preventing complications, and restoring the body chemistry to its normal state. Depending on the cause of acute renal failure, it can often be reversed with no permanent damage to the kidney.

Because there is no cure for chronic renal failure, the treatment is directed at control. In the very early stages of chronic renal failure, the treatment may include restricting water to an amount equal to urine output, carefully monitoring body weight, and managing the diet to provide adequate nutrition without overtaxing the kidney with metabolic waste products. As renal failure progresses, additional measures, such as dialysis, may be instituted.

Renal failure affects all other body systems, and other conditions, such as congestive heart failure or hypertension (see Chapter 2), may result from kidney damage. In these cases, the treatment is directed toward control of the secondary condition as well. In some instances of renal failure, kidney transplantation may be indicated.

DIAGNOSTIC PROCEDURES

Urinalysis

Urine may be examined by direct visualization, under a microscope, or through other laboratory tests. The report of such a **urinalysis** contains information about the concentration, acidity, and appearance of the urine, as well as the presence of any other components such as protein, sugar, blood, bacteria, or various types of cells in the urine. A urinalysis not only provides a gross estimate of kidney function, but also permits the identification of other potential problems (e.g., infection) or systemic conditions (e.g., diabetes) that may exist. A urinalysis is often a screening test to help determine what, if any, other tests are needed. The collection of urine can be external or, if a sterile specimen (one that is uncontaminated by organisms outside the urinary tract) is needed, through a tube or catheter that is passed through the external opening or **urinary meatus** into the bladder.

Urine Culture

A laboratory examination of a sterile urine specimen, a **urine culture,** is done in order to determine whether there is an infection within the urinary tract and, if so, which organisms are responsible. It is preferable to obtain the specimen for a urine culture through catheterization.

Blood Urea Nitrogen (BUN) Determination

A blood test in which the level of urea nitrogen (a waste product of protein metabolism) in the blood is measured can be helpful in the evaluation of kidney function. Because urea nitrogen is normally excreted by the kidneys, an evaluation of this substance in the blood can reveal kidney impairment. The urea level may also be elevated in conditions other than renal disease, however, such as starvation, dehydration, or conditions in which the blood supply to the kidneys is poor.

Serum Creatinine Determination

Creatinine is a waste product of a high-energy compound (creatine phosphate) found in skeletal muscle tissue. An elevation in the creatinine level in the blood indicates damage to a large number of nephrons. The determination of the creatinine level is a more sensitive test than that of the blood urea nitrogen level and is a better reflection of kidney function.

Creatinine Clearance Test

Used to determine the kidneys' glomerular filtration rate, the **creatinine clearance test** involves a comparison of the amount of creatinine in the blood serum (serum creatinine) with the amount of creatinine excreted in the urine over a specified period of time. For the test, individuals collect and save all their urine during a specified period of time. Blood tests are performed at various points during that time period, and the amounts of creatinine in the blood serum and in the urine are compared. A decreased creatinine clearance rate indicates decreased glomerular function and, thus, kidney dysfunction. The creatinine clearance rate is a better indicator of renal dysfunction than is the measurement of serum creatinine alone. Creatinine clearance tests may be used to diagnose kidney dysfunction or to evaluate the progress of renal disease.

Kidney, Ureters, and Bladder Roentgenography (KUB)

A simple roentgenogram of the kidney, ureters, and bladder may be taken. The x-ray film outlines the size, shape, and location of these structures, but does not indicate kidney function.

Intravenous Pyelography

A radiologic examination of the kidneys, ureters, and bladder, an **intravenous pyelogram** may be done on an outpatient basis. During the test, a special dye is injected into a vein in the arm. The dye is filtered by the kidney and excreted through the urinary tract, during which time x-ray films are taken at intervals for approximately 1 hour. The intravenous pyelogram helps to identify not only any structural abnormalities of the kidney, but also any problems with the passage of the dye through the urinary system. Because some individuals are hypersensitive to the components of the dye and may have severe allergic reactions, questions about known allergies and skin tests are usually routine prior to testing.

Cystoscopy

A **urologist** (a physician who specializes in the diagnosis and the treatment of disease in the urinary tract) may visualize the urethra and bladder directly through a special tube, called a **cystoscope**, inserted through the urinary meatus and urethra into the bladder. Cystoscopy can be used either as a diagnostic procedure or as a part of treatment. It may be done on an outpatient or inpatient basis and may be performed under local or general anesthesia. The cystoscopic examination makes it possible to identify any abnormalities in the internal structure of the bladder, as well as to remove foreign objects or calculi from the bladder, to remove tumors or other abnormal tissue from the bladder, or to perform a **retrograde pyelogram**.

Retrograde Pyelography

In a **retrograde pyelogram**, a small catheter is inserted through a **cystoscope** and then directed into the ureters to the pelvis of the kidney. A special dye is injected through the catheter, and x-ray films are taken to visualize the collecting system. A retrograde pyelogram is performed to assess the function of the kidneys and the ureters, and to detect possible abnormalities or obstructions in the collecting system. The procedure may be done on an outpatient or in-patient basis.

Renal Biopsy

In some cases, it is necessary to remove a small piece of kidney tissue for the diagnosis of kidney disease. Called a renal biopsy, the procedure may be done in several ways. One method involves a surgical incision over the kidney so that the physician can directly view the kidney and remove the specimen. Because this procedure is done under a general anesthetic in a hospital setting, it has a prolonged recuperation period.

The second, more commonly used method involves the insertion of a specially designed needle through the skin over the kidney. The needle is then inserted into the kidney, and a small amount of kidney tissue is removed. This technique is called a **percutaneous renal biopsy**. It is generally performed under a local anesthetic in a hospital setting.

Renal Arteriography

In order to examine the vascular function of the kidney, a diagnostic procedure called renal arteriography may be done. The procedure is performed by inserting a needle into the femoral artery, which is located in the groin. A small catheter is passed through the needle into the femoral artery and advanced through the artery until it reaches the renal arteries. Dye is then injected through the catheter, and x-ray films are taken at 2- to 3-second intervals to examine the functioning of the renal artery.

TREATMENT

Lithotomy

When kidney stones do not pass out of the body with the urine flow, it may be necessary to remove them surgically. This procedure is called **lithotomy**. There are several surgical techniques that may be used. The surgeon may make an incision in the lower part of the abdomen (a **suprapubic** incision) and remove the stone through the incision. At times, the surgeon can remove stones from the bladder by inserting a cystoscope into the bladder through the urethra, passing a special instrument through the cystoscope, and then grasping and crushing the stone with the instrument; this procedure is called **litholapaxy**. The crushed fragments of stone are then passed in the urine.

Depending on the location of the stone, other surgical procedures may be used. A special instrument called a **nephroscope** may be inserted through the skin directly into the kidney to remove the stone. If the kidney pelvis is entered the procedure is called **pyelolithotomy**. If the renal calix is entered, the procedure is called a **nephrolithotomy**. The surgical removal of stones from the ureter is called **ureterolithotomy**. In this procedure, an incision is made through the lower abdomen or flank, the affected ureter is surgically opened, and the stone is removed.

Extracorporeal Shock Wave Lithotripsy

A noninvasive procedure, **extracorporeal shock wave lithotripsy** disintegrates kidney stones with shock waves. Because it is not a surgical procedure, it may be performed on an outpatient basis or, if done in the hospital, with only a minimal hospital stay. An individual who is undergoing the procedure may be positioned in a padded chair that is lifted into a stainless steel tub of warm water, or a fluid bag may be placed between the individual and the source of the shock waves in order to serve as a buffer to the shock waves. Once the individual is positioned to receive maximum effect, shock waves from a machine called a **lithotriptor** are directed to the stones, which are visualized radiographically. The stones are broken apart by the sound waves, and the fragments can then be passed in the urine.

Nephrectomy

If trauma has severely injured the kidney, if stones have caused severe damage or are too large to remove, or if the kidney is chronically infected or nonfunctional, the entire kidney may be removed. This surgical procedure is called **nephrectomy**. Individuals can live normal lives with one functioning kidney, but should guard against infection or injury that could compromise the function of the one remaining kidney.

Dialysis

When the kidneys fail, a process called **dialysis** may be used to perform the kidneys' function. Dialysis may be used temporarily, as in the case of acute renal failure, or it may be used to sustain life when the kidney damage is irreversible, as in end-stage renal disease. If individuals with chronic renal failure or end-stage renal disease are suitable candidates for renal transplantation, dialysis may be used until an appropriate donor kidney is available. Individuals with end-stage renal disease must remain on dialysis the rest of their lives, unless they receive a transplanted kidney.

There are two types of dialysis, **peritoneal dialysis** and **hemodialysis**. Both types are performed to remove the end products of metabolism from the blood, to maintain an appropriate balance in the body chemistry, and to remove excess fluid from the blood. Both types of dialysis involve the use of a semipermeable membrane to simulate kidney function for filtering wastes and water from the body. The blood of the individual who is undergoing dialysis is on one side of the membrane, and a specially prepared solution called a **dialysate** is on the other side of the membrane. The difference in the concentrations of the two fluids allows certain particles—but not others—to pass from the blood, through the membrane, and into the dialysate, where they can then be removed through dialysis.

Peritoneal Dialysis

The abdominal cavity is lined with a membrane called the **peritoneum**. This membrane is the semipermeable membrane used for **peritoneal dialysis** (Figure 4-2). Peritoneal dialysis may be chosen as the dialysis method for individuals who have, in addition to kidney disease, other medical conditions that increase the risk of complications associated with hemodialysis. In other instances, peritoneal dialysis may be chosen because of the relative ease of the procedure and the limited use of sophisticated equipment, factors that enable individuals to use peritoneal dialysis in the home. Depending on the type of procedure used, individuals may enjoy more mobility with peritoneal dialysis than with hemodialysis. If severe vascular disease interferes with the blood supply to the peritoneum or there is an increased vulnerability to infection, however, peritoneal dialysis may be contraindicated.

Although there are several different types of peritoneal dialysis, some procedures are common to all. A peritoneal catheter is surgically implanted through the abdominal tissue layers into the peritoneal cavity, and the dialysate is infused into the abdominal cavity through the catheter. The catheter is clamped, and the dialysate is left in the abdominal cavity for a specified amount of time. During this time, waste products and excess fluid pass from the blood, through the peritoneal membrane, and into the dialysate. At the end of the specified period, the catheter is unclamped, and the dialysate, which now contains the waste products and excess fluid, is drained from the body through the catheter.

Peritoneal dialysis may be performed manually or with the use of a machine. In **continuous ambulatory peritoneal dialysis**, the dialysate is instilled into the abdominal cavity manually by using gravity. A bag of dialysate solution is connected to the catheter. Raising the bag causes the dialysate to flow into the

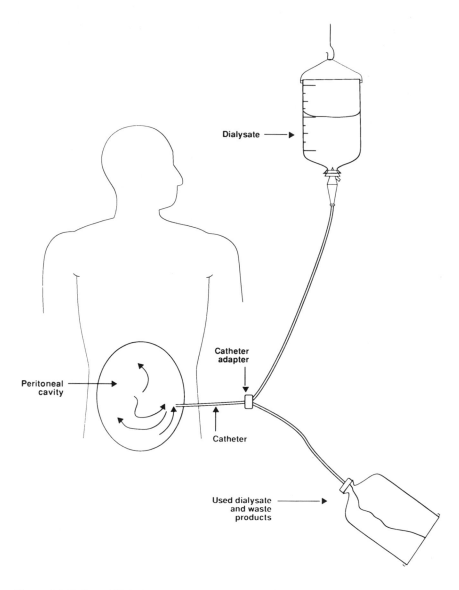

Figure 4-2 Peritoneal Dialysis

abdominal cavity. The catheter is clamped and the dialysate left in place for 4 to 8 hours. The catheter is then unclamped and the bag lowered so that the dialysate drains from the abdominal cavity. When the bag is full, the individual detaches the bag from the catheter, attaches a new bag of dialysate, and begins the process again. Individuals who use this type of peritoneal dialysis may continue their regular daily activities, stopping only for periodic intervals to drain the dialysate and attach a fresh bag.

Continuous cycling peritoneal dialysis is usually done at home with a cycling machine. The catheter is connected to the cycling machine, which performs multiple solution exchanges while the individual sleeps. In the morning, the individual disconnects the catheter from the machine and is able to engage in regular activities. **Intermittent peritoneal dialysis** is also done with a cycling machine; this procedure is usually performed three or more times each week, with each treatment lasting 10 or more hours. Like continuous cycling peritoneal dialysis, the intermittent procedure is usually performed during sleep, enabling individuals to engage in their regular activities during the day.

Although generally a safe procedure, peritoneal dialysis can have a number of associated complications. The most common is **peritonitis** (inflammation of the peritoneum) caused by contamination by bacteria. If peritonitis develops, antibiotics may be used to treat the infection, or peritoneal dialysis may be discontinued and hemodialysis begun. Other complications that may occur as a result of peritoneal dialysis are plugging or displacement of the catheter, development of hernias, or pain during dialysis. Over time, infection or the dialysate concentration itself may damage the peritoneum. Peritoneal dialysis is usually a limited procedure because of the loss of membrane function.

Hemodialysis

The most common type of dialysis used for individuals with renal failure is **hemodialysis**, in which an artificial kidney machine (**dialyzer**) filters the blood to remove waste products and excess fluid. The artificial kidney has two compartments, one for the individual's blood and one for the dialysate solution. A synthetic semipermeable membrane separates these compartments within the artificial kidney. Blood cells and other important substances are too large to pass through the pores of the membrane, so they remain in their compartment. Most waste products, however, are small enough to pass through the membrane into the dialysate, and they are washed away. The cleansed blood then returns to the individual. Hemodialysis may be performed temporarily for acute kidney failure; however, when there is permanent damage such as in chronic renal failure or end-stage renal disease, the dialysis must be continued throughout the individual's life unless a successful kidney transplant is performed.

Hemodialysis requires access to the individual's blood. Access routes may be through a graft, an external arteriovenous shunt (less commonly used today), or an internal arteriovenous fistula (Figure 4-3), or through a subclavian cannula (Figure 4-4).

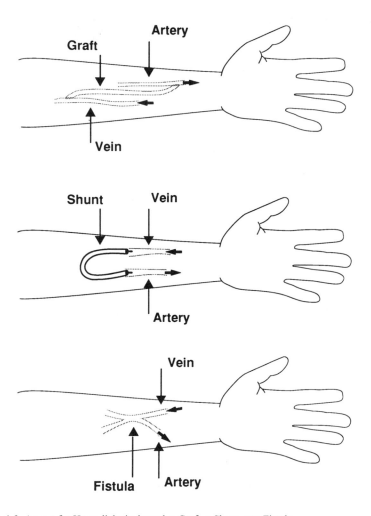

Figure 4-3 Access for Hemodialysis through a Graft, a Shunt, or a Fistula

A graft is surgically implanted to connect an artery and a vein. The graft may be made of synthetic material, or it may be a vein that has been removed from another part of the individual's body.

The external **arteriovenous shunt** requires surgical placement of a tube (**cannula**) under the skin to connect an artery to a vein. For hemodialysis, the tube is punctured with needles and connected to the dialysis machine. Blood flows from the artery into the dialysis machine, where it is filtered and cleansed. The filtered blood then returns to the individual's vein through the tube.

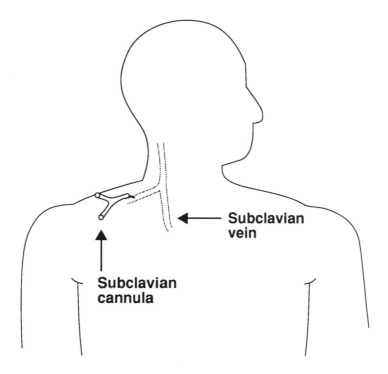

Figure 4-4 Access for Hemodialysis through a Subclavian Cannula

---

The **internal arteriovenous fistula** is also created surgically, most often in the forearm. In this procedure, an artery is joined to a vein, establishing an opening called a **fistula** between the two. The leakage of arterial blood into the vein causes the vein to become engorged and enlarged so it can be used for dialysis. Engorgement provides better blood flow and accessibility for dialysis. This process may take 2 to 6 weeks to develop so that the fistula can be used. In the meantime, temporary access may be maintained through the subclavian artery. Once the fistula has developed, one needle is placed in the artery side, and another is placed in the vein side of the fistula. Tubes are attached to the needles and connected to the dialysis machine. Blood moves from the first tube to the dialysis machine, where it is cleansed and filtered. The cleansed blood is then returned to the individual through the second needle in the vein. Hemodialysis is usually performed from 3 to 6 hours a day three times a week. It has also been performed successfully on a daily basis for 2 hours a day. Hemodialysis can be performed at a kidney dialysis center or, in some instances, at home. Because home hemodialysis requires a high degree of individual control, self-destructive tendencies in the individual or the unwillingness of family members or caregivers to participate in the procedure is a contraindication for home hemodialysis. The stress associated with home hemodialysis often leads to problems, and it should be carefully evaluated and monitored before the implementation of such a program.

The success of hemodialysis depends on the individual's level of motivation, the presence of other medical conditions that may cause complications, and the development of complications from the hemodialysis itself. The numerous potential complications related to hemodialysis range from technical problems with the access route to more generalized complications that could result in death. Arteriovenous grafts and subclavian catheters are especially prone to infection that can result in **septicemia** (toxins in the blood), a potentially life-threatening complication. Cardiac-related complications, such as **pericarditis**, **endocarditis**, **arrhythmias**, or **tamponade**, may also occur (see Chapter 2). Another possible complication of hemodialysis is stroke or some other thrombolytic event. Because of the risk of clot formation in the access route, individuals on hemodialysis may receive anticoagulant medication during the procedure; the administration of this medication, however, may also increase the risk of bleeding.

The hemodialysis procedure itself is painless, although there may be some slight discomfort when the needles are inserted for dialysis. Some individuals complain of nausea, vomiting, headaches, or cramps in association with hemodialysis. Some may become anemic, and some experience sleep disturbances or mental cloudiness. In individuals on prolonged hemodialysis, changes in the nerves of the extremities may result in **peripheral neuropathy** (loss of sensation and weakness in the arms and legs).

Hemodialysis can relieve many of the symptoms of renal disease, but not all. Individuals on hemodialysis may develop secondary conditions that increase the risk of bone fractures, or the procedure may not adequately clear all wastes, leading to feelings of weakness. The degree of functional capacity varies from individual to individual. Many continue to lead near-normal lives, however, except for their dialysis treatments.

Renal Transplantation

In a **renal transplantation**, a kidney is surgically replaced with another kidney from a donor. Although commonly performed because of end-stage renal disease, the procedure may also be performed if one kidney has been removed and the second kidney is injured or ceases to function. A renal transplant frees the individual from the restrictions associated with dialysis, diminishes many symptoms of chronic renal failure, and improves the individual's overall quality of life. Before being considered for transplantation, recipients undergo careful medical and psychological screening.

The major factor that inhibits renal transplantations is the scarcity of donor kidneys, although they may be obtained from either cadaver donors or living donors. In both instances, compatibility of tissue type and blood type, and a variety of other factors determine the degree of the success of the transplantation. The most desirable sources of kidneys for transplantation are closely related, living donors, but surgeons in new protocols are attempting to use living, unrelated, and blood type–incompatible donors. Tissue typing is most important in decreasing the possibility of rejection. Once the donor kidney has been transplanted, it begins to function almost immediately.

The major complication of kidney transplantation is rejection, which can destroy the transplanted kidney. The body's defense system, or immune system, naturally attacks foreign substances in the body. Unfortunately, the immune system does not distinguish between a life-saving transplanted kidney and harmful substances. If rejection takes place immediately, it may be necessary to remove the transplanted kidney in order to avoid a generalized body reaction that could be fatal. Rejection most commonly occurs within the first 6 weeks after the transplantation; however, chronic rejection may occur months or years later.

In order to prevent rejection, medications called **immunosuppressants** are prescribed. These medications block the body's normal immune response. The use of immunosuppressants is not without risk, however. The complications of immunosuppressant use include an increased rate of **malignancy** (cancer), an increased susceptibility to infection, formation of cataracts, and degeneration of bone.

FUNCTIONAL IMPLICATIONS

Psychological Issues

Not all kidney conditions are life-threatening, nor do they all impose major changes in functional capacity. Although they may cause some pain and discomfort, conditions such as cystitis frequently leave no functional or psychological sequelae. End-stage renal disease has a profound impact on all areas of the individual's life, however, causing severe psychological stress. Psychological changes are associated both with the emotional reactions to a life-threatening disease and with the physiological changes that occurr with end-stage renal disease. Elevated levels of toxic waste in the blood can produce cognitive changes, such as impaired judgment, drowsiness, and difficulty with concentration. Other possible cognitive changes include memory loss, speech impairments, and irritability. The physical discomforts associated with dialysis, such as interrupted sleep patterns, nausea, lethargy, and shortness of breath, may increase the individual's psychological distress.

The initial diagnosis of end-stage renal disease and its ramifications may be immobilizing. Reactions vary in degree from severe depression to total denial. Feelings of sadness, hopelessness, and despair may become so severe that the individual considers suicide as a way to resolve the problems surrounding the illness. Suicide attempts may be overt, or they may be more covert, such as a failure to cooperate with treatment. Denial can be helpful in reducing the level of stress, but it can be life-threatening if it leads to noncompliance with the recommended treatment.

The fear of death is common. A loss of self-esteem and feelings of helplessness and inadequacy are also common, as these individuals come to realize that they are dependent on the dialysis machine for their existence. In the early sessions of dialysis, individuals frequently become anxious and concerned about machine malfunction. Fears of death may then conflict with fears of continuing to live a life sustained by dialysis with its subsequent restrictions.

Anger and hostility are frequent manifestations of conflicts between dependency and independency—even conflicts between living and dying. Feelings of hostility may be expressed openly, but they may also be internalized as these individuals on dialysis realize the degree of their dependence not only on a machine, but also on those who provide their care. These internalized feelings can be self-destructive if these individuals rebel against the necessary care and treatment.

Transplantation involves a number of psychological issues. Individuals identified as eligible recipients of a transplanted kidney are often elated about the anticipated improvement in their quality of life after the transplantation. Consequently, rejection of the transplanted kidney can be devastating. Even if rejection does not occur and their quality of life is significantly improved, individuals who have a transplanted kidney may express disappointment that long-term care and evaluation are still necessary. In addition, they may be disappointed that the transplantation has not restored the state of health that was theirs before the onset of end-stage renal disease. Even after the initial postoperative period, the chance of later rejection or the risk that infection will damage the transplanted kidney may be sources of anxiety.

Despite the significant psychological preparation that is usually done prior to transplantation, postsurgical psychological reactions, including guilt, anxiety, or depression, may still occur. Often, the donor is also affected. In fact, the identification of a potential donor can create stress, conflict, or guilt if that person should choose not to donate a kidney.

Life Style Issues

The life style changes that many conditions of the urinary tract require are short-term or preventive in nature. Individuals with renal failure, however, face changes in the activities of daily living that are profound. When kidney function is impaired or nonexistent, the intake of foods and fluids must be carefully monitored. Such restrictions are necessary to minimize the amount of waste products and to avoid the presence of too much or too little fluid in the body.

The intake of foods containing protein, sodium, and potassium must be limited or totally restricted in chronic renal failure. Consequently, the amounts of meats, poultry, fish, eggs, and dairy products that an individual may eat are limited because of protein content of these foods. In addition, a number of fruits and vegetables must be restricted because of the potassium content. Sodium restrictions affect not only the intake of salt, but also the intake of processed and smoked meats such as ham, bacon, sausage, and cold cuts. Food products such as ketchup, mustard, most canned and processed foods, and soft drinks are also high in sodium and must be avoided.

Because the kidney is no longer able to excrete adequately in chronic renal failure or end-stage renal disease, total fluid intake between dialysis sessions must also be monitored. Fluid intake includes not only beverages, but also water contained in foods. Individuals are weighed before and after each dialysis treatment in order to monitor fluid gain so that the dialysis procedure may be adjusted accordingly.

Individuals on dialysis may have to alter their activities, both because of their physical condition and because of the dialysis schedule. Those with shunts should avoid any activity that could expose the shunt area to potential injury. Because heat intolerance is often associated with end-stage renal disease, activities that require exposure to heat should be avoided.

Although there are no limitations or restrictions regarding sexual activity, sexual function is impaired in many individuals on dialysis. Some men with end-stage renal disease experience impotence or have a diminished interest in sexual activities. Women with end-stage renal disease often report a general disinterest or a diminished interest in sexual activities, or a decreased response to sexual stimulation. Sexual dysfunction among individuals on dialysis probably results from a combination of their generally poor health and their emotional reactions to a life-threatening illness. The reproductive capacity of both men and women on dialysis is severely diminished.

Sexual function may improve after renal transplant, although it rarely returns to the pre-illness state. If the transplant is rejected or the individual is heavily medicated, sexual function may be impaired. After successful transplantation, conception is possible.

Social Issues

Renal conditions may not affect an individual's social activities until the kidneys become dysfunctional, causing restrictions or alterations in regular activities. Although family, friends, and associates play an important supportive role in an individual's adjustment to kidney failure, an overindulgent attitude on their part can impede the individual's return to the earlier level of independence.

Problems that previously existed in relationships may be amplified after a diagnosis of end-stage renal disease. The additional stress brought on by dialysis or the wait for transplantation may intensify marital discord. If dialysis is conducted at home, the spouse may feel burdened and strained by the added responsibility and regimen of the dialysis program. Activities must be programmed around the dialysis schedule. The individual's physical complaints, fatigue, and loss of interest in sexual activities may compound the problem. Although financial assistance for dialysis is usually available through government or private agencies, the overall financial burden of medical bills, dialysis, and lost income if the individual with kidney disease is not able to continue working exerts additional stress on relationships.

Even if these individuals feel well enough to participate in social activities, they must avoid many activities because of their dietary and fluid restrictions. They may be reluctant to accept the dinner invitations of friends, or they may themselves give up entertaining because of the limitations involved. Their increasing social isolation can increase their loss of self-esteem, feelings of depression, and hopelessness.

Vacations are still possible, but require careful planning for individuals who are on hemodialysis. Dialysis units near the vacation spot must be located, and arrangements must be made for dialysis at the center prior to departure.

Although transplantation can free individuals from some limitations, other issues may arise. If the donor is a family member or friend, a strong bond may develop between the donor and the recipient; in some cases, however, problems occur in the relationship. The donor may resent the attention paid to the recipient or may feel abandoned. The recipient may feel guilty because of the potential jeopardy to the donor, who is left with only one kidney.

Vocational Issues

Many renal and urinary tract disorders have no long-term impact on an individual's ability to work. When kidney damage occurs, however, a variety of alterations may be necessary. The degree to which kidney disease affects employment depends on the condition and its treatment. Individuals in beginning end-stage renal disease can generally continue their previous job, especially if it is sedentary and does not require strenuous activity. If they are no longer capable of the physical activity that the work requires, a job modification or change may be necessary.

As end-stage renal disease progresses and symptoms become more pronounced, its impact on vocational function increases. Fatigue may necessitate a shortened workday or rest periods during the day. Problems of impaired judgment, difficulty with memory, or irritability may interfere with adequate job performance. Peripheral neuropathy may make it difficult or impossible to perform tasks such as lifting or to complete tasks that require manual dexterity.

Individuals on dialysis may need a flexible work schedule to accommodate the dialysis schedule. Many dialysis centers are operational 24 hours each day, enabling individuals to arrange dialysis in off-hours. Blood access routes, such as shunts, require protection; occupations that pose a potential threat of damage to the shunt should be avoided. Fatigue or the decreased ability to walk caused by peripheral neuropathy may necessitate a job change to a more sedentary line of work. Environmental issues should also be considered. Work that requires exposure to high temperatures should be avoided because of the heat intolerance associated with kidney diseases.

BIBLIOGRAPHY

Barber, T.C., and Langfitt, D.E. *Teaching the Medical/Surgical Patient—Diagnostics and Procedures.* Bowie, Md.: Robert J. Brady Co., 1983.

Bastl, C.P.; Cutler, R.E.; McClennan, B.L.; Salusky, I.B.; Van Stone, J.C.; Kaiser, H.B.; and Teaque, R.C. "As End-Stage Renal Disease Approaches." *Patient Care* 20(1986):49–61.

Berkman, A.H.; Katz, L.A.; and Weissman, M.A. "Sexuality and the Lifestyle of Home Dialysis Patients." *Archives of Physiology and Medical Rehabilitation* 63(1982):272–275.

Berkow, R., and Fletcher, A.J., eds. *The Merck Manual of Diagnosis and Therapy.* Rahway, N.J.: Merck Sharpe and Dohme Research Laboratories, 1987.

Brunner, L.S.; Emerson, C.P.; Ferguson, L.K.; and Suddarth, D.S. *Textbook of Medical-Surgical Nursing.* Philadelphia: W.B. Saunders Co., 1970.

Cass, A.S. "Extracorporeal Shock Wave Lithotripsy." *Postgraduate Medicine* 83(1988):185–204.

Coleman, E.A. "When the Kidneys Fail." *RN* (July 1986):28–37.

Corbett, J.V. *Diagnostic Procedures in Nursing Practice.* Norwalk, Conn.: Appleton-Century-Crofts, 1982.

Corbett, J.V. *Laboratory Tests in Nursing Practice.* Norwalk, Conn.: Appleton-Century-Crofts, 1983.

Goodenough, G.K.; Lutz, L.J.; and Gregory, M.C. "Home-Based Renal Dialysis." *American Family Physician* 37(1988):203–214.

Guyton, A.C. *Human Physiology and Mechanisms of Disease.* Philadelphia: W.B. Saunders Co., 1982.

Held, P.J.; Pauly, M.V.; and Diamond, L. "Survival Analysis of Patients Undergoing Dialysis." *Journal of the American Medical Association* 257(1987):645–650.

Keele, C.A.; Neil, E.; and Joels, N. *Samson Wright's Applied Physiology.* New York: Oxford University Press, 1982.

Levy, N.B. *Sex and Intimacy for Dialysis and Transplant Patients*. Bethesda, Md.: Virgil Smirnow Associates, 1978.

Luckman, J., and Sorensen, K.C. *Medical-Surgical Nursing: A Psychophysiologic Approach*. Philadelphia: W.B. Saunders Co., 1987.

McGovern, M.M. *Diet and Kidney Disease*. Bethesda, Md.: Virgil Smirnow Associates, 19.

Moore, J., and Maher, J.F. "Management of Chronic Renal Failure." *American Family Physician* 30(1984):204–213.

National Institute of Handicapped Research. "Rehabilitation and End-Stage Renal Disease." *Rehab Brief* 7(1984):1–4.

Nursing 87 Books. *Patient Teaching*. Springhouse, Pa.: Springhouse Corporation Book Division, 1987.

Rakel, R.E. *Conn's Current Therapy 1990*. Philadelphia: W.B. Saunders Co., 1990.

Scheer, S.J., ed. *Medical Perspectives in Vocational Assessment of Impaired Workers*. Gaithersburg, Md.: Aspen Publishers, 1991.

Smith, D.W., and Hanley-Germain, C.P. *Care of the Adult Patient*. Philadelphia: J.B. Lippincott Co., 1975.

Smolens, P. "Acute Renal Failure." *Hospital Medicine* (August 1984):95–132.

Stolov, W.C., and Clowers, M.R. *Handbook of Severe Disability*. Washington, D.C.: U.S. Department of Education, Rehabilitation Services Administration, 1981.

Toth, J.M. "When Your Patient Faces a Urostomy." *RN* (November 1985):50–55.

Twardowski, Z.J. "Peritoneal Dialysis." *Postgraduate Medicine* 85(1989):161–182.

Vander, A.J.; Sherman, J.H.; and Luciano, D.S. *Human Physiology: The Mechanisms of Body Function*. New York: McGraw-Hill Book Co., 1985.

Wyngaarden, J.B., and Smith, J.H. *Cecil Textbook of Medicine*. Philadelphia: W.B. Saunders Co., 1988.

chapter 5

Endocrine Disorders

NORMAL STRUCTURE AND FUNCTION

The endocrine system consists of a number of glands that produce chemical substances called hormones (Figure 5-1). Secreted directly into the bloodstream, hormones influence a number of activities throughout the body. The endocrine system operates with the nervous system to keep all body organs and response mechanisms working together in a controlled manner. The endocrine system's main function is regulatory, and different hormones can speed up or slow down various body processes in order to maintain the body's internal balance (**homeostasis**).

Although each has its own unique and independent function, the endocrine glands often work in concert. The hormones that are secreted by the endocrine system control and integrate a variety of body activities, establishing a delicate chain of communication between various body systems. Hormones set in motion a number of body processes.

- physical and intellectual growth
- reproductive maturity and function
- metabolism
- reaction to internal and external stress
- water balance

The overproduction or underproduction of one hormone can affect a number of other endocrine glands and a variety of body functions.

The **thyroid gland** is located in the neck, in front of and on either side of the trachea (windpipe). It secretes a hormone called **thyroxine**, which regulates the rate of metabolism. When the level of the hormone in the blood is high, metabolism speeds up; when it is low, metabolism slows down.

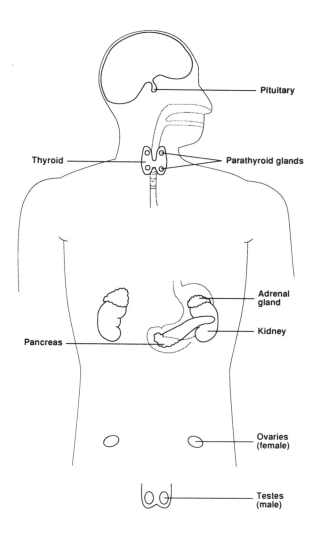

Figure 5-1 Endocrine System

The **parathyroid glands** are tiny, bean-shaped glands that are buried within the thyroid gland. They secrete **parathyroid hormone**, which regulates the concentrations of calcium and phosphate in the body. Excessive amounts of the hormone in the blood can result in the demineralization of bone, causing bones to become fragile so that they are easily broken. Insufficient amounts of the hormone in the blood can cause spasm and involuntary contraction of the muscles (**tetany**). If the parathyroid hormone is to be effective, vitamin D must be present.

The **adrenal glands** are small glands that lie on top of the kidneys. Each adrenal gland has two parts, and each part has a different function. The inner part of the adrenal gland (**medulla**) secretes the hormones **epinephrine** and **norepinephrine** at times of stress to enable the body to prepare physiologically for emergencies; for example, these hormones increase the heart rate, increase muscle tone, and constrict blood vessels in times of stress. The outer portion of the adrenal glands (**cortex**) secretes hormones called **steroids**, which are concerned with many essential functions, such as electrolyte and water balance in the body, metabolism, immune responses, and inflammatory reactions. The adrenal cortex is essential to life. If it dysfunctions, death will occur within a few days unless the hormones that it normally secretes are replaced.

The **pituitary gland** is located in the skull, just above the roof of the mouth, and is connected to the brain by a slender stalk. It is divided into two parts, the anterior and the posterior lobes. The **anterior lobe** secretes **thyroid-stimulating hormone**, which is necessary for thyroid function; a growth hormone; hormones involved with reproductive function; and corticotropin, a hormone necessary for the function of the adrenal cortex. The **posterior lobe** of the pituitary gland stores hormones produced in the portion of the brain called the **hypothalamus**, which coordinates the functions of the nervous system and the endocrine system. **Antidiuretic hormone**, which increases water reabsorption by the kidneys, is produced by the hypothalamus, but is stored in and secreted by the posterior lobe of the pituitary gland.

Embedded in the pancreas are endocrine glands called the **islets of Langerhans**. Special cells within the islets of Langerhans produce the hormones **insulin** and **glucagon**, which are necessary for the metabolism of carbohydrates, proteins, and fats.

The testes in males and the ovaries in females are also endocrine glands. Hormones produced by the testes and ovaries are important not only to reproductive function, but also to normal growth and development.

ENDOCRINE DISORDERS

Various medical conditions result from endocrine dysfunction. Because the symptoms of endocrine disorders are often similar to those associated with a number of mental disorders, some endocrine disorders may go unrecognized or misdiagnosed as psychiatric disorders. Likewise, the administration of hormones in the treatment of an endocrine deficiency may have side-effects similar to those of some mental disorders. Clearly, the endocrine system, in addition to regulating internal body functions and maintaining homeostasis, has a role in human behavior and emotions.

Hyperthyroidism (Grave's disease, Thyrotoxicosis, Exophthalmic Goiter)

Hyperthyroidism is the overproduction of thyroid hormone, resulting in an increased metabolic rate. The thyroid gland may become so enlarged that there is a visible swelling in the neck, a condition sometimes referred to as a **goiter**. Other symptoms of hyperthyroidism include restlessness, irritability, nervousness, and weight loss. The increased rate of metabolism causes an intolerance to heat; thus, environmental temperatures that seem comfortable to others seem unbearably warm to individuals with hyperthyroidism. **Exophthalmos** (abnormal protrusion of the eyeball) may also develop with hyperthyroidism. Once exophthalmos develops, the effects are permanent, giving the individual a wide-eyed and startled appearance. With early diagnosis and treatment, hyperthyroidism usually causes no permanent disability.

Hypothyroidism (Myxedema)

In individuals with **hypothyroidism,** the production of thyroid hormone is inadequate. The symptoms of hypothyroidism are in many ways the opposite of those of hyperthyroidism. Individuals with hypothyroidism have a slowed metabolic rate; they may feel tired, lack energy, and gain weight. The hair becomes dry, brittle, and thin, and the voice is low-pitched and coarse. Emotional responses are subdued and mental processes slowed. The complications of hypothyroidism include the rapid development of atherosclerotic heart disease, including angina pectoris, myocardial infarction, and congestive heart failure (see Chapter 2). Individuals with severe hypothyroidism can also develop psychosis, with associated paranoia and delusions. Unless complications develop, however, appropriate treatment usually prevents any permanent disability.

Cushing's Syndrome (Adrenal Cortex Hyperfunction)

The overproduction of hormones by the adrenal cortex leads to Cushing's syndrome. The symptoms include a rounded moon face, obesity of the trunk of the body, and fat pads at the back of the neck (**buffalo hump**). The skin of those with this syndrome becomes thin and fragile; wound healing is poor, and bruising is frequent. Women with Cushing's syndrome may have menstrual irregularities and facial hair growth. Mood and mental acuity may also be altered. The appropriate treatment usually alleviates the symptoms, enabling these individuals to return to normal, productive lives.

Addison's Disease (Adrenocortical Insufficiency)

In contrast to Cushing's syndrome, Addison's disease results from an under-production of hormones by the adrenal cortex. Weakness and fatigue are early symptoms; skin pigmentation increases later. Individuals with Addison's disease may also experience weight loss, loss of appetite, and decreased cold tolerance. Because the hormones secreted by the adrenal cortex play a prominent role in the body's adaptive response to stress, individuals with Addison's disease may have severe, potentially life-threatening reactions such as extremely low blood pressure and severe electrolyte imbalance to situations (e.g., uncomplicated surgical procedures) that do not normally elicit such a response. With continued treatment, individuals are generally able to lead full lives.

Diabetes Insipidus

Although there are a number of causes of diabetes insipidus, the most common cause is damage to the posterior lobe of the pituitary gland that reduces the secretion of antidiuretic hormone. As a result, water pours out the kidneys (**polyuria**). Excessive and constant thirst (**polydipsia**) is present, with individuals consuming as much as 30 quarts of water per day. **Diabetes insipidus** may be temporary or chronic. The condition is permanent, but symptoms can be controlled with medication, enabling individuals in most instances to live a normal life.

Diabetes Mellitus

A chronic, incurable disorder of carbohydrate metabolism, **diabetes mellitus** involves an imbalance of the supply of and demand for insulin. The condition affects every body system. The cause of diabetes mellitus is unknown, but there may be a familial tendency to develop the disease. Diabetes mellitus can also occur as a complication of other conditions, such as **pancreatitis** (inflammation of the pancreas) or tumors of the pancreas; as a side-effect of medications that cause an abnormal tolerance to **glucose** (sugar); or as a result of specific conditions that increase the body's demand for insulin, such as **gestational diabetes** (diabetes which occurs during pregnancy). In these cases, the correction of the underlying cause may reverse the diabetes.

Body tissues need insulin in order to use glucose as a source of energy. In diabetes mellitus, insufficient insulin is available to meet this need because of (1) the failure of the islets of Langerhans to produce enough insulin, (2) the destruction of the insulin before it can be used, or (3) the inability of body tissues to use the insulin that is present. Consequently, large amounts of glucose accumulate in the blood. This condition is known as **hyperglycemia**.

As blood is filtered by the kidney, glucose is normally channeled back into the blood. Because individuals with diabetes mellitus have such a large amount of glucose in the blood, however, some glucose spills over into the urine (**glycosuria**). Owing to the large concentration of glucose in the urine, the kidney excretes large quantities of water, a symptom called **polyuria**. As a result, the individual wants to drink large quantities of water to replace the excess fluid lost (**polydipsia**).

There are two types of diabetes mellitus. In **insulin-dependent (type I)** diabetes, the more severe form, little or no insulin is available. Individuals with insulin-dependent diabetes require external sources of insulin for their survival. External sources of insulin may or may not be taken to control the symptoms of **non–insulin-dependent** diabetes (**type II**), but survival does not depend on an external insulin source.

The inability of the body to use glucose means that the food or energy available to body tissues is inadequate. To compensate, individuals with diabetes increase their food intake dramatically (**polyphagia**). Despite the increased food intake, the lack of insulin prevents them from using the food as an energy source. They begin to lose weight and become increasingly weak. Unless supplemental insulin is available, they literally enter a state of starvation.

Because its need for energy remains unmet, the body metabolizes its own stores of fat and proteins for energy. Ketones, the byproducts of fat metabolism, are formed. Normally, ketones are broken down and excreted. In individuals with diabetes mellitus, however, ketones accumulate more rapidly than they can be excreted; when the ketone level becomes toxic, **ketosis**, **ketoacidosis**, or **diabetic coma** occurs. Having too little or no insulin available for the amount of food ingested may also cause a diabetic coma.

The onset of diabetic coma may be gradual; few symptoms may appear until the level of sugar in the blood becomes severely elevated. Individuals in this condition may become confused, feel drowsy, and eventually slip into unconsciousness. There may be difficulty in breathing, nausea and vomiting, and flushing of the skin, which remains dry. Water depletion and dehydration are common. Characteristically, the breath has a fruity odor. Diabetic coma is a medical emergency that without treatment may end in death. Medical treatment is directed toward lowering the level of blood sugar through the injection of insulin and correcting dehydration and electrolyte imbalance through the intravenous infusion of fluids.

Insulin shock is the opposite of diabetic coma. It occurs when there is too much insulin in the blood for the amount of glucose present. Insulin shock may result from injecting too much insulin, from engaging in an unusual amount of exercise that burns up the glucose normally available, or from failing to take in sufficient amounts of food for the amount of insulin injected. Individuals going into insulin shock may feel hungry, weak, and nervous. They may perspire profusely although their skin is cold to the touch. Confusion and personality changes may also occur during insulin shock. If insulin shock is untreated, the individual may lapse into unconsciousness. If it continues to go untreated, brain damage and eventual death can result. The treatment of insulin shock is directed toward raising the blood sugar level. If the individual is conscious, simple sugars such as candy, orange juice, or honey may be ingested orally; if the individual is unconscious, glucose must be infused intravenously.

Gastric juices inactivate insulin. Consequently, individuals who are insulin-dependent *must* inject insulin into the subcutaneous, fatty layer of tissues rather than take it orally. The amount and type of insulin is balanced with the number of calories consumed and the amount of physical activity performed daily. Conditions that increase the metabolism rate or cause the body to consume more of the available glucose, such as fever or infection, alter the amount of insulin needed. Consequently, individuals with insulin-dependent diabetes who become ill with flu, fever, or other types of illness should consult their physician regarding adjustments to their normal insulin dosage.

Individuals who are non–insulin-dependent must also follow a carefully regulated diet, but, depending on their needs, they may not take insulin. Instead of insulin, they may take **hypoglycemic agents** (oral medications that are effective in lowering blood sugar). Some individuals can control their blood sugar by diet alone.

A number of complications of diabetes mellitus can affect a number of different body systems and result in a major disability. The exact reason that individuals with diabetes mellitus develop these complications is unknown. Some complications are related to the circulatory system. Vascular changes can contribute to **myocardial infarction** (heart attack) or **cerebral vascular accident** (stroke). They may also lead to such poor circulation in the extremities that even minor injuries are prone to become infected. Furthermore, tissues recover from infections more slowly. Thus, because it is combined with poor circulation, a minor injury of the lower extremities may become so severely infected that amputation is necessary. Vascular changes may also deprive the kidney of an adequate blood supply, causing kidney failure. Changes in blood vessels in the retina (**retinopathy**) can result in blindness.

Other complications associated with diabetes mellitus may involve changes in the nervous system. Changes in the peripheral nerves, **peripheral neuropathy**, may result in the loss of sensation in the extremities. Other effects of neuropathy may be sexual impotence in men, and decreased genital sensation in women.

The risk that individuals with diabetes mellitus will develop complications is variable. Factors such as the type of diabetes, the age of onset, the duration of the disease, and the degree to which individuals follow the prescribed protocol must be considered. Individuals whose diabetes was diagnosed at an earlier age and those who have insulin-dependent diabetes generally have a greater risk of associated complications.

DIAGNOSTIC PROCEDURES

Blood Tests for Thyroid Function

A number of tests are available to assess thyroid function. Examples of blood tests are **serum thyroxine** or **T4** and **T3**. These tests measure the level of thyroid hormone in the blood. In addition, another type of blood test that measures the level of **thyroid stimulating hormone (TSH)** in the blood may also be used.

Radioiodine Uptake Test (^{131}I)

The ^{131}I test is a radioisotope study in which a radioactive substance, in this case radioactive iodine ^{131}I, is ingested orally or injected. The radioactive iodine concentrates in the thyroid gland, and a device called a scintillation scanner is then passed back and forth over the thyroid to measure the concentration. The procedure is simple and painless. The dose of radioactivity of iodine 131 is so small that the body absorbs a minimal amount of radiation.

Blood Tests for Diabetes Mellitus

The major blood tests used in the diagnosis of diabetes mellitus are determinations of the **fasting blood sugar (FBS)** and **postprandial blood sugar** levels, and the **glucose tolerance test**. In the fasting blood sugar test, blood is drawn after the individual has not eaten for a number of hours. For a postprandial blood sugar test, blood is drawn several hours after the individual has eaten. Blood is drawn for the glucose tolerance test while the individual is fasting. The individual is then given concentrated glucose in liquid form to drink, and blood samples are drawn at 1-, 2-, and 3-hour intervals. All three tests make it possible to compare the level of glucose in the individual's blood with the level expected in a person without diabetes mellitus under similar circumstances.

TREATMENT

For many endocrine conditions, treatment involves the replacement of hormones if there is insufficient production or the administration of medication to decrease the production of hormones that are being overproduced.

Hyperthyroidism (Grave's disease, Thyrotoxicosis, Exophthalmic Goiter)

In hyperthyroidism, treatment is directed toward curtailing the secretion of the thyroid hormone. **Antithyroid** medication that blocks the production of the hormone may be used. Symptoms usually subside within weeks or months after the treatment begins. Treatment does not, however, alleviate exophthalmos.

Some physicians recommend the oral administration of **iodine 131** The radioactive iodine destroys the cells that produce the thyroid hormone, and symptoms usually subside within weeks or months. This type of treatment causes some individuals to become hypothyroid, however, and these individuals may require thyroid medication for life.

Surgical treatment of hyperthyroidism is sometimes indicated. In these instances, a **subtotal thyroidectomy**, which involves the removal of most, but not all, of the thyroid gland, is performed. Because some of the thyroid gland is left in place, replacement therapy with thyroid hormone is not usually necessary.

Hypothyroidism (Myxedema)

The goal in the treatment of hypothyroidism is to correct the thyroid hormone deficiency. Consequently, replacement therapy is the primary treatment. The medication of choice for thyroid hormone replacement is levothyroxine (**Synthroid**), a synthetic thyroid preparation. Individuals with hypothyroidism may have to remain on this medication for life. Their appearance and their level of physical and mental activity usually improve gradually as the level of thyroid hormone rises. The blood levels of thyroid hormone in individuals on thyroid hormone replacement therapy should be measured regularly. These individuals should be cautioned not to alter the medication regimen without consulting a physician.

Cushing's Syndrome (Adrenal Cortex Hyperfunction)

The treatment of Cushing's syndrome involves the prescription of medication to reduce the production of corticosteroids. Unless the condition has been caused by a tumor, surgical intervention is not usually needed.

Addison's Disease (Adrenocortical Insufficiency)

Although Addison's disease was once fatal, replacement therapy with synthetic corticosteroids now enables individuals with Addison's disease to live normal lives. The medication must be taken daily, however. Careful monitoring for the development of the symptoms of excessive corticosteroid ingestion is necessary.

Diabetes Insipidus

Depending on the cause, different hormonal preparations may be used to correct diabetes insipidus or to treat the symptoms. If the condition has been caused by a pituitary tumor, surgical resection of the tumor may be indicated.

Diabetes Mellitus

There is no cure for diabetes mellitus. Treatment is directed toward controlling the level of glucose in the blood and preventing complications. Individuals with non–insulin-dependent diabetes may be able to control their blood glucose level with diet alone, or with a combination of diet and oral hypoglycemic agents. In some instances, insulin may also be used for non–insulin-dependent diabetes. Individuals with insulin-dependent diabetes control their blood glucose level through diet and the use of supplemental insulin. Individuals with either type of diabetes must consider the amount of energy expended through exercise and balance it with calories available from food.

All diabetic diets are designed to balance the number of proteins, carbohydrates, and fats ingested and to exclude foods that contain large amounts of sugar. Because individuals with insulin-dependent diabetes take a predetermined amount of insulin, they must be especially careful to consume a specified number of calories at consistent times throughout the day to maintain a balance of insulin and glucose in the blood.

Diabetic diets are individualized based on many personal factors, such as weight, age, and type of daily activity (e.g., sedentary, moderately active, very active). Individuals who are overweight may be placed on a low-calorie reduction diet so that the body will need less insulin. Because of their growth needs, adolescents may be placed on a higher calorie diet than is an older individual of the same size. Individuals who engage in sedentary activities throughout the day do not require as many calories as do individuals who are very physically active in their job or at home. Compliance with the prescribed diet is usually better if life style, religious, and cultural habits are considered as much as possible when dietary recommendations are made.

Exercise is important for the general health and well-being of all individuals. For individuals with diabetes mellitus, however, calories must be balanced with the amount of activity to be performed, as well as with the amount of insulin taken. Unplanned exercise that is not coordinated with caloric intake can create an imbalance between the amount of insulin previously taken and the amount of glucose remaining available in the blood. Insulin shock can result.

Sources of insulin include beef, pork, and a commercially prepared insulin called "human" insulin. There are several different types of insulin, grouped according to the speed with which they work within the body. Rapid-acting insulins usually act within 30 minutes to 1 hour after injection, while intermediate types work within 1 to 2 hours. Long-acting insulin works within 4 to 6 hours. Each type of insulin also has a different time of peak action and duration.

Individual need determines the amount and type of insulin prescribed. Thus, a physician should prescribe the insulin type and dosage only after carefully evaluating the individual's specific needs. Some individuals may be required to take several different types of insulin and/or to inject insulin at several different times throughout the day. Monitoring of blood glucose levels helps to determine the efficiency of the insulin dosage prescribed. Individuals may monitor their own blood glucose levels at home by lancing their finger and using a small portable machine called a **glucometer** to assess the glucose content of the blood.

Stress, illness, infection, and pregnancy all alter insulin requirements and, consequently, may necessitate an alteration in an individual's insulin dosage. Individuals may learn to alter their own insulin levels in accordance with their home blood glucose reading; however, such alterations should always be done with the advice and supervision of a physician.

In order to maximize independence, individuals who have diabetes mellitus should learn to inject their own insulin. Disposable syringes eliminate the need for cleaning and decrease the possibility of contamination and subsequent infection. Insulin injection devices that resemble fountain pens, containing cartridges of insulin, may be carried unobtrusively in a purse or pocket for use away from home. For the most part, insulin no longer requires refrigeration for storage, but exposure to extremes in temperatures and to intense light should be avoided. Individuals should rotate the injection site to avoid a buildup of scar tissue that can interfere with the absorption of the insulin.

Insulin can also be administered through an infusion pump. When a pump is used, a needle is inserted into the fatty tissue of the abdomen and connected to an insulin pump that is worn externally. The pump provides a slow, continuous supply of insulin throughout the day, eliminating the need for daily injections.

Because even small cuts or scratches can become infected, causing serious complications, individuals with diabetes mellitus should be careful to avoid injury. If injury does occur, the injured area requires particular care in order to prevent the development of complications. These individuals should undergo regular medical checkups so that other possible complications of diabetes mellitus, such as changes in vision or cardiovascular problems, can be identified and promptly treated.

FUNCTIONAL IMPLICATIONS

Psychological Issues

The change in hormonal patterns associated with disorders of the endocrine system may cause behavioral changes. For example, individuals with thyroid disease may experience emotional outbursts, irritability, or anxiety symptoms that are not always recognized as manifestations of their disease. In most cases, such changes in behavior are temporary and steadily improve as the endocrine condition is corrected. Changes in physical appearance, such as the exophthalmos associated with thyroid disease or the physical changes associated with Cushing's syndrome, can disturb an individual's body image, causing subsequent emotional reactions. The treatment of many endocrine conditions involves the long-term or lifelong ingestion of medications. For some individuals, taking medication daily creates a sense of frustration and resentment, leading to noncompliance with treatment and the development of subsequent complications or a recurrence of the disease.

Diabetes mellitus involves not only lifelong treatment, but also multifaceted treatment that has a significant impact on individuals' daily lives and futures, if complications should develop. Psychological, as well as physiological, factors frequently determine the course of diabetes mellitus. Psychological factors may affect the management of diabetes directly by inducing metabolic changes that can affect the individual's ability to control blood glucose levels or indirectly by altering the degree to which the individual follows instructions related to medication, diet, and exercise. The motivation to follow the prescribed treatment is paramount in the control of diabetes mellitus.

Diabetes mellitus is a hidden disability, as its symptoms are not always present. Others may see no indication of a condition that imposes restrictions. If the individuals have not adapted to the diabetes or if they fear social nonacceptance because of the condition, they may attempt to hide the condition from others, ignoring dietary restrictions or engaging in activities outside their treatment plan. Some individuals may believe that following a diabetic diet draws attention to the condition and, therefore, may neglect the diet.

In some instances, the benefit of careful adherence to the recommended regimen is not always apparent to the individual with diabetes mellitus. Even though instructions have been followed carefully, the blood glucose level may remain elevated, or complications may develop. Such occurrences frequently result in discouragement and depression.

If emphasis is placed on the restrictions imposed by the condition, individuals may feel depressed and hopeless. The fear of complications that may lead to blindness or possible amputation may create additional anxiety. For some individuals, these feelings are overwhelming. Self-destructive behaviors, such as skipping insulin injections and/or abandoning the diet—both of which can imperil their life—may result.

Life Style Issues

For most individuals with endocrine disorders, after the condition has been stabilized and unless there are complications, the primary life style changes revolve around remembering to take the medication at the same time every day. Many additional life style changes are necessary for individuals with diabetes mellitus, however, especially for those with insulin-dependent diabetes.

Although diet and insulin dosage can be adjusted to account for different types of activities, advance planning is essential for individuals with diabetes mellitus. Activities, including exercise, and meal times should generally be consistent from day to day. Eating on the run or skipping meals is not feasible. If the schedule changes, the food intake and insulin dosage must be changed accordingly. If activities involve additional walking, comfortable and well-fitting shoes should be worn to avoid the formation of blisters that could become infected.

Individuals with diabetes mellitus should check with their physician about insulin and food schedules before traveling, especially across time zones. If traveling by plane, they should request special meals ahead of time, and they should be served at the time required for the regimen. They should carry insulin with them and should protect the insulin against extremes of temperature.

With guidance from physicians or dieticians, individuals can learn to accommodate in their diet meals served at restaurants or in other people's homes. The quantity and types of foods must be taken into account, however. Individuals with diabetes must learn to judge calories and portions. Fatty, rich foods should be eliminated from the diet. Although concentrated sweets and alcohol should usually be avoided, planning may permit the incorporation of small quantities into the diet for special occasions.

Diabetes mellitus does not usually affect sexual activity unless there are complications. Neuropathy may be the cause of impotence in men and decreased sensation in women. Frequent vaginal infections in a woman with diabetes may also alter her sexual activity because of the physical discomfort involved. Reproductive function is not affected in men who are not impotent. Women with diabetes mellitus who become pregnant generally have more complicated pregnancies and need special medical attention to monitor the progress of the pregnancy and to alter insulin and caloric requirements.

Social Issues

Many of the social issues associated with endocrine disorders depend on the specific condition. For example, individuals with hyperthyroidism may suffer social isolation because of the behavior changes that occur before treatment is instituted. The physical changes caused by endocrine conditions, such as those associated with Cushing's syndrome, may lead to self-consciousness and cause the individual to withdraw from social activities.

The effects of any chronic disease are not limited to those on the individual alone. This is especially true of diabetes mellitus, because so many life style factors are involved in the adequate management of the condition. Often, the degree to which individuals with diabetes mellitus follow the prescribed treatment protocol depends on the degree of social support that they receive. The eating habits of family members, as well as their understanding of the importance of the diet prescribed for the individual, can contribute significantly to the individual's willingness to adapt to and follow the diabetic diet. The acceptance and understanding of the condition and its restrictions by friends and colleagues also contribute to the individual's self-concept and subsequent acceptance of the condition. Individuals with diabetes mellitus are constantly aware of the need to comply with dietary restrictions, the need to eat at regular times, the need to balance activity with calories, and the need to stick themselves several times a day to inject insulin or to test their blood glucose level. These factors can make them feel alone and different if they do not have social support at work or home.

The effect that a diagnosis of diabetes has on the individual's family depends on the composition of the family, the family's usual coping mechanisms, the age of the individual at the onset of diabetes, the regimen prescribed, the perception of future disability, and the functioning of the family before the diagnosis was made. If the individual with diabetes does not control the diet or prepare the meals, the family member who assumes this responsibility has new status and influence. This can create another source of support or, in some instances, a source of sabotage of the regimen itself.

The impact of diabetes on other social relationships varies. In social situations where food and alcohol are the major focus of activity, individuals with diabetes mellitus may need to modify their participation, although they need not totally avoid such situations. Depending on the individual and others in the social setting, modifications may or may not have an impact on the social relationship itself.

As diabetes mellitus is an invisible disability, couples who are planning to marry may not discuss diabetes and its effect on the marital relationship or on plans for children. Depending on the maturity, understanding, and expectations of both individuals in the marital relationship, problems related to the presence of diabetes may emerge, especially in the decision to have children or in the management of complications, should they arise.

Vocational Issues

In most instances, individuals with disorders of the endocrine system that have been identified and are being treated have no special vocational needs. When hormone replacement therapy is part of the treatment, however, the importance of compliance with the prescribed medical regimen cannot be overstated.

The special needs of individuals with diabetes mellitus in the work environment are determined by the degree to which the prescribed protocol controls the condition. Individuals with non–insulin-dependent diabetes who can control the condition by diet alone or with a combination of diet and oral medications will probably have few vocational problems. Those individuals with insulin-dependent diabetes may be able to control their condition effectively, but certain modifications in employment may also be necessary. First, the activity level should be somewhat consistent, or it should be planned in order to balance activity with food intake and insulin dosage. If at all possible, rotating shifts or irregular schedules should be avoided because of the alterations in insulin and food schedules that would be required. Because of the danger of infections, work in which there is a risk of even minor cuts and scratches should be avoided. As emotional stress has a direct impact on the blood glucose level, individuals with diabetes mellitus should learn coping strategies that enable them to deal effectively with job stress, or they should avoid overly stressful job situations, if possible.

An employer should generally be informed of an employee's diagnosis of diabetes mellitus so that misunderstandings about the need for regular meal schedules, routine activities, and avoidance of injury do not develop. In addition, the employer should be alerted to the symptoms of diabetic coma or insulin shock so that appropriate action may be taken if either of these events should occur.

There need be no emphasis on the complications that may develop, but potential complications should be considered in vocational planning. Although not a guarantee that complications will not develop, maintaining good control of the individual's blood glucose level decreases the number of days lost from work due to minor complications. When complications do develop, alterations in employment are specific to the type of complication. For example, individuals with peripheral neuropathy or poor circulation to the lower extremities may need to avoid occupations that require excessive walking or standing. Because of the possibility of diabetic coma or insulin shock, individuals with diabetes mellitus should probably not work in isolation.

BIBLIOGRAPHY

American Diabetes Association. *Diabetes in the Family: Your Guide to a Healthy Life-Style*. New York: Prentice-Hall, 1987.

Barber, T.C., and Langfitt, D.E. *Teaching the Medical/Surgical Patient—Diagnostics and Procedures*. Bowie, Md.: Robert J. Brady Co., 1983.

Berkow, R., and Fletcher, A.J., eds. *The Merck Manual of Diagnosis and Therapy*. Rahway, N.J.: Merck Sharpe and Dohme Research Laboratories, 1987.

Bluhm, H.P., and Stone, J.B. "Diabetic Retinopathy Patients: Characteristics and Rehabilitation Implications." *Journal of Rehabilitation* 49(1983):50–53.

Brunner, L.S.; Emerson, C.P.; Ferguson, L.K.; and Suddarth, D.S. *Textbook of Medical-Surgical Nursing*. Philadelphia: W.B. Saunders Co., 1970.

Cohen, M.P.; Field, J.B.; Krosnick, A.; Lebovitz, H.E.; and Pfeifer, M.A. "Diet and Exercise in Type II Diabetes." *Patient Care* 20(1988):117–122.

Cohen, M.P.; Field, J.B.; Krosnick, A.; Lebovitz, H.E.; and Pfeifer, M.A. "Screening for Type II Diabetes." *Patient Care* 22(1988):38–53.

Corbett, J.V. *Diagnostic Procedures in Nursing Practice*. Norwalk, Conn.: Appleton-Century-Crofts, 1982.

Corbett, J.V. *Laboratory Tests in Nursing Practice*. Norwalk, Conn.: Appleton-Century-Crofts, 1983.

Dangel, R.B. "How To Use an Implantable Infusing Pump." *RN* (September 1985):40–43.

Gerding, D.N.; Piziak, V.K.; and Rowbotham, J.L. "Problems in Diabetic Foot Care." *Patient Care* 22(1988):102–118.

Gilden, J.L. "Benefits from Self-monitoring of Blood Glucose." *Consultant* 28(1988):29–34.

Greene, D.A. "Diabetic Complications—Retinopathy." *Drug Therapy* (July 1987):16–37.

Greene, D.A. "Diabetic Complications—Retinopathy." *Drug Therapy* (August 1987):33–42.

Guyton, A.C. *Human Physiology and Mechanisms of Disease*. Philadelphia: W.B. Saunders Co., 1982.

Hollander, P. "Type II Diabetes—More Than 'Just a Touch' of Diabetes." *Postgraduate Medicine* 85(1989):211–232.

Houston, M., and Hay, I.D. "Practical Management of Hyperthyroidism." *American Family Physician* 41(1990):909–916.

Keele, C.A.; Neil, E.; and Joels, N. *Samson Wright's Applied Physiology.* New York: Oxford University Press, 1982.

Lachman, T. "Clinical Aspects of Peripheral Neuropathy." *Hospital Medicine* (July 1987):56–74.

Lawson, G.W., and Cooperrider, C.A. *Clinical Psychopharmacology: A Practical Reference for Nonmedical Psychotherapists.* Gaithersburg, Md.: Aspen Publishers, 1988.

Levin, M.E. "The Diabetic Foot: Preventing Its Morbidity and Mortality." *Medical Times* 116(1988):23–31.

Luckman, J., and Sorensen, K.C. *Medical-Surgical Nursing: A Psychophysiologic Approach.* Philadelphia: W.B. Saunders Co., 1987.

Manley, G. "Diabetes and Sexual Health." *Diabetes Educator* 12:366–369.

Martin, R.A. "Management of Peripheral Neuropathy in Diabetes Mellitus." *Postgraduate Medicine* 82 (1987):183–188.

Mengel, M.B. "Functional Assessment of Families with a Diabetic Person." *Primary Care* 15(1988):297–310.

Molitch, M.E. "Diabetes Mellitus—Control and Complications." *Postgraduate Medicine* 85 (1989):182–194.

National Institute of Handicapped Research. "Diabetes and Its Complications: Implications for Rehabilitation," *Rehab Brief* 12(1989):1–4.

Nursing 87 Books. *Patient Teaching.* Springhouse, Pa.: Springhouse Corporation Book Division, 1987.

O'Hare, J.A., and Warfield C.A. "The Diabetic Neuropathies." *Hospital Practice* (November 1984):37–48.

Porte, K.L.; Oliveri-Sulo, D.; and Wood, W.S. "Thyroid Disease and Sexual Dysfunction." *Medical Aspects of Human Sexuality* (February 1987):39–45.

Rakel, R.E. *Conn's Current Therapy 1990.* Philadelphia: W.B. Saunders Co., 1990.

Scheer, S.J., ed. *Medical Perspectives in Vocational Assessment of Impaired Workers.* Gaithersburg, Md.: Aspen Publishers, 1991.

Schwarz, L.S. "A Biopsychosocial Approach to the Management of the Diabetic Patient." *Primary Care* 15(1988):409–421.

Smith, D.W., and Hanley-Germain, C.P. *Care of the Adult Patient.* Philadelphia: J.B. Lippincott Co., 1975.

Spencer, M. "Type I Diabetes—Control with Individualized Insulin Regimens." *Postgraduate Medicine* 85(1989):201–209.

Stolov, W.C., and Clowers, M.R. *Handbook of Severe Disability.* Washington, D.C.: U.S. Department of Education, Rehabilitation Services Administration, 1981.

Stone, J.B., and Gregg, C.H. "Juvenile Diabetes and Rehabilitation Counseling." *Rehabilitation Counseling Bulletin* 24(1981):283–291.

Surwit, R.S.; Feinglos, M.N.; and Scovern, A.W. "Diabetes and Behavior." *American Psychologist* 38(1983):255–262.

Vander, A.J.; Sherman, J.H.; and Luciano, D.S. *Human Physiology: The Mechanisms of Body Function.* New York: McGraw-Hill Book Co., 1985.

Wyngaarden, J.B., and Smith, J.H. *Cecil Textbook of Medicine.* Philadelphia: W.B. Saunders Co., 1988.

chapter **6**

Gastrointestinal Disorders

NORMAL STRUCTURE AND FUNCTION

The **gastrointestinal tract**, or **alimentary canal**, is a hollow, muscular tube approximately 30 feet long (Figure 6-1). Its principal purpose is to provide a mechanism whereby nutrients and liquids can be taken into the body for energy and tissue growth, and through which wastes from the digestive process can be eliminated.

The digestive process begins in the **mouth**, sometimes called the **oral** or **buccal cavity**, where teeth break food into smaller particles. The teeth at the front of the mouth (**incisors**) provide a cutting action, while the teeth at the back of the mouth (**molars**) provide a grinding action. Chewing is important to the digestive process. Breaking food into smaller particles not only facilitates the passage of the food into the stomach, but also enlarges the surface area available for the gastric juices as the digestive process continues in the stomach. While still in the mouth, the smaller particles of food are mixed with **saliva**, which lubricates and softens the food, also facilitating its passage. Saliva, produced by the **parotid glands**, **submaxillary glands**, and **sublingual glands**, contains an enzyme that begins the breakdown of starches.

Food passes from the throat (pharynx) into a muscular tube called the **esophagus**, which leads from the mouth to the stomach. The esophagus and windpipe (trachea) have a common opening at the pharynx. Consequently, a flap called the **epiglottis** closes over the opening to the windpipe when food is swallowed, ensuring that food will pass into the esophagus rather than the windpipe. The esophagus is approximately 10 inches long and moves food along through rhythmic, muscular movements called **peristalsis**.

A muscular wall called the **diaphragm** separates the thoracic (chest) cavity from the abdominal cavity. The esophagus passes through the diaphragm in

111

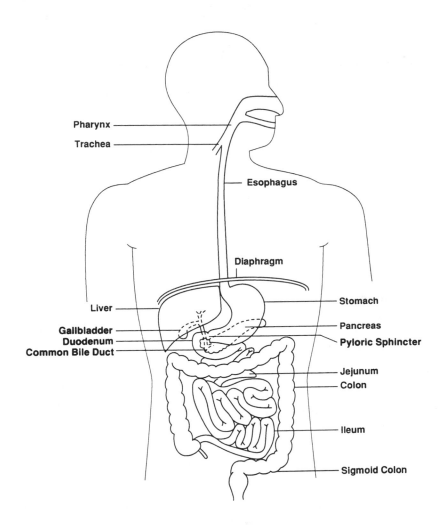

Figure 6-1 Gastrointestinal System

order to reach the stomach. The cavity contains the stomach, intestines, and other abdominal organs; it is lined with a thin membrane called the **peritoneum**.

Food enters the stomach from the esophagus through an opening called the **lower esophageal sphincter**, sometimes called the **cardia**. Pressure gradients around this opening prevent the backflow of food and gastric juices into the esophagus from the stomach, a muscular organ that continues the digestive process by storing, mixing, and liquefying food. The stomach contains some gastric juice at all times. Small glands in the stomach lining secrete a thin mucus to protect the stomach from irritation and from the action of gastric enzymes. The nervous system, via the **vagus nerve**, and the presence of food in the stomach stimulate gastric secretion.

In the stomach, food is mixed with **gastric juice** secreted by glands contained within the walls of the stomach and liquefied through a churning or mixing action. One component of gastric juice, **hydrochloric acid**, has a sterilizing effect, killing most organisms that enter the stomach. **Pepsin**, the primary enzyme of gastric juice, digests protein in the presence of hydrochloric acid. Also produced in the stomach is a substance called the **intrinsic factor** that is necessary for the absorption of vitamin B_{12}.

Some alcohol, water, sugars, and drugs are absorbed in the stomach, but most digestion and absorption take place in the small intestine. From the stomach, food passes through an opening called the **pyloric sphincter** into the small intestine. The small intestine is approximately 22 feet long and is divided into three parts. The first part of the small intestine, the **duodenum**, is approximately 10 inches long and is connected to the stomach at the pyloric sphincter. The middle section, the **jejunum**, is approximately 8 feet long; the last part, the ileum, which connects to the large intestine, is approximately 12 feet long. Digested food continues to move through the gastrointestinal tract by peristaltic movements. Although some fluid is absorbed in the small intestine, most fluid is absorbed in the large intestine. Thus, the contents of the small intestine tend to be liquid in nature.

The small and large intestines are connected by the **ileocecal valve,** which allows the contents of the small intestine to flow into the large intestine, but prevents any backflow. The large intestine collects food residue and is the place where the remaining water is absorbed from the intestinal contents, which makes the waste products (**feces**) more solid. Waste continues to move through the large intestine into the rectum and is finally excreted from the body through the anus. The brown color of feces is due primarily to bile pigments.

The large intestine is only about 5 feet long, but, like the small intestine, it is divided into parts. The part attached to the small intestine at the ileocecal valve is the **cecum**, to which the **appendix** is attached. The major portion of the large intestine, the colon, is divided into **ascending colon**, the **transverse colon**, the **descending colon**, and the **sigmoid colon**. The sigmoid colon leads to the **rectum** and, thence, to the **anus**, the opening from which feces are expelled.

Sometimes called accessory organs of digestion, the liver, the gallbladder, and the pancreas are located together in the upper abdominal cavity. The **liver** is the largest single organ in the body and is necessary for survival. In addition to aiding in digestion, the liver is important to carbohydrate, protein, and fat metabolism. The liver (1) converts a product of carbohydrate metabolism, **glucose**, into an energy source, **glycogen**, and then stores the glycogen until the body needs it; (2) converts the end products of protein metabolism into **urea**, which is later excreted by the kidneys; (3) manufactures and secretes bile for the digestion and absorption of fat; and (4) breaks down red blood cells and produces substances important for clotting of blood. Bile contains—along with bile salts—**bilirubin**, an orange pigment formed from the breakdown of red blood cells. The liver also serves as the detoxification center of the body, detoxifying poisonous chemicals and drugs.

Two major blood vessels enter the liver. The **hepatic artery** carries oxygenated blood for the organ itself. The **portal vein** carries blood to the liver from the pancreas, spleen, stomach, and intestine. Blood in the portal vein contains nutrients and toxins for either metabolism or detoxification by the liver.

The **gallbladder**, a small sac that stores bile, is located on the underside of the liver. Bile leaves the liver via the **hepatic ducts** and enters the gallbladder through the **cystic duct**. When the gallbladder contracts, bile flows through the **common bile duct** into the small intestine. Bile salts participate in fat digestion and absorption.

In addition to its endocrine function of producing the hormone insulin (see Chapter 5), the **pancreas** plays an important role in digestion. The pancreas lies behind the stomach and produces pancreatic juice, which contains enzymes to digest fats, carbohydrates, and proteins. Pancreatic juices enter the common bile duct through the **pancreatic duct** and then continue to the small intestine.

GASTROINTESTINAL DISORDERS

Disorders of the Mouth

Although not always disabling, disorders of the mouth can contribute to illness and disability by interfering with nutrition. Tooth decay (**dental caries**) and **periodontal disease** (disease of the tissues that surround and support the teeth) can lead to the loss of the teeth. Periodontal disease may separate the gum from the tooth, leading to the destruction of the underlying tissues. The early form of the disease is called **gingivitis** (inflammation of the gums). If untreated, **periodontitis**, a more severe form of gum disease, may develop. Periodontitis can affect the supporting structures of the teeth, causing the teeth to become loose and possibly fall out. Dentures cannot replace the natural teeth for effective chewing. The best treatment for dental caries and periodontal disease is prevention, early detection, and treatment.

Other disorders of the mouth that can interfere with proper nutrition are **stomatitis** (inflammation of the mouth) and **parotitis** (inflammation of the parotid glands). Stomatitis can result from infection, injury, toxic agents, or systemic illness. Parotitis can result from inactivity of the glands because of lack of oral intake or infection, or it can be a side-effect of some medications or general anesthesia. The treatment of both stomatitis and parotitis is directed toward correcting or alleviating the underlying cause.

Disorders of the Esophagus

Dysphagia (difficulty in swallowing) is a major symptom of a variety of disorders: **strictures** (narrowing) of portions of the esophagus due to injury or obstruction; neurological disorders, such as stroke or multiple sclerosis; or cardiovascular conditions, such as an enlarged heart. **Achalasia** (cardiospasm) is a type of dysphagia that is believed to be caused by a degeneration of the nerves that supply the muscles of the esophagus. As a result, the motility of the lower portion of the esophagus is decreased, and food is unable to pass into the stomach efficiently. Thus, food accumulates within the lower esophagus, causing esophageal irritation and regurgitation. Emotional upsets can aggravate the problem. In addition to the discomforts of esophagitis and the embarrassment of regurgitation, aspiration of undigested food particles into the lungs may occur, resulting in atelectasis (see Chapter 3).

Dyspepsia (indigestion) is also a common symptom of esophageal disease. Dyspepsia may be experienced alone or in combination with dysphagia. Among the causes of dyspepsia is **esophageal reflux**, in which the contents of the stomach flow back into the esophagus, irritating the esophageal lining.

Hiatus Hernia (Esophageal Hernia, Diaphragmatic Hernia)

The esophagus passes through an opening in the diaphragm to the stomach. When the opening becomes stretched or weakened, the stomach may protrude through the opening in the diaphragm into the thoracic cavity; this condition is called a **hiatus hernia**. It allows gastric juices to come into contact with the esophageal wall, causing **esophagitis**, **dyspepsia**, and possible ulceration of the esophagus. Individuals with a hiatus hernia may experience mild to severe pain and discomfort with the development of esophagitis.

A hiatus hernia may not cause extensive debilitation; however, the discomfort and potential complications may interfere with the individual's sense of well-being and subsequent productivity. In order to decrease the frequency of the symptoms, individuals with a hiatus hernia may be advised to refrain from any activity that increases intra-abdominal pressure, such as strenuous exercise and bending. In addition, it may be helpful to modify the timing and size of meals (such as having four to six small meals a day) in order to decrease the amount of gastric acid that the stomach produces. Raising the head of the bed approximately 6 inches while sleeping may also improve symptoms. If symptoms become severe, surgical repair may be indicated.

Gastritis

An inflammation of the lining of the stomach, **gastritis** can be caused by a variety of irritants or infectious agents. Acute gastritis is of short duration, with symptoms of nausea, vomiting, and pain; it is generally self-limiting and requires little except symptomatic treatment. Chronic gastritis, which is of longer duration, may consist of nondescript upper abdominal distress with vague symptoms. Extensive evaluation may be necessary to identify the causative factors. Food, beverages, or medications that seem to irritate the stomach lining should be avoided. Untreated, chronic gastritis can progress to scarring of the stomach lining, ulceration, or hemorrhage.

Peptic Ulcer

A break or loss of tissue in the lining of any part of the gastrointestinal tract that comes in contact with digestive juices is a **peptic ulcer**. Such ulcers occur when there is an imbalance between the secretion of gastric juices and the protective mechanism of the lining of the gastrointestinal tract. Consequently, peptic ulcers occur when the concentration or activity of gastric secretions is increased or when the resistance of the gastrointestinal tract lining to irritation is decreased. Peptic ulcers in the upper portion of the small intestine are called **duodenal ulcers**; those in the stomach are called **gastric ulcers**. Duodenal ulcers occur more frequently than do gastric ulcers.

The exact cause of peptic ulcer disease is unknown; however, several factors have been associated with the development of peptic ulcers. There is a high incidence of ulcer disease in some families, suggesting the possibility of a genetic predisposition. Cigarette smoking has been associated with a higher incidence of ulcer disease. Some medications, such as aspirin, nonsteroidal anti-inflammatory drugs, and steroids, can irritate the lining of the gastrointestinal tract and are believed to contribute to the formation of peptic ulcers. In some individuals, emotional stress has been associated with the development of peptic ulcer disease. Although some foods and beverages (e.g., alcohol and caffeine-containing beverages) increase gastric secretion and can irritate the lining of the gastrointestinal tract, there is no evidence that the intake of these substances causes ulcer disease.

The most common symptom of peptic ulcer is **epigastric pain**, which is located in the lower chest above the heart. Often, the pain occurs several hours after eating, when the stomach is empty, and is relieved by the ingestion of food, especially in the case of a duodenal ulcer. If there is bleeding in the area, individuals may have **hematemesis** (vomiting of blood) or **melena** (black, tarry bowel movements).

In addition to causing discomfort, peptic ulcers can interfere with adequate food intake and, thus, contribute to malnutrition. Hemorrhage and perforation are also serious complications of peptic ulcers. **Perforation**, the erosion of the ulcer through the gastric lining, allows the contents of the gastrointestinal tract to escape into the peritoneal cavity. Because the resulting irritation of the peritoneal lining (**peritonitis**) can be fatal, perforation is a medical emergency.

Effective treatment controls peptic ulcer disease. There is, however, a high incidence of recurrence once there has been an attack.

Another type of peptic ulcer, a "stress ulcer," may develop after an acute medical crisis, such as a severe injury or a catastrophic illness. Special names are given to stress ulcers that develop with some conditions. For example, stress ulcers associated with burns are called **Curling's ulcer**s; those associated with head injury are called **Cushing's ulcers**. The reason that these ulcers develop is unknown; however, they develop rapidly, sometimes within 72 hours of the injury or illness. Symptoms may not appear until the ulcer perforates and massive gastric hemorrhage occurs.

Inflammatory Bowel Disease

In **inflammatory bowel disease**, there is a chronic inflammation of different sites of the gastrointestinal tract. **Remissions** (times when symptoms subside) alternate with **exacerbations** (times when symptoms become worse). The exact cause of inflammatory bowel disease is unknown. Included in inflammatory bowel disease are Crohn's disease and ulcerative colitis.

Crohn's Disease (Regional Enteritis, Granulomatous Ileitis)

Individuals with **Crohn's disease** have an inflammation of segments of the **ileum** (small intestine). It results in scarring, thickening, and small inflammatory nodules of the intestinal wall that can cause **stenosis** (narrowing) of the intestine. It is characterized by chronic diarrhea, abdominal pain, fever, loss of appetite, and weight loss. Crohn's disease may be complicated by obstruction of the intestine because of the stenosis or by the formation of abscesses. In addition, an abnormal tubelike passage (fistula) may form between the small intestine and other parts of the abdominal cavity.

If there are no complications, complete recovery may follow a single isolated attack; however, Crohn's disease is frequently characterized by lifelong exacerbations.

Ulcerative Colitis

In contrast to Crohn's disease, which affects segments of the small bowel, **ulcerative colitis** is an inflammatory condition of the **colon**, or large intestine. It starts at the rectum or lower end of the colon and spreads upward, at times involving the entire colon. The colon lining becomes **edematous** or swollen, thickened and congested; small ulcers that ooze blood form on the colon lining. Ulcerative colitis may develop slowly or rapidly. The usual symptoms include crampy abdominal pain and bloody diarrhea. In severe cases, shock may result.

Ulcerative colitis can be a serious, debilitating disease with systemic complications that range from malnutrition to arthritis and ankylosing spondylitis. Nearly one-third of individuals with ulcerative colitis eventually require surgical intervention. Because individuals with ulcerative colitis have an increased risk of developing cancer of the colon, regular cancer screening is essential.

Diverticulitis

A **diverticulum** is an outpouching of the wall of a structure such as the bladder or intestine. **Diverticulosis** is the presence of numerous such outpouchings in the intestinal wall. Individuals with diverticulosis are often symptom-free and even unaware of the condition until it is found accidentally through a radiologic examination for another reason or until **diverticulitis** (i.e., the obstruction, infection, and inflammation of a diverticulum) develops. The symptoms of diverticulitis include crampy pain in the lower abdomen and, occasionally, mild fever. Its complications include perforation with resulting peritonitis and hemorrhage.

Individuals with no symptoms usually experience little debilitation, but they may need to avoid activities that increase intra-abdominal pressure, such as bending, lifting, and stooping. Some individuals with diverticulitis may require surgical intervention, however.

Irritable Bowel Syndrome (Spastic Colon, Mucous Colitis)

Called a **functional** bowel disorder, **irritable bowel syndrome** has no apparent organic or anatomic cause. Irritable bowel syndrome is characterized by chronic, excessive spasms of the large intestine, resulting in diarrhea, constipation, or both. Individuals with this syndrome also frequently experience abdominal pain, especially after eating. The symptoms vary in intensity. The impaired function of the intestine is generally associated with stress, and individuals with irritable bowel syndrome are frequently anxious, tense, depressed, and nervous. The degree of debilitation produced by irritable bowel syndrome depends on the individual and his or her ability to cope with the symptoms.

Hernia (Rupture)

The protrusion of an organ through the tissues that normally contain it is called a **hernia**. The most common types of abdominal hernia are the **inguinal** and **femoral** hernias, in which the intestine protrudes through a weakened part of the lower abdominal wall. Men are more likely to develop inguinal hernias, and women are more likely to develop femoral hernias. The symptoms are often mild, consisting of little more than a lump or swelling on the abdomen underneath the skin. The protrusion may appear when the individuals cough or lift something heavy, but the application of manual pressure over the area often pushes it back into place (reduces it). The protruding structure can become swollen and constricted by the opening, however, making it impossible to move the protrusion back into place. If this condition, called **incarceration**, is not treated, the blood supply to the herniated portion of the intestine may be cut off, causing tissue death. Called a **strangulated hernia**, this condition is a surgical emergency.

Uncomplicated hernias cause little disability, although it may be necessary to avoid such activities as lifting or pushing heavy objects. Even though there may be little discomfort or disability, the danger of hernia strangulation makes it important for individuals to seek treatment even if they are not in pain.

Pancreatitis

Individuals may develop **pancreatitis**, inflammation of the pancreas, in association with gallbladder disease, certain surgical procedures, some viral infections (e.g., mumps), or chronic alcohol abuse. Pancreatitis may be acute or chronic. **Acute pancreatitis** can result in **necrosis** or death of pancreatic tissue. As the pancreatic enzymes begin to digest the pancreas itself, hemorrhage and death may result. **Chronic pancreatitis** involves the progressive scarring and calcification of the pancreas; it is most frequently associated with chronic alcoholism.

The most common symptom of pancreatitis is severe abdominal pain, often radiating to the back. If there are no complications, the inflammation and symptoms subside once the causative factors have been eliminated and early treatment implemented.

Cholecystitis

Although **cholecystitis** (inflammation of the gallbladder) can occur without stones, especially in individuals with severe trauma or other critical illness, an obstruction of the cystic duct by a gallstone is the most common cause. The presence of gallstones is called **cholelithiasis**. Stones may injure the gallbladder and block the passage of the bile that is stored there.

Gallbladder disease can be acute or chronic. The symptoms of acute cholecystitis include severe pain in the upper abdomen, often with nausea and vomiting. When stones block its passage, bile may back up to the liver, interfering with the production of more bile. As a result, the level of bilirubin circulating in the blood becomes excessive, causing **jaundice** (a yellowish appearance of the skin and whites of the eyes).

The possible complications of cholecystitis include infection and/or perforation of the gallbladder, damage to the liver, and pancreatitis. The usual treatment for cholecystitis is surgical removal of the gallbladder.

Hepatitis

There are many different causes of **hepatitis** (inflammation of the liver), including viruses, the abuse of alcohol and drugs, and the ingestion of other toxic chemicals. Hepatitis is categorized according to the cause.

Acute Viral Hepatitis

Several different viruses can cause hepatitis. The viruses are transmitted in different ways, but they all produce an inflammatory process in the liver that interferes with its effective functioning.

Hepatitis caused by the type A virus is called **hepatitis A**. The type A virus is usually transmitted through the ingestion of food or water that has been contaminated because of poor sanitation or poor personal hygiene. Spread through direct person-to-person contact, it may be called **infectious hepatitis**. **Hepatitis B** is caused by the type B virus, which is transmitted through an injection with a contaminated needle or fluid, or through contact with contaminated body fluids. It is sometimes called **serum hepatitis**.

Hepatitis non-A, non-B, which is caused by an unidentifiable virus, is contracted primarily through the transfusion of contaminated blood or blood products and has some characteristics of both hepatitis A and hepatitis B. It may also be transmitted through direct personal contact and, possibly, through the ingestion of contaminated food and water. It may be spread through **carriers** (i.e., persons who appear healthy, but who carry the virus in their body).

Hepatitis may begin with flulike symptoms, such as **anorexia** (lack of appetite), distaste for cigarettes, chills and fever, nausea and vomiting, or headache. Eventually, **jaundice** may appear because of **hyperbilirubinemia** (an excess of bilirubin in the blood). Individuals may complain of **pruritus** or itching of the skin.

Hepatitis usually resolves spontaneously after a 1- to 2-month illness. Hepatitis B, although generally more prolonged than hepatitis A, is self-limited in most instances. On occasion, however, it may become chronic. Complications of both hepatitis A and hepatitis B may include destruction of liver tissue, liver failure, coma, and death. These complications occur more frequently in individuals with hepatitis B than in those with hepatitis A. The same complications may result from hepatitis non-A, non-B. Individuals with hepatitis non-A, non-B have a greater chance of developing chronic hepatitis.

Chronic Hepatitis

When liver inflammation continues longer than 3 to 6 months, individuals are said to have **chronic hepatitis**. This condition may lead to progressive fibrous changes in the liver or **cirrhosis**. The prognosis is variable, depending on the cause.

Toxic Hepatitis

Because the liver metabolizes and detoxifies many drugs, as well as other toxic or poisonous substances, the overexposure or the presence of **hepatotoxins** (substances that are harmful to the liver) can cause liver damage and chronic liver disease. The prognosis depends on the extent of the liver damage and the prevention of associated complications.

Cirrhosis

In cirrhosis, liver function is disorganized and altered because of fibrous changes in the structure of the liver. Such changes can occur for a wide variety of reasons, such as infection of the liver, as in viral hepatitis; obstruction of bile flow, as in gallbladder disease; or overexposure to hepatotoxins, such as toxic chemicals, drugs, and alcohol.

Some individuals with cirrhosis have no symptoms. As the disease progresses, symptoms may consist of **anorexia**, nausea, and vomiting. Individuals with advanced cases of cirrhosis may gain weight because of their retention of fluid and the presence of fluid in the abdominal cavity, a condition called **ascites**. Finally, there may be vomiting of blood (**hematemesis**) and a general bleeding tendency. Complications of cirrhosis include hemorrhage, coma, and, eventually, death.

The prognosis depends on the severity of the condition and the associated complications.

DIAGNOSTIC PROCEDURES

Barium Swallow (Upper Gastrointestinal Series)

A radiologic (x-ray) study of the upper gastrointestinal tract, a **barium swallow** makes it possible to identify abnormalities of the esophagus, stomach, and the upper portion of the small intestine. Immediately before the procedure, the individual drinks a white, chalky liquid called barium so that the radiologist can visualize the structures of the upper gastrointestinal tract on x-ray film. The test aids in the medical diagnosis of structural abnormalities, ulcers, and tumors of the upper gastrointestinal tract. The test is usually performed by a radiologist (a physician specializing in diagnostic or therapeutic use of x-ray film).

Barium Enema (Lower Gastrointestinal Series)

Like the barium swallow, a **barium enema** is a radiologic (x-ray) study. In the case of the barium enema, however, the large intestine is filled by an enema with barium. This procedure enables the radiologist to visualize the large intestine on x-ray film for the diagnosis of structural abnormalities, diverticula, and tumors.

Esophageal Manoscopy (Manometry)

Although done infrequently, **esophageal manoscopy** is a diagnostic procedure to evaluate the function of the sphincter between the esophagus and the stomach. During the procedure, the individual swallows a catheter that has a small instrument or transducer attached to it. When the transducer reaches the lower end of the esophagus, the pressure around the sphincter is measured.

Gastroscopy (Endoscopy)

When there are indications of abnormalities in the esophagus, stomach, or small intestine, the physician may visualize the walls of these organs directly through a specially lighted, flexible tube called a **gastroscope** or **endoscope**. Usually, a **gastroenterologist**, a physician who specializes in the diagnosis and treatment of gastrointestinal conditions, performs the gastroscopy. During the procedure, the individual's throat is sprayed with an anesthetic medication to numb the gagging reflex. The gastroscope is then inserted through the mouth, into the esophagus, into the stomach, and, at times, into the small intestine. Through the tube, the physician not only can visualize ulcerations or other abnormalities, but also can remove stomach contents for analysis, if needed.

Proctoscopy and Sigmoidoscopy

The procedure used to detect abnormalities of the rectum is called a **proctoscopy**. It involves the direct visualization of the anus and rectum through a special instrument called a **proctoscope** inserted into the rectum. Similarly, **sigmoidoscopy** permits the direct visualization of the sigmoid colon through a special instrument called a **sigmoidoscope** inserted through the anus and rectum up into the colon. This procedure is performed by a physician, often a gastroenterologist, a **family physician,** or a general **internist**. The procedure is performed to identify problems of the rectum and large intestine, including tumors, obstruction, and bleeding.

Cholecystography

If gallbladder disease is suspected, a **cholecystogram** may be performed to detect abnormalities, inflammation, or the presence of stones. Before the procedure, the individual swallows special pills or liquid, or receives an intravenous injection of a special substance that allows the gallbladder to be visualized on x-ray film. A **radiologist** (a physician who specializes in the diagnostic or therapeutic use of x-ray) usually performs the procedure.

Cholangiography

A study called a **cholangiogram** is used to visualize the bile ducts on x-ray film. Dye is injected into a vein or into a drain called a T tube that has been inserted into the bile duct (usually after gallbladder surgery). A radiologist performs the procedure to identify any obstruction of the bile ducts.

Abdominal Sonography (Ultrasonography)

In **ultrasonography**, sound waves are passed into the body and converted to a visual image or photograph of a body structure. **Abdominal sonograms** focus on organs contained within the abdomen and can be used to identify disorders of the pancreas, liver, gallbladder, or any other abdominal organ.

Computed Tomography (CT Scan, CAT Scan)

A special kind of x-ray procedure, **computed tomography** produces three-dimensional pictures of a cross section of a part of the body. The radiologist studies the image produced to identify problems and to determine if further tests are needed. This procedure can be used to diagnose pancreatic disease, tumors, or abscesses in the abdominal area.

Radionuclide Imaging

For **radionuclide imaging**, individuals are given a small amount of a radioactive chemical (**radionuclide**) that gives off energy in the form of radiation. Different radionuclides concentrate in different organs. Special types of equipment, such as counters, scanners, and gamma cameras, are used to detect the radiation, producing an image on film or on a special type of screen. A physician who has specialized in nuclear medicine then examines and evaluates the image. In the gastrointestinal system, radionuclide imaging is helpful in detecting tumors, abscesses, or cirrhosis of the liver and in diagnosing gallbladder disease.

Biopsy

The removal of a specimen of tissue from a specified site for examination is a **biopsy**. Common sites of biopsy in the gastrointestinal tract are the esophagus, stomach, rectum and colon, and liver. Biopsies are performed by a physician and can be performed on an outpatient basis under local anesthesia.

Abdominal Paracentesis

A procedure to remove fluid from the abdominal cavity, **abdominal paracentesis** involves a puncture of the abdominal cavity with a hollow needle through which accumulated fluid can be withdrawn. A physician performs the procedure. It may be done for diagnostic purposes to determine the nature of the fluid present, or for therapeutic purposes to remove accumulated fluid in the abdominal cavity that may be causing respiratory difficulty, pain, or other problems.

Laparoscopy

The abdominal cavity may be directly examined through a hollow tube called a **laparoscope** or peritoneoscope. The instrument is inserted into the abdominal cavity through a small incision. Individuals who have undergone laparoscopy may remain in the hospital overnight for observation after the procedure.

TREATMENT

Medications

Various medications are used in treating conditions of the gastrointestinal system; they may act on either muscular or glandular tissues. The specific classifications of medications frequently used in the treatment of gastrointestinal conditions are

- **antacids** to counteract excess acidity.
- **antiemetics** to prevent nausea and vomiting. A side-effect of these medications may be drowsiness.
- **digestants** to replace missing enzyme secretions when there is an enzyme deficiency in the gastrointestinal tract.
- **antidiarrheals** to prevent diarrhea.
- **laxatives** and **cathartics** to relieve constipation. Generally, laxatives have mild actions, while cathartics have stronger actions.
- **anticholinergics** to inhibit the action of the involuntary nervous system. In gastrointestinal conditions, these medications may be given to reduce the activity of the intestine or to decrease secretions.
- **histamine H₂ receptor antagonists** (e.g., cimetidine) to inhibit cells in the stomach lining from producing acid.
- **antimicrobials** (e.g., **sulfonamides**) to inhibit the growth of microorganisms.

Hyperalimentation (Total Parenteral Nutrition)

It is possible to bypass the gastrointestinal tract in providing nourishment. **Hyperalimentation** is the infusion of a special nutritional solution into a vein. Because of the nature of the solution, infusion usually takes place in a large vessel, such as the subclavian vein, which is located in the upper body. Hyperalimentation may be used in the treatment of any condition that compromises the individual's nutritional status. It may also be used when there is a need to rest the gastrointestinal tract, as in inflammatory bowel disease, or when there is an obstruction or malabsorption problem in the bowel.

Stress Management

Although stress management may be helpful in the treatment of a variety of chronic illnesses and disabilities, it may be especially useful in the treatment of conditions of the gastrointestinal tract. Stress itself may not be a direct cause of many conditions of the gastrointestinal tract, but it may exacerbate or prolong an acute episode in some patients with existing disease.

The body has a number of defensive mechanisms that take action in the face of threat or danger. When stress is encountered, a variety of physiological reactions take place in the body, including the gastrointestinal tract. The digestive system responds differently to different kinds of emotional stimuli. For example, it may become more or less active, and it may secrete more or less gastric juice. The intensity of the physiological reaction depends on the individual and on the situation.

Stress management helps individuals to control their reactions to stress. Programs in stress management may vary from exercise to techniques that alter the body's response to stress, such as biofeedback.

Treatment of Specific Disorders

Esophageal Disorders

In cases of **narrowing** or **constriction** of the esophagus, the goal of treatment is to widen the opening of the passageway. The physician may dilate the opening repeatedly with a dilating instrument or may determine that surgical repair is necessary. If the narrowing is due to a tumor, surgical removal of the tumor or part of the esophagus may be indicated.

Esophageal reflux may be treated with medications (e.g., antacids or cimetidine) that decrease acidity, avoidance of smoking, and avoidance of foods or beverages that seem to increase gastric acidity and discomfort. Mechanical measures of treatment may include sleeping with the head of the bed raised in order to minimize the amount of reflux by gravity.

The aim of the treatment of **achalasia** is to reduce the amount of pressure at the lower end of the esophagus, thus reducing the extent of the obstruction. The physician may dilate the opening between the esophagus and stomach mechanically with the use of a dilating instrument. In more severe cases, however, surgery to cut the muscle fibers of the sphincter of the lower esophagus may be indicated.

Hiatus Hernia

If the symptoms are mild, the treatment of hiatus hernia may be similar to the treatment of esophageal reflux, as described earlier. In other instances, hiatus hernia may be repaired surgically. Surgery returns the stomach to its normal position and makes the opening in the diaphragm smaller so that the stomach cannot again move above the diaphragm.

Gastritis

Acute gastritis is generally self-limiting, requiring little except symptomatic treatment. With chronic gastritis, however, it may be necessary to identify the cause and to avoid factors that irritate the stomach lining, such as certain foods or beverages.

Peptic Ulcer

The overall goals in the treatment of peptic ulcer are to relieve discomfort, heal the ulcer itself, and prolong the intervals between recurrences. The nonsurgical or medical treatment of ulcer disease may be directed toward cure or toward control of the disease. Medications such as **cimetidine** that decrease the acidity of the stomach contents are widely used to control peptic ulcer disease. Compliance with the daily dosage is essential, however, if medication is to have maximum effect.

There is little evidence that dietary intake causes peptic ulcer disease or that dietary therapy is useful in its treatment. Even so, individuals are generally encouraged to avoid foods that produce discomfort and to use alcohol and coffee only in moderation. Other substances that irritate the stomach lining, such as tobacco, aspirin, and nonsteroidal anti-inflammatory medications, are generally discontinued. Individuals who must continue using aspirin, for example, in the treatment of arthritis, may be encouraged to use aspirin that is buffered or aspirin that has a special enteric coating.

If the ulcer does not respond to medical therapy or if there are complications, such as uncontrollable bleeding or perforation, surgery is indicated. Several types of surgery may be performed. One procedure, a **vagotomy**, involves cutting the vagal nerve in order to eliminate its ability to stimulate acid secretion in the stomach. Another procedure, **pyloroplasty**, involves widening the opening between the stomach and the small intestine in order to facilitate stomach drainage. A **gastroenterostomy** is a surgical procedure in which the bottom of the stomach and the small intestine are both opened; the two openings are then connected, creating a passage between the body of the stomach and the small intestine to facilitate stomach drainage. In some instances, the acid-secreting portions of the stomach are removed; this procedure is called an **antrectomy** or **subtotal gastrectomy**.

The possible complications of surgical resection of the stomach include pernicious anemia (vitamin B_{12} deficiency) and a condition known as dumping syndrome. **Pernicious anemia** may occur after the removal of a portion of the stomach because of the absence of the intrinsic factor. In this case, lifelong treatment with injections of supplemental vitamin B_{12} is necessary. Other nutritional problems such as reduced absorption of calcium or vitamin D may also be experienced due to the rapid emptying of food into the bowel. **Dumping syndrome** occurs after the individual eats because food enters the small intestine more rapidly and is not adequately mixed. Individuals with dumping syndrome may experience dizziness, sweating, fainting, rapid heartbeat, and nausea 5 to 30 minutes after eating. The treatment of dumping syndrome involves decreasing the amount of food taken at one time, lying down after meals, and not taking liquids with meals. Dumping syndrome usually subsides 6 months to 1 year after surgery.

Inflammatory Bowel Disease

The treatment of inflammatory bowel disease depends on the location, severity, and chronicity of the disease. **Steroid** therapy may be used to reduce inflammation in acute exacerbations of the disease. A **sulfonamide** known as **sulfasalazine** is frequently prescribed for individuals with inflammatory bowel disease to prevent or to control infections, as the inflamed bowel is susceptible to infection.

During acute attacks, individuals with inflammatory bowel disease should keep physical activity to a minimum. They may continue working, but may need rest. Individuals with severe symptoms may be debilitated to the extent that bed rest is indicated.

Specific dietary restrictions vary with different individuals. In general, individuals with this condition should avoid foods that cause flare-ups. Low-fiber diets may be appropriate for those who have a propensity toward bowel obstruction, while a high-fiber diet that stimulates the bowel may be advisable for others.

When medical management fails to resolve inflammatory bowel disease or if complications occur, surgery may be indicated. The type of surgery depends on the location and severity of the inflammatory bowel disease.

In Crohn's disease, surgery is usually indicated for complications such as obstruction or abscess formation. The surgical treatment of Crohn's disease may involve removing or resecting the diseased portion of the intestine and surgically connecting the two ends of the intestine. This surgical connection is called an **anastomosis**. Surgical intervention in Crohn's disease is not curative, however.

The most common surgical procedure for **ulcerative colitis** is the removal of all or part of the colon, a procedure called a **colectomy**. If removing the entire colon, the surgeon passes a portion of the small intestine through a surgically created opening to the outside of the abdomen and establishes an **ileostomy**. The part of the intestine that is exposed to the outer surface of the abdomen is called a **stoma**. In this instance, the ileostomy is permanent, and all waste from the small intestine passes through this opening rather than through the rectum. The removal of the entire colon is curative for ulcerative colitis.

If only part of the colon is removed, a surgically created opening between the remaining portion of the colon and the external surface of the abdomen is formed. This opening, called a **colostomy**, is the opening through which solid wastes (feces) will be excreted. Colostomies may be temporary or permanent.

Because there is no sphincter in the stoma of either an ileostomy or a colostomy, individuals have no control over the elimination of waste through the stoma. Consequently, they wear a plastic bag over the stoma to collect fecal waste. Individuals with an ileostomy have more liquid and more frequent bowel movements than do individuals with a colostomy, because a great deal of liquid is removed from waste products in the large intestine. Thus, although individuals with a colostomy may be able to control the timing of their bowel movements through regular daily colostomy irrigation, individuals with an ileostomy may be unable to regulate eliminations by this means.

Some individuals with an ileostomy have a continent ileostomy in which an intra-abdominal pouch or **Kock pouch** is surgically constructed from a portion of the small intestine. Fecal waste collects in the pouch until they drain the pouch through the stoma with a catheter. Those who have such a pouch need not wear an external appliance. They insert a catheter three or four times a day, as needed, to remove the waste.

It is possible to create an **ileoanal pouch** for some individuals. In this procedure, after the colon is removed, the small intestine is sutured to the rectum so that the individual is able to have bowel movements through the anus. A temporary ileostomy may be necessary until the area around the ileoanal pouch heals, but, after 2 to 3 months, the ileostomy may be closed and anal elimination resumed.

Diverticulosis and Diverticulitis

Individuals with diverticulosis who have no symptoms usually require no special treatment; however, they may be advised to avoid activities that increase intra-abdominal pressure and to avoid constipation through the ingestion of a high-fiber diet and plenty of fluids.

For diverticulitis, however, it may be necessary to provide the colon with a period of rest. During this time, the individual is permitted to have nothing by mouth and may be given antibiotics. Surgery may be indicated for those who develop complications of diverticulitis, such as hemorrhage, abscess, or perforation. Surgery usually involves a colon resection, in which a portion of the bowel with the inflamed diverticula is removed and the healthy portions of the bowel are rejoined. Individuals who undergo surgery for diverticulitis may be able to resume their normal activities within 2 to 4 weeks after surgery, but they are usually advised to continue the therapeutic measures recommended for diverticulosis.

Irritable Bowel Syndrome

The treatment of irritable bowel syndrome is directed toward relieving its symptoms and eliminating stress. Foods and beverages that appear to aggravate the symptoms should be avoided. Medications may be prescribed to reduce intestinal activity or to relieve tension and anxiety. Individuals may be referred to special programs where they can learn techniques to control emotional tension. Because the bowel responds to stress, individuals with this syndrome should maintain a healthy life style that includes adequate nutrition, rest, exercise, and recreation.

Hernia

The surgical procedure used to repair hernias is called a **herniorrhaphy**. In this surgery, the protruding organs are replaced and the weakened area in the abdominal wall repaired. Because of the danger of hernia strangulation, it is important for individuals who have a hernia to seek treatment, even though they may have no pain. This is especially true if the individuals engage in strenuous work.

Pancreatitis

Individuals with acute pancreatitis should fast until the inflammation subsides. Hyperalimentation and the intravenous administration of fluids are generally indicated to meet nutrition and fluid needs.

Cholecystitis

For individuals with cholecystitis, treatment may begin with the elimination of fatty and highly seasoned foods that aggravate the condition from the diet. The curative treatment is surgical removal of the gallbladder, a procedure called **cholecystectomy**. Unless complications develop, there are usually no special limitations after surgery.

Hepatitis

There is no specific medication or treatment that directly affects the viruses that cause hepatitis. Usually, hepatitis resolves spontaneously after 1 to 2 months. During that interval, the treatment is directed toward alleviating the symptoms and maintaining the individual's state of health so that he or she may withstand the infection. Rest and adequate nutrition are the cornerstones of therapy. Individuals with hepatitis may generally return to work after jaundice disappears and they feel sufficiently strong to resume their duties.

Cirrhosis

The treatment of cirrhosis is based on its cause and any complications that may be present. Treatment of cirrhosis is discussed in further detail in Chapter 14.

FUNCTIONAL IMPLICATIONS

Psychological Issues

Conditions that affect the physical processes of eating and elimination have many psychological implications. Throughout life, eating is often associated with pleasure and social interaction. The treatment of gastrointestinal conditions frequently requires avoidance of substances that irritate the gastrointestinal tract or cause the excessive secretion of gastric juices. When certain types of food and beverages are restricted or when special diets are required, individuals may have difficulty in giving up something that they enjoyed.

Elimination is associated with privacy and personal cleanliness. The modification of elimination habits is learned in childhood as part of the socialization process. Individuals with problems of elimination may fear embarrassment and social ridicule as a result of their condition. Those with an ileostomy or a colostomy may fear the loss of physical and sexual attractiveness because of odor or embarrassing sounds. Individuals who have inflammatory bowel disease accompanied by diarrhea may fear fecal incontinence and concomitant humiliation.

There are other reasons for psychological reactions as well. Individuals with hepatitis may fear the transmissibility of the disease, while individuals with ulcerative colitis may be preoccupied with their increased risk of cancer. Depression is common in individuals with irritable bowel syndrome. The identification and resolution of these reactions may be crucial to the rehabilitative process.

Emotions affect the involuntary nervous system, which, in turn, affects the gastrointestinal tract. Thus, psychological factors may aggravate conditions of the gastrointestinal tract. For example, anxiety may contribute to flare-ups of conditions such as inflammatory bowel disease. Although rest and relaxation are of prime importance in the treatment of many gastrointestinal conditions, individuals may find it difficult to modify their schedules, to adjust to new life patterns, or to alter stressful situations at home or work. Often, directions to "rest and relax" are useless, unless individuals are assisted with methods and techniques to do so.

Although many conditions of the gastrointestinal tract do not affect body image, individuals with an ileostomy or a colostomy may encounter problems with body image and self-concept. They may perceive themselves as different from others. They may visualize themselves as unattractive and may believe that they must wear shapeless, dowdy clothes to hide the ileostomy or colostomy bag. It is often helpful if the individual is able to meet another person who has a similar condition and is leading a normal, active life.

Many conditions of the gastrointestinal tract require permanent alterations in life style and constant control over emotional tension. At times, individuals with such conditions exhibit illness behavior and disability that are out of proportion to the objective findings. These individuals should be helped to make the recommended alterations and encouraged to maintain as normal a life style as possible.

Life Style Issues

Individuals with any chronic disease must have a healthy life style, including adequate nutrition, rest, and exercise, in order to reach their maximal functional capacity. This is especially true of gastrointestinal conditions, because stress, fatigue, and emotions appear to have some direct effect on the digestive system. Individuals who are accustomed to performing in high-pressure, high-stress situations may need to learn ways either to decrease the stressful aspects of their daily life or work, or to cope better with the stress that is present.

Although not always required, dietary modifications are frequently a part of the treatment plan for conditions of the gastrointestinal tract. The alterations and restrictions of diet are often based on avoiding foods that appear to cause distress. Depending on the meaning of these foods to the individual, it may be difficult for him or her to abide by such restrictions. In most instances, eating well-balanced, regular meals is part of the therapeutic regimen. For individuals whose work or daily schedule is somewhat erratic, even this simple task may be difficult.

Alcohol intake should not necessarily be totally restricted, but may be limited. Tobacco use is restricted for many individuals with gastrointestinal conditions. Depending on the former habits of these individuals, both of these recommendations may be difficult to follow.

In most instances, conditions of the gastrointestinal tract do not directly affect sexual function. Individuals may be reluctant to engage in sexual activity, however, if their gastrointestinal condition affects their body image or if they fear fecal incontinence. Those with an ileostomy or a colostomy may have fears of defecation during sexual contact or may be self-conscious about the stoma itself. In some cases, men may become impotent as a result of nerve damage caused by the surgical procedure. Open discussion about such issues is important to uncover such fears and concerns, as well as to provide information that can help individuals and their partners deal with such issues.

Social Issues

Social situations that are stressful for the individual with gastrointestinal disease may cause a flare-up of symptoms. In order to avoid such stress, some individuals with gastrointestinal symptoms may withdraw from many social activities. Those who fear fecal incontinence, or odors or spillage from ileostomy or colostomy bags, may withdraw from social interactions to avoid potential embarrassment.

For individuals with an ileostomy or a colostomy, problems may arise if family members are repelled by the condition or find it impossible to fit the care of a stoma into the household routine. If these individuals have not accepted responsibility for their own personal care, they may become overly demanding or sloppy in the care of the stoma, antagonizing family members. The acceptance of the individual by family members and friends often determines to a great degree the acceptance of the condition by the individual.

Vocational Issues

In most instances, special work restrictions are not necessary for individuals with gastrointestinal disorders. Those with diverticular disease or hernia may need to avoid activities that increase intra-abdominal pressure, such as lifting or bending, however. Modifications may occasionally be necessary for those with other gastrointestinal conditions. For example, erratic or rotating schedules may make it difficult for an individual with a peptic ulcer to eat regular, well-balanced meals, aggravating the condition. Work situations that cause undue stress may contribute to a flare-up of the symptoms of some gastrointestinal conditions. If schedules or workload cannot be changed, individuals may need to learn different ways of expressing tension and coping with stress.

Special considerations, such as readily available bathrooms with privacy in the work place, may be necessary for individuals who experience diarrhea as a symptom of a gastrointestinal disorder or for those who have an ileostomy or a colostomy that may need attention during the day.

BIBLIOGRAPHY

Barber, T.C., and Langfitt, D.E. *Teaching the Medical/Surgical Patient—Diagnostics and Procedures.* Bowie, Md.: Robert J. Brady Co., 1983.

Bayless, T.M.; Drossman, D.A.; and Scherl, E. "Managing Inflammatory Bowel Disease." *Patient Care* 22(1988):20–43.

Bayless, T.M.; Drossman, D.A.; and Scherl, E. "Help Your IBP Patient Help Himself." *Patient Care* 22(1988):139–156.

Berkow, R., and Fletcher, A.J., eds. *The Merck Manual of Diagnosis and Therapy.* Rahway, N.J.: Merck Sharpe and Dohme Research Laboratories, 1987.

Brinberg, D.E., and Berkeley, B.E. "Crohn's Disease." *Postgraduate Medicine* 86(1989):257–265.

Brooks, D.V. "Diverticulitis." *Medical Times* 117(1989):17–23.

Brunner, L.S.; Emerson, C.P.; Ferguson, L.K.; and Suddarth, D.S. *Textbook of Medical-Surgical Nursing.* Philadelphia: W.B. Saunders Co., 1970.

Clearfield, H.R., and Wright, R.A. "Update on Peptic Ulcer Disease." *Patient Care* 24(1990):28–40.

Clementz, G.L., and Schade, S.G. "The Spectrum of Vitamin B_{12} Deficiency." *American Family Physician* 41(1990):150–161.

Corbett, J.V. *Diagnostic Procedures in Nursing Practice.* Norwalk, Conn.: Appleton-Century-Crofts, 1982.

Corbett, J.V. *Laboratory Tests in Nursing Practice.* Norwalk, Conn.: Appleton-Century-Crofts, 1983.

Crenshaw, T.L. "Impotence Following Colorectal Surgery." *Medical Aspects of Human Sexuality* (November 1986):51–57.

Farmer, R.G. "Differentiating Crohn's Disease from Ulcerative Colitis." *Diagnosis* (July 1987):66–74.

Guyton, A.C. *Human Physiology and Mechanisms of Disease.* Philadelphia: W.B. Saunders Co., 1982.

Hines, C.; Rogers, A.; and Weakley, F.L. "When Colonic Diverticula Cause Trouble." *Patient Care* 21(1987):38–42.

Katz, K.D., and Hollander, D. "Outpatient Management of Duodenal Ulcer Disease." *Hospital Medicine* (January 1988):95–117.

Keele, C.A.; Neil, E.; and Joels, N. *Samson Wright's Applied Physiology.* New York: Oxford University Press, 1982.

Klein, K.B. "Irritable Bowel Syndrome: Rational Use of Drugs." *Drug Therapy* (August 1987):17–29.

Koester, D.R., and Ryan, J.G. "Recognizing Major Sexually Transmitted Diseases, Part 4: Hepatitis B." *Family Practice Recertification* 12(1990):50–61.

Luckman, J., and Sorensen, K.C. *Medical-Surgical Nursing: A Psychophysiologic Approach.* Philadelphia: W.B. Saunders Co., 1987.

Nursing 87 Books. *Patient Teaching.* Springhouse, Pa.: Springhouse Corporation Book Division, 1987.

Peppercorn, M.A. "New Approaches to Ulcerative Colitis." *Drug Therapy* (February 1987):38–50.

Rakel, R.E. *Conn's Current Therapy 1990.* Philadelphia: W.B. Saunders, 1990.

Rhodes, J.B., and Payne, K.M. "Management of Irritable Bowel Syndrome." *Modern Medicine* 56(1988):66–72.

Sabesin, S.M. "Guidelines to Counseling Patients with Peptic Ulcer Disease." *Hospital Practice* (June 1985):38–44.

Scheer, S.J., ed. *Medical Perspectives in Vocational Assessment of Impaired Workers.* Gaithersburg, Md.: Aspen Publishers, 1991.

Smith, D.W., and Hanley-Germain, C.P. *Care of the Adult Patient.* Philadelphia: J.B. Lippincott Co., 1975.

Stolov, W.C., and Clowers, M.R. *Handbook of Severe Disability.* Washington, D.C.: U.S. Department of Education, Rehabilitation Services Administration, 1981.

Vander, A.J.; Sherman, J.H.; and Luciano, D.S. *Human Physiology: The Mechanisms of Body Function.* New York: McGraw-Hill Book Co., 1985.

Wyngaarden, J.B., and Smith, J.H. *Cecil Textbook of Medicine.* Philadelphia: W.B. Saunders Co., 1988.

chapter 7

Musculoskeletal and Connective Tissue Disorders

NORMAL STRUCTURE AND FUNCTION

The Skeletal System

Bones make up the general framework of the body. The skeletal system, which is made up of 206 bones, supports the surrounding tissues and assists in movement by providing leverage and attachment for muscles (Figure 7-1). It also protects vital organs, such as the heart and brain. The tough outer covering of bone is called the **periosteum**. Bones also have a network of sensory nerves and a network of tiny vessels to supply blood.

Bones have many functions other than support, movement, and protection. Red blood cells are manufactured in the red bone marrow by means of a process called **hematopoiesis**. Bone also stores calcium and other mineral salts. New bone is constantly being produced and old bone removed, creating a dynamic relationship between calcium in the bone and calcium in the blood.

Bones are classified according to shape. Long bones are found in the arms and legs (e.g., the **humerus** and the **femur**). Short bones are found in the hands and feet (e.g., the **carpals** and the **tarsals**). Flat bones are those like the skull (cranium) and ribs, while irregular bones have differing shapes, such as the vertebrae and **mandible** (jaw bone).

Connective tissue supports and, as its name implies, connects other tissues and tissue parts. Not only bones, but also ligaments, tendons, and cartilage are connective tissue. **Ligaments** are tough bands of fiber that connect bones at the joint site and provide stability during movement. **Tendons** are bands of tissue that connect muscle to bone, enabling muscle movement. **Cartilage** is a dense type of connective tissue that can withstand considerable tension. There are

137

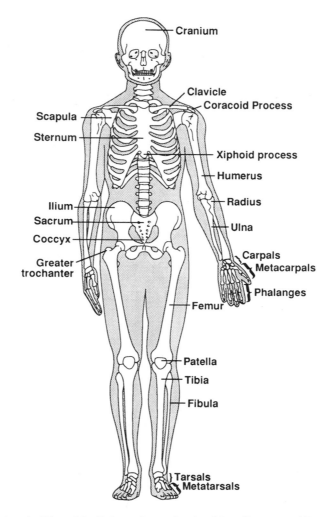

Figure 7-1 Anterior View of the Skeleton. *Source*: Reprinted from *Structure and Function in Man*, 4th ed., by S.M. Jacob, C.A. Francone, and W.J. Lossow, p. 93, with permission of W.B. Saunders, © 1978.

several different types of cartilage. For example, the cartilage between the vertebral disks of the spine is called **fibrocartilage**, while the cartilage in the external ear is called **elastic cartilage**.

The bones in the back that surround the spinal column are called **vertebrae**. They support the head and trunk of the body, protect the spinal cord, and enable bending and flexibility. The seven vertebrae at the neck and upper back are called **cervical vertebrae**. The twelve that extend from the upper to lower back are called **thoracic vertebrae**. In the lower back, there are five **lumbar vertebrae**; a bony prominence called the **sacrum** that consists of fused bone; and the **coccyx**, or small residual "tail bone," that extends from the end of the sacrum. Between each two vertebrae are disks of cartilage; these **intervertebral disks** act as cushions against shock. The tough, fibrous outer portion of the disk is called the **annulus**, and the spongy inner portion is called the **nucleus pulposus**. Vertebrae are connected by ligaments and surrounded in part by a joint capsule containing synovial fluid like other synovial joints.

A **joint** is the place where two or more bones are bound together. The coming together of two bones at a joint is called **articulation**. Some joints, such as those in the skull, are **fibrous** or **fixed** and provide no movement. Other joints, such as the **pubis symphysis** in the pelvis, are **cartilaginous** and provide slight movement. **Synovial joints** are freely movable, enabling both motion and change of position (Figure 7-2). They are enclosed in a sac called the **bursa**, which is lined with a synovial membrane. This membrane secretes synovial fluid, which aids joint movement by acting as a lubricant. Synovial fluid also helps cushion the joint against the shock produced by joint movement. **Articular cartilage** lines the end of each bone, helping to absorb shock. It receives its nourishment from the synovial fluid.

Synovial joints are capable of a variety of different types of movements.

- **circumduction**: circular movement
- **eversion**: movement in which a body part is turned outward
- **inversion**: movement in which a body part is turned inward
- **flexion**: bending movement
- **extension**: straightening movement
- **abduction**: movement of a body part away from the midline of the body
- **adduction**: movement of a body part toward the midline of the body
- **ulnar deviation**: lateral movement of the hand away from the body
- **radial deviation**: lateral movement of the hand inward, toward the body
- **pronation**: turning movement of a body part downward
- **supination**: turning movement of a body part upward
- **dorsiflexion**: backward movement of a body part

The motion of a particular synovial joint depends on the type of joint. **Ball-and-socket** joints, such as those found in the hip and shoulder, permit circular motion; **hinge** joints, such as those in the elbow and knee, provide back-and-forth motion. The joints of the vertebrae provide a **gliding** motion, while the vertebrae that connect the head and the spine provide a **pivotal** motion.

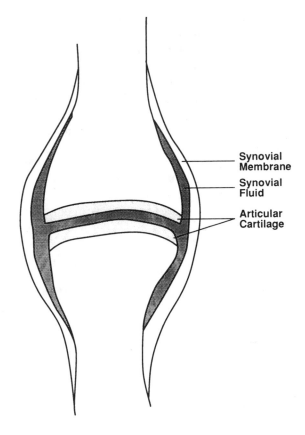

Figure 7-2 Synovial Joint

The Muscular System

There are several types of muscles in the body. Some muscles are **involuntary muscles** and work automatically, such as the cardiac muscle (**myocardium**) of the heart and the **smooth muscle** found in the digestive tract. In contrast, **striated** or **skeletal muscle**, which makes up 40 percent to 50 percent of an individual's body weight, is under voluntary control. A **muscle sheath** of connective tissue that contains blood vessels and nerve fibers surrounds every muscle. Each of the two ends of the muscle is attached to a different bone. The muscle attachment closer to the midline of the body is called the **origin** of the muscle, while the attachment of the end farther from the midline of the body is called the **insertion**.

Muscles produce movement by the contraction of opposite muscle groups. Muscles are classified by their function. Those muscles that bend a limb are called **flexors**; those that straighten a limb are **extensors**. Muscles that move a limb laterally, away from the body, are called **abductors,** while muscles that move a limb closer to the body are called **adductors**. Muscles that bend a body part backward are called **dorsiflexors**. Muscles maintain a partial state of contraction or **tone** even at rest because of continuous nerve stimulation.

MUSCULOSKELETAL AND CONNECTIVE TISSUE DISORDERS

Rheumatoid Arthritis

The term **arthritis** refers to joint inflammation; the term **rheumatic disease** describes approximately 100 types of conditions that usually produce arthritic symptoms and damage surrounding tissue. **Rheumatoid arthritis** is one type of arthritis and one of the most common rheumatic diseases. It is a chronic systemic disease of unknown cause that is characterized by recurrent inflammation of the synovial membrane of joints. **Rheumatic diseases**, including rheumatoid arthritis, are thought to result in part from an **autoimmune response** in which the body's normal mechanisms of defense produce an inflammatory type of reaction against itself, leading to cell destruction.

During the disease process in rheumatoid arthritis, the synovial membrane becomes inflamed; the joints become warm, swollen, and painful; and the synovial membrane thickens. As the condition progresses, a layer of scar tissue forms over the synovial membrane. This tissue, called **pannus**, interferes with the provision of nutrients to the cartilage of the joint, thereby leading to erosion and joint destruction. The scar tissue becomes so tough and fibrous that **ankylosis** (stiffness and fixation of the joint) occurs, impeding movement.

Rheumatoid arthritis may not affect all joints, or it may affect different joints at different times. The joints that are affected, however, are usually affected symmetrically. For example, both knees, rather than one knee, are affected. Joint pain and stiffness are generally worse in the morning, subside somewhat during the day, and again become painful at night.

Rheumatoid arthritis is a progressive disease, but not all individuals are affected to the same degree. The disease may be severe in some individuals, causing moderate joint deformity in a relatively short amount of time. In others, the condition may progress more slowly or may never become severely debilitating. The disease may be characterized by a series of **remissions**, in which symptoms subside for a period of weeks to years, and **exacerbations**, in which symptoms become worse. During exacerbations, joints may sustain increased damage so that they never return to their normal state, even during remissions.

Because rheumatoid arthritis is a systemic disease, individuals experience symptoms such as fatigue, weight loss, or fever, as well as joint pain and deformity. The inflammatory process may affect other body organs (e.g., the eyes, heart, lungs, or spleen), causing changes that alter organ function. The prognosis for individuals with rheumatoid arthritis is variable. Some individuals may experience rapid progression of debilitating symptoms, while others remain in a state of remission for years, continuing their normal employment and full activity.

Systemic Lupus Erythematosus

An autoimmune disease of unknown cause, **systemic lupus erythematosus** is most common in young women; it does not usually develop in those past middle age. The disease produces inflammation and structural changes in many body organs. It may progress rapidly or slowly, or it can become chronic with associated remissions and exacerbations. The symptoms vary with the individual, but may include a characteristic "butterfly rash" on the face, increased sensitivity to sunlight, loss of appetite, and weight loss. As the disease progresses, it may have more serious effects, such as kidney damage; accumulation of fluid around the heart or lungs; and mental changes, including forgetfulness, confusion, and, in some instances, seizures or convulsions.

The prognosis for individuals with systemic lupus erythematosus depends on which organs are involved and the degree of autoimmune reaction experienced. The condition is not curable and requires long-term management. For many individuals, however, appropriate treatment controls or suppresses the symptoms. Some individuals experience years of remission in which they are almost symptom-free, while others rapidly develop kidney damage. Women may experience flare-ups of disease activity at certain periods of the menstrual cycle and during or after pregnancy.

Osteoarthritis (Degenerative Joint Disease)

Associated with "wear and tear" of the joints, **osteoarthritis** is a local joint disease, not a systemic disease. Therefore, its symptoms are centered around the affected joint. Bone spurs (osteophytes) develop on the surface of the joints, eroding the cartilage so that it can no longer serve as a cushion or shock absorber. Consequently, the ends of the bones at the joint rub on each other, causing pain and inflammation. Weight-bearing joints, such as the knees, hips, and spine, are frequently affected. Finger joints may also be affected.

The joints affected by osteoarthritis may be those that had been injured previously or had been exposed to long-term strain. Obesity places extra strain on joints and is thought to be one predisposing factor for osteoarthritis. The reason that some individuals who have no known predisposing factor develop osteoarthritis is unknown, although the disease may be associated with the aging process.

Osteoarthritis is generally progressive and unremitting. Overuse of the affected joints, cold and damp weather, or other factors may intensify the symptoms. The amount of disability experienced depends on the type and magnitude of the joint damage, the number of joints involved, the particular joints involved, and the daily activity of the individual.

Gout (Gouty Arthritis)

Hyperuricemia, a buildup in the body of a substance called **uric acid**, characterizes **gout**. Uric acid is a waste product of the metabolism of substances called **purines**, which are found in a variety of foods. It is normally carried in the blood until it is excreted by the kidneys. With gout, the uric acid level in the blood increases, either because the kidneys are not excreting uric acid fast enough or because the body is making too much uric acid. The excess uric acid changes into crystals, called **urate crystals**, which settle in the joints, causing swelling and excruciating pain. Individuals with gout are more likely than are others to develop kidney stones (see Chapter 4), which occasionally cause obstruction and severe kidney damage.

Gout can be inherited, or it can be a complication of another condition. The symptoms, which appear suddenly, may be precipitated by the intake of foods rich in purines, alcohol intake, minor injury, stress, or fatigue. Attacks may last only a few days at first, but, if the condition is not adequately controlled, later attacks may last weeks. If untreated, gout may result in chronic joint symptoms with permanent joint deformity and limitation of motion. Although gout cannot be cured, prophylactic treatment can control its symptoms.

Ankylosing Spondylitis

A systemic rheumatic disorder that occurs primarily in young men, **ankylosing spondylitis** affects the joints and ligaments of the spine. At times, it may also affect the hips, ankles, or elbows. The inflammatory process around these joints causes pain and can result in a fusing of the joints with subsequent loss and/or restriction of motion.

Back pain, which is of varying intensity and often worse at night, is the most common initial complaint. Other complaints may include morning stiffness that is relieved by activity and systemic symptoms, such as fatigue, weight loss, loss of appetite, and anemia. Postural abnormalities may develop; if the condition is untreated, a permanent postural deformity called **kyphosis** (hump back) may occur.

With proper treatment, many individuals with ankylosing spondylitis have little permanent disability. There may be occasional flare-ups when the symptoms become worse, but there may also be long periods with no symptoms.

Osteoporosis

With **osteoporosis**, the bone mass (the amount of bone) is reduced, causing bones to become weakened, fragile, and easily broken. Although osteoporosis commonly occurs in individuals after middle age, **secondary osteoporosis** may occur as a result of other medical disorders such as gastric resection (see Chapter 6) or as a side-effect of the overuse of steroid medication.

Individuals with osteoporosis commonly have no symptoms until a bone is broken and there has been little or no trauma. Frequent sites of bone fractures are the hip, especially in the elderly, and the wrist (**Colles' fracture**). **Crush** or **compression** fractures may occur in the vertebrae. In some instances, although there has been no bone fracture, individuals may complain of aching in the various bones and, often, chronic backache.

Osteoporosis is progressive, but appropriate treatment may slow the disease process.

Osteomyelitis

There are several ways in which **osteomyelitis**, an infection of the bone, can occur. The pathological organism can enter the bone directly through an injury, such as an **open** or **compound fracture** in which the broken bone fragment has broken the skin, allowing pathological organisms to enter and invade the bone. An infection of surrounding tissue may extend to the bone; for example, an ulceration of tissue in a lower extremity that occurs because of vascular insufficiency (e.g., due to arteriosclerosis or diabetes) may become infected, and that infection may then extend to the bone. In other instances, pathological organisms that are present in the blood may settle and localize in the bone.

Osteomyelitis is often difficult to cure. If the initial treatment is ineffective, osteomyelitis can lead to chronic infection or amputation.

Bursitis

An inflammation of the **bursa** (the sac that contains the synovial fluid in the synovial joints), **bursitis** may be acute or chronic. It may result from chronic overuse of a joint, trauma to the joint, or the invasion of the bursa by infectious organisms. Although it may affect any synovial joint, bursitis commonly occurs in the shoulder, in the elbow (**olecranon bursitis**), or in the knee (**suprapatellar bursitis** or **housemaid's knee**).

Bursitis is characterized by pain and tenderness over the joint and by limitation of joint motion. Acute attacks may last for days to weeks, and they may recur. Splinting and rest of the joint are generally recommended. Bursitis may become chronic, causing varying degrees of disability.

Tendinitis and Tendosynovitis

The term **tendinitis** describes a condition in which there is an inflammation of a tendon; the term **tendosynovitis** describes a condition in which there is an inflammation of the sheath of tissue that surrounds the tendon. The two conditions usually occur simultaneously. Although the exact cause is unknown, tendinitis may be associated with trauma, strain, or unaccustomed exercise.

The primary symptom is pain on motion at the site of the inflammation. The condition usually subsides with appropriate treatment, although surgery may be indicated on rare occasions.

Carpal Tunnel Syndrome

The compression of the median nerve in the wrist causes pain and **paresthesia** (tingling, pricking sensation) in the hand. Known as **carpal tunnel syndrome**, this condition may be a complication of rheumatoid arthritis or other systemic disease, or it may result from strenuous or repetitive use of the hand. The symptoms may be mild and of short duration; if they become chronic, however, surgery may be indicated.

Herniated or Ruptured Disc (Herniated Nucleus Pulposus)

The rupture of the soft, inner portion of the intervertebral disc (**nucleus pulposus**) through a tear in the tougher outer portion of the disc (**annulus**) is called a herniation (Figure 7-3). A sprain or strain of the back or a disease that weakens the annulus may cause such a herniation of the disc. It results in back pain, often

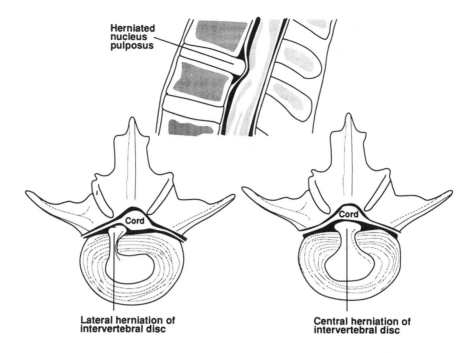

Figure 7-3 Forms of Vertebral Herniation. Reprinted from *Medical Surgical Nursing: A Psychological Approach*, 1st ed., by J. Luckman and K.C. Sorenson, p. 407, with permission of W.B. Saunders, © 1974.

accompanied by spasms of the back muscles. The protrusion of the **herniated disc** exerts pressure on the nerves that surround the area. The pressure on the nerves may cause a partial loss of sensation and/or weakness in lower extremities. In severe cases, the pressure on the nerves can cause problems with bowel or bladder function as well.

The pain experienced with a herniated disc is frequently exacerbated by straining, coughing, or lifting. The symptoms may be intermittent at first, but later progress to continuous pain or loss of sensation. Treatment usually eliminates the pain. Although surgery is sometimes necessary to repair the damaged disc, treatment may consist of physical therapy and the use of anti-inflammatory medications.

Low-Back Pain and Sciatica

Pain in the lumbar or sacral region, or low back pain, may be experienced in the erect, nonmoving spine (**static pain**) or during movement (**kinetic pain**).

Occasionally, **sciatica** (pain that radiates down the sciatic nerve of the hip and leg) may accompany low back pain; however, it may also occur alone.

Low back pain may result from any condition that stretches the back muscles or ligaments abnormally. For example, swayback posture (**lordosis**), poor conditioning, or overuse or misuse of the muscles and ligaments of the back may all result in stretched and painful back muscles.

Back pain can also result from **spondylolysis** (the breakdown of a vertebra), **spondylolisthesis** (the forward slipping of a vertebra), or the herniation of an intervertebral disc, as discussed earlier. Low back pain can be a symptom of other conditions, such as diseases that involve the internal organs of the abdomen. At other times, back pain may be psychogenic in origin, as no organic cause for the pain can be found. Because of the subjective nature of pain and the different meaning of pain to different individuals, the diagnosis and treatment of back pain in these individuals may be different, especially when there is no indication of an organic cause. Even if back pain is psychogenic in nature, however, the pain that the individual experiences is real and no less debilitating.

Acute low back pain that results from unusual strain or activity generally subsides with rest. Preventive measures, such as conditioning of the muscles of the back or the use of proper body mechanics, should be helpful in avoiding recurrences. It may be more difficult to resolve chronic low back pain, depending on the cause, and extensive, long-term therapy may be necessary.

Scoliosis

A lateral, S-shaped curvature of the spine, **scoliosis** can be **congenital** (present at birth), or it can be a complication of amputation or of a medical condition such as poliomyelitis or cerebral palsy. With early recognition and proper treatment, scoliosis can be corrected. If the spinal deformity becomes fixed, however, the condition is difficult to reverse. In severe cases, the deformity can interfere with respiratory capacity and can cause pressure on organs in the thoracic or abdominal cavity.

Fractures

Any break or disruption in the continuity of bone is a fracture. There are several types of fractures with different levels of severity.

- **closed or simple fracture**: an uncomplicated break in a bone with no breaking of skin. If the fracture extends straight across the bone, it is said to be a **transverse fracture**. If the fracture is at a slant, it is called an **oblique** fracture. A fracture that occurs in a spiral around the bone is usually caused by a twisting injury and is called a **spiral fracture**.

- **complete fracture**: a break in a bone that extends through the bone from one side to the other, including the periosteum or outer cover.
- **incomplete** or **partial fracture**: a break that does not extend all the way through the bone.
- **impacted fracture**: a break in which one portion of the bone is impacted, or forcibly driven, into another portion of the bone.
- **comminuted fracture**: a break in which the bone has been shattered, leaving fragments of bone at the site of the break.
- **displaced fracture**: a break in a bone in which the two ends of the bone are separated.
- **complicated fracture**: a break in a bone in which the tissue surrounding the bone, such as blood vessels and nerves, has also been injured.
- **compression fracture**: a break in which the ends of the bones are pressed against each other. Compression fractures often occur in the **vertebrae**.
- **pathologic fracture**: a break in a bone due to disease of the bone itself, rather than to an injury.
- **Colles' fracture**: a break in a bone near the wrist.
- **stress fracture**: a small break in a bone that occurs as the result of prolonged or unaccustomed activity.
- **open** or **compound fracture**: a break in a bone in which the skin is broken so that the bone protrudes through it. Open fractures may become infected, leading to osteomyelitis.

Some fractures may be treated by **closed reduction**, a procedure in which bone fragments are realigned manually, without surgery, and immobilized with a plaster cast. Other fractures must be treated by **open reduction**, a procedure in which bone fragments are realigned and stabilized surgically. Traction may be used in combination with either closed or open reduction.

Fractures seldom result in permanent disability unless complications develop. Complications that can contribute to a permanent disability are damage to surrounding nerves and blood vessels, and infection.

Dislocation

The displacement or separation of a bone from its normal joint position is called a **dislocation**. If the bone is not totally separated from the joint, the condition is called a **subluxation**. In addition to causing extreme pain, a dislocation causes a partial loss of movement at the joint and can impede the blood supply to the surrounding tissue.

Dislocations can result from trauma or from a congenital weakness or abnormality of a joint that predisposes the individual to dislocation on certain movements of the joints. The shoulder and the hip are common sites of dislocation, although any joint can be dislocated. In order to prevent complications, such as nerve damage or injury due to the decreased blood supply, prompt treatment is necessary. The bones can usually be slipped back into place manually. If there has been no damage to the nerves, blood vessels, or surrounding tissue, there is usually no permanent disability. If dislocations recur in the same joint, however, it may be advisable for the individual to avoid the movements that appear to contribute to the dislocation. If the dislocation recurs frequently, surgical fixation of the joint may be necessary.

Injuries to Tissues and Underlying Structures

Musculoskeletal injuries may not always involve bone; sometimes the injury involves underlying structures, such as the soft tissue under the skin. A **contusion** is a soft tissue injury that results from a blunt, diffuse blow. Although the skin is not usually broken nor are any bones broken, local hemorrhage with associated bruising, swelling, and damage to the deep soft tissue under the skin occurs. The bleeding under the skin is responsible for the purplish discoloration at the site of injury—the bruise (**ecchymosis**). When a major vessel or a muscle is injured, a **hematoma** (a sac filled with accumulated blood) may develop under the skin.

Strains and sprains are also soft tissue injuries. Although the terms *strain* and *sprain* are often used interchangeably, they refer to two different types of injuries. A **strain** is an overstretching or overuse of tendons and muscles, while a **sprain** is an injury or overstress of a ligament and its attachment site. Strains may be acute, resulting from a sudden twisting or wrenching movement, or they may occur with unaccustomed vigorous exercise. Chronic strain may be the result of repetitive muscle overuse. Sprains are categorized as mild, moderate, or severe. A severe sprain tears a ligament completely from its attachment and may require surgical repair.

An injury that has torn or cut the skin and underlying tissues is referred to as a **laceration**. **Puncture** and **penetration** injuries generally have a small entrance wound, but cause extensive damage to tissues under the skin. Stabbing wounds and gunshot wounds are puncture and penetration wounds, respectively. The degree of disability experienced with lacerations, puncture wounds, or penetration wounds depends on the location; the amount of damage to the underlying tissues, such as nerves, blood vessels, and internal organs; and associated complications, such as infection. The risk of infection is dependent on the source and circumstances of the injury.

Amputation

The loss of all or a portion of a body part is an **amputation**. It may be the result of an injury (**traumatic amputation**), such as the severance of an extremity in an accident; a surgical procedure performed to treat disease; or a congenital condition. Although amputations may involve any extremity, upper extremity amputations are more frequently associated with accidents, burns, explosions, or other types of injury. Lower extremity amputations are more frequently associated with disease, such as peripheral vascular disease.

A body part that has been totally severed by an injury can sometimes be surgically reattached to the body with partial restoration of function. The degree of success of a surgical reimplantation is dependent on the general condition of the individual, the availability of rapid transport to a reimplantation center, and appropriate care of the severed body part prior to reimplantation.

The type of surgical amputation performed because of underlying disease, such as cancer or arteriosclerosis, as well as the postoperative course and rehabilitation, depend to a great extent on the circumstances surrounding the amputation and the individual's general condition. Individuals who have had an amputation because of underlying disease are at risk of further amputations because of the disease process itself or of additional complications as a result of the disease.

An amputation of an extremity may be performed at different levels. In order to provide for maximal length of the stump and, thus, maximal function with a prosthesis, surgeons usually perform an amputation as **distal** (farthest from the center body) as possible.

The levels of upper extremity amputation are

1. **forequarter or interscapular-thoracic amputation**: the most severe upper extremity amputation, in which the entire arm, clavicle, and scapula are removed
2. **shoulder disarticulation** (S/D): the removal of the arm at the shoulder joint
3. **above the elbow** (A/E): the removal of the arm anywhere between the shoulder and the elbow joints
4. **elbow disarticulation** (E/D): the removal of the arm at the elbow joint
5. **below elbow** (B/E): the removal of the arm anywhere between the elbow and the wrist
6. **wrist disarticulation** (W/D): the removal of the hand at the wrist
7. **partial hand**: the amputation of one or more fingers or the loss of a portion of the hand

The levels of lower extremity amputation are

1. **hemipelvectomy or hindquarter amputation**: the most severe lower extremity amputation, in which the entire lower limb and half of the pelvis are removed
2. **hip disarticulation** (H/D): the removal of the leg at the hip joint
3. **above the knee** (A/K): the removal of the leg anywhere between the hip and the knee joints
4. **knee disarticulation** (K/D): the removal of the lower leg at the knee
5. **below the knee** (B/K): the removal of the lower leg anywhere between the knee and the ankle
6. **Syme's amputation**: the removal of the foot at the ankle
7. **transmetatarsal or partial foot**: the removal of a portion of the foot

It is especially important to retain the maximal length of the stump in lower extremity amputations, where the amount of energy required to use an artificial limb increases with the height of the amputation. Individuals with a below-the-knee amputation, for example, require approximately 25 percent more energy for movement than do individuals without an amputation.

Use of Prostheses

A **prosthesis** is a fabricated substitute for a missing body part, such as an artificial limb that replaces an amputated limb. The prosthesis may enable individuals to regain their independent function, or it may serve cosmetic purposes. The type of prosthesis, its purpose, and maximal use are dependent on the reason for the amputation, the type and level of the amputation, the presence of any underlying disease, the development of any complications, and, most important, the motivation of the individual to use the prosthesis. The physician, usually the **orthopedic** surgeon who performed the surgery, prescribes the prosthesis on the basis of the individual's daily activities, occupation, and cosmetic needs. A **certified prosthetist**, an individual who specializes in making prosthetic devices, then fabricates the prosthesis.

In some instances, the surgeon may place a temporary prosthesis on the stump of a lower extremity immediately after surgery. In this case, a rigid total contact dressing is applied to the stump in the operating room, and a **pylon** or adjustable rigid support structure is attached. An ankle-foot assembly is then attached to the lower end of the pylon. The immediate placement of a temporary prosthesis may have a psychological benefit for the individual, fostering a sense of independence and optimism as soon as he or she wakes from surgery. It also promotes early ambulation, thus reducing the risk of complications associated with immobility. The immediate placement of a temporary prosthesis is contraindicated, however, if there is severe underlying disease, such as diabetes or infection, or if there has been extensive damage as a result of injury. It is also contraindicated for individuals who have limited mental capabilities and may not be able to understand instructions or to regulate the weight placed on the stump in the early postoperative period.

When an immediate prosthetic fitting is not advisable, individuals receive a temporary prosthesis 2 to 3 weeks after surgery. The placement of a temporary prosthesis is necessary, whether the fitting is immediate or delayed, so that **edema** or swelling can subside and the stump can shrink before the permanent prosthesis is fitted. A permanent prosthesis can usually be placed within 3 months.

As much as possible, lower extremity prostheses are designed to enable ambulation. Generally, the lower the level of amputation, the easier the use of the lower extremity prosthesis. The ankle-foot attachment may be immovable or movable. A commonly used ankle-foot mechanism is the **SACH (solid ankle–cushion heel) foot**. In above-the-knee amputations, the prosthesis must also replace knee function, providing a joint that is stable for both standing and walking. Good alignment and fit of the socket of the prosthetic device are crucial for optimal balance and support. Because the proper alignment varies with the heel heights of shoes, individuals who wish to wear shoes with different heel heights on occasion may need several removable prosthetic feet designed to accommodate the varying heel heights.

Prosthetic devices for use after hemipelvectomy are more difficult to use. The increased energy needed for ambulation often makes the use of a prosthesis after hemipelvectomy unrealistic for other than cosmetic use, although such a prosthesis can be functional. For example, a prosthesis may be worn after hemipelvectomy to help the individual maintain proper posture while sitting in a wheelchair. When using the prosthesis for ambulation, the individual can walk only at a slow pace and only on level ground, however. Most individuals who have undergone hemipelvectomy choose to use crutches or a wheelchair for their daily activities, reserving the prosthesis for special events when cosmetic appearance is more important than ambulation.

Upper extremity prostheses vary in type and purpose; they are custom-made according to individual need. Complex function of the hand cannot be replaced, but functions such as lifting, grasping, and pinching can often be restored with a prosthesis. A **terminal device** is a prosthesis that substitutes for a hand. The level of amputation and the individual's needs determine the type of terminal device used. In general, the greater the cosmetic appearance of the device, the less its functional capacity. For an individual who needs grasping, holding, or lifting, a hook may be the most beneficial prosthesis. For others, a prosthetic hand that has grasp or pinch function for light objects may be most useful. Some individuals value the cosmetic appearance rather than the function of a prosthetic hand.

Activation of the function of a prosthesis is obtained by the using of muscles in the remaining portion of the limb. For this reason, a prosthesis placed after a high upper extremity amputation may have limited function. A prosthesis placed after a shoulder disarticulation or an interscapular-thoracic amputation, for example, may be mostly cosmetic with little, if any, functional capacity.

Myoelectrical prostheses, the function of which is activated by electrical potentials produced by muscles, may be considered in some instances. Electrodes are placed over the skin of the muscles to be used. These electrodes pick up electrical impulses from the muscles, transferring them to a motor in the prosthesis that then activates the hand to open and close. The function does not approximate the function of normal hand movement and dexterity, however. Myoelectrical prostheses are best suited for individuals with below-the-elbow prostheses. They are heavier because of the battery and motor that they contain, and they are more expensive than are regular prosthetic devices.

Complications of Amputation

Complications may develop after either upper or lower extremity amputation. It is extremely important that the prosthesis fit well and that there is no undue pressure or rubbing that could lead to ulceration. All individuals, but especially those whose amputation was the result of underlying peripheral vascular disease, must be careful to avoid skin ulceration that could become infected and necessitate a higher level amputation. Swelling or edema of the stump after the permanent prosthesis has been placed not only can interfere with the proper fit of the prosthesis, but also can increase the pressure and restrict the blood flow to the stump, contributing to the likelihood of ulceration. An improper fit, rubbing, or swelling should be immediately brought to the attention of the physician and prosthetist so that they can make appropriate adjustments of the prosthesis.

Individuals who have undergone an amputation should concentrate on preserving the range of motion in the remaining joints of the amputated limb. **Contractures** (deformities in which a permanent contraction of a muscle makes a joint immobile) may occur because of improper positioning or limited activity of remaining joints, and contractures impede or prevent the effective use of the prosthetic device. Contractures are easier to prevent through regular range-of-motion exercises of joints than they are to cure. When contractures develop, they may be corrected with extensive physical therapy and, occasionally, surgery.

Other complications of amputation include bone spurs, scoliosis, and phantom pain. Bone spurs or bone overgrowth may develop at the end of the stump, changing its shape and causing pain. **Scoliosis** may occur after a lower extremity amputation because of the improper alignment or the improper use of the prosthesis. After a higher upper extremity amputation, scoliosis may develop if the prosthetic device unbalances the trunk. In both instances, scoliosis can be prevented by making sure that the prosthesis is in good alignment. Individuals who have had an upper extremity amputation may also perform exercises to strengthen the muscles that support the prosthesis.

Although all amputees experience some degree of **phantom sensation**, in which there is a sensation that the amputated extremity is still present, the sensation usually diminishes over time. Some, however, experience a chronic, severe pain sensation in the amputated extremity called **phantom limb pain**. This pain may also gradually diminish over time, but it sometimes becomes disabling. In some instances, treatment to block the nerves that serve the amputated extremity may alleviate the pain. At times, **neuromas** (bundles of nerve fibers) that are imbedded in the scar tissue of the stump may cause pain and can be removed; however, this may not totally alleviate phantom limb pain. Individuals with chronic disabling phantom pain may need chronic pain management.

Pain

The purpose of pain is mainly protective; pain is a signal or warning that an area of the body needs attention. Pain and pain-related problems may be associated with a number of body systems and disease conditions. It is particularly prevalent in conditions of the musculoskeletal system.

Pain is one of the most complex human experiences. It is subjective, is difficult to quantify, and has different meanings to different individuals. Pain intensity is not always a reliable index of the seriousness of the condition. An individual's response to pain is influenced by a number of cognitive, emotional, behavioral, and cultural factors. Some cultures encourage a stoic response to pain, for example, while other cultures permit a free expression of feelings in response to pain. Different individuals may not respond to the same pain stimuli in the same way. Similarly, the same person may react differently to pain in different circumstances. Anxiety and fear tend to enhance the perception of pain and the intensity of the pain response, whereas distractions tend to lessen the perception of and response to pain.

Pain is classified as acute or chronic. **Acute pain** may be defined as pain that has an identifiable cause, such as injury, surgery, or acute illness. As healing occurs or the cause of pain is corrected or removed, the pain usually decreases within an established course of time. **Chronic pain** is defined as pain that continues more than 3 months. As it persists over time, chronic pain loses its biological function of signaling injury or disease and imposes psychological and physical stress on the individuals who are experiencing it. Chronic pain may be of three types.

1. pain that persists beyond the normal healing time (e.g., pain at the site of a fractured bone after the bone has healed, phantom pain in an amputated limb)
2. pain related to a chronic, degenerative, or malignant disease (e.g., rheumatoid arthritis, osteoporosis, cancer)
3. pain that persists for months or years, but has no readily identifiable organic cause (e.g., low back pain with no identifiable physical cause)

Chronic pain may be associated with a number of conditions of the musculoskeletal system. Often, it is the most debilitating factor of the condition.

Individuals who experience chronic pain may develop **chronic pain syndrome**, a condition characterized by physical, social, and behavioral dysfunction. Individuals with chronic pain syndrome often have a marked alteration of behavior, as shown by depression or anxiety, restriction in daily activities, excessive use of medications, and frequent use of multiple medical services. The pain becomes a central issue in their lives.

DIAGNOSTIC PROCEDURES

Roentgenography (Radiography, X-Rays)

The most widely used diagnostic tool for musculoskeletal disorders is roentgenography. The painless procedure involves positioning the body part to be studied against photographic film and exposing the film by irradiation. A radiographic technician generally takes the x-ray films, and a **radiologist** (a physician who specializes in radiation and the use of radioactive materials for the diagnosis and treatment of disease) reads them. For musculoskeletal conditions, roentgenography is useful for identifying deformity or injury of bones.

Arthrography

In order to perform an **arthrogram**, a radiographic study of a joint, the radiologist first injects the joint to be examined with a local anesthetic and then injects a special material or contrast medium and/or air into the joint cavity. The joint is then moved through its range of motion and a series of x-ray films taken. This diagnostic procedure is done to identify injury to the joint or supporting ligaments.

Discography and Myelography

Although discography and myelography are similar to arthrography, they involve the study of different areas of the body. **Discography** is a radiographic study of the cervical or lumbar disks, while **myelography** is a radiographic study of the spinal cord.

Arthroscopy

A joint may be visualized directly through a small instrument, called an **arthroscope**, inserted into the joint to be studied. Videotaped pictures may be taken of the internal joint structures.

Arthrocentesis

In **arthrocentesis**, the physician aspirates synovial fluid with a needle that has been inserted into the joint cavity. The synovial fluid is then examined for abnormalities, such as blood, crystals, or infection. In some instances, arthrocentesis may be used to remove fluid from the joint in order to relieve pain. If the joint has been injured or is infected, the examination of blood or pus in the synovial fluid can help in determining the type or degree of injury or infection.

Bone Scan

When a bone scan is to be done, radioactive substances, called **radioisotopes**, are injected intravenously. The radioisotopes concentrate in the bone, and the amount of concentration is measured by a special machine called a scanner. The scanner produces a picture of the bone (scan), enabling a physician to identify any abnormalities.

Magnetic Resonance Imaging

In a painless, noninvasive procedure, **magnetic resonance imaging** produces rapid detailed pictures of body tissue. The procedure requires no radiation and no intravenous injections. For magnetic resonance imaging, individuals are placed in a horizontal cylinder, where they are exposed to a magnetic field much greater than the earth's. As a result, hydrogen atoms within the body line up parallel to the magnetic field. Low-energy radio waves are then directed into the individual's body, causing the protons in the body to move out of alignment; this process is called resonance. When the radio waves are discontinued, the protons realign. The machine picks up the amount of energy released by the protons as they swing back into alignment and converts it into an image of the body part being studied.

Because of the strength of the magnetic field used for the procedure, individuals with metal in their body should not undergo magnetic resonance imaging. Thus, the procedure is contraindicated for individuals with a cardiac pacemaker, metal clips that have been placed in the body as part of a prior surgical procedure, or small pieces of metal embedded by injury (e.g., shrapnel).

Magnetic resonance imaging is used for diagnosing diseases of many body systems. In the musculoskeletal system, magnetic resonance imaging is helpful in diagnosing diseases of the joints, confirming infection of the bone (osteomyelitis), discovering small fractures of the bone that may not be detectable by other means, and identifying soft tissue and bone tumors.

Computed Tomography (Computed Axial Tomography, CAT Scan, CT Scan)

In order to determine if a disk has ruptured, computed tomography may be used to examine disks between vertebrae.

Blood Tests

In and of themselves, blood tests are not diagnostic of specific disorders of the musculoskeletal system; however, some blood tests indicate inflammation or tissue injury and, thus, may be used as part of the diagnostic process. For example, a determination of the **erythrocyte sedimentation rate** may be part of the diagnostic workup for conditions such as rheumatoid arthritis. Another test, **C-reactive protein,** may also be used to identify inflammatory processes or tissue destruction.

A blood test commonly used in the diagnosis of rheumatoid arthritis is the **rheumatoid factor (latex fixation** or **agglutination test).** The blood test determines whether there is abnormal protein in the serum. Many individuals with rheumatoid arthritis have such protein, although individuals with many other conditions (e.g., tuberculosis and bacterial endocarditis) may also have the factor in their serum.

Other blood tests that may be used, especially in the diagnosis of systemic lupus erythematosus, are the **LE prep** and the **antinuclear antibodies (ANA)** tests. The LE prep is the examination of a specific cell in the blood (a particular type of neutrophil) that is changed due to systemic lupus erythematosus. Antinuclear antibodies are proteins found in the blood of some individuals with autoimmune diseases. The antinuclear antibody test is a blood test that identifies the presence of these proteins. However, since the test may be positive in many different autoimmune diseases or may be positive as a result of some medications, the test is not definitive.

TREATMENT

Physical Therapy

Many types of musculoskeletal disorders can be improved through physical therapy techniques. The type of physical therapy administered depends on the particular musculoskeletal condition. Physical therapy may be directed toward increasing or maintaining a joint's range of motion, increasing muscle strength, relieving pain or muscle spasms, or teaching techniques for ambulation.

Some techniques used in physical therapy involve therapeutic exercise, which may be passive or active. In **passive exercise**, the therapist or a mechanical device exercises the body part. In **active exercise**, the individual independently performs a specified exercise regimen under the direction or supervision of the physical therapist or physical therapy technician. Exercise may be designed to increase or maintain range of motion, prevent **atrophy** (shrinking of the muscles), prevent deformity due to contractures, or increase muscle strength.

Other physical therapy techniques may involve the application of heat or cold, or the massage of muscles for relaxation or relief of pain. Heat may be applied through hot packs, hot soaks, infrared radiation, or whirlpool baths. Another procedure for applying heat is **diathermy**, a process in which the temperature of the body part is raised through high-frequency ultrasonic waves. Because cold has a numbing effect, it may also be used to relieve pain. Cold packs or chemical packs may be applied to the painful area. Massage, the manipulation of muscles through rubbing or kneading, may be used to relax muscles, improve muscle tone, relieve muscle spasm, or increase blood flow to the area.

Casts

The treatment of a variety of musculoskeletal conditions includes casting. Although casts may be synthetic, they are more commonly made of plaster of Paris. Casts provide immobilization and support for a body part while it is healing. They may also be used to prevent or correct various musculoskeletal deformities. The type and size of cast depends on the condition and the purpose of the casting. In addition to the casts used on extremities, there are **spica casts**, which extend the entire length of the lower extremity from the middle of the trunk of the body. In some instances, a full body cast is necessary.

Assistive Devices

Individuals with musculoskeletal disorders may use assistive devices to aid in ambulation, to prevent undue strain on a body part, to correct or prevent a deformity, or to restore function. Assistive devices may be used therapeutically in the healing period after musculoskeletal injury, or they may be used on a continuing basis.

Canes, crutches, and walkers are assistive devices that aid in ambulation or prevent excessive weight bearing on a lower extremity. The assistive devices used to straighten or correct a deformity (**orthosis**) are mechanical devices applied to the body to control the motion of joints and the force or weight distribution to a body part. A brace, for example, is an orthotic device used to provide support or to prevent or correct a deformity. The type of device used depends on the purpose of the bracing and the condition itself. An **orthotist** is an individual who constructs orthotic devices to meet individual needs.

Orthoses may be prescribed for any musculoskeletal area, depending on the nature of the problem. For example, **lower limb orthoses** are orthopedic shoes or orthoses for the foot, ankle, knee, or hip. **Spinal orthoses** may be used to relieve compression forces on the spine, to restrict the movement of the spine, or to modify the alignment of the spine. There are at least 50 types of spinal orthoses, classified according to the level of application. **Cervical orthoses** may be prescribed for a wide variety of problems, ranging from whiplash to fracture of the cervical spine. The **Taylor**, the **Jewett Hyperextension TLSO**, and the **C.A.S.H.** are spinal orthoses that are prescribed to restrict trunk flexion and rotation, or to provide hyperextension and reduce flexion in the thoracic-lumbar spine. **Lumbar-sacral spinal orthoses**, such as the **Knight Chairback** and **Williams**, are prescribed primarily for low back pain and may consist of flexible or semirigid corsets that provide support and protection. The **Milwaukee brace** is an orthotic device designed for the treatment of scoliosis.

Orthotic devices may also be used for the upper extremities. In these instances, they are most frequently prescribed because of injury. **Upper extremity orthoses** may be applied to the shoulder, elbow, or wrist/hand.

Newer orthotic devices, called **fracture orthoses**, are designed to allow early ambulation on fractures of the lower extremity. These devices permit the functional use of the extremity much earlier than does conventional casting. Recently, some upper extremity fractures have also been treated with fracture orthoses.

Traction

Individuals with a variety of musculoskeletal conditions may benefit from **traction**, a therapeutic method in which a mechanical or manual pull is used to restore or maintain the alignment of bones, or to relieve pain and muscle spasm. It may be applied in several ways. When traction exerts a constant pull, it is said to be **continuous**. If the pull is relieved periodically, the traction is said to be **intermittent**.

Traction may be applied externally or internally. **Skin traction** is applied by fastening straps, belts, or other external devices around the body and then to a source of countertraction. In contrast, **skeletal traction** is applied internally; metal wires (**Kirschner wires**), pins (**Steinmann pins**), or tongs (**Crutchfield tongs**) are inserted through the bone surgically and attached to a source of countertraction outside the body. Kirschner wires and Steinmann pins are typically used to **reduce** (align) fractures of the long bones of the extremities in order to promote bone healing or to stabilize the fracture until surgical treatment can be undertaken to correct the fracture. Crutchfield tongs are inserted into the skull for injuries of the cervical spine.

The use of traction may prevent surgical intervention in some cases, and it offers more freedom of movement than does a cast. It usually requires prolonged hospitalization, however. Furthermore, in the case of skeletal traction, there is a risk of complications, such as osteomyelitis, that can contribute to permanent disability.

Surgical Treatment

Individuals with musculoskeletal conditions may require surgical treatment to correct, remove, or replace injured or diseased structures. Surgery may be performed on an emergency basis in the case of injury or on an elective basis in the case of disease, deformity, or an old injury. There are several types of surgical interventions.

- **open reduction** of fractures: the surgical alignment of the fractured bone. **Internal fixation** is the placement of screws, pins, wires, rods, or other devices through the bone to hold the bone fragments together.
- **arthroplasty**: the replacement of all or part of a joint with a prosthetic device in order to relieve pain or to restore function. Common sites of arthroplasty are the hip, shoulder, knee, and elbow. Reasons for arthroplasty include a broken hip (total hip replacement) or arthritis.
- **arthrodesis**: the surgical **fusing** (joining) of two joint surfaces, making them permanently immobile. The procedure was once commonly performed

in order to relieve joint pain; with improved arthroplasty procedures, however, arthrodesis is now less common.

- **synovectomy**: the surgical removal of the synovial membrane surrounding a joint. Synovectomy prevents recurrent inflammation, thus reducing joint pain and further joint destruction.
- **laminectomy**: the surgical removal of a portion of a vertebra, exposing the spinal cord. It is usually performed to facilitate the removal of any source of pressure on the spinal cord. For example, the procedure may be used to remove bone fragments after a spinal injury, to remove the herniated area of a disk (**diskectomy**), or to remove tumors from the spinal cord. Whereas laminectomy once involved a long recuperative period, new microsurgical techniques enable surgery to be performed with minimal trauma so that the individual can return to function in a much shorter period of time.
- **spinal fusion**: the grafting of bone from another area of the body into the disk interspace after a surgical procedure on the spine (e.g., laminectomy). After spinal fusion, mobility at the point of the fusion is lost.
- **carpal tunnel repair**: a surgical procedure indicated for carpal tunnel syndrome in which the median nerve is decompressed by the transection of surrounding ligaments. It is performed when the symptoms are severe and of long duration or when there is progressive sensory loss in the fingers and hand.

Medical Treatment

Pain and inflammation are common manifestations of many musculoskeletal and connective tissue disorders. **Salicylates** (e.g., aspirin) are commonly the first choice of medication to reduce pain and inflammation. For some conditions, such as rheumatoid arthritis, it may be necessary to prescribe as many as 15 or more tablets of salicylate a day to reach a therapeutic dosage, however. This high concentration of aspirin in the blood may exceed the liver's ability to metabolize it. The side-effects of a high salicylate dosage include gastric irritation and ringing in the ears (**tinnitus**).

Nonsteroidal anti-inflammatory drugs may also be used to reduce the pain and inflammation associated with musculoskeletal conditions. Like salicylates, these drugs can irritate the stomach lining, causing pain and, in some instances, bleeding. **Corticosteroids** can produce dramatic short-term anti-inflammatory effects, but they do not prevent the progression of joint destruction and, because of their potency and subsequent side-effects, can be used only on a short-term basis. Some of the side-effects of prolonged use include cataracts, demineralization of bone, delayed wound healing, poor resistance to infection, and symptoms similar to those of Cushing's syndrome (see Chapter 5). More serious systemic effects may involve severe adrenal insufficiency following withdrawal (see Chapter 5).

Steroid use should always be carefully monitored by a physician and should never be discontinued suddenly. Although steroids for musculoskeletal conditions are generally taken orally, they are sometimes injected directly into an inflamed joint for the temporary suppression of the inflammation.

Treatment of Chronic Pain

When possible, pain is best managed by treatment of the underlying cause. When pain becomes chronic, however, it is often treated as a condition in itself. The treatment of pain that cannot be controlled or eradicated is directed toward helping the affected individual learn to cope with the pain. Physicians may treat chronic pain, but they more often refer individuals with chronic pain to a **clinic** that uses multiple, simultaneous therapeutic approaches to chronic pain. Alternate forms of pain control may be used alone or in combination with analgesic medication.

Generally, **medications** are used more often in the treatment of acute pain rather than chronic pain. When medications are used as a part of pain management, the type chosen depends on the cause and the type of pain. **Muscle relaxants** may be prescribed to relax tight muscles; **analgesics**, to relieve pain. In most instances, the use of narcotic analgesics for the long-term treatment of chronic pain is inadvisable because of the possibility of physical and/or psychological dependence or addiction. Because individuals with chronic pain frequently experience depression as well, **antidepressant** medications may occasionally be prescribed.

Physical therapy may be prescribed to help individuals with chronic pain gradually increase their exercise tolerance. It may also be prescribed to help individuals increase their activity. Splints or braces may be used to support the painful body part.

Transcutaneous electrical nerve stimulation may help to relieve pain. In this technique, the electrodes of a small, battery-operated device are placed over the painful area.When the unit is on, it stimulates nerve fibers electrically, providing a counterirritation that, in turn, blocks pain impulses. The treatment itself is painless. The length of time that the individual wears the unit varies, ranging from all day to only 1 or 2 hours a day. The success of transcutaneous electrical nerve stimulation depends to some degree on the individual's understanding of the technique and motivation to use it.

The technique of **stress management** includes specific procedures designed to reduce stress and promote relaxation. Stress management may be useful in the treatment of a variety of disorders, but it may be particularly useful in the treatment of chronic pain. Because tension and anxiety tend to accentuate pain perception, the removal of tension and anxiety can serve to reduce pain perception. There are a variety of different types of stress management. Some individuals may be helped to identify the sources of stress and learn ways to control their reaction to it. Other individuals may learn specific relaxation techniques.

Some individuals find **biofeedback** helpful in controlling pain, especially if the pain is due in part to muscle tension. Electrodes are placed on the skin over localized muscles. Wires from the electrodes are attached to an **electromyogram** machine, and the electrical activity of the muscles is measured. The individual receives this information through a tone or lights. After learning different methods to reduce the amount of muscle tension, the individual can monitor the effectiveness of these methods in controlling muscular activity through the feedback system.

Acupuncture is an ancient Chinese form of analgesia in which long, fine needles are inserted into selected points of an individual's body to eliminate the pain sensation. There is no simple explanation for the mechanisms that underlie the analgesic effects of acupuncture. Although it is considered an invasive technique, it has few, if any, complications when it is done under sterile conditions by those who have been trained and certified in acupuncture techniques.

Meditation, another ancient technique, removes the individual's focus from the painful sensation. Individuals concentrate on a variety of other focuses, such as breathing, chanting, or a visual image.

Hypnosis is a procedure by which individuals are induced into a trance state, during which suggestion is used to alter attitudes, perceptions, or behavior. For individuals with chronic pain, hypnosis may be used to alter the reaction to painful stimuli or the perception of pain. Hypnosis should be conducted only by trained, certified individuals. It has varying degrees of success in the management of chronic pain.

Individuals who undergo **progressive relaxation training** are taught to tighten and relax different muscle groups gradually. The procedure promotes relaxation, decreases anxiety, and lessens muscle tension.

A behavioral technique designed to decrease the functional impairment associated with chronic pain, **operant conditioning** does not cure or reduce the pain itself, but rather alters the individual's behavioral response to the pain. The technique is based on theories of learning and conditioning. The experience of pain often results in a series of behaviors that communicate discomfort (e.g., grimacing, guarding, or limping) and usually elicit responses from others in the form of sympathy, decreased expectations for performance or success, or even monetary compensation. Behavioral responses to pain may also be reinforced by the fact that they may help individuals to avoid activities that they find unpleasant. Such reinforcement of these pain behaviors may condition individuals to display them and, as a result, may increase the functional impairment associated with the pain behaviors. Operant conditioning involves withdrawing reinforcement for "pain" behaviors and reinforcing "well" behaviors.

Nerve blocks eliminate pain locally. They are commonly used for surgical procedures, as well as in the treatment of chronic pain. Local anesthetics are injected close to nerves, thus blocking their ability to conduct the painful stimuli. Generally, nerve blocks are given for the temporary relief of pain; however, in cases of severe pain, such as in terminal cancer, nerve blocks may be performed so that the effects are irreversible.

Neurosurgical procedures in which the surgeon severs the sensory nerves to the painful area may be used when severe pain cannot be ameliorated or controlled by other means. Cutting the nerves removes not only the sensation of pain, but also the sensations of pressure, heat, and cold. Consequently, individuals who have undergone these procedures must be aware of the necessity of protecting the area from injury. The type of neurosurgical procedure used depends on the type and location of the pain. For example, **sympathectomy** involves the autonomic nervous system; **neurectomy**, either the cranial or the peripheral nerves; **rhizotomy** and **chordotomy**, the nerves close to the spinal cord.

Treatment of Specific Disorders

Rheumatoid Arthritis

For individuals with rheumatoid arthritis, treatment is aimed toward decreasing joint destruction, maintaining joint function, and preventing deformity. The cornerstones of therapy are rest and exercise. Complete bed rest may be recommended for short periods during the acute phases of the condition. In other instances, rest periods throughout the day may be prescribed. Splinting of specific joints may occasionally be prescribed in order to reduce local inflammation; in order to prevent deformity due to lack of use, however, joints should be immobilized only under the direction of a physician.

Although activity alone is not necessarily therapeutic, prescribed exercise is important in the treatment of rheumatoid arthritis in order to restore muscle strength, to maintain joint mobility, and to prevent contractures. Individuals should follow the specific exercise plan recommended by their physician.

Salicylates (e.g., aspirin) are considered the mainstay of treatment, together with other medications such as nonsteroidal anti-inflammatory agents. **Steroids** are added to the treatment regimen only in more severe cases when symptoms and inflammation cannot be adequately controlled.

Gold compounds may be injected intramuscularly if other medications do not bring sufficient relief. Given over a series of weeks, the injections are tapered off when maximum improvement has been achieved. Some individuals may remain on a maintenance dosage of gold to prevent relapse. Gold compounds have potential toxic effects on the kidneys and bone marrow, however, so that those on this therapy should have regular blood check ups and urinalyses for the identification of damage. If there are signs of toxic effects, such as changes in blood chemistry, **pruritus** (itching), or **proteinuria** (protein in the urine), gold therapy is discontinued.

A medication called **penicillamine** may also be given in severe cases of rheumatoid arthritis to alleviate the symptoms. Like gold, penicillamine has potential toxic effects on the kidney, so individuals on penicillamine require careful monitoring by the physician. In some instances, **immunosuppressant** medications (medications that suppress the immune system) have also been helpful in reducing symptoms, but the use of immunosuppressants increases the susceptibility of these individuals to infection.

Most individuals with rheumatoid arthritis are treated with a combination of medication, exercise, and rest. Severe inflammation and joint deformity may be indications for surgery, however. Common surgical procedures for rheumatoid arthritis are synovectomy and arthroplasty with joint replacement, as discussed earlier.

Systemic Lupus Erythematosus

Mild cases of systemic lupus erythematosus may require little or no therapy. When therapy is necessary, the type and location of the disease determine the therapy prescribed. If major organs such as the heart or kidney are involved, treatment is directed toward preserving function and preventing an organ failure that could result in disability or death. In mild cases, **salicylates** or nonsteroidal anti-inflammatory agents may be used. In more severe cases, **steroids** may be indicated. Such complications as cardiac symptoms or renal damage are treated as appropriate. Persons with severe kidney involvement may require dialysis (see Chapter 4).

Individuals with systemic lupus erythematosus may need more than the normal amount of rest. The more active the disease, the more rest they need. Exercise to the point of exhaustion and stressful situations should be avoided, because both can cause exacerbations of the disease.

Osteoarthritis

The treatment of osteoarthritis is directed toward increasing function and preventing further dysfunction. Specific exercises, including range-of-motion and other strengthening exercises, are often part of the treatment prescribed to meet this goal. It may be necessary to balance rest of the joint with its use. The use of assistive devices, such as canes or crutches, may prevent undue weight bearing on joints. If the individual with osteoarthritis is obese, weight reduction may be advisable to remove undue pressure on the joints. The oral administration of aspirin or nonsteroidal anti-inflammatory agents, as well as the injection of steroids into the joint, may also be helpful. Occasionally, if all other treatment has failed, surgical joint replacement may be considered.

Gout

The objectives in the treatment of gout are to terminate the acute attack and to prevent recurrent attacks. During acute attacks, the affected joint is placed at rest and anti-inflammatory agents are prescribed. The prevention of further attacks may require the daily use of medications for lowering the level of uric acid in the blood or for increasing its excretion by the kidneys. Occasionally, surgery is necessary to remove **tophi** (deposits of crystals in the joints).

Individuals with gout should increase their fluid intake in order to decrease the risk of kidney stones; follow a diet that excludes foods high in purines and fats, such as sardines, anchovies, organ meats, veal, or bacon; and avoid excessive alcohol intake. Gradual weight reduction may be indicated in those individuals who are obese.

Ankylosing Spondylitis

The management of ankylosing spondylitis involves relieving pain and inflammation, and maximizing function through physical therapy and exercise. **Nonsteroidal anti-inflammatory** agents may be administered to decrease inflammation and pain, thereby facilitating exercise. The exercises prescribed are designed to strengthen supporting muscles and to maintain good posture and function. Physical therapy should begin early in order to keep the spine as straight as possible and, thus, to preserve the chest's ability to expand. In the case of severe deformity, arthroplasty may be indicated.

Osteoporosis

The best treatment for osteoporosis is prevention through the daily intake of adequate amounts of dietary calcium; the combination of weight-bearing exercise throughout life; and the avoidance of the long-term use of steroid medications, which promote bone loss. When osteoporosis does occur, analgesics, heat, or rest may relieve the pain. In some instances, braces or splints may be indicated. Exercise that strengthens muscles, thus providing additional support, may be beneficial. Although general activity is encouraged, heavy lifting or any activity that increases the risk of falls should be avoided.

Calcium supplements are usually prescribed for both men and women with osteoporosis. Women with osteoporosis may be given the hormones to decrease bone loss and increase absorption of calcium. When calcium absorption is impaired, supplemental **vitamin D** may also be given.

Osteomyelitis

The treatment of osteomyelitis may be medical or surgical. Medical treatment consists of the administration of **antibiotics** to treat the infection and bed rest until the infection has been eradicated. Surgical intervention may be indicated to remove infected tissue, replace a portion of bone with a graft, or replace an infected prosthetic joint. In some instances, amputation may be required.

FUNCTIONAL IMPLICATIONS

Psychological Issues

The emotional needs of individuals with musculoskeletal conditions often relate to prolonged dependence on others, the long-term nature of the condition, and uncertainty about their ability to resume their normal responsibilities and activities. The restrictions on their mobility and natural movements because of casts, braces, or traction, or because of pain or deformity are, for many individuals, unbearable. Depending on the extent of their immobility, they may have a sense of powerlessness leading to anger, hostility, and, later, depression. If the musculoskeletal disorder necessitates giving up some valued activity permanently, depression may deepen. Some individuals who have a strong athletic identity may fail to disclose the disorder, continuing the activity even though it may cause additional damage.

The prolonged pain that is associated with many disorders of the musculoskeletal system consumes energy and may contribute to individuals' becoming more self-centered and dependent as pain becomes the central issue in their lives. Discomfort, as well as the limitations on their mobility, can contribute to irritability, discouragement, and depression. The perception of pain is related not only to various personality factors, but also to factors such as workers' compensation, litigation, or other benefits that may decrease an individual's motivation to reduce pain or restore function.

Individuals who are planning to undergo musculoskeletal surgery may experience a mixture of fear and anticipation regarding the extent to which the surgery will restore lost function. Those who are having repeated surgery, such as a second joint replacement for arthritis, or continuing treatment for osteomyelitis may lose patience and hope.

Individuals with chronic conditions of the musculoskeletal system may force themselves to do more than they comfortably can because they fear being a burden on others. Their inability to maintain their levels of activity at previous standards may keep them perpetually frustrated. The unpredictability of diseases that have remissions and exacerbations (e.g., rheumatoid arthritis) may also be a source of tension.

The deformity associated with many musculoskeletal conditions, such as rheumatoid arthritis, ankylosing spondylitis, osteoporosis, or amputation, alters the body image of individuals with such conditions. Most individuals react to any body image change with anxiety and fear of rejection. The value and subjective meaning of appearance influence their reactions to the alteration of appearance. Concerns about acceptance of family, friends, and acquaintances can preoccupy their thoughts.

Amputation forces individuals to make a major adjustment not only to a change in body image, but also to a change in functional capacity. Those who require an amputation because of a chronic disease that had been associated with pain and immobility may find it less difficult to adjust than do those who lost a limb because of traumatic injury. The suddenness of traumatic amputation allows the individual no time to prepare for the loss. In any case, it is important to understand the individual's interpretation of the loss.

The individual's ability to adapt to an amputation depends on the circumstances surrounding the amputation, the usefulness of the prosthetic device, and the individual's perception of the disability. Some individuals who have lost a limb no longer consider themselves whole. They may fear that they will never again be able to function as they did prior to the amputation. For these individuals, a prosthesis is a reminder of perceived inadequacy rather than a means to restore function. In some instances, the loss of a limb is comparable to the loss of a loved one. Individuals may need sufficient time to grieve and adjust to their loss.

Life Style Issues

Although many conditions of the musculoskeletal system require only short-term treatment and impose only temporary disability, some conditions require lifelong adaptation and significant life style changes. The restrictions in body movement that result from a loss of muscle strength, deformity of joints, or pain alter the activities of daily living, as well as social and recreational activities. Individuals may need to learn new ambulation and transfer techniques, and to find alternatives to activities that place undue stress on joints. It may be necessary to install grab bars and safety rails in the home to provide stability and prevent falls.

Conditions that affect the ankles or the feet may require the wearing of special shoes for protection of the joints and for comfort. Sitting while performing many tasks, such as meal preparation, may save wear and tear on weight-bearing joints. Conditions that affect the joints of the hands, such as rheumatoid arthritis, may require the use of assistive devices, such as hooks, zipper pulls, special openers, or other self-help aids, if the individual is to perform the activities of daily living independently. Adaptive handles for combs and brushes may be of help for grooming. Soft lead pencils and felt-tipped pens are useful for decreasing the pressure on finger joints when writing.

Organizing and planning daily tasks help to reduce strain and fatigue. The pace of travel should be slower. At home, work centers may be established where all the items needed for a specific task are kept within easy reach. It may be necessary to lower tables and cabinets so that individuals with a musculoskeletal disorder may be seated while they work and to raise beds, toilet seats, and chairs so that sitting and arising are easier for these individuals.

If obesity places extra strain on joints, a weight reduction diet may be prescribed. Specific conditions, such as gout, require dietary modifications. Individuals who have pain or deformity in the hands or who have undergone upper extremity amputation may need special adaptive eating utensils for activities such as cutting meat.

Many conditions of the musculoskeletal system require some form of therapeutic exercise to maintain joint function, restore strength and/or joint motion, or prevent deformity. Such exercise programs must be incorporated into the daily routine. Some conditions, such as rheumatoid arthritis, may require specified rest periods during the day.

Individuals with systemic lupus erythematosus are often sensitive to sunlight, which may trigger symptoms. They may need to give up outdoor activities, or at least activities that entail exposure to the sun. When they cannot avoid sunlight, they may need to wear extra clothing or hats, or use umbrellas to protect themselves from the sun. Other musculoskeletal conditions may become worse in cold, damp environments.

Individuals who have undergone an amputation, especially of a lower extremity, must guard against injury and infection to the stump. Consequently, skin care is a vital part of their rehabilitation. Bathing in the evening rather than in the morning is advisable, since damp skin may swell and stick to a prosthesis, causing irritation and rubbing. Many limitations of activity depend on the level of the amputation. Most individuals who have had a lower extremity amputated can bicycle, swim, dance, and participate in many athletic activities with adaptive equipment. Driving a car is usually not a problem, although automatic transmissions may allow these individuals to drive more easily. Activities such as climbing, squatting, and kneeling may be more difficult. Individuals who have had an upper extremity amputated may require a number of assistive devices, in addition to the prosthesis, in order to perform a number of activities of daily living.

Most musculoskeletal disorders do not hamper sexual activity. Pain, deformity, lack of range of motion of joints, or alteration in body image may affect sexual function, however. Positioning may be difficult or painful, as in the case of rheumatoid arthritis or low back pain. The steroids prescribed for a number of musculoskeletal conditions may decrease libido, and pain may inhibit sexual desire. Women with systemic lupus erythematosus tend to have complicated pregnancies. Conception is often difficult, and almost one-half of the pregnancies of women with systemic lupus erythematosus end in miscarriage. Although the amputation of an extremity has no direct effect on sexual activity, psychological factors and/or the reaction of sexual partners to the amputation may alter sexual function.

Social Issues

Because musculoskeletal disorders often impair mobility and individuals with such disorders must depend on others for assistance, the support and understanding of family and friends are paramount. Although reassurance that physical changes or deformities are unimportant can be valuable to individuals' self-esteem and confidence, such reassurance by family and friends is not always forthcoming.

Depending on the discomfort, limitation of motion, and deformity of the individual with the musculoskeletal disorder, other family members may have to share in his or her household or outdoor chores. Their willingness to accept such necessary alterations in home life can facilitate the individual's adjustment. In some instances, the condition may lead to unemployment, bringing about role changes within the family structure that can pose a threat to the individual's social identity. If work or other social activities must be altered, the friendships that developed around these activities may also be affected.

It may be necessary to plan vacations around the condition, taking the individual's limited mobility into consideration. Individuals with systemic lupus erythematosus may have to avoid hot, sunny beaches, whereas individuals with other musculoskeletal conditions may need to avoid colder climates. Individuals who are experiencing severe pain may be reluctant to venture on vacation at all.

Family and friends may have difficulty in coping with the feelings of hostility, frustration, or irritability expressed by individuals because of pain or increased dependency. Others may view these individuals as demanding, manipulative, and difficult, thereby further decreasing the individuals' self-esteem.

Individuals with musculoskeletal disorders, especially those involving ongoing pain, are especially vulnerable to those who promote unproved "miracle cures." Such measures may include medications, dietary supplements, special devices, or treatments. In addition to the expense, many fraudulent measures have dangerous side-effects that, in some instances, can be fatal. Even if there are no side-effects, individuals may use these methods in place of recommended treatment, thus losing the therapeutic effects of legitimate treatment.

Vocational Issues

The impact of musculoskeletal disorders on vocational function depends on the type of job previously held, as well as on the type of musculoskeletal disorder. The amount of sitting, bending, stooping, or lifting that the job requires must be considered. Modification of the work environment, such as by raising or lowering worktables or chairs, may be necessary. Generally, it is important that individuals return to their work and daily activities as soon as possible in order to maintain good work habits.

Assistive devices such as crutches, walkers, or canes may make ambulation slower and more difficult. In addition, the use of such devices makes it difficult, if not impossible, to carry objects from one point to another. Individuals with amputation who wear a prosthesis may need to avoid hot humid environments that can cause skin breakdown or contribute to the deterioration of the prosthesis. Dust or grit can be abrasive to the skin, exacerbating skin problems, and can interfere with the functioning of the movable parts of the prosthesis.

In the case of lower extremity amputation, the physical demands of the job, such as walking, climbing, or pushing, should be evaluated and altered, if necessary. The increased energy expenditure required in the use of a prosthesis should also be considered part of the physical demands of the the job. Individuals in professional or managerial careers may have fewer limitations following the amputation of either an upper or a lower extremity. Those who have had an upper extremity amputation may have a greater cosmetic need for a prosthesis, however, than do those workers whose jobs require the prosthesis for tasks such as lifting.

Rheumatoid arthritis, ankylosing spondylitis, systemic lupus erythematosus, and a number of other connective tissue disorders are progressive in nature and often unpredictable. Although not all individuals with these conditions become severely disabled, ongoing medical care and evaluation are necessary. There will be periods of remission and periods of exacerbation during which these individuals may miss work. Their need to avoid overexertion, stress, and fatigue may necessitate altered or shortened work schedules to accommodate periods of rest.

The overuse of damaged joints should be avoided. For example, individuals with osteoarthritis of the knees should avoid excessive walking; those with carpal tunnel syndrome should avoid repetitive activities with the hands. The deformity of joints not only may interfere with occupational function, but also may be potentially embarrassing to the individual in personal interactions at work.

Occasionally, there are barriers to the effective rehabilitation of individuals with musculoskeletal disorders. Such barriers may involve financial disincentives, the status of legal claims, and other disability and compensation protocols. Individuals may be hesitant to learn new skills or use devices that help them to maintain their independence if, in so doing, they imperil possible financial benefits or will be expected to return to a work environment that they did not or will not enjoy.

BIBLIOGRAPHY

Aronoff, G.M., and Whitkower, A.B. "Chronic Pain: Common Problems and Practive Solutions." *Medical Times* (1988):39–47.

Barber, T.C., and Langfitt, D.E. *Teaching the Medical/Surgical Patient—Diagnostics and Procedures*. Bowie, Md.: Robert J. Brady Co., 1983.

Bennett, R.M.; Bickel, Y.B.; Clayton, M.L.; Goergen, T.G.; Wilske, K.R.; Reeves, J.E.; and Norman, F.W. "Treating RA Medically." *Patient Care* 17(1983):75–119.

Bennett, R.M.; Bickel, Y.B.; Clayton, M.L.; Goergen T.G.; Wilske, K.R.; Reeves, J.E.; and Norman, F.W. "When RA Requires Surgical Management." *Patient Care* 17(1983):73–194.

Berkow, R., and Fletcher, A.J., eds. *The Merck Manual of Diagnosis and Therapy*. Rahway, N.J.: Merck Sharpe and Dohme Research Laboratories, 1987.

Bienenstock, H. "Diagnosis: Arthritis." *Hospital Medicine* (October 1984):238–282.

Birnhaum, N.S.; Gerber, L.H.; and Panush, R.S. "Self-help for Arthritis Patients." *Patient Care* 23(1989):69–91.

Block, A.R. "Multidisciplinary Treatment of Chronic Low Back Pain: A Review." *Rehabilitation Psychology* 27(1982):51–63.

Boachie-Adjei, O. "Conservative Management of Low Back Pain." *Postgraduate Medicine* 84(1988):127–133.

Brunner, L.S.; Emerson, C.P.; Ferguson, L.K.; and Suddarth, D.S. *Textbook of Medical-Surgical Nursing*. Philadelphia: W.B. Saunders Co., 1970.

Clark, H.M., and Kaufman, M.E. "Effective Management of People with Chronic Pain." *Journal of Rehabilitation* 53(1987):51–53.

Corbett, J.V. *Diagnostic Procedures in Nursing Practice*. Norwalk, Conn.: Appleton-Century-Crofts, 1982.

Corbett, J.V. *Laboratory Tests in Nursing Practice*. Norwalk, Conn.: Appleton-Century-Crofts, 1983.

Covington, E.C. "Management of the Patient with Chronic Benign Pain: Diagnosis." *Modern Medicine* 57(1989):75–100.

Cummings, V. "Sexual Problems of the Amputee." *Medical Aspects of Human Sexuality* (November 1987):82–88.

Deluca, S.A., and Castronova, F.P. "Hazards of Magnetic Resonance Imaging." *American Family Physician* 41(1990):145–146.

Empting-Koschorke, L.D.; Hendler, N.; Kolodny, A.L.; and Kraus, H. "Tips on Hard-To-Manage Pain Syndromes." *Patient Care* 24(1990):26–46.

Frierson, R.L., and Lippmann, S.B. "Psychiatric Consultation for Acute Amputees." *Psychosomatics* 28(1987):183–189.

Frymoyer, J.W. "Back Pain and Sciatica." *New England Journal of Medicine* 318(1988):291–300.

Goodgold, J.; Grynbaum, B.B.; Lehnis, H.R.; Dong, C.; and Ragnarsson, K.J. "Using Prosthetics To Aid Independence." *Patient Care* (1983):45–70.

Greenspan, J. "Carpal Tunnel Syndrome." *Postgraduate Medicine* 84(1988):34–43.

Guyton, A.C. *Human Physiology and Mechanisms of Disease.* Philadelphia: W.B. Saunders Co., 1982.

Hamerman, D. "The Biology of Osteoarthritis." *New England Journal of Medicine* 320(1989):1322–1330.

Hennig, L.M., and Burrows, S.K. "Keeping up on Arthritis Meds." *RN* (February 1986):32–38.

Keele, C.A.; Neil, E.; and Joels, N. *Samson Wright's Applied Physiology.* New York: Oxford University Press, 1982.

Lisse, J.R. "Ankylosing Spondylitis." *Postgraduate Medicine* 86(1989):147–153.

Luckman, J., and Sorensen, K.C. *Medical-Surgical Nursing: A Psychophysiologic Approach.* Philadelphia: W.B. Saunders Co., 1987.

Mendelson, R.L.; Burech, J.G.; Polack, E.P.; and Kappel, D.A. "The Psychological Impact of Traumatic Amputations. A Team Approach: Physician, Therapist, and Psychologist." *Hand Clinics* 2(1986):577–583.

National Institute of Handicapped Reasearch. "Chronic Pain." *Rehab Brief 5* (1982):1–4.

Nursing 87 Books. *Patient Teaching.* Springhouse, Pa.: Springhouse Corporation Book Division, 1987.

Rakel, R.E. *Conn's Current Therapy 1990.* Philadelphia: W.B. Saunders Co., 1990.

Rapoport, S. "Common Peripheral Nerve Injuries." *Hospital Medicine* (June 1984):33–60.

Reagles, S. "Chronic Pain: Principles for Rehabilitation Counselors." *Rehabilitation Counseling Bulletin* (1984):15–25.

Rosenberg, S.A.; Blaiss, M.S.; and Springgate, C.F. "Emerging Therapies for Autoimmune Disease, Such As Systemic Lupus Erythematosus." *Modern Medicine* 56(1988):44–47.

Roush, S.E. "Vocational Outcomes Following Elective Hip and Knee Arthroplasties." *Journal of Rehabilitation* (1985):49–52.

Scheer, S.J., ed. *Medical Perspectives in Vocational Assessment of Impaired Workers.* Gaithersburg, Md.: Aspen Publishers, 1991.

Silby, H. "Conservative Management of Lumbar Disc Herniation." *Postgraduate Medicine* 84(1988):157–172.

Smith, D.L., and Lucas, L.M. "Sjogren's Syndrome." *Postgraduate Medicine* 82(1987):123–131.

Smith, D.W., and Hanley-Germain, C.P. *Care of the Adult Patient.* Philadelphia: J.B. Lippincott Co., 1975.

Smith, J.K., and Crisler, J.R. "Chronic Low Back Pain: The Treatment Dichotomy and Implications for Rehabilitation Counselor." *Journal of Applied Rehabilitation Counseling* 16(1985):28–31.

Sparks, J.A., and Clark, D.W. "Social, Psychological, and Medical Aspects of Chronic Pain." *Rehabilitation Counseling Bulletin* 25(1981):292–287.

Steinberg, A.D. "Systemic Lupus Erythematosus." *Hospital Medicine* (September 1987):131–148.

Stolov, W.C., and Clowers, M.R. *Handbook of Severe Disability.* Washington, D.C.: U.S. Department of Education, Rehabilitation Services Administration, 1981.

Vander, A.J.; Sherman, J.H.; and Luciano, D.S. *Human Physiology: The Mechanisms of Body Function*. New York: McGraw-Hill Book Co., 1985.

Wyngaarden, J.B., and Smith, J.H. *Cecil Textbook of Medicine*. Philadelphia: W.B. Saunders Co., 1988.

Yocum, D.E. "The Immunology of Rheumatoid Arthritis." *Drug Therapy* (September 1987):41–54.

chapter 8

Nervous System Disorders

NORMAL STRUCTURE AND FUNCTION

The nervous system is a complex network that serves as the communication center for a variety of body functions (see Exhibit 8-1). The nervous system controls and coordinates activities throughout the body by sending, receiving, and sorting electrical impulses.

No matter how simple or how complex, behavioral responses require nervous system activity. The nervous system organizes and directs motor activities (movement) in response to the internal and external environment. It monitors the outside world so that the individual perceives and acts on physical and sensory stimuli. It is crucial in cognitive processes, such as learning, memory, and thinking. In addition, it coordinates the function of internal organs so that the body functions as a unit. The disruption of any part of the nervous system affects body function in some way, either internally or externally.

Specialized cells called **neurons** are the functional unit of the nervous system (Figure 8-1). Neurons transmit neural impulses. Each neuron consists of a **cell body**, processes that emerge from the cell body called **dendrites**, and a singular process called the **axon**. The dendrites receive information *from* other neurons. The axon passes information *to* other neurons.

Information is passed from neuron to neuron by both electrical and chemical impulses. The electrical impulse picked up by the dendrites is passed through the cell body to the axon. At the tip of the axon are tiny processes that release special chemicals known as **neurotransmitters**. These neurotransmitters make it possible to transmit nerve impulses between neurons. The space between neurons where this chemical action takes place is called the **synapse**. After their release, the neurotransmitters are either taken up again by the neuron or destroyed.

Exhibit 8-1 The Nervous System

I. Central nervous system
    A. Brain
    B. Spinal cord
II. Peripheral nervous system
    A. Afferent (sensory)
    B. Efferent (motor)
       1. Somatic nervous system
       2. Autonomic nervous system
          a. Sympathetic nervous system
          b. Parasympathetic nervous system

The axons of many neurons are covered with a fatty sheath called **myelin**. Like the insulation that surrounds electrical cords, myelin acts as an insulator, enabling electrical impulses to be conducted reliably.

Central Nervous System

The brain and the spinal cord make up the **central nervous system.** The **white matter** of the central nervous system is composed of myelinated fibers that conduct nerve messages; white matter fibers make up the *inner* part of the brain and the *outer* portion of the spinal cord. **Gray matter**, or nonmyelinated nerve fibers, make up the *outer* portion of the brain and the *inner* portion of the spinal cord. Gray matter of the brain receives, sorts, and processes nerve messages. Gray matter of the spinal cord serves as a center for **reflex** action (automatic response to a stimulus).

Embedded deep within the white matter of the brain are masses of gray matter called **basal ganglia**, which are part of the **extrapyramidal** system. (Extrapyramidal denotes nerve fiber tracts that lie outside the pyramidal tract, a relatively compact group of nerve fibers that originate from cells in the outer layer of the brain.) Extrapyramidal function is concerned with postural adjustment and gross voluntary and automatic muscular movements. Basal ganglia help to maintain contractile tone in muscles in the trunk and extremities, enabling individuals to maintain balance and posture, as well as to react swiftly, appropriately, and automatically to stimuli that demand an immediate response.

Bony coverings protect both the brain and the spinal cord. The **cranium** or **cranial bones** cover the brain, while **vertebrae** surround the spinal cord. The vertebral column has seven **cervical vertebrae** located in the neck area; twelve

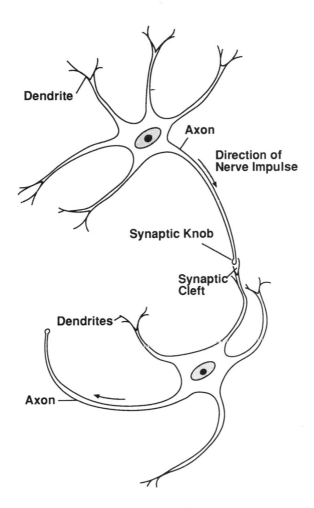

Figure 8-1 The Neuron. *Source*: Reprinted from *Pathopsysiology: Principles of Disease* by M.J. Miller, p. 369, with permission of W.B. Saunders, © 1978.

thoracic vertebrae located in the upper and middle back; and five **lumbar vertebrae** located in the lower back. The **sacrum** located below the lumbar vertebrae consists of fused (joined) bone. At the tip of the sacrum is the **coccyx** or tail bone.

On the interior of the bony coverings of both the brain and the spinal cord are three membranes (**meninges**) that provide additional protection. The outer membrane that covers the brain and the spinal cord is called the **dura mater**. The **arachnoid membrane**, a cobweb-appearing membrane, is the middle mem-

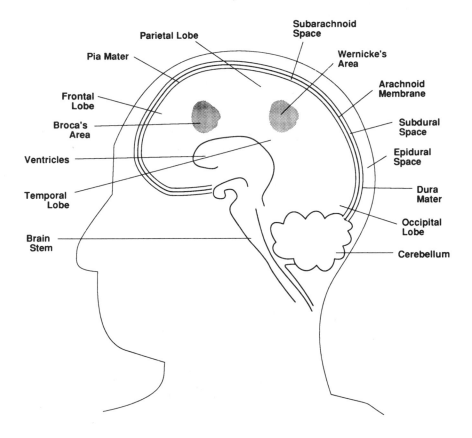

Figure 8-2 The Brain.

brane. The inner membrane, which lies next to the brain and spinal cord, is the **pia mater**. Between each of the membrane layers are spaces. The space between the dura mater and the inner surface of the bony covering is the **epidural space**. The space between the dura mater and arachnoid membrane is the **subdural space**. The space between the arachnoid membrane and the pia mater is the **subarachnoid space** (Figure 8-2).

The central nervous system is also protected and cushioned by cerebrospinal fluid. **Cerebrospinal fluid (CSF)** is formed by the choroid plexus in chambers within the brain called **ventricles**. It escapes into the subarachnoid space, where it bathes the brain and spinal cord and is then reabsorbed.

The brain serves as the primary center for the integration, coordination, initiation, and interpretation of most neural messages. The largest part of the brain is the **cerebrum**, which consists of a right and left hemisphere. The gray matter that makes up the outer layer of the cerebrum is called the **cortex**, and it has three major areas of function: (1) motor, (2) sensory, and (3) associational. The **motor cortex** coordinates voluntary movements of the body. The recognition or perception of sensory stimuli, such as touch, pain, smell, taste, vision, and hearing, takes place in the **sensory cortex**. The **associational cortex** is involved in cognitive functions, such as memory, reasoning, abstract thinking, and consciousness.

The hemispheres of the cerebrum are divided into lobes that contain areas related to specific functions. The **frontal lobe**, located in the front part of each hemisphere, contains the primary motor areas that initiate voluntary movement and skilled movements (e.g., those involved in writing). Also contained within the frontal lobe are areas that deal with higher intellectual functions (e.g., foresight, analytical thinking, and judgment). The **parietal lobe** is located in the middle of each hemisphere; it is primarily a sensory area, integrating and interpreting sensation (e.g., light touch, pressure, pain, and temperature). It also has some memory functions, especially storage of sensory memory. The **temporal lobe**, located under the frontal and parietal lobes, is primarily responsible for the interpretation of and distinction between sounds. The **occipital lobe**, in the posterior portion of each hemisphere, is the primary area for the reception and interpretation of visual stimuli.

Several parts of the cerebrum are involved in language function, which consists of receiving, interpreting, and integrating visual and auditory stimuli as well as expressing thoughts in a coordinated way to communicate meanings to others. Language function is located in the left hemisphere of the cerebrum in virtually all right-handed individuals and in most left-handed individuals. **Wernicke's area**, located over the temporal and parietal lobes, is the major area of receptive function. The major area of expressive function (**Broca's area**) is anterior to Wernicke's area.

Beneath the occipital lobe of the cerebrum is an oval structure called the **cerebellum**. The cerebellum is primarily responsible for the coordination and integration of voluntary movement, and for the maintenance of equilibrium and balance of the body.

The **brain stem** is located at the base of the brain, between the cerebrum and the spinal cord. It acts as a relay station, transmitting impulses between the spinal cord and the higher cerebral centers. The brain stem is the center of involuntary functions, such as heart and respiratory functions, and reflex actions, such as coughing and swallowing. Also within the brain stem are scattered groups of cells, called the **recticular formation**, that are involved in the initiation and maintenance of wakefulness and alertness.

The spinal cord extends from the base of the brain down to the level of the second lumbar vertebra. The outer white matter of the spinal cord conveys electrical impulses up and down the spinal cord between the peripheral nervous system and the brain. The inner gray matter of the spinal cord acts as a co-ordinating center for reflex and other activities. Motor and sensory spinal nerve roots leave the spinal cord through openings between the vertebrae that surround the spinal cord. These spinal nerve roots are named for the vertebral level at which they exit (Figure 8-3). For example, the nerve roots that leave the spinal cord at the cervical level are labeled C-1 through C-8, while the nerve roots that leave at the thoracic level are labeled T-1 through T-12. Nerves at each level travel to specific parts of the body, conveying information between that area and the central nervous system. For instance, nerve roots C-5 through T-1 innervate the muscles of the upper extremities, and nerve roots from the sacral areas (S-2 through S-4) innervate the muscles that are involved in bowel and bladder function.

The Peripheral Nervous System

All the nerves that extend from the brain and spinal cord make up the **peripheral nervous system**. A **nerve** is a bundle of fibers outside the central nervous system that transmits information between the central nervous system and various parts of the body. In order to function effectively, the peripheral nerves must be connected to the central nervous system. The 12 pair of peripheral nerves that connect and transmit messages directly to the brain are called **cranial nerves**. Some cranial nerves contain only sensory fibers (e.g., the olfactory nerve for smell and the optic nerve for vision) that carry information only to the brain, whereas others contain both sensory and motor fibers. Cranial nerves mediate many aspects of sensation and muscular activity in and around the head and neck. The 31 pair of peripheral nerves that connect and transmit messages directly to the spinal cord are called **spinal nerves**. Because these nerves carry both sensory and motor information, they are called mixed. The cranial and spinal nerves are essential links between the rest of the body and the central nervous system.

The nerves in the peripheral nervous system that carry impulses *toward* the central nervous system from other parts of the body are **sensory** nerves. They are part of the **afferent** division of the peripheral nervous system. The nerves that carry impulses *from* the central nervous system to other parts of the body are called **motor nerves**; they are part of the **efferent** division of the peripheral nervous system. The efferent division is further subdivided according to nerve function. Some nerves in the efferent division of the peripheral nervous system are called **somatic** nerves, and they innervate body structures that are under *voluntary* control, such as muscles of the extremities. Other nerves in the efferent division are concerned with control of *involuntary* functions. These nerves are part of the **autonomic nervous system**.

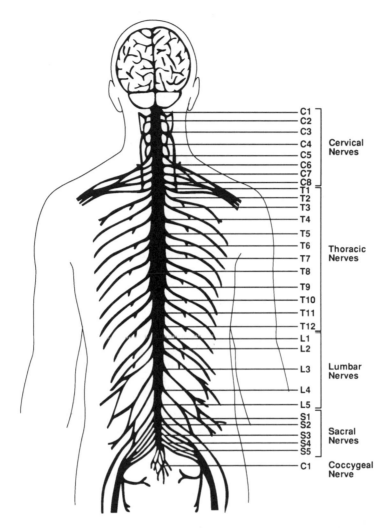

Figure 8-3 Spinal Nerves: Posterior View. *Source*: Reprinted from *Pathophysiology: Principles of Disease* by M.J. Millcr, p. 380, with permission of W.B. Saunders, ©1978.

The autonomic nervous system integrates the work of vital organs, such as the heart and lungs. Its primary function is to coordinate the activity of internal organs so that they can make adaptive responses to changing external situations. The autonomic nervous system is further divided into the **sympathetic** and **parasympathetic nervous systems**, which work together and in opposition to control visceral reflexes and to regulate the function of internal organs. Hormones and emotions can affect both systems.

The sympathetic nervous system becomes active during stress and emergencies. It prepares the body for action, deepening respirations, making the heart beat faster, dilating the pupils, decreasing gastrointestinal secretions, and increasing the blood supply to the large muscles of the body.

The parasympathetic nervous system dominates when the body is at rest. The parasympathetic nervous system focuses on bold conservation such as decreasing the heart rate and constricting the pupils of the eye. The parasympathetic nervous system is also important for innervation of the bladder and for sexual function.

NEUROLOGICAL DISORDERS

Traumatic Brain Injury

Defined as an injury to the brain from an external physical force, a **traumatic brain injury** is not degenerative, is not the result of a disease process, and is not congenital. The traumatic brain injury may result from a closed or open (penetrating) head injury. A **closed head injury** is an injury in which the skull has not been broken. This type of brain injury can result from a blow to the head or from a violent movement of the head that slams the brain against the skull. Because the brain is confined within the skull and suspended in cerebrospinal fluid, the external force is transmitted diffusely. The injury can be primary, occurring at the time of the injury as a direct result of the force, or it can be secondary, occurring later as an indirect result of **edema** (swelling), hemorrhage, or the formation of a **hematoma** (sac filled with blood) in the brain that increases intracranial pressure. Because the brain as a whole has been traumatized, the injury may be more diffuse.

An **open (penetrating) head injury**, in contrast, is an injury in which the skull is broken or penetrated (e.g., a gunshot wound). In open head injuries, not only is the brain injured from the external force, but also bone fragments may lacerate and injure the brain, blood vessels, and the meninges surrounding the brain. The functional impairments experienced with open head injury may be more localized and are usually related to the specific area of the brain affected.

When the brain is injured, bleeding and/or **edema** (swelling) may occur as they do when any other organ is injured; however, because the brain is encased in bone, there is no space available for expansion. Thus, bleeding and edema compress the brain, increasing intracranial pressure and interfering with brain function. Unless recognized and treated promptly, these events can cause permanent brain damage or death.

Brain injuries are classified as mild, moderate, or severe. One basis for classification is the length of time the individual is unconscious. Mild to moderate head injuries are characterized by a **concussion**, in which there is a loss of consciousness for a period varying from a few minutes to 24 hours after the injury. Bruising of the brain (**cerebral contusion**) and lacerations of the brain are more severe injuries. Individuals who remain unconscious for 1 or more days are considered to have severe head injuries.

The length of **coma** (state of unconsciousness) is also used as a predictor of prognostic outcome. Generally, the longer the period of unconsciousness, the more severe the injury to the brain and the greater the subsequent residual effects. An instrument called the **Glasgow Coma Scale** is frequently used to assess the level of consciousness on a continuum ranging from alert to a coma state. Points are assigned according to the level of response in each of three areas: eye opening, motor response, and verbal response. The maximum number of points that can be accumulated on the scale is 15. The lower the number of points, the deeper the level of unconsciousness. The Glasgow Coma Scale provides a means whereby the individual's level of consciousness can be assessed systematically. An initial assessment provides a baseline from which changes in neurological status can be measured. The scale is also sometimes used as an indication of the severity of injury and consequently as an outcome indicator. For example, a score of 13 to 15 indicates minor injury; 9 to 12, moderate injury; and 3 to 8, severe injury. When the injury to the brain is so severe that little function aside from control of the vital organs remains, individuals are said to exist in a **persistent vegetative state.**

Conditions Associated with Head Injury

Bleeding within the cranial vault is called **intracranial hemorrhage**. Bleeding and blood clots (**hematomas**) compress the brain, increasing intracranial pressure. An **epidural hematoma** is bleeding that occurs in the space between the dura mater and the skull. Although bleeding generally occurs rapidly, it may not be recognized immediately after an injury. Individuals who have been injured may carry on a lucid conversation, only to slip into drowsiness and unconsciousness hours later. Epidural hematomas carry a high mortality rate. A **subdural hematoma** is a hemorrhage in the space beneath the dura mater. Although symptoms may be apparent immediately, they may also appear more gradually, becoming evident days or even weeks after the injury. In both instances, immediate action is essential to stop the bleeding and relieve the intracranial pressure.

Some individuals experience **post-traumatic epilepsy** after a traumatic brain injury. In the early postinjury period, seizures may be related to increased intracranial pressure or other direct results of injury. Seizures that occur later may be due to the formation of scar tissue in the brain.

Individuals who have had a traumatic brain injury may also develop **post-traumatic hydrocephalus,** in which there is interference with the reabsorption of cerebrospinal fluid. Post-traumatic hydrocephalus can cause increasing neurological or functional deterioration. It may be treated by surgically implanting a shunt in the brain to divert and drain the cerebrospinal fluid. The prognosis for individuals who develop post-traumatic hydrocephalus is variable.

Residual Effects of Traumatic Brain Injury

Although many mild head injuries have no readily apparent residual effects, the possible residual effects of such an injury range from severe headaches to a lack of concentration and mild memory loss. Severe brain injury always has residual effects of some degree. The type and degree of residual effects depend on the extent and location of the brain damage. Severe brain injury has physical, cognitive, behavioral, and emotional implications. There are often drastic changes in personality, as well as in physical and cognitive abilities.

The residual effects of severe brain damage may include motor coordination difficulties. There may be motor deficits, such as paralysis, weakness, or spasticity of muscles. The impairment in muscle coordination (**ataxia**) may produce a loss of balance, causing the individual to walk with a staggering gait. Other motor deficits may include **dyskinesias** (abnormal movement) or **dystonia** (abnormal muscle tone). Even when the motor function of muscles remains intact, the individual may lose the ability to organize and sequence specific muscle movements in order to perform a task (**apraxia**).

Motor difficulty may also affect speech. Coordination and accuracy of movement of the muscles, lips, tongue, or other parts of the speech mechanism may be impaired secondary to weakness or paralysis of these muscles. This condition is called **dysarthria**. The impairment may range from speech that is slightly slurred to speech that is unintelligible. Vocal cord dysfunction may also affect voice quality. Swallowing reflexes may also be affected so that the individual salivates excessively. Difficulty with swallowing reflexes may result in buildup of saliva with subsequent drooling. In severe cases, tube feedings may be necessary in order to prevent aspiration.

Other speech and language problems may result from articulation disorders in which there is no significant weakness or incoordination for reflexive action, but there is the inability to position and sequence muscle movements. For example, the individual may be able to scrape a food particle off the teeth with the tongue, but may be unable to position the tongue to the teeth in order to produce a "t" sound. This condition is known as **apraxia of speech**. Individuals have more difficulty with complex speech tasks and with longer words. Apraxia of speech rarely occurs in isolation and is frequently associated with aphasia.

Aphasia refers to impairment in the ability to comprehend and use language. Aphasia can affect verbal or written communication and is the result of dysfunction of language centers in the brain, rather than impairment of musculature, involved in producing speech. Although there are a number of types of aphasia, two common categories are **nonfluent** (expressive or motor) **aphasia** and **fluent** (receptive or sensory) **aphasia**.

Broca's aphasia is a type of nonfluent aphasia characterized by misarticulation, laborious speech, hesitancy, and reduced vocabulary. Individuals may be able to understand and read simple material; however, as the complexity or length of the message increases, difficulty becomes more apparent. Although individuals are able to comprehend, they may have difficulty in expressing their thoughts in speech and writing. Reading ability may be better than writing ability. Speech may be labored, slow, and/or difficult to understand. Small connecting words, such as prepositions, may be omitted. Another type of nonfluent aphasia is **global aphasia,** in which individuals have limited ability to communicate. There may be only utterances of sterotypic words such as "O.K.," and inability to respond appropriately to simple questions.

Wernicke's aphasia is a type of fluent aphasia in which there is effortless speech, relatively normal grammatical structure, and increased verbal output, but with reduced information content, so that what the individual says makes little sense. Auditory and reading comprehension are usually poor. Individuals with Wernicke's aphasia are typically unaware of their communication difficulties.

Perceptual problems may also be present. Even though the eye itself may not be injured, there may be visual problems if the part of the brain that receives, perceives, or interprets nerve impulses from the eye has been injured. Visual problems may include total blindness, **diplopia** (double vision), cuts in the peripheral field of vision or blind spots, **hemianopsia** (loss of vision in half the visual field), or color blindness. The individual's comprehension of a variety of other stimuli may also be affected. There may be a loss of the comprehension of sensations (**agnosia**); for example, these individuals may be unable to interpret sounds or visual images, or to distinguish objects by touch. Individuals may experience residual **tinnitus** (ringing in the ears) or sensorineural hearing loss. If the olfactory nerve or the corresponding area of the brain has been damaged, the individual may have no sense of smell (**anosmia**), which can affect the ability to detect hazards such as smoke, gas leaks, or other important warning signs. Visual-spatial deficits may cause individuals to misjudge distances, lose depth perception, or lose the ability to appreciate the concept of whole objects rather than fragmented parts. As a result, these individuals may have difficulty in interpreting visual information accurately in order to orient position and movement within the environment.

A traumatic brain injury may alter a variety of cognitive skills. Memory encompasses the ability to analyze and store perceptions of the external world and to categorize those perceptions for later recognition and recall. Memory impairments caused by severe brain injury may involve recent or remote memory. Individuals may be unable to complete simple daily tasks, such as dressing, because they are unable to remember the steps involved or because, after completing the first steps of the task, they forget their original goal. Individuals with remote memory impairments may have forgotten their own personal history or may be unable to remember skills that were once very familiar. Other possible cognitive impairments include decreased organizational skills, attention and/or concentration deficits, and decreased reasoning and problem-solving ability.

There are behavioral and emotional manifestations as well as personality changes associated with almost all severe brain injuries. The development of a personality and emotional disorder may be the most disabling factor in traumatic brain injury. At times, it is difficult to discern the extent to which personality changes are the direct consequence of physiological damage to the brain and the extent to which they are a personal reaction to the losses associated with the disability itself. After a traumatic brain injury, individuals may exhibit sudden mood swings from happy to sad, or complacent to volatile, with little or no provocation. They may experience difficulty in initiating behavior or carrying out self-directed behavior. They may behave impulsively, appearing to act quickly without thinking or without anticipating the consequences of their behavior.

A poor self-awareness may also be a direct physiological result of a severe brain injury. Individuals may lack insight into the inappropriateness of their behavior and may be unaware of their deficits. They may demonstrate unrealistic expectations or appraisals of their abilities, or they may deny or disagree with others' observations regarding their behavior or performance. They may show disinhibition and lack the social skills needed to function adequately within the environment. They may regain some degree of self-awareness with experience and appropriate feedback, however.

Aggressive behavior may be a sequel to traumatic brain injury. It can result from frustration, or it can be a direct physiological consequence of the injury. Aggression can be expressed actively or passively, verbally or physically. Aggressive behaviors may include violent verbal or physical acts toward people or objects, lack of cooperation, and failure to perform certain tasks or duties.

Depression, anxiety, and reduced self-esteem are commonly associated with traumatic brain injury. As individuals become increasingly aware of the losses, restrictions, and alterations in life style that frequently follow traumatic brain injury, they may be overwhelmed by hopelessness and anxiety. They may become preoccupied with feelings of worthlessness and grief. Suicide ideation is not uncommon and should always be taken seriously.

Most individuals who have experienced a traumatic brain injury must abstain from alcohol or other substances that have not been medically prescribed. They may view such restrictions as additional losses caused by the injury, and they may need considerable education and support in order to adhere to these limitations. The use of alcohol and other substances can increase the potential for seizures after a traumatic brain injury, however, and the interaction of such substances with prescribed medications can have dangerous effects. In addition, alcohol and other substances potentiate any existing impairment of psychomotor and cognitive function, thus increasing the chances of accident and additional injury.

Cerebrovascular Accident (Stroke)

In a **cerebrovascular accident**, there is a sudden loss of brain function due to the decreased blood flow to a part of the brain. Although cerebrovascular accidents can be caused by congenital defects in the vasculature of the brain, they are more frequently associated with systemic conditions, such as arteriosclerosis and hypertension, but a number of other conditions may also interfere with the blood supply to the brain. One of the most common is the blocking of a cerebral artery by a clot (**thrombus**) that has formed inside the artery, a condition referred to as **cerebral thrombosis**. In other instances, a clot that has formed in another part of the body may break off, travel to the brain, and lodge in one of the cerebral arteries. This condition is referred to as a **cerebral embolism**.

Stroke is usually the culmination of progressive disease that has occurred over the course of many years. In addition to arteriosclerosis and hypertension, heart disease and diabetes are associated with stroke. When individuals have both arteriosclerosis and high blood pressure, a weakened, diseased cerebral artery may burst because of the increased pressure, resulting in cerebral hemorrhage and subsequent stroke. A ruptured **cerebral aneurysm**, a weakened spot in the arterial wall that balloons out and can burst if placed under increased pressure, may also lead to cerebral hemorrhage and stroke. Aneurysms can be congenital, or they can be associated with vascular disease (e.g., arteriosclerosis).

At times, temporary blocking of cerebral arteries causes slight, temporary neurological deficits. These "mini-strokes" are referred to as **transient ischemic attacks**. Although the neurological deficits experienced are usually temporary, their occurrence forewarns the individual of the possibility of a larger stroke unless treatment controls the underlying condition.

Many manifestations and residual effects of stroke are the same as those of traumatic brain injury. Like the damage sustained after an open (penetrating) head injury, damage to the brain from stroke is generally localized rather than diffuse. The symptoms experienced depend on how extensive the damage is and whether it affects the left or the right hemisphere of the brain. Paralysis of the side of the body opposite the damaged cerebral hemisphere is common. Consequently, right cerebral damage results in paralysis of the left side of the body (**left hemiplegia**), while left cerebral damage results in paralysis of the right side of the body (**right hemiplegia**).

Individuals with left cerebral damage may find problem solving difficult. When presented with a new problem, individuals whose left hemisphere has been damaged may respond slowly and in a cautious, disorganized fashion. In most instances, it is helpful to divide tasks into smaller steps in order to avoid confusion in performance. These individuals may need frequent feedback throughout even simple tasks, such as dressing, in order to be assured that they are performing the task correctly. In addition, because the center of language function is located in the left cerebral hemisphere for most individuals, communication deficits (**aphasia**) may occur when stroke involves the left side of the brain.

Individuals with right cerebral damage have language function, but they commonly have visual-spatial defects. Because the ability to communicate is intact, the other skills and abilities that remain may be overestimated. **Visual-spatial deficits**, however, cause problems with depth perception and the judgment of distance, size, position, rate of movement, form, and the relation of parts to wholes. Because these judgments are normally automatic, those who come into contact with the individual may not immediately recognize the impairment. Inappropriate judgment of space or distance may, therefore, be misinterpreted as carelessness or clumsiness. Individuals with right cerebral damage may behave as if unaware of the deficits present, acting fast and impulsively. Because they often have difficulty in understanding visual cues from their environment, simplification of the surroundings and good lighting are crucial to their ability to move about without difficulty.

Individuals who have had a stroke, especially in the right hemisphere, may experience **anosognosia** (one-sided neglect). In some instances, anosognosia is visual; the affected individuals are unable to perceive objects on either the right or the left of the central field of vision. Sometimes, signals from all senses on one side of the body are involved so that individuals may not recognize their own arm or leg or are unresponsive to verbal stimuli that originate from one side of the body. Nonresponsiveness to verbal stimuli on the impaired side is different from merely losing the hearing in one ear. All stimuli on the impaired side are ignored, while stimuli on the individual's unimpaired side do evoke a response.

Some individuals who have had a stroke have no paralysis, but experience intellectual deficits. Others have a paralysis, but few other deficits. In most instances, however, as does traumatic brain injury, stroke involves some behavioral and emotional changes. Individuals who once were very neat and tidy may become unkempt or sloppy in appearance. Those who were once jovial and outgoing may become quiet and withdrawn. Such behavior may at first be misinterpreted as laziness, disinterest, or uncooperativeness rather than as a symptom of the condition itself. Once these deficits are recognized as symptoms associated with stroke, individuals can learn compensatory behaviors to overcome them.

Depending on the extent of permanent damage that the brain has sustained, individuals who have had a stroke can, with physical, speech, and occupational therapy, use assistive devices to perform a variety of functions and activities. Because stroke is generally associated with other systemic disease, however, control of the underlying cause of the stroke affects the extent of the recovery and the potential for strokes in the future.

Cerebral Palsy

Injury to the brain during the fetal period, during birth, or in early childhood may result in **cerebral palsy**. The type of cerebral palsy and the symptoms experienced depend on the location and the extent of the injury. Some individuals have minor, barely detectable symptoms, while others have severe impairments. There is generally some difficulty with the control and coordination of muscles. There may be an abnormality of muscle tone, resulting in muscle stiffness (**spasticity, hypertonia**) that, in turn, interferes with dexterity and the ability to perform various movements. Some individuals with cerebral palsy have **ataxia** (disorder in the accuracy of muscle movement), which affects their balance and coordination of gait. Still others have **dyskinesia**, involving unwanted, involuntary muscle movements. Specific types of dyskinesia include slow writhing; purposeless movements, especially of the hands (**athetosis**); or abrupt and jerky movements (**choreoathetosis**). Some individuals have a combination of spasticity, ataxia, or dyskinesia.

Because cerebral palsy is due to permanent brain damage, symptoms are lifelong. The brain injury itself is not progressive, but because of the altered tone and/or activity of muscles, disorders such as **contractures** (loss of range of motion or fixation of a joint) or scoliosis (see Chapter 7) may occur. The administration of **muscle relaxants** may be helpful in reducing increased muscle tone and muscle spasms. Physical therapy and, in some instances, surgery may postpone or prevent such complications.

Although cerebral palsy affects primarily muscle control, additional problems, including visual or hearing impairments, seizures, or mental retardation, may occur if other parts of the brain are also affected.

Epilepsy

In **epilepsy**, neurons in the brain create abnormal electrical discharges that cause **seizures** (temporary loss of control over certain body functions). There are many different types of epilepsy with a variety of symptoms: muscle spasms, confusion, or loss of consciousness. Seizures usually last only a short time, and function is normal between seizures. Epileptic seizures can be mild or severe, can occur frequently or rarely, and can change in their pattern of occurrence over time. The symptoms experienced with seizures depend on the area of the brain affected, the number of brain cells involved, and the duration of the abnormal discharge.

Epilepsy can result from damage to the brain, as in traumatic brain injury or stroke. It can also be caused by a defect that was present in the brain at birth or by disease or inflammation of the brain, as in meningitis. Although epilepsy due to damage or injury to the brain can occur at any age, it frequently appears in childhood when due to other causes.

The general prognosis for individuals with epilepsy depends on the type of seizure, the underlying cause, the administration of appropriate treatment, and the individual's willingness and ability to follow the prescribed treatment regimen. If their condition is accurately diagnosed and appropriately treated, most individuals with epilepsy can live active, productive lives.

Epilepsy is classified according to the type of seizure experienced. Seizures may be generalized (nerve cells discharge throughout the brain) or more localized.

Generalized Tonic-Clonic Seizure (Grand Mal Epilepsy)

An abnormal discharge of nerve cells throughout the brain results in a **generalized tonic-clonic seizure**. Some individuals experience an **aura** (warning), such as a flash of light or other unusual sensation, immediately before the seizure begins. As the seizure develops, the affected individual loses consciousness and falls down, entering a **tonic state** in which there is a generalized body rigidity. The muscles then enter a **clonic state**, in which they undergo jerking movements. The teeth are clenched tightly together. Control of the bladder or the bowel may be lost. The seizure generally lasts less than 4 minutes. When the seizure ends, the individual gradually regains consciousness, but may experience confusion, difficulty in speaking, and headache. Although these symptoms usually disappear within several hours, fatigue may be overwhelming, often necessitating rest or sleep.

Although a tonic-clonic seizure may be frightening to those who witness it, the individual is usually in no imminent danger unless there are hard, sharp, or hot hazards within the immediate environment. Individuals who are having a seizure should not be moved except to protect them from such hazards. There should be no attempt to restrain an individual during a tonic-clonic seizure or to pry open the clenched teeth, nor should hard objects that could cause injury be placed in the mouth. The individual will not "swallow" the tongue, but may inadvertently bite its edge. The individual should be placed on his or her side during the seizure so that secretions can drain from the mouth and cannot compromise the airway.

Absence Seizure (Petit Mal Epilepsy)

Like tonic-clonic seizures, **absence seizures** are generalized, because nerve cells discharge throughout the brain. Children most commonly experience these seizures, which are characterized by brief blank spells or staring spells and a loss of awareness of the surroundings. The seizure generally lasts for several seconds. The individual does not fall, and there are usually no outward motor manifestations of absence seizures, although abnormal blinking or slight twitching may occur occasionally. Observers often misinterpret this type of seizure as daydreaming or inattentiveness. Absence seizures that occur frequently may disrupt school performance. These seizures may disappear spontaneously with age, but some individuals who have had absence seizures begin to have tonic-clonic seizures.

Partial Seizures

When nerve cells discharge in an isolated part of the brain, **partial seizures** occur. One type of partial seizure is a **focal seizure**, in which there is no loss of consciousness and symptoms are very localized, depending on the part of the brain affected. A **Jacksonian (simple-partial)** seizure begins with convulsive symptoms in one part of the body, such as a hand or foot. The convulsive muscle movement then progresses in an orderly manner up the extremity. Jacksonian seizures can develop into full-blown tonic-clonic seizures.

Other types of partial seizures may have more complex symptoms. **Complex-partial (psychomotor)** seizures are characterized by a loss of awareness of the surroundings. The individual may pace, wander aimlessly, make purposeless movements, and utter unintelligible sounds. The seizure can last up to 20 minutes with mental confusion for a few minutes after the seizure is over. Observers may misinterpret complex-partial seizures, often attributing the symptoms to alcohol or drug abuse.

Multiple Sclerosis

Multiple sclerosis is a progressive disease of the central nervous system in which the myelin is destroyed in localized areas of the brain and spinal cord. Scar tissue forms over the patches of destroyed myelin, interfering with the transmission of electrical impulses and causing neurological deficits. The cause of multiple sclerosis is unknown, although it has been speculated that a virus, an autoimmune response, or both may be responsible. It most often affects young adults between the ages of 20 and 40.

Individuals with multiple sclerosis have various combinations of symptoms, including dizziness, weakness, spasticity, unsteadiness, numbness, visual problems, or poor bladder control. Symptoms may come and go, with some remaining, some progressing slowly, others progressing rapidly—all in varying combinations and patterns. None of the combinations or patterns are predictable. The part of the brain or spinal cord involved determines the symptoms experienced. The initial symptoms may be vague and are sometimes attributed to fatigue or stress—or even laziness and withdrawal. Later symptoms become more pronounced, causing permanent dysfunction in a variety of areas. Characteristic of the disease are periods of **remission** and periods of **exacerbation**. Although the symptoms may partly resolve when the disease is in remission, every exacerbation leaves permanent residual defects. Often, the condition is not recognized or diagnosed immediately, because the symptoms have resolved by the time the individual sees a physician.

Motor, sensory, intellectual, or emotional deficits may be associated with multiple sclerosis, depending on the part of the central nervous system affected. Symptoms vary greatly from person to person and from time to time in the same person. The progression of the disease is also variable. In some individuals, it progresses very rapidly, leading to disability within months or years. Other individuals may have only mild symptoms, or the disease may remain in remission for years, enabling these individuals to lead active, productive lives.

Common early symptoms are **paresthesia** (a sensation of numbness or tingling in some part of the body); weakness of an extremity; visual disturbances, such as **diplopia** and dimness of vision; and **vertigo** (dizziness or false sensation of circular movement). Individuals with multiple sclerosis may develop difficulty with coordination and balance, giving them the appearance of someone who is drunk. There may be a partial or complete paralysis of any part of the body or spasticity of muscles. There may be a tremor of the hands, commonly called **intention tremor** because it occurs only when the individual tries to engage in a purposeful activity, such as reaching for a glass. Speech may be slurred, or there may be **scanning** speech, in which the individual enunciates slowly with frequent hesitations at the beginning of a word or syllable. Individuals with multiple sclerosis may also have difficulty in swallowing (**dysphagia**). The disease may affect the genito-urinary tract, causing **incontinence** (loss of control of the bladder or bowel). Some individuals may experience **urinary retention** (the inability to empty the bladder of urine). Men may become impotent, and women may experience numbness in the genital area.

Cognitive changes may occur in multiple sclerosis, although intellectual function often remains intact. For some individuals, however, impairment may be noted on performing tasks that require conceptualization, memory, or new learning, as well as on measures that require either rapid or precise motor responses. Depression is common, although the degree to which it is a reaction to the disease and the degree to which it is a manifestation of neurological dysfunction is not known. Some individuals experience an inappropriate euphoria.

There is no cure for multiple sclerosis, nor is there a formula for estimating the general outcome for all individuals. Treatment may improve symptoms somewhat or help to prevent or delay future exacerbations of symptoms. Each treatment, however, has risks that must be carefully weighed by each individual. The general prognosis is unpredictable, with varying rates of progression and varying rates of disability. Approximately one-third of individuals with multiple sclerosis continue their normal life style; one-third must modify their life style somewhat; and one-third become severely disabled.

Parkinson's Disease (Paralysis Agitans, Shaking Palsy)

A slowly progressive disorder of the central nervous system, **Parkinson's disease** involves extensive degenerative changes in the basal ganglia and the loss of or decrease in the levels of dopamine (a neurotransmitter) in the brain. Although Parkinson's disease occurs most commonly after the age of 40, greater awareness and improved methods of detection have increased the number of diagnosed cases of Parkinson's disease among younger individuals. The exact cause of Parkinson's disease is unknown.

Secondary parkinsonism is a term used to describe the parkinsonian syndrome that has been associated with the ingestion of certain drugs (prescription or others) or exposure to toxic substances, such as carbon monoxide or other chemicals. Secondary parkinsonism gained attention in the early 1980s when the "designer drug" MPTP, which mimicked the action of heroin, entered the street market. A number of young adults, after taking the drug, suddenly developed permanent signs and symptoms of severe Parkinson's disease. These individuals have shown no signs of recovery in long-term follow-up.

A variety of other conditions mimic Parkinson's disease, causing similar symptoms. These symptoms are collectively called **parkinsonism** and should be distinguished from Parkinson's disease. Some medications used in the treatment of mental illness have reversible parkinson-like symptoms as side-effects.

The symptoms of Parkinson's disease include disorders of movement, tremor, muscle rigidity, and abnormalities of postural reflexes. Movement disorders consist of extreme slowness of movement (**bradykinesia**), or complete or partial absence of movement (**akinesia**). Individuals who have Parkinson's disease may walk with small, shuffling steps and may have difficulty in rising from a chair or bed. They may find it difficult to initiate or to stop voluntary movements. While walking, for example, they may suddenly freeze, taking seconds to regain motion; in other instances, they may continue five or six more steps beyond where they want to stop. The impairment experienced with bradykinesia can interfere with activities such as shaving, buttoning clothes, or cutting food, all of which take longer and become more difficult to perform as the disease progresses.

Individuals with Parkinson's disease are sometimes said to have a poverty of spontaneous movement. They may blink less frequently and may develop a masklike, expressionless face. Their decreased ability to swallow results in saliva accumulation and drooling. Their speech may be decreased in volume and may have no verbal inflections. The amplitude of movement may also be decreased so that handwriting gradually becomes smaller and smaller (**micrographia**) until it is no longer legible.

The tremor of a limb, usually most noticeable in one hand, is the most frequent early symptom. The tremor intensifies when the hand rests in the lap (**resting tremor**) and diminishes with voluntary movement. The tremor is not present during sleep, however.

The posture of individuals with Parkinson's disease becomes stooped, and their arms fail to swing with their stride when they are walking. The loss of postural reflexes makes it difficult for these individuals to maintain an upright position if they are suddenly bumped, increasing the risk of falls. To keep from falling, individuals may inadvertently quicken their steps as if to "catch up" with their own center of gravity.

Muscle tone is increased, creating muscle rigidity, which also interferes with movement and causes severe immobility. Because greater effort is necessary to engage in voluntary movement, fatigue is also increased.

Mental and behavioral changes do not always occur, but Parkinson's disease can cause a mild impairment in recent memory, as well as changes in emotions and behavior. Apathy, passivity, depression, and loss of initiative may be noted. The degree to which these reflect physiological changes and the degree to which they reflect a reaction to the disease itself are not known. Dementia is common late in the course of the illness. As the individual becomes aware of his or her decreasing cognitive abilities, depression related to losses may result.

There is no cure for Parkinson's disease. The disease is characterized by progressive debilitation, although the progression occurs slowly over years. Treatment, usually in the form of medication, physical therapy, and exercise—along with maintenance of general health—can reduce the effects of the symptoms so that individuals with this condition may remain active longer.

Infections of the Central Nervous System

Any infection of the brain or the membranes that surround it can cause serious neurological effects, some of which may be permanent. **Meningitis** is an inflammation of the meninges, the layers of membrane that lie between the bones of the skull and the brain tissue. Bacteria are usually responsible for meningitis, although viral or fungal infections may also cause meningitis. The infecting organism reaches the meninges by traveling through the bloodstream or by spreading from nearby infected structures, such as the sinuses. Individuals with meningitis are usually acutely ill and have severe neurological symptoms, such as confusion, seizures, or coma. The use of antibiotics has greatly reduced the number of fatalities from meningitis; however, if it occurs in individuals whose physical state is weakened or if diagnosis and treatment are delayed, it can still be fatal. Although most individuals with meningitis recover completely, some may have residual neurological deficits. Meningitis is a life-threatening condition. In some instances, individuals may die of overwhelming infection, even with the best medical care.

Encephalitis is an inflammation of the brain due to the direct invasion of a virus. It may be caused by an endemic virus, such as a mosquito-borne virus, or it may occur as a complication of a viral infection, such as measles or chickenpox. Some individuals with encephalitis experience only fever and fatigue, while others may experience severe headache, stiff neck, and coma. There is no adequate treatment for encephalitis, except for maintaining comfort and preventing complications. The symptoms usually subside in a few weeks, leaving no permanent damage. Some individuals, however, develop irreversible neurological changes as a result of the infection.

Guillain-Barré Syndrome (Acute Postinfectious Polyneuropathy)

An acute and rapidly progressive condition, **Guillain-Barré syndrome** is characterized by a muscular weakness that usually begins in the lower limbs and spreads upward (ascending paralysis). The amount of paralysis varies: some individuals experience only mild footdrop, while others develop complete paralysis and weakness of all extremities and, at times, even the facial muscles. Sensation or feeling, especially in the lower extremities, is often experienced to some degree, but, unlike the paralysis, is not progressive.

The exact cause of Guillain-Barré syndrome is unknown, but the symptoms develop rapidly, often after an infection or immunization. Generally, the symptoms have reached their maximum intensity within 3 to 8 weeks. For the most part, the symptoms are reversible, and recovery occurs within a month after the progression of the symptoms ceases. The treatment is primarily symptomatic, although almost all individuals require hospitalization during the initial stages of the disease. Most individuals recover completely, but permanent disability or even death may result in some instances.

Post-Polio Syndrome

Poliomyelitis, a common disabling disease in the 1940s and 1950s, is now rare because of the development of the Salk and Sabin vaccines in the mid-1950s.

The disease, caused by the polio virus, varied widely in its severity. The virus attacked the motor neurons of the nervous system, leaving the muscles weak and/or paralyzed. Although some individuals recovered motor function after the attack, others experienced varying degrees of permanent paralysis. For some individuals, the muscles of respiration were so severely affected that they required ventilatory aids.

Many individuals who had been infected with the polio virus years ago are now experiencing new symptoms that range in severity from mild to severely debilitating. As a group, these symptoms have been labeled **post-polio syndrome**. Individuals with post-polio syndrome experience severe fatigue that necessitates more frequent rest periods, increased muscular weakness, and joint and muscle pain.

Those who adjusted to and compensated for their disability, attaining active, independent lives, may find the occurrence of new symptoms and the limitations of post-polio syndrome difficult to accept. No specific treatment is available. The treatment focuses on assisting these individuals to maintain their functional status and independence as long as possible. Good health practices, including proper nutrition and adequate rest, are important to maintain function. In addition, these individuals may need to control their weight in order to avoid unnecessary stress on weight-bearing joints. For individuals whose respiratory muscles were affected by the initial infection, weight control can prevent increased respiratory difficulty. Some individuals may require the use of additional assistive devices if their symptoms become more debilitating. For example, those who have been ambulatory with crutches or braces may need to use a wheelchair at times.

Spinal Cord Injuries

An injury to the vertebrae can also injure the spinal cord, interrupting the transmission of nerve impulses between the brain and other parts of the body below the level of injury. In some instances, swelling, bleeding, or a bone fragment may compress the cord. In these cases, if the spinal cord is still intact, the removal of the source of compression can restore function. When the spinal cord has been severed, however, the interruption of the nerve pathways cannot be repaired. In such an injury, referred to as a complete injury, there is no voluntary motor or sensory function below the level of the injury, and the paralysis is permanent. At times, the spinal cord injury is incomplete, and some motor or sensory function remains below the level of the injury. One portion of the spinal cord may be nonfunctional, while another portion is functional; or certain nerve tracts may still be functioning, but in an abnormal way. The term **paraparesis** indicates that some function remains below the level of injury.

When an individual can no longer move the muscles voluntarily because of a spinal cord injury, the muscles of the extremities below the level of injury **atrophy** (become smaller). Even when there is no voluntary muscle function, spasticity often causes sudden involuntary movements of the legs. In some instances, spasticity may be severe enough to impede the effective use of wheelchairs or other assistive devices.

Although direct trauma causes most spinal cord injuries, conditions such as osteoporosis may cause the fracture or dislocation of vertebrae, injuring the spinal cord as a result. Other causes of impairment in spinal cord function are herniated disks, multiple sclerosis, or spinal cord tumors. The amount of impairment experienced with spinal cord injury is dependent on the level at which the injury occurs. The higher the level of injury, the greater the degree of impairment. However, in most spinal cord injuries there is a loss of sensory and motor function, loss of bowel and bladder control, and some loss of sexual function, including diminished or absent sensation. In males, in addition to sensation loss, psychologically stimulated erections can no longer occur, but reflex erections are possible.

Injuries to the Spinal Cord at the Cervical Level (C-2 through C-7)

Diving accidents, auto accidents, or a blow on the head with a heavy object may cause fractures of the cervical vertebrae. An injury to the spinal cord at the cervical level results in paralysis of both the upper and lower extremities (**quadriplegia**).

Spinal cord injuries that occur at the C-2 (second cervical vertebra) level and above usually result in death, because the functioning of all muscles, including the muscles of respiration, is lost. Individuals who survive these injuries require ventilatory support. Individuals with injuries at C-3 or C-4 may have some impairment in respiratory capacity and are almost totally dependent on others for self-care, although they may use a mouth stick to manipulate an electric wheelchair. Some gross movement of the upper extremities is possible after injuries at C-5 or C-6 so that, with the aid of special equipment, individuals who have been injured at these levels can retain some independence in feeding, dressing, and propelling a wheelchair. Individuals with C-7 injuries can straighten their arms and may be able to achieve almost total independence with some adaptations in their home. Although fine motor movements of the hands are impaired, writing may be possible with the use of a special device that can be strapped to the hand. Driving a motor vehicle is also possible with use of hand controls.

Spinal Cord Injuries at the Thoracic Level (T-1 through T-12)

Spinal cord injuries that occur at T-1 or below result in **paraplegia** (paralysis of the lower extremities). The upper extremities are unimpaired. In most cases, individuals are able to attain total independence in self-care, wheelchair activity, and transfer. Individuals with injury between T-1 and T-3 may need a brace or other support in order to sit in an upright position because muscles of the trunk and body are paralyzed even though upper extremities are functional. Operation of a motor vehicle is possible with the use of hand controls.

Spinal Cord Injuries at the Lumbar Level (L-1 through L-5)

Many of the muscles of mobility are intact, with possible functioning of all upper body muscles and many of the leg muscles. Ambulation with braces may be possible, especially for short distances. Individuals gain total independence in care. Hand controls may still be necessary, however, for driving a motor vehicle. Although bowel and bladder function are still impaired, reflex emptying may be possible.

Spinal Cord Injuries at the Sacrum

Ambulation is usually possible with little or no equipment after an injury to the spinal cord at the sacrum. Bowel and bladder function may, however, be impaired.

Complications of Spinal Cord Injury

As a result of the immobility and other physiological changes that occur because of a spinal cord injury, a number of complications may develop that not only can cause discomfort, but also can contribute to further debilitation, hospitalization, and, in some instances, death. For example, **autonomic dysreflexia** commonly occurs in individuals who have experienced an injury to the upper spinal cord. It is characterized by a sudden rise in blood pressure, profuse sweating, and headache. It is the result of an excessive neural discharge from the autonomic nervous system and may be triggered by the overdistention of the bowel or bladder.

Decubitus ulcers (pressure sores) are a major problem for individuals with a spinal cord injury. These ulcers develop when pressure on a part of the body interferes with the blood supply to that part, eventually resulting in the breakdown and ulceration of the skin. Because individuals with a spinal cord injury have no sensation below the level of injury, they are unable to feel such pressure; furthermore, because of the paralysis, they are unable to shift their weight to relieve the pressure. Ulcerations may develop over any bony prominence; however, they occur most frequently over the sacral area or the buttocks.

Contractures (loss of range of motion, or fixed deformity of a joint) may occur in paralyzed limbs if the joints are not moved through their range of motion. Depending on their location, contractures can interfere with the use of assistive devices. If located in the hip or knee, they can even interfere with comfortable positioning in a wheelchair. Passive exercise of the joints by another person can prevent such contractures, however.

Infections of the urinary tract are recurring problems for many individuals with a spinal cord injury. Because these individuals are generally unable to control their bladder, they may need to have a catheter inserted into the bladder to drain urine and prevent incontinence. The bladder and its contents normally contain no pathological organisms, but there is always the potential for the introduction of infectious organisms when a catheter is inserted into the bladder. For individuals with a spinal cord injury, urinary tract infections can be a serious, debilitating, and, at times, life-threatening problem.

Amyotrophic Lateral Sclerosis

In **amyotrophic lateral sclerosis**, there is a degeneration of the **motor neurons** (nerve cells that convey impulses to initiate muscular contraction). The cause of the disease is unknown. It is a progressive, incurable disease characterized by muscular weakness, a decrease in muscle size (**atrophy**), spasticity, and hyperactive reflexes. It does not usually affect intellectual function, sensation, or bowel and bladder function. The degree of disability experienced depends on the muscles affected. An increasing number of neurons are destroyed, but at an unpredictable rate. Activity becomes more and more difficult as the disease progresses, and ambulation aids, such as a wheelchair, are needed. The condition generally progresses fairly rapidly over a course of 3 years. Amyotrophic lateral sclerosis that lasts longer than 3 years suggests a misdiagnosis, and the individual should undergo a reexamination. There is no effective treatment for amyotrophic lateral sclerosis, other than physical therapy to maintain muscle function and to forestall complications, such as respiratory infections and decubitus ulcers.

Huntington's Chorea (Huntington's Disease)

A slowly progressive, hereditary disease of the central nervous system, **Huntington's chorea** is characterized by jerky involuntary movements and mental deterioration (**progressive dementia**). Most symptoms begin in young adulthood or middle age. There is no known treatment or cure for Huntington's chorea. The length of time from the onset of the symptoms to total disability or death varies, but averages approximately 15 years.

DIAGNOSTIC PROCEDURES

Skull and Spine Roentgenography (X-ray)

Roentgenograms (radiographic studies or x-rays) of the skull and spine are helpful in identifying damage to bony structures, such as the skull and vertebrae surrounding the spinal cord.

Computed Tomography (CT Scan, CAT Scan)

A special kind of radiographic technique, **computed tomography** produces images of cross sections of the body. Unlike conventional roentgenography, computed tomography produces an image of one "slice" of the structure being studied at a time, in sequence. On regular x-ray films, bone (e.g., the skull) can block the view of parts lying behind it (e.g., the brain). Computed tomography scans show both the bone and the underlying tissue.

A scan of the head by computed tomography can detect tumors and blood clots inside the brain. It can also reveal an enlargement of the ventricles of the brain due to inadequate drainage of cerebrospinal fluid (**hydrocephelus**), as well as other types of abnormalities in the brain and skull. It can also be used to identify tumors or other sources of pressure on the spinal cord.

Individuals who are undergoing a scan by computed tomography are placed within a large cylinder that contains an x-ray tube and a receptor mounted opposite each other. Usually, a special substance (contrast medium) is administered to the individual intravenously to highlight certain structures and make the results more readable. The tube is rotated around the individual. X-rays are sent from the tube to the receptor, which measures the amount of radiation that each body tissue or organ absorbs during each rotation. A computer converts this information to a visual image on a screen. Images are monitored on a video screen and later photographed for more careful study by the **radiologist**.

Brain Scan

With the use of radionuclides (radioisotopes), **brain scans** make it possible to identify changes in the brain tissues. A radionuclide that localizes in the brain is given to the individual, and the amount of radiation emitted from the brain is measured. The radiation hazard is very slight, because the dosage of the radionuclide is very small and the duration of the exposure brief.

Positron Emission Transaxial Tomography (PET Scan)

In order to study the biochemical or metabolic activities in the cells of body tissue, **positron emission transaxial tomography** may be used. Individuals are injected with or inhale a biochemical substance tagged with a radionuclide. When the particles from the radionuclide combine with particles normally found in the cells of certain tissues, they emit special rays (gamma rays) that a scanner can detect. The scanner then translates these emissions into color-coded images. Such scans can be used to evaluate the function of many different body tissues. In the brain, this type of scan can be used to evaluate tumors or disorders that may alter cerebral metabolism, such as Parkinson's disease, multiple sclerosis, or epilepsy.

Magnetic Resonance Imaging

Magnetic resonance imaging may be used for the diagnosis or evaluation of the following conditions of the nervous system: brain tumor, stroke, multiple sclerosis, dementia, encephalitis or meningitis, and seizure disorders. It may also be useful in determining the extent of traumatic brain injury. In spinal cord injury, magnetic resonance imaging may be used in conjunction with regular x-rays films, myelograms, and scans done by computed tomography to identify cord compression, swelling, or bleeding of the cord. (See Chapter 7.)

Myelography

A radiographic (x-ray) examination of the spinal canal is sometimes performed by **myelography**. A special dye is injected into the spinal canal and x-ray films are taken. The test may be performed to identify injury to the spinal nerves, tumors of the spinal cord, or other conditions that block the flow of cerebrospinal fluid around the spinal cord.

Cerebral Angiography

The blood circulation in the brain may be visualized by **cerebral angiography**. A catheter is inserted into an artery and a contrast medium injected. A series of x-ray films are then taken.

Digital Venous Subtraction Angiography

For **digital venous subtraction angiography**, a procedure that allows the physician to visualize the blood vessels in the head and neck, a catheter is inserted into a vein and a special contrast medium injected into the catheter. A series of x-ray films are then taken. Digital venous subtraction angiography requires much less contrast medium than does conventional angiography. It uses a computerized digital video subtraction system in which data are stored in digital form and can be retrieved at any time. Those images that provide the best visualization of the vasculature of the brain are then electronically manipulated to improve the detail of the image.

Lumbar Puncture (Cerebrospinal Fluid Analysis, Spinal Tap)

When a laboratory analysis of an individual's cerebrospinal fluid is needed, a **lumbar puncture** is done. To remove the fluid, a physician inserts a needle into the subarachnoid space of the spinal column at the lumbar area. The test may be done to determine whether there is a blockage of the flow of spinal fluid, to detect any bleeding or infection in the area, and to identify other central nervous system disorders. Although a lumbar puncture is often performed for diagnostic purposes, it can also be done for therapeutic reasons, such as to reduce increased pressure or to instill medications. It is often performed in an outpatient setting under local anesthesia.

Electroencephalography (EEG)

The electrical activity of the brain (brain waves) can be measured through **electroencephalography** (EEG). Electrodes are placed in various areas of the scalp and connected to a machine that records the brain waves graphically. The procedure is helpful in identifying tumors, seizure disorders, and other types of brain dysfunction.

Electromyography and Nerve Conduction Velocity

Electromyography (EMG) is a procedure used to evaluate the electrical activity of certain muscles and is helpful in the diagnosis of certain muscle diseases. A small needle that is attached to an electrode is inserted into the muscle being examined, and the electrical activity of the selected muscle is recorded both at rest and during exercise. Nerve conduction studies are often performed in conjunction with EMG and are helpful in diagnosing conditions affecting peripheral nerves. For the nerve conduction portion of the procedure, a stimulating electrode that delivers a mild electrical charge is placed on the skin over a nerve. An electrode placed over a muscle records the activity of the nerve distally at the nerve-muscle junction. Electromyography makes it possible to identify defects in the transmission of impulses from nerves to muscles. It may be used in the diagnosis of a number of neuromuscular disorders and peripheral nerve injuries.

Neuropsychological Tests

Neuropsychological tests are procedures that may be used to assess major functional areas of the brain and may be used when an individual has a cognitive impairment. Information gained from these tests may be used for diagnosis, monitoring changes, or for planning. In addition to assessing cognitive processes, most neuropsychological tests also assess perceptual and motor skills.

TREATMENT

Neurological disorders have widespread effects. Physical deficits can prevent the individual with such a disorder from performing even routine self-care. Problems with speech may alter means of communication. Emotional lability or cognitive deficits may interfere with productive activity. The symptoms of some conditions of the nervous system, such as epilepsy, can be controlled with medication. Other conditions, such as multiple sclerosis and Parkinson's disease, involve progressive deterioration, and treatment must focus on counteracting symptoms, preventing complications, and promoting function and independence as long as possible. When there has been permanent damage to the nervous system, such as that caused by head injury or spinal cord injury, the treatment is directed toward rehabilitation and prevention of complications.

In many instances, the treatment of nervous system disorders involves helping individuals to compensate for neurological deficits or to learn alternative methods of performing routine tasks. Assistive devices, such as canes, braces, and wheelchairs, may be indicated for individuals with special motor needs. Other means of assistance for individuals with neurological disorders that interfere with motor function are "help animals," such as dogs or monkeys that have been especially trained to retrieve various items or to perform other tasks that are difficult or impossible for an individual with a neurological disorder.

Traumatic Brain Injury

The initial treatment after a traumatic brain injury is intended to stabilize the condition and to enhance the recovery process. Special attention is given to maintaining the individual's nutritional status and preventing complications, such as infections and contractures. Careful observation is essential to detect early signs of increased intracranial pressure, which, unless relieved, can cause additional damage or even death. Intracranial pressure is monitored by inserting a catheter through the skull into a ventricle of the brain, into the subarachnoid space around the brain, or into the epidural space around the brain.

The treatment of increased intracranial pressure can be surgical or nonsurgical. Surgical intervention may involve the placement of a shunt that allows excess cerebrospinal fluid to drain into the general body circulation. If the individual has an open skull fracture, surgery may be necessary to remove fragments of bone or other foreign materials and to repair the skull. When a blood clot (e.g., a subdural or epidural hematoma) or hemorrhage is responsible for the increased intracranial pressure, two small holes (**burr holes**) may be placed in the skull and the blood clot removed or the bleeding controlled. In other instances, individuals with these injuries may undergo a **craniotomy**, a surgical procedure in which the skull is opened and the clot or foreign object removed or bleeding controlled through the surgical incision. Nonsurgical interventions for increased intracranial pressure consist of giving medications such as **diuretics** that remove fluid from the brain, thus helping to relieve the pressure. Steroids may also be used, although the exact reason that they work is unknown.

After the condition has stabilized, appropriate treatment requires early and active intervention by a complete interdisciplinary team that includes specialists in physical and occupational therapy, speech and language therapy, psychological evaluation and therapy, and cognitive retraining. In the early phases of brain injury, physical therapy focuses on activities to prevent joint and muscular complications. Later, physical therapy may be directed toward improving balance, muscle control, and ambulation and other physical movements. Occupational therapy may help brain-injured individuals to integrate available sensory information so that they can use it as a basis for motor activity and to increase their ability to perform the activities of daily living. Individuals may also need assistance to increase their awareness or orientation to time, place, and person. Speech and language therapies may focus on the mechanical difficulties of speech, as well as on the formation and execution of language, or on the development of alternative communication systems. Psychotherapy may be directed toward both the individual and the family in order to facilitate the adjustment process.

Often, cognitive deficits, rather than physical deficits, hamper the effective daily functioning of brain-injured individuals. In these instances, cognitive remediation strategies that are designed to ameliorate sensory/perceptual, language-related, and problem-solving deficits of brain-injured individuals may be a major focus of the rehabilitation effort. The goal of therapy is to return the individual to as much independent functioning as possible in as many areas as possible. Depending on the individual and the extent of the brain damage, long-term supportive care may be needed. If the individual is unable to return to the community, placement in a skilled nursing or extended care facility may be necessary.

Brain-injured individuals who are medically stable and have good potential for independent living may be placed in residential community reentry or transitional living programs. These programs may offer therapies designed to improve the functioning of these individuals and to develop their social behaviors, or they may provide care and supervision for those who require some assistance in meeting basic needs, as in a supervised living arrangement.

Cerebral Vascular Accident

Many aspects of the treatment of traumatic brain injury also apply to the treatment of cerebral vascular accidents. Because the latter are often precipitated by another disease process, such as hypertension and arteriosclerosis, one aspect of treatment is to prevent a second stroke by treating the underlying cause: treatment of hypertension with the administration of **antihypertensive** medications (see Chapter 2); reduction of clot formation through the administration of **anticoagulants** (see Chapter 2); or decrease of overall risk by avoiding tobacco, controlling weight, and living a generally healthy life style. A surgical procedure called an **endarterectomy** may be performed to open clogged arteries and clean out obstructing arteriosclerotic material.

As with traumatic brain injury, the immediate treatment of stroke is directed toward stabilizing the condition and preventing complications. Although many individuals have minimal deficits after a stroke, many others experience hemiplegia and need special instruction in ambulation techniques (**gait training**). Braces or splints may be necessary to help these individuals increase their functional capacity and become independent (see Chapter 7). The use of special tools (e.g., cups, spoons, and pencils) may be of help in daily living activities. As a stroke frequently impairs speech and language, a speech pathologist may help the individual with both verbal and nonverbal communication. The speech pathologist can also help those around the individual learn techniques to maximize communication and ways to structure the environment to maximize communication effectiveness. In some instances, alternative methods of communication, such as writing or using a picture board, may be used.

Individuals with hemiplegia may have a prescribed exercise program in order to maintain the range of motion of the joints and prevent complications. Because the weight of a paralyzed arm can cause a separation of the shoulder joint (**subluxation**), individuals with this condition may wear a sling to support the arm. The paralysis of an arm may also necessitate special feeding aids, such as a plate guard to keep food from sliding off the plate.

Epilepsy

The treatment of epilepsy is dependent on the cause of the seizure activity and the types of seizures experienced. The standard treatment of most types of epileptic seizures is the regular use of one or more **anticonvulsant** or **anti-epileptic** medications. Although the medications do not cure epilepsy, they can effectively control seizures and permit many individuals to carry on full and productive lives. Often, however, the successful control of seizures requires the individual's strict, long-term compliance with medication instructions.

The medication is prescribed according to what type of seizure the individual experiences and whether the individual has more than one type of seizure. The physician monitors the levels of the medication in the blood periodically and may alter medication dosages on occasion, depending on the blood levels and the effectiveness of the current medication in controlling seizure activity. In some cases, even when individuals take anticonvulsants regularly, seizure activity remains uncontrolled. Individuals on anticonvulsants should never discontinue their medication abruptly because of the danger of continuous seizures (**status epilepticus**), which is life-threatening. Because alcohol lowers seizure threshold and therefore could precipitate seizures, individuals who have epilepsy should avoid alcohol.

If seizures are caused by a tumor, scar tissue, or another abnormality that can be corrected, surgical intervention (e.g., craniotomy) may be indicated. Individuals often continue to need anticonvulsant medications even after surgery, however.

Individuals with epilepsy should be helped to identify the factors that may trigger a seizure. They should also avoid activity that would be hazardous if a seizure should occur, such as swimming alone or operating heavy equipment. Individuals with epilepsy should also wear a medical identification bracelet at all times.

Multiple Sclerosis

There is no specific therapy for multiple sclerosis. The treatment is usually directed toward controlling symptoms and preventing exacerbations and complications. In general, individuals with multiple sclerosis should remain as active as they can without developing excessive fatigue. Steroids do not affect the progression of the disease, but they may be prescribed during exacerbations to suppress the symptoms. Because of their potential effects, however, steroids cannot be taken over long periods of time.

If individuals experience muscle spasm, **muscle relaxant**s or **antispasmodics** may be prescribed. Specific exercises that help to decrease calcium loss from bones, strengthen weak muscles, and maintain muscle strength and joint mobility may also be prescribed. Physical therapy that includes massage and passive range-of-motion exercises may also be beneficial. Physical therapy may be prescribed to help individuals with problems of mobility or with the use of assistive devices, such as walkers. Individuals with multiple sclerosis who experience speech problems may have phonation exercises prescribed, or they may use assistive devices, such as a communication board and voice amplifier.

Anticholinergic medications, which inhibit the effect of the parasympathetic nervous system, are sometimes helpful in relieving bladder symptoms such as frequency and urgency. Conversely, **cholinergic** medications, which stimulate the effect of the parasympathetic nervous system, may be helpful in relieving urinary retention. Some individuals may have to learn to insert a catheter into their bladder in order to drain accumulated urine.

Parkinson's Disease

Currently, there is no cure for Parkinson's disease; however, the administration of a medication called **L-dopa** (Sinemet) frequently decreases its symptoms. L-dopa works by helping to increase the level of the neurotransmitter dopamine in the brain. Small amounts are usually prescribed at first, and the dosage is gradually increased. Some individuals may experience side-effects, such as nausea or abnormal involuntary movements called **dyskinesia**. These effects are generally related to the dosage of the medication, occurring more frequently with higher dosages. In some individuals, L-dopa causes mental confusion or decreases alertness.

Exercise and activity are especially important for individuals with Parkinson's disease because of the tendency of the muscles to be stiff and rigid. The muscles can atrophy without the stimulation that exercise provides, decreasing the individual's ability for self-care. Other aspects of treatment are directed toward preventing complications, such as infection. Surgical intervention for Parkinson's disease fell out of favor with the introduction of new and improved medications in the 1960s, but recently developed surgical approaches in which tissue from the adrenal medulla is transplanted into the brain in order to generate additional dopamine have gained attention. At present, however, the risks and benefits of this type of surgery are still being debated.

Spinal Cord Injuries

The initial treatment of spinal cord injuries focuses on stabilizing the individual's physical condition. Individuals with injuries to the cervical spine are usually placed in skeletal traction in order to immobilize the spine (see Chapter 7). In some instances, cervical orthoses, such as a **halo brace**, may be used to allow mobility while keeping the head and neck in proper position. Metal pins are inserted into the skull and attached to a metal "halo" that surrounds the head. The halo is attached with two metal rods to a "vest" worn on the torso of the individual. Traction is usually not used to stabilize and immobilize thoracic or lumbar fractures because there is no effective way to provide it.

Physical therapy begins as soon as possible in order to prevent deformities, such as contractures or footdrop. An immediate treatment goal for individuals with either paraplegia or quadriplegia is to place them in an upright position as soon as possible in order to prevent complications such as respiratory problems. This is done with a device called a tilt board or circular bed. The individual is strapped securely to the board or bed while in a prone position. The board is gradually raised or the circular bed rotated until the individual is upright.

As the individual's condition stabilizes, treatment is directed toward teaching self-care. Most individuals with a spinal cord injury become mobile with a wheelchair. Many types are available with a variety of options, including detachable armrests and footrests, removable back panel, lapboard, and carryall bag. Power-operated wheelchairs are available for individuals who have little or no use of their upper extremities; they are battery-operated and can be controlled with a switch adapted to the particular individual's ability. Because of the size of the battery, power-operated wheelchairs are heavy and, therefore, difficult to transport.

Individuals are taught a variety of self-care skills, including dressing, hygiene, and grooming. It may be necessary to install specific adaptive devices, such as grab bars and a raised toilet seat, in the home. Because most spinal cord injuries affect bladder and bowel function, instructions in catheter care and bowel retraining may also be helpful. Most individuals are eventually able to control bowel movements by conditioned reflex activity.

FUNCTIONAL IMPLICATIONS

Psychological Issues

The adjustment to any chronic illness or disability can be a difficult process. Individuals with neurological disorders may face particular challenges, because their disorders affect many different areas of function. As with all disabling conditions, psychological reactions are individually determined, based in part on the way in which the individual has dealt with life problems in the past. Individuals with traumatic brain injury, stroke, or multiple sclerosis may have cognitive and emotional impairments, as well as motor function impairments, as a direct result of their injury or disease. Because they need to learn compensatory strategies for a number of activities and social interactions, their psychological adaptation to the disorder becomes multifaceted. It is often difficult to determine the degree to which behavioral and affective changes are physiological and the degree to which they are situationally induced.

For many neurological conditions, the available treatment is limited and directed mainly toward control of symptoms or prevention of complications. As a result, individuals with these conditions may feel that they have little control over their condition or their future. When a condition is progressively debilitating, as multiple sclerosis and Parkinson's disease are, individuals must continually readjust as additional functional capacity is lost. Under these circumstances, they may experience a helpless rage or bitterness at being afflicted with a condition over which they have no control. The rate of progression and degree of loss of functional capacity are often unpredictable, and the substantial uncertainty about whether they will have minimal disability or will progress to a wheelchair or bed can produce stress and hardship for these individuals. Although the use of a wheelchair can provide mobility and an added sense of freedom and independence, some individuals have a negative emotional reaction to the wheelchair, viewing it as a symbol of lost function.

Often, conditions of the nervous system not only impose permanent loss of functional capacity, but also involve complex self-concept and body image changes. Traumatic brain injury, stroke, and spinal cord injury provide no time for gradual adjustment; previously active individuals are suddenly disabled, losing both their functional capacity in many areas and their former physical appearance. Individuals may react with hostility, depression, anger, or withdrawal.

Those injured through accidents may feel remorse or self-recrimination for their failure to prevent the accident that resulted in their disability. If the accident was the fault of another, the injured individual may feel chronic anger toward the offender or may turn the anger inward, with resultant depression. In some instances, the quest for retribution becomes a negative force, eroding the life of the individual who is seeking some kind of justice. In other cases, however, the quest for retribution becomes a positive force directed toward a possible broader social issue, such as seat belts in automobiles, helmets for motorcyclists, or laws against drunk driving.

By their very nature, the symptoms of many neurological conditions necessitate assistance in care and function. Individuals may harbor resentment over the dependency imposed by the condition. They may feel an increased sense of vulnerability, especially when paralysis is involved, fearing that escaping from a dangerous situation or defending themselves against threat would be difficult or impossible. Individuals' reactions may vary from overdependence to overcompensation, in which they take unnecessary risks in order to test or prove their independence and strength.

Most individuals with neurological disorders learn to be self-reliant, despite the fact that their ability to care for their most basic physical needs is decreased. The loss of this capacity is difficult to accept. Learning to accept the necessary assistance of others for basic needs, such as feeding, personal hygiene, and bowel and bladder care, requires reconstituting views of privacy and self-reliance. The impairment of bladder and bowel control may be an especially difficult area of adjustment. Not only are such activities private and mishaps a potential source of embarrassment, but both may also be associated with shame and humiliation experienced in early childhood when control of these most basic body functions is a central issue of development.

Life Style Issues

The effects of neurological disorders on an individual's life style are varied and complex. The activities of daily living are often altered in that help from family members or other individuals is necessary. The subsequent loss of privacy for the most intimate details of daily life, such as bathing or other aspects of self-care, may be part of the general condition. Even when individuals are able to manage their own personal care, the additional time required to carry out most activities may be considered a liability. Special adaptations within the environment, such as widening doorways for wheelchairs, lowering countertops in kitchens, raising toilet seats, and adding ramps and railings, may be necessary, especially if the individual uses a wheelchair or other assistive device.

Although not all neurological conditions require the use of a wheelchair, most require some consideration of environmental factors. For example, individuals with epilepsy may need to avoid environmental factors (e.g., flashing lights) that may precipitate seizures. Because individuals with multiple sclerosis may be especially sensitive to hot, humid conditions, they may need to remain in a cool environment with decreased humidity. Individuals with balance or coordination problems caused by brain injury may need to avoid situations in which they may fall or be thrown off balance.

Alterations in daily schedules and routines may be necessary to allow additional time for dressing, bathing, and other self-care needs. The accessibility of the environment often determines the ease of movement from place to place if wheelchairs are utilized. Wheelchairs can provide more freedom of movement for those who are paralyzed, for those who have difficulty in walking because of problems with coordination, or for those who fatigue easily and use the wheelchair to conserve energy. Freedom of movement is limited, however, if there are stairs, but no elevator; bathrooms that are too small to accommodate a wheelchair; or public transportation without lifts or mechanisms for transporting individuals in wheelchairs.

Individuals who have neurological disorders can usually drive, even if there is paralysis, if the vehicle is equipped with special controls. If the disability includes cognitive or perceptual deficits, however, driving may not be possible. Although regulations vary from state to state, individuals with epilepsy may have to demonstrate that they have been seizure-free or that medication has adequately controlled their seizures over a number of months or years before they are permitted to drive a motor vehicle.

When fatigue exacerbates the symptoms of a neurological disorder, as in multiple sclerosis, or when fatigue is part of the symptomatology, as in post-polio syndrome, it may be necessary to space out activities or to arrange for frequent rest periods during the day. It is sometimes helpful to divide activities that were once completed in a short amount of time into a series of subsections of tasks, allowing rest periods in between.

A number of conditions of the nervous system may lead to sexual difficulties. Generally, physiological responses require an intact nervous system. Sexual function may be most disrupted by spinal cord injury. Although women with a spinal cord injury are still capable of intercourse, sensory loss in the genitals is common in both men and women. Men may still experience reflex erections, but are usually incapable of psychologically stimulated erections. Reproductive function may also be a concern after a spinal cord injury. Women with such an injury generally remain fertile and are capable of conceiving and delivering a child. Men with a spinal cord injury may be infertile, however, because of the inability to ejaculate, retrograde ejaculation, or decreased sperm formation.

Conditions that involve spasticity, such as cerebral palsy or multiple sclerosis, may make sexual intercourse more difficult. In some instances, the stimulation and arousal experienced as a part of sexual excitement may make the spasms worse. Women with multiple sclerosis may still be able to conceive and deliver a child, although the pregnancy itself sometimes exacerbates symptoms. Some individuals with brain damage may exhibit sexual disinhibition and must learn to substitute appropriate social behaviors.

Sexuality is more than genital acts. Some form of sexual expression is possible for almost all individuals with a disability. Although the loss or alteration of sexual function is initially a severe blow to their self-esteem and sense of attractiveness, these individuals can express their sexual and intimacy needs through a variety of alternate means. Individuals with neurological disorders can develop long-term interpersonal relationships that include love, respect, and a mutually satisfying expression of sexual feelings.

The financial impact of many neurological diseases can be devastating. The cost of medical care, rehabilitation, assistive devices, and environmental restructuring can be great. The costs and financial adjustments that must be made have a significant impact on the individual's general life style.

Social Issues

Many factors associated with disorders of the nervous system may affect social function. A supportive environment, including family, plays an instrumental role in an individual's response to the disorder. Some barriers to effective social interaction may result from others' misinterpretation or misperception of the individual's limitations, however. Although some limitations associated with neurological disorders are visible, such as the mobility restrictions indicated by the use of a wheelchair, others are not so readily recognizable. The fatigue experienced in multiple sclerosis, the visual or perceptual problems experienced with brain injury or stroke, or the difficulty with bladder control may create a conflict of expectations; others may characterize the behavior as laziness or attempts to avoid work, clumsiness, or neurotic preoccupation with the location of restroom facilities. If cognitive deficits that involve emotional lability, memory, attention, or judgment are part of the "invisible" disability, others may perceive these individuals as insensitive, rude, or irresponsible. When the neurological disorder affects gait or balance, or results in slurred speech, others may misinterpret the symptoms as intoxication, even though the individual may abstain from alcohol.

In addition to the stigma that is often attached to disability, some conditions have myths or misinformation attached. Individuals with epilepsy, for example, may encounter this type of social stigma. Seizures can frighten those who observe them. Not understanding the nature of the disability or of the seizure itself, people may avoid social contact with those who have epilepsy so as to also avoid the possibility of witnessing a seizure. Individuals with communication difficulties or a social skills deficit because of brain damage may also be avoided in social settings because of discomfort and misunderstanding about the condition.

All chronic illness and disability affect family members and social interactions. Family members may react by becoming overly protective, taking away the individual's own sense of responsibility. Family members may find it difficult to express anger toward the individual and may essentially exclude him or her from the family structure and interactions. At times, some of the symptoms or behaviors manifested in the neurological disorder may be more troublesome to others than to the individual. If extended assistance in care is needed, the individual may fear becoming a burden on family members and may withdraw from close personal interactions with others in order to avoid the pain of possible resentment or later rejection.

The use of a wheelchair may also affect social function. Not all social events are accessible to the individual in a wheelchair, who must, therefore, either avoid the activity or make special arrangements in order to attend it. In addition, the different angle of eye contact can create multiple emotional impacts for individuals in wheelchairs, who must continually look upward at their peers. This can create an impression of differing social stature, both in the individuals and in those with whom they engage in conversation.

Individuals who display an impaired capacity for social perceptiveness, an absence of social initiation, or behavior problems (e.g., disinhibition or impulsivity) may need social skills training or continuing supervision in the social setting. Distractibility, which may be a manifestation of brain damage, may also disrupt social interaction.

The social interaction difficulties associated with neurological disorders may be manifest in social performance, social anxiety, and self-esteem. The individual with such a disorder may experience considerable frustration, as well as lowered self-esteem and self-assurance, in the struggle to cope with social demands.

Vocational Issues

The capabilities of individuals with disorders of the nervous system vary widely, depending on the nature of the disorder. For progressive conditions or those that are characterized by remissions and exacerbations, such as multiple sclerosis, ongoing evaluation of limitations and remaining function is necessary. For other conditions, such as spinal cord injury or brain injury in which the damage is permanent, but not progressive, the initial evaluation of capabilities and remaining function may suffice.

Brain damage affects a number of functions, all of which should be assessed. Not only should cognitive functions, such as memory, problem-solving ability, and spatial and temporal orientation, be assessed, but also motor abilities, such as coordination, balance, speed of performance, and muscle dexterity, should be evaluated.

The degree of job stress is a factor to be considered for those with a number of neurological disorders. In some instances, stress in the work place may add to the fatigue that is part of the condition itself. In other instances, stress may precipitate symptoms, as it does in epilepsy or multiple sclerosis. Moreover, if individuals with poor motor speed or decreased processing ability are rushed or feel stressed, the quality of their work performance may suffer.

When the disorder affects an individual's communication skills, it may be necessary to establish alternate means of communication in the work place or to modify the job in order to incorporate this limitation. In many instances, even though the individual may be difficult to understand, patience and practice allow co-workers to establish basic patterns of communication that make interchange in the work place possible.

Some conditions have specific characteristics that must be considered in an assessment of the work place. For example, when working with individuals with epilepsy, it is important to assess the degree to which seizures are controlled and to identify whether any stimuli in the work environment may possibly precipitate seizures. Individuals with multiple sclerosis should avoid hot, humid environments. Those with high thoracic spinal cord injuries or cervical injuries should not be exposed to extremes of temperature, as they often have difficulty with body heat regulation. In addition, because of the loss of sensation in the extremities they should avoid situations in which there is a possibility of burn or frostbite. Individuals with spinal cord injuries, multiple sclerosis, or Parkinson's disease may be especially susceptible to upper respiratory problems; consequently, they must consider exposure to pollutants, upper respiratory infections, or other situations in the work place that could threaten respiratory function.

The accessibility of the work place must be evaluated for individuals who use a wheelchair. The availability of elevators as opposed to stairs, desk or workbench height, width of doorways, and size of bathrooms are all important environmental considerations.

In all instances, a realistic appreciation of the disability is particularly crucial for individuals with disorders of the nervous system. Others' expectations for performance may not match the individual's abilities. In addition to the disability itself, a variety of factors may interfere with the individual's reaching his or her full vocational potential. Such factors include the availability of transportation, environmental barriers in the work place, and stigma or misinformation regarding the disability.

BIBLIOGRAPHY

Ahlskog, J.E., and Wilkinson, J.M. "New Concepts in the Treatment of Parkinson's Disease." *American Family Physician* 41(1990):574–584.

Barber, T.C., and Langfitt, D.E. *Teaching the Medical/Surgical Patient—Diagnostics and Procedures.* Bowie, Md.: Robert J. Brady Co., 1983.

Berkow, R., and Fletcher, A.J., eds. *The Merck Manual of Diagnosis and Therapy.* Rahway, N.J.: Merck Sharpe and Dohme Research Laboratories, 1987.

Berry, S. "Rehabilitation Planning for the Severely Head Injured." *Journal of Applied Rehabilitation Counseling* 16(1985):46–48.

Braunling-McMorrow, D.; Lloyd, K.; and Fralish, K. "Teaching Social Skills to Head Injured Adults." *Journal of Rehabilitation* 52(1986):39–44.

Bressman, S.; and Fahn, S. "Parkinson's Disease." *Hospital Medicine* 23(1987):82–96.

Brunner, L.S.; Emerson, C.P.; Ferguson, L.K.; and Suddarth, D.S. *Textbook of Medical-Surgical Nursing.* Philadelphia: W.B. Saunders Co., 1970.

Burnfield, A., and Burnfield, P. "Common Psychological Problems in Multiple Sclerosis." *British Medical Journal* 1(1978):1193–1194.

Calesnick, B. "Selegiline for Parkinson's Disease." *American Family Physician* 41(1990):589–591.

Casas, M.S. "Experience in Coping with Stroke: A Survey of Caregivers." *Journal of Rehabilitation* 55(1989):37–43.

Cook, D.W.; Bolton, B.; and Taperek, P. "Rehabilitation of the Spinal Cord Injured: Life Status at Follow-up." *Rehabilitation Counseling Bulletin* 25(1981):110–121.

Corbett, J.V. *Diagnostic Procedures in Nursing Practice.* Norwalk, Conn.: Appleton-Century-Crofts, 1982.

Corbett, J.V. *Laboratory Tests in Nursing Practice.* Norwalk, Conn.: Appleton-Century-Crofts, 1983.

Devins, G.M., and Seland, T.P. "Emotional Impact of Multiple Sclerosis: Recent Findings and Suggestions for Future Research." *Psychological Bulletin* 101(1987):363–375.

Dew, M.A.; Lynch, K.; Ernst, J.; and Rosenthal, R. "Reaction and Adjustment to Spinal Cord Injury: A Descriptive Study." *Journal of Applied Rehabilitation Counseling* 14(1983):32–39.

Dreifuss, F.E.; Gallagher, B.B.; Leppik, I.E.; and Rothner, A.D. "Epilepsy: Management by Medication." *Patient Care* 22(1988):52–71.

Fowler, R.S., and Fordyce, W.E. *Stroke: Why Do They Behave That Way.* Dallas: American Heart Association, 1974.

Fraser, R.T. "A Needs Review in Epilepsy Rehabilitation: Toward Solutions in the 1980s." *Rehabilitation Literature* 44(1983):261–269.

Fraser, R.T., and Clemmons, D. "Epilepsy Rehabilitation: Assessment and Counseling Concerns." *Journal of Applied Rehabilitation Counseling* 14(1983):26–31.

Fraser, R.T.; McMahon, B.T.; and Vogenthaler, D.R. "Vocational Rehabilitation Counseling with Head-Injured Persons." In *Contemporary Challenges to the Rehabilitation Counseling Profession,* edited by S.E. Rubin and N.R. Rubin, 217–242. Baltimore: Brookes Publishing Co., 1988.

Frick, N.M., and Bruno, R.L. "Post-Polio Sequelae: Physiological and Psychological Overview." *Rehabilitation Literature* 47(1986):106–111.

Goldstein, G., and Hersen, M. *Handbook of Psychological Assessment.* New York: Pergamon Press. 1984.

Green, B.C.; Pratt, C.C.; and Grigsby, T.E. "Self-Concept among Persons with Long-Term Spinal Cord Injury." *Archives of Physical and Medical Rehabilitation* 65(1984):751–754.

Guyton, A.C. *Human Physiology and Mechanisms of Disease.* Philadelphia: W.B. Saunders Co., 1982.

Harrower, M. *Mental Health and MS.* New York: National Multiple Sclerosis Society, 1953.

Hill, J.A., and Kaasam, S.H. "Sexual Competence in Multiple Sclerosis." *Female Patient* 9(1984):81–84.

Holman, K.G. "Post-Polio Syndrome." *Postgraduate Medicine* 79(1986):44–53.

Jankovic, J.; Kurlan, R.M.; and Young, R.R. "Managing the Patient with Tremor." *Patient Care* 23(1989):33–38.

Keele, C.A.; Neil, E.; and Joels, N. *Samson Wright's Applied Physiology.* New York: Oxford University Press, 1982.

Kreed, M.M.; Kaplan, L.I.; Klinger, J.L.; and Strebel, M.B. "Improving Life for the Wheelchair User." *Patient Care* 18(1984):48–86.

Langston, J.W. "Parkinson's Disease: Current View." *American Family Physician* 35(1987):201–206.

Lehman, L.B. "Injury of the Cervical Spine." *Postgraduate Medicine* 82(1987):193–200.

Luckman, J., and Sorensen, K.C. *Medical-Surgical Nursing: A Psychophysiologic Approach.* Philadelphia: W.B. Saunders Co., 1987.

Mayer, T., and Andrews, H.B. "Changes in Self-Concept Following a Spinal Cord Injury." *Journal of Applied Rehabilitation Couseling* 12(1981):135–137.

McMahon, B.T., and Fraser, R.T. "Basic Issues and Trends in Head Injury Rehabilitation." In *Contemporary Challenges to the Rehabilitation Counseling Profession*, edited by S.E. Rubin and N.R. Rubin, 197–215. Baltimore: Brookes Publishing Co., 1988.

McSherry, J.A. "Cognitive Impairment after Head Injury." *American Family Physician* 40(1989): 186–190.

National Institute of Handicapped Research. "Neuromuscular Diseases." *Rehab Brief 11* (1988):1–4.

National Institute of Handicapped Research. "Stroke." *Rehab Brief 11* (1989):1–4.

Newton, A., and Johnson, D.A. "Social Adjustment and Interaction after Severe Head Injury." *British Journal of Clinical Psychology* 24(1985):225–234.

Nursing 87 Books. *Patient Teaching.* Springhouse, Pa.: Springhouse Corporation Book Division, 1987.

Ojemann, L.M., and Ojemann, G.A. "Treatment of Epilepsy." *American Family Physician* 30(1984):113–128.

Osokie, J.N. "Epilepsy: Implications for Rehabilitation." *Journal of Applied Rehabilitation Counseling* 15(1984):12–15.

Paty, D.W.; Poser, C.M.; and Schapiro, R.T. "The Challenge of Detecting MS." *Patient Care* 23(1989):62–75.

Raderstorf, M.; Hein, D.M.; and Jensen, C.S. "A Young Stroke Patient with Severe Aphasia Returns to Work: A Team Approach." *Journal of Rehabilitation* 50(1984):23–26.

Rakel, R.E. *Conn's Current Therapy 1990.* Philadelphia: W.B. Saunders Co., 1990.

Rothrock, J.; Taft, B.J.; and Lyden, P.D. "A New Approach to Stroke Management." *American Family Physician* 36(1989):189–197.

Scheer, S.J., ed. *Medical Perspectives in Vocational Assessment of Impaired Workers.* Gaithersburg, Md.: Aspen Publishers, 1991.

Schiebel, R.S., and Isensee, S. "Multiple Sclerosis." *Journal of Family Practice* 23(1986):543–550.

Schuchmann, J.A. "Stroke Rehabilitation." *Postgraduate Medicine* 74(1983):101–111.

Smith, D.W., and Hanley-Germain, C.P. *Care of the Adult Patient.* Philadelphia: J.B. Lippincott Co., 1975.

Stolov, W.C., and Clowers, M.R. *Handbook of Severe Disability.* Washington, D.C.: U.S. Department of Education, Rehabilitation Services Administration, 1981.

Sudarsky, L. "Management of Parkinson's Disease: 1987." *Medical Times* 115(1987):29–34.

Szekely, B.C.; Kosanovich, N.N.; and Shepphard, W. "Adjunctive Treatment in Parkinson's Disease: Physical Therapy and Comprehensive Group Therapy." *Rehabilitation Literature* 43(1982):72–76.

Torkelson, R.M.; Jellinek, H.M.; Malec, J.F.; and Harvey, R.F. "Traumatic Brain Injury: Psychological and Medical Factors Related to Rehabilitation Outcome." *Rehabilitation Psychology* 28(1983):169–176.

Vander, A.J.; Sherman, J.H.; and Luciano, D.S. *Human Physiology: The Mechanisms of Body Function*. New York: McGraw-Hill Book Co., 1985.

Vogenthaler, D.R. "Rehabilitation after Closed Head Injury: A Primer." *Journal of Rehabilitation* 53(1987):15–21.

Wedl, L. "Rehabilitation Counseling and Persons with Multiple Sclerosis." *Journal of Applied Rehabilitation Counseling* 5(1984):27–28.

Wehman, P., and Kreutzer, J.S. *Vocational Rehabilitation for Persons with Traumatic Brain Injury*. Gaithersburg, Md.: Aspen Publishers, 1990.

Wepman, J.W. *Aphasia and the Family*. Dallas: American Heart Association, 1966.

Wyngaarden, J.B., and Smith, J.H. *Cecil Textbook of Medicine*. Philadelphia: W.B. Saunders Co., 1988.

Zarski, J.J.; Hall, D.E.; and DePompei, R. "Closed Head Injury Patients: A Family Therapy Approach to the Rehabilitation Process." *American Journal of Family Therapy* 15(1987):62–68.

chapter 9

Hearing Disorders

NORMAL STRUCTURE AND FUNCTION

The ear consists of three divisions: the outer, middle, and inner ear (Figure 9-1). The **outer ear** includes the **auricle** and the **external ear canal**. The **auricle (pinna)**, the visible portion of the ear, is made up of elastic cartilage covered with skin; it functions to collect sound. The **external ear canal** is a little longer than 1 inch and extends from the opening of the ear to the eardrum. It contains special glands that produce **cerumen** (earwax), which protects the ear against the entry of foreign material. Behind the outer ear in the temporal bone is a bony prominence called the **mastoid process**; it contains many air cells, each of which connects directly to the middle ear.

The middle ear **(tympanic cavity)** is located in the temporal bone of the skull. It is separated from the outer ear by the **tympanic membrane** (eardrum). The tympanic cavity is an air-filled cavity that is connected to the throat by the **eustachian tube**. Normally, the eustachian tube opens with yawning or swallowing in order to equalize the air pressure in the middle ear to that of atmospheric pressure.

Three small movable bones **(ossicles)** are located in the middle ear: the malleus, the incus, and the stapes. The chained movement of these small bones conducts sound vibrations from the eardrum to the inner ear. The **malleus** sits on the upper portion of the eardrum. The opposite end of the malleus connects to the **incus**, which is joined to the neck of the **stapes**. The foot of the stapes fits into an opening called the **oval window**, which communicates with the inner ear.

The **inner ear (labyrinth)** is a fluid-filled cavity lying deep within the temporal bone of the skull. The inner ear is important not only for hearing (as part of the **auditory system**), but also for maintaining body balance and equilibrium (as part of the **vestibular system**). Impulses from both the auditory system and the

219

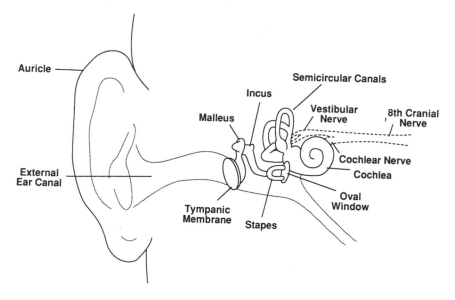

Figure 9-1 The Outer, Middle, and Inner Ear.

vestibular system are converted into nerve impulses and transmitted from the inner ear to the brain by the **eighth cranial nerve**, sometimes called the **acoustic** or **auditory nerve**. The acoustic nerve has two parts: the **cochlear nerve branch**, which conducts sensory information about sound, and the **vestibular nerve branch**, which conducts impulses regarding body balance and movement.

The oval window opens into the **vestibule** (chamber) of the inner ear. The vestibule communicates with two fluid-filled chambers of the inner ear: the **cochlea**, which is part of the auditory system, and the **semicircular canals**, which are part of the vestibular system.

The cochlea has a snail-like appearance and contains tiny hair cells within the **organ of Corti**, the end organ for hearing. Sound waves enter the external ear and move through the external ear canal to the eardrum, causing it to vibrate. The vibration of the eardrum moves the malleus, which transmits the vibration to the incus; in turn, the incus transmits the vibration to the stapes. The stapes vibration moves the fluid in the vestibule and the sensory portion of the cochlea, which stimulates the tiny hair cells in the organ of Corti. The movement of the hair cells stimulates the nerve endings located around their bases to transmit impulses to the cochlear nerve, which carries the impulses to the auditory center of the brain.

The semicircular canals contain the nerve endings through which balance is controlled. Like the organ of Corti, they contain numerous hair cells that project into the fluid of the inner ear. The movement of the head sets the fluid in motion and moves the hair cells, stimulating the nerve endings, which then transmit the impulses to the vestibular nerve. These impulses are carried to the portion of the brain that is involved with maintaining equilibrium and coordinating movement.

HEARING DISORDERS

Types of Hearing Disorders

A **hearing impairment** is a hearing loss of any degree and type, while **deafness** is the inability to discriminate conversational speech through the ear. Deafness is the most severe type of hearing impairment.

There are three types of hearing impairments: conductive, sensorineural, and mixed. In **conductive hearing impairments**, an obstruction or defect in the external or middle ear prevents sound waves from reaching the cochlea in the inner ear. In most cases, correction of the underlying problem can restore diminished hearing. A conductive loss alters the loudness of sound, but does not reduce its clarity. Therefore, when the cause of a conductive hearing impairment cannot be corrected, hearing aids may be used to amplify sound and restore normal loudness. Conductive hearing losses are generally moderate types of losses.

In **sensorineural hearing impairments**, there is some interference with either the reception or the transmission of nerve impulses—or both—so that sound is not perceived. The problem may be due to a disorder of the cochlea or of the eighth cranial (auditory) nerve, which carries impulses to the brain, or to a disorder of the auditory centers of the brain. Sensorineural damage can lead to total deafness. If the hearing impairment results from damage to the auditory processing system of the brain, as may be experienced with trauma or stroke, the individual is said to have **central deafness**. Sensorineural hearing impairments are almost exclusively irreversible. Because some sensorineural losses may reduce clarity without much or any change in loudness, hearing aids may not be of assistance.

In **mixed hearing impairments**, there is a combination of conductive hearing loss and sensorineural hearing loss. The conductive component is often treatable, but the sensorineural component is usually not treatable. Consequently, the extent of the hearing loss experienced with mixed hearing impairments and the success of intervention depend on the degree and type of sensorineural damage.

Hearing loss may also be categorized by the age of onset. A **prelingual** hearing loss occurs before the individual acquires language, usually before the age of 3. A **prevocational** hearing loss occurs after the individual acquires language, but before he or she enters the work force. Hearing impairments that occur after the individual has started to work are categorized as **postvocational** hearing losses.

Hearing impairments may be congenital or acquired. **Congenital hearing loss** is present at birth. The major causes of congenital hearing loss are genetic transmission, the mother's ingestion of drugs that are harmful to the developing auditory system of the fetus, or prenatal exposure to rubella. Inherited hearing impairments may be part of specific genetically linked conditions that involve a variety of other abnormalities, or they may be isolated. The degree, progression, and age of onset of inherited hearing impairments vary widely, depending on the specific condition or syndrome.

Acquired hearing loss occurs after birth or later in life. Premature birth can be a cause of very early hearing loss, while recurrent ear infections (e.g., otitis media) with complications often cause conductive hearing loss in young children. Noise-induced hearing loss is a common, but preventable, type of acquired hearing loss. Avoiding loud noises or wearing ear protectors when exposed to loud noise could drastically reduce the incidence of noise-induced hearing loss. **Presbycusis** (hearing loss associated with aging) is an acquired hearing loss. The extent to which the degeneration of portions of the auditory system as part of the aging process or cumulative noise trauma throughout life causes presbycusis is unknown.

The type and degree of hearing impairment experienced with hearing loss, regardless of the cause, is varied. Hearing impairments usually involve more than a reduction in the loudness of sound. Some hearing impairments also result in a distortion of sound so that words may be heard, but are difficult to understand or garbled. In this case, increasing the loudness is unlikely to enhance the individual's ability to understand what is being said.

Hearing loss may lead to **recruitment**, a symptom characterized by an abnormally rapid increase in the perception of loudness with small changes in signal energy. In the recruiting ear, there is a narrow range between a level of sound that is loud enough to be understood and a level of sound that is loud enough to cause discomfort or pain. Individuals with recruitment cannot tolerate loud sounds. Unexpected sounds may startle them and distract them from the interpretation of the sounds' meaning. Therefore, increasing the loudness of sound does not correct the individual's hearing problem, and can actually cause considerable discomfort.

Conditions That Affect the Outer Ear

Although conditions of the outer ear may not have a major impact on hearing, conditions that are disfiguring can cause cosmetic concerns. Deformities of the outer ear may result from congenital conditions or from trauma.

Deformities or abnormalities that obstruct the external ear canal can interfere with the transmission of sound in the middle ear, decreasing the acuity of hearing. A buildup of earwax, foreign bodies in the ears, and growths (e.g., polyps) may cause such an obstruction.

For the most part, partial occlusion of the external ear canal has no influence on the efficiency of sound transmission and causes no hearing loss. Complete occlusion, however, generally results in a moderate conductive loss. Conditions of the outer ear that cause temporary conductive hearing impairments can usually be corrected or alleviated by surgical or mechanical intervention.

Conditions That Affect the Middle Ear

Conditions of the middle ear may cause temporary or permanent hearing impairment. A **perforated tympanic membrane** (ruptured eardrum) may or may not impair hearing. Rupture of the eardrum may result from an injury (e.g., a blow to the ear or head, or an explosion) or from **otitis media** (infection of the middle ear).

Although otitis media is the most common cause of conductive hearing loss, a condition called **otosclerosis** may also cause a conductive impairment when the eardrum is still intact. The linkage of the ossicular bridge of bone that transmits sound impulses to the inner ear becomes hardened, reducing the efficiency of the transfer of sound impulses to the inner ear. Otosclerosis appears in part to be hereditary. Hearing can often be restored or improved with surgical intervention. Furthermore, in almost all instances, the use of hearing aids effectively restores normal hearing.

Mastoiditis, another cause of hearing impairment, is not as prevalent as it once was because of the earlier detection of otitis media and treatment with antibiotics. **Mastoiditis** is an infection of the mastoid cells within the mastoid process located in the skull. Because of the proximity of the mastoid cells to other important structures in the head, mastoiditis may lead to a number of complications, including paralysis of the facial muscles and infection or abscess of the brain. Chronic mastoiditis and associated complications may be the result of previously untreated ear infections.

Conditions That Affect the Inner Ear

Many conditions of the inner ear cause permanent hearing loss. One condition, **labyrinthitis** (inflammation of the labyrinth of the inner ear), may be acute without resulting in permanent hearing loss. Labyrinthitis may occur as a complication of otitis media, influenza, or upper respiratory infections. Because the inner ear is involved, symptoms of **vertigo** (dizziness), nausea, and vomiting frequently accompany the condition.

Ménière's disease is a disorder of the inner ear that encompasses the triad of recurrent severe vertigo, hearing loss, and **tinnitus** (noise or ringing in the ears). The cause of Ménière's disease is unknown. One or both ears may be affected. Vertigo usually appears suddenly and is often accompanied by nausea and vomiting. Tinnitus may be intermittent, or it may be constant, even between attacks, and become worse during an attack. The hearing loss associated with Ménière's disease is variable. Typically, the loss becomes progressively greater with repeated active phases. The lower tones may be affected at first, but all tones are affected as the disease progresses.

Hearing loss may also result from damage to the inner ear or to the acoustic nerve. Among the causes of sensorineural deafness are traumatic head injury or stroke; hypertension and arteriosclerosis, which produce vascular changes in the central nervous system; exposure to high levels of noise, which can damage the hair cells in the inner ear; the ingestion of **ototoxic agents** (drugs or other chemicals that destroy the hair cells of the inner ear or damage the eighth cranial nerve); and infections, such as meningitis. Growths or tumors inside the head may cause hearing loss by mechanically impinging on the acoustic nerve or by involving it directly.

Presbycusis is caused by degenerative changes in the inner ear, neural pathways, or both; however, the reason that presbycusis occurs is unknown. The onset is slow, and the loss can vary in degree from mild to severe. The ability to hear higher tonal frequencies is usually affected first, but the ability to hear lower frequencies is gradually affected as well. The hearing loss experienced with presbycusis most often reduces word discrimination or understanding because of interference with the higher pitched consonants that control understanding.

DIAGNOSTIC PROCEDURES

Identification of Hearing Deficits

Before a hearing loss can be evaluated or treated, it must be identified. Individuals with hearing impairments may not be aware of the degree of loss, or they may deny that they have a hearing impairment. An important tool in the diagnosis of hearing loss may be simple observation of behaviors that may be indicative of such an impairment.

The indications of a possible hearing problem in infants and small children include unresponsiveness to sound, delayed development of speech, and behavior problems (e.g., tantrums, inattention, and hyperactivity). School-aged children with undiagnosed hearing impairments may have speech impairments, may demonstrate attentional disorders, or may demonstrate below average ability in school.

Adults with undiagnosed hearing impairments may be irritable, hostile, or hypersensitive. They may deny their inability to understand or respond appropriately by blaming others for not enunciating distinctly. They often have a tendency to avoid situations in which hearing is more difficult, such as events that involve crowds or large groups. Individuals with undiagnosed hearing impairments may also speak in excessively loud tones and may require increased volume to hear the television and radio.

Heightened sensitivity and patience are often necessary when encouraging individuals with a suspected hearing loss to obtain evaluation and treatment. An initial resistance to these recommendations is not unusual.

Use of Tuning Forks

Physicians sometimes use tuning forks in routine physical examinations in their offices as a cursory, initial screening method for hearing impairments. Although this method may reveal the existence of conductive or sensorineural hearing disorders, it does not quantify the degree of impairment. Because of the gross nature of this screening method, it has been widely replaced by other methods.

Tuning forks can be used as a screening method to detect problems in both air conduction and bone conduction of sound. The ability to hear by air conduction is tested by placing a vibrating tuning fork in the air near the ear, but out of the individual's sight. The inability to hear the sound is an indication of a hearing loss that requires further evaluation. Hearing by bone conduction is evaluated by placing a vibrating tuning fork in different positions on the individual's skull, which causes vibration throughout the skull, including the inner ear. Both conductive and sensorineural impairments can be detected in this manner. An abnormal test result warrants further testing and evaluation.

Audiometric Testing

In audiometric testing, the degree of hearing loss is measured with an electronic device called an **audiometer**. An **audiologist**, a person with a master's degree who specializes in the evaluation and rehabilitation of individuals with hearing disorders, usually performs the test.

Tonal Audiometry

An audiometer emits sounds (pure tones) through earphones worn by the individual being tested. As the tones are transmitted through the earphones, the individual indicates when he or she first hears sound. The individual's responses to the calibrated tones are plotted as thresholds on a graph called a **pure tone audiogram**. The test takes place in a sound-proof booth to eliminate distracting sounds.

Audiometric testing measures the ear's ability to detect and discriminate changes in sound intensity or loudness. Changes in sound intensity are measured in **decibels** and heard as changes in loudness. Changes in sound frequency are measured in **hertz** and heard as changes in pitch. The individual's ability to detect and discriminate sound intensity and pitch in each ear is plotted on the audiogram (Figure 9-2).

The numbers along the side of the audiogram represent intensity in decibels and range from −10 to 110 decibels. The hearing level scale is constructed so that average normal hearing equals 0 decibel; normal hearing sensitivity ranges from −10 to 25 decibels. The higher the number on the decibel scale, the greater the degree of hearing loss. The numbers across the top of the audiogram, ranging from 125 to 8,000 hertz, represent the tonal frequencies used to test hearing. **Speech frequencies** range from 250 to 8,000 hertz. The inability to discriminate frequencies within this range interferes with everyday communication for children. Adults who have had normal hearing and have developed a rich language system can hear and understand speech over a more restricted range (approximately 500 to 2,000 hertz).

When audiometric testing reveals a hearing loss, the audiologist conducts further testing to determine whether the hearing loss is sensorineural, conductive, or mixed. Tests used for this purpose include pure tone bone conduction tests and impedance audiometry. The procedure for **bone conduction audiometry** is similar to that for air conduction audiometry, except that a vibrator rather than an earphone set is placed on the individual's mastoid process. Calibrated tones are then transmitted through the vibrator directly into the inner ear, bypassing the external and middle ear systems. The individual's responses to the thresholds are plotted on the audiogram and contrasted with the air conduction test results.

Impedance audiometry is a technique used to measure the amount of impedance to or admittance of sound energy into the ear. As sound energy strikes the eardrum, some is transmitted to the middle and inner ear, but some is reflected back into the ear canal. The less impedance, the more sound energy admitted to the middle and inner ear. An increased level of impedance is diagnostic of middle ear pathology. Impedance audiometry may also be used to measure the **acoustic reflex** (movement of the muscles attached to the malleus and stapes as

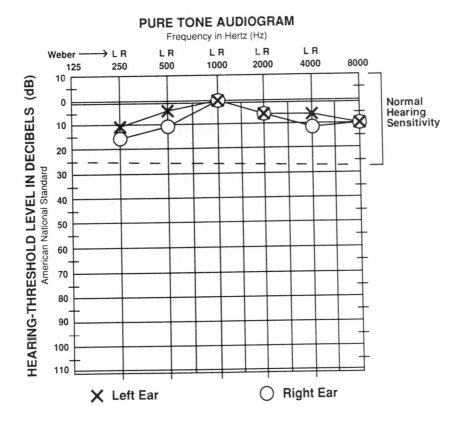

Figure 9-2 Pure Tone Audiogram.

a response to intense sound), which may be helpful in diagnosing conditions or problems that involve the cochlea or auditory nervous system.

One type of impedance testing used to evaluate middle ear function is **tympanometry**. In this test, the status of the eardrum is assessed by altering the air pressure in the ear canal and measuring the response of the eardrum to sound transmissions under these varying conditions. The results are plotted on a graph called a **tympanogram**. The ear's response is plotted on the vertical dimension of the graph, and the air pressures are plotted on the horizontal dimension.

No form of impedance audiometry requires voluntary responses from the individual. Consequently, tympanometry is frequently used to detect or rule out conductive hearing loss in children or in mentally or physically handicapped adults who are unable to cooperate fully during pure tone testing.

Speech Audiometry

Although tonal audiometry is used to determine individuals' ability to hear spoken language, speech audiometry provides measurements that indicate more directly their ability to understand speech in everyday situations. Two types of **speech audiometry** are speech reception threshold testing and speech discrimination testing.

Individuals with hearing impairments may be able to hear words spoken, but unable to understand them. A **speech reception threshold** test helps identify the lowest intensity (decibels) at which an individual first understands speech by testing the individual's ability to understand two-syllable words presented through earphones. Frequently, the speech reception threshold corresponds closely to average pure tone air conduction thresholds. The higher the decibel level required for either threshold, the greater the hearing loss. A speech reception threshold or average tonal threshold of 25 decibels, for instance, is considered borderline normal hearing for adults. (Limits for children are reduced to 15 to 20 decibels.) A threshold of 35 decibels is considered a mild hearing loss.

A **speech discrimination** test provides a measure of the individual's ability to understand words at a comfortable listening level. The test requires the individual to repeat one-syllable words that are presented through earphones. The result of the speech discrimination test is reported as the percentage of words repeated correctly. The lower the percentage, the greater the problem in understanding. Obviously, the words presented in both tests should be in the language of the individual being tested.

Evaluation of the Vestibular System (Disorders of Balance)

Individuals who experience vertigo or dizziness, or who have problems with balance are frequently tested for inner ear and sensorineural disorders related to vestibular function. These tests are performed either by a physician or under a physician's supervision.

In one test of vestibular nerve function, the **caloric test**, either cold or hot water is introduced into the external auditory canal. The water stimulates the fluids within the inner ear, thus stimulating the vestibular nerve. The introduction of the water into the ear creates a reflex response of the eye called **nystagmus** (involuntary horizontal eye movement). By monitoring the direction of eye movements, the physician can determine what the origin of the dizziness is and whether there is nerve damage. Eye movement may be monitored visually or with **electronystagmography**, a procedure in which electrodes are placed near the eye to record eye muscle activity.

TREATMENT

Both medical and nonmedical interventions may be used in the treatment of hearing impairments. Medical interventions may involve surgery or medications, while nonmedical interventions may include the use of hearing aids or other assistive listening devices and special training programs. Treatment in most cases involves a variety of professionals.

An **otolaryngologist**, a physician who specializes in disorders of the ear and related structures, provides professional assistance concerning medical problems and the treatment of hearing impairments. The **audiologist**, in addition to conducting evaluations of hearing function, may also determine if hearing aids would be useful and, if so, what type would be most beneficial. Individuals with hearing impairments may also have difficulty in speaking because of the lack of auditory feedback; therefore, **speech and language therapists** may work with these individuals on particular aspects of speech, language, or both in order to increase intelligibility.

Auditory training is often helpful to individuals with special problems in communication. Such training may be included in hearing aid orientation and/or special programs on listening for the sounds of speech and other environmental sounds.

Surgery

Surgical procedures may be performed in order to eliminate pathological conditions and to restore or improve hearing.

Myringotomy

When the middle ear is infected, as in otitis media, or when there is a fluid buildup in the middle ear, surgical intervention may be necessary to drain pus or fluid, thus relieving pressure and preventing rupture of the eardrum. A **myringotomy** is a procedure in which an incision is made into the eardrum for this purpose. Because the procedure is performed under controlled conditions, it seldom leaves enough scar tissue to have a negative effect on hearing. If fluid has accumulated in the middle ear, the physician may perform a **needle aspiration** to remove it. Needle aspiration may not remove fluid that has invaded the mastoid air cell system, however, and additional intervention may be necessary if the mastoid system is to be rendered dry.

Mastoidectomy

Since the advent of antibiotics for treatment of mastoiditis, mastoidectomy is performed less frequently. It is a surgical procedure for the removal of infected mastoid air cells, which are located in the mastoid process. Because the mastoid is a portion of the acoustic system of the middle ear, there may be a permanent hearing loss after surgery, depending on the nature of the surgery. For example, an individual who has had a radical mastoidectomy in which other structures in addition to the mastoid cells are removed may have a greater degree of hearing loss or permanent hearing loss. An individual having a simple mastoidectomy in which only the mastoid cells are removed may have hearing unaffected.

Tympanoplasty

Surgical procedures that involve the middle ear are referred to generally as **tympanoplasty**. **Myringoplasty** is a specific type of tympanoplasty in which a damaged eardrum is repaired. Other types of tympanoplasty may be performed for the surgical repair or reconstruction of the ossicles of the middle ear. Repairing or reconstructing the middle ear's conductive mechanisms may improve or restore the conductive component of the individual's hearing.

Stapedectomy

The most common surgical treatment for otosclerosis is **stapedectomy**, a surgical procedure in which the stapes is removed and replaced with a prosthesis. The surgery, which reestablishes a more normal sound pathway between the middle and inner ear, usually improves hearing, but does not totally restore it.

Cochlear Implant

Profoundly hearing-impaired individuals who cannot benefit from a traditional hearing aid may benefit from a cochlear implant. An electronic device, a **cochlear implant** consists of a microphone that picks up sound; a battery-powered processor, typically worn on a belt, that converts sound into electric current; a transmitter implanted into the exterior surface of the mastoid that transmits electrical impulses into the head; and a receiver in the middle ear and an electrode inserted directly into the cochlea that receive the impulse and stimulate the auditory nerve directly.

The microphone is mounted at ear level and picks up sounds in the environment. The processor converts sound into electrical energy, amplifies it, alters it and sends it to the transmitter (a disk the size of a nickel that is surgically implanted behind the ear under the skin near the mastoid process). The transmitter then sends the electrical impulses to the receiver. Implanted in the middle ear, the receiver is connected to electrodes implanted in the inner ear, which receive impulses from the receiver and stimulate the auditory nerve with these electrical impulses.

Individuals with cochlear implants learn to read coded signals so that they can distinguish environmental sounds and warning signals (e.g., ringing telephones and horns), although they will not actually "hear" the sound in the way that individuals without hearing impairments hear them. Cochlear implants help in speech-reading by enabling individuals to distinguish the beginnings and endings of words, as well as the intonation and rhythm patterns being used. Not all deaf individuals are candidates for cochlear implants. Those who do receive a cochlear implant should have realistic expectations for hearing ability after the implantation.

Vibrotactile Aids

For individuals with a profound hearing loss or deafness, a vibrotactile aid is a nonsurgical alternative to a cochlear implant. A vibrotactile aid consists of a microphone, a processor with a battery supply, and one or more vibrators placed on the skin. Aids are currently available with one to seven vibrators. Incoming signals are processed to produce patterns of vibrations delivered as a code to the skin.

Results from studies of individuals using cochlear implants or vibrotactile aids indicate that the more channels (the more electrodes or the more vibrators), the more effective the device. For the same number of channels, performance is comparable in the two devices, but varies markedly from person to person for users of either system.

Hearing Aids

Any mechanical or electronic device that improves hearing is a hearing aid. Although hearing may improve, it does not often return to a normal level with the use of a hearing aid because most users have sensorineural rather than conductive hearing losses. Thus, not all individuals can benefit from the use of a hearing aid. These devices must be prescribed and fitted according to individual need.

Hearing aids come in different shapes and sizes; however, all hearing aids function by amplifying sound. Most hearing aids used today are air conduction aids. Individuals with mild to moderate hearing losses may use a **canal type** hearing aid, which fits entirely within the ear canal, making it almost invisible. Those with mild to moderate hearing impairments may benefit from an **in-the-ear type** of hearing aid that fits in the opening to the outer ear and extends into the ear canal. The **behind-the-ear type** of hearing aid consists of a plastic earmold worn in the ear and connected to an instrument worn behind the ear. The **eyeglass model** of hearing aid is similar to the behind-the-ear model, except that the amplification system is housed in the eyeglass frame. Both the behind-the-ear aids and the eyeglass model aids may be used by individuals with mild to severe hearing losses.

The larger body aids carried in the shirt pocket and bone conduction aids are rarely used today. The larger body-carried aids are capable of accommodating users with greater hearing losses than can be handled by a head-worn aid. Body-carried aids can be worn by individuals who cannot wear an air conduction system aid inserted into the ear canal because of some condition of the canal, such as the congenital absence of the canal.

An optional feature that may be built into some hearing aids is **telecoil circuitry** that is activated with a **T switch** located on the hearing aid case. A telecoil is a very small coil of wire that acts as an antenna picking up electromagnetic energy that is then delivered to the hearing aid's receiver and converted into sound. This type of device enables individuals to use other assistive listening devices discussed later in the chapter.

Hearing aids should be carefully prescribed to meet individual needs. There should be a trial period of at least 1 month before the finalization of a hearing aid purchase. Hearing aids should not be dispensed without prior evaluation or without accompanying orientation to their use and care. Orientation is important so that the individual knows what the hearing aid can and cannot do. Hearing aid orientation helps individuals learn ways to enhance communication and to minimize communication problems.

Hearing aids are delicate devices that need routine care and maintenance to ensure maximum function. Batteries must be replaced on occasion and must be protected from decay. Hearing aids should not be exposed to extremes in temperatures and should not be worn in situations where they may become wet, such as while showering or swimming. Because of the delicate mechanisms in the hearing aid, they can be easily broken or damaged if dropped.

Alerting Devices

In addition to creating difficulties in communication, hearing impairments can hamper an individual's ability to respond to everyday environmental sounds, such as a baby crying, a doorbell ringing, or an alarm clock buzzing. Various devices and systems are available commercially to alert individuals with hearing impairments to these cues. They may use visual cues, such as flashing lights; auditory cues, such as increased amplification of sound; or tactile cues such as a vibrator.

Telephone Aids

Several types of telephone aids are available for use with a telephone. Some of these devices use telecoil circuitry with a hearing aid, as discussed previously.

Telephone adapters using telecoil circuitry do not amplify sound but rather use electromagnetic energy that is converted into sound. When using a hearing aid with a telecoil, a portable adapter is slipped over the receiver of the telephone so that a magnetic field is generated. Electromagnetic energy is transferred to the receiver of the hearing aid and converted into sound. This special adapter can only be used with hearing aids with telecoil circuitry. Not all phones, however, are compatible with the adapter or telecoil.

Other telephone aids use amplification, and may be used without a hearing aid. Portable telephone amplifiers that can be carried and slipped over a regular telephone receiver may be useful for hearing-impaired individuals who travel or who may not have a specially wired telephone available. Portable telephone amplifiers are not compatible with all phone models, however. Other telephone amplification devices may be wired to the telephone handset so that volume is increased and controllable by the user. These devices may be used with or without a hearing aid.

Public telephones equipped with amplifier handsets, although still not readily available, are becoming more common. These telephones are usually identified with an access sign.

Telecommunication devices (TDD) are used to transmit conversations in printed format over regular telephone lines. Individuals on both ends of the line must have compatible devices with which to type their messages and visualize the printed message on a screen or paper. If one individual does not have a TDD, a third party system may be used in which a message relay operator transmits the message to the other individual.

Assistive Listening Devices (ALD)

Several types of assistive listening devices have been designed to enhance hearing with or without the associated use of a hearing aid. Individuals with hearing impairments may have more difficulty perceiving high-pitched sounds common in speech. In addition, background noise in the environment further interferes with the perception of these sounds. Assistive listening devices intensify high-pitched sounds and reduce environmental sounds that interfere with hearing.

Hard-Wired Devices

In hard-wired systems, the receiver or hearing aid worn by the user is connected to a sound source, such as television or radio. Such a system enables hearing-impaired individuals to increase the volume on their receiver or hearing aid without altering the volume for others in the room. Hard-wired systems are not useful in group settings, but are useful in one-to-one communication. The microphone of the system is placed near the speaker, and a wire is connected to the user's receiver or hearing aid. Speech is easier to understand, because the system makes it louder than the surrounding noise.

Group Access Systems

Background noises may make it difficult for individuals with hearing aids to hear speakers in large rooms. Several types of electronic devices are available to enhance their ability to hear in these situations. Among these devices are Audio Loop Systems, AM and FM systems, and infrared systems. In each case, the device must be installed in the room. For most systems, the hearing-impaired person must also have a hearing aid equipped with a T switch or must use a special receiver.

When electronic devices are not available or their use is not feasible, certified interpreters may convey the speaker's words simultaneously to persons trained in sign language or some other symbol system.

Speech-Reading (Lip-Reading)

Speech-reading is a type of communication skill in which spoken words are identified by watching the formation of the words on the speaker's lips. Because not all words are identifiable in this manner, individuals who are speech-reading may supplement information about the meaning of what is being said by observing the speaker's facial expressions and by taking into account the overall context of the message.

Speech-reading requires good lighting. The speaker must face the individual who is speech-reading and be close enough to allow the individual to see the word formation on the lips. Speech-reading is more difficult when the speaker speaks very rapidly or enunciates poorly, or when hand movements, a beard, or a mustache obstructs the individual's view of the lips.

Sign Language

Language is a set of symbols combined in a certain way to convey concepts, ideas, and emotions. There are many ways of transmitting language. **Speech** is the verbal expression of language concepts. **Sign language** is a means of communication in which specific hand configurations symbolize language concepts.

There are several types of sign language, the two most common being **American Sign Language** and **Signed English**. American Sign Language is the native language of individuals who are deaf. It has its own grammar and syntax; more-over, it is conceptual in nature, rather than word-oriented. Signed English follows the syntax and linguistic structure of English. Often, people who use Signed English also mouth the words that they sign. This process is called **si-multaneous communication**.

Fingerspelling, used to supplement sign systems, consists of different hand shapes for each letter of the alphabet. It may be used to convey proper names or to clarify a concept being conveyed.

FUNCTIONAL IMPLICATIONS

Psychological Issues

Deafness can pervade every aspect and activity of an individual's life. Because hearing is vital to verbal communication and to the perception of environmental cues, all hearing impairments interfere with daily function to some degree. An individual's ability to cope with a hearing impairment depends on the type and degree of the impairment, the age of onset, and the extent to which it interferes with daily communication and activity.

Individuals with congenital deafness or with a hearing impairment that was acquired before speech development need special programs to help them learn to communicate. Unfortunately, hearing impairments in the very young are not always recognized immediately and may be misinterpreted as intellectual deficits, mental retardation, or behavior disorders. Normal development and healthy adjustment of children with a hearing impairment are dependent to a large degree on early diagnosis and treatment, early social and cultural influenc-es, and parental attitudes and acceptance. The diagnosis of deafness in a child often results in parental guilt, overprotection, or rejection. Professional as-sistance for the family of a newly diagnosed deaf infant may be critical to their acceptance of the child's needs and to their competence in providing a nurturing environment for the child's emotional development.

Individuals who have acquired a hearing impairment during adulthood have memories of sound, language, and of previous function. They have already learned speech patterns and can maintain them through speech and conversation therapy. When a hearing impairment occurs in adulthood, however, individuals may feel uncomfortable and fear that others will reject them if they admit their disability. As a result, they may withdraw from situations in which they have difficulty in hearing. Being unable to understand what is being said, individuals with impaired hearing may believe that the laughter and talking of others is being directed toward them. Some individuals exhibit aggressive and dominat-ing behavior as a reaction to their hearing impairment.

A hearing loss can lead to isolation, loneliness, and frustration, as well as to sensory deprivation. Hearing helps individuals communicate on a daily basis with family and friends, and in the social and work setting. At the most basic level, hearing helps individuals keep in touch with the environment. Background sounds, such as the wind in the trees, children playing down the street, or a train whistle in the distance, keep individuals aware of what is happening in the outside world. Hearing also acts as a signal to action. The sounds of a telephone ringing, a baby crying, or the horn of an approaching car are all cues for some type of action. Thus, not only must individuals with a loss of hearing alter their activities for which hearing is vital, but also they carry a sense of vulnerability because of their inability to hear sounds that once served as cues to action or danger. The sound of footsteps from behind, once a warning signal that someone is approaching, may no longer be heard.

Grief reactions are not uncommon for individuals with acquired hearing impairments. These individuals have memories of sounds. Their inability to hear cherished sounds, such as the voices of loved ones, music, or the chirping of birds, may be a difficult loss to accept.

Because hearing impairments are invisible disabilities, denial is common, especially for those who acquire a hearing impairment later in life. They may react with increased sensitivity or irritability when they do not understand words. The increased social pressure to understand may cause anxiety and frustration, and they may avoid activities and interactions that they once enjoyed. Their unwillingness to acknowledge their impairment may result in their refusal to participate in hearing evaluations or their reluctance to wear hearing aids.

Individuals with an acquired hearing loss, especially if the onset is sudden, may experience depression. Because of the suddenness of the loss, the individual has not had an opportunity to adapt gradually as hearing diminishes and is unlikely to have developed signing skills. Depression can interfere with learning and using new communication skills, however. Its effects are circular; depression is a barrier to communication, thus intensifying feelings of isolation and making the individual more depressed. Counselors trained in sign language may not be readily available, and the use of an interpreter for counseling sessions may increase the individual's reluctance to participate or to disclose feelings openly.

Any and all of the emotional states that are experienced by the adult who is hearing-impaired may be experienced by the parents of children who have been identified as hearing-impaired. Just as hearing-impaired adults must work through their feelings in order to achieve a healthy adjustment, so must parents before they can be of optimal assistance to their child.

Individuals who have a hearing impairment depend heavily on visual channels and on manual means of communication. The development of additional medical conditions that threaten these resources is of increasing concern. A visual impairment or conditions that affect the hands, such as rheumatoid arthritis, can seriously hamper the hearing-impaired individual's accustomed means of communication, necessitating additional training in new ways of communicating.

Life Style Issues

Many daily activities involve the sense of hearing. For individuals with hearing impairments, simple transactions, such as purchasing items from a local store, communicating with a repairman, or obtaining directions, require additional means of communication. In some instances, the use of a third party as an interpreter may be a solution; however, hearing-impaired individuals may resent the loss of privacy or the loss of the sense of independence associated with the use of an interpreter. Signal dogs ("hearing ear" dogs) trained to alert their deaf owners to environmental sounds or signals are increasing in popularity. Special devices are necessary to make daily environmental sounds, such as a knock on the door, known to the hearing-impaired individuals. Technology and special aids become, in many instances, a necessity.

Everyday activities with family members may require more effort on the part of all involved. For instance, without the awareness and sensitivity of other family members, hearing-impaired individuals may not be able to participate actively in family conversations at mealtime. Small talk between the individuals and others while performing various tasks may no longer be possible.

Depending on the degree of impairment, special activities, such as watching television or attending movies, plays, and concerts, may also be affected. The special devices mentioned previously may help these individuals participate more fully in such activities. In addition, television decoders that provide captioned programming may be available to enable hearing-impaired individuals to enjoy television.

Although hearing impairments do not directly affect sexual activity, an individual's self-concept or perception of the reactions of others to the hearing impairment may affect sexual activity. Verbal communication during love-making may no longer be possible, and an individual with a hearing impairment may view this as an emotional loss.

Social Issues

Individuals with hearing impairments may limit their social contacts to family members and a few close friends, or they may avoid social contacts altogether because of their inability to understand what is being said. The difficulty in understanding verbal communication can cause them to withdraw from social situations in order to avoid the embarrassment of giving inappropriate responses to questions or statements.

The lack of understanding by others can contribute to social isolation. New acquaintances, unfamiliar with hearing impairments or unaware of the individuals' disability, may perceive them as aloof or even rude because of their failure to respond to a friendly statement that they did not hear. It may be particularly difficult for these individuals to keep up with conversations in group settings, especially if others in the group are unaware of or insensitive to their needs. Group settings with poor lighting, which makes lip-reading more difficult, or with competing sounds, such as the rattling of dishes in a restaurant, may make communication difficult even for individuals with milder hearing losses.

Engaging in conversation requires cooperation from others. Some people may feel uncomfortable or impatient while attempting to communicate with hearing-impaired individuals and, consequently, they may avoid contact with them. Some may consider deafness a social stigma because of myths and misconceptions about hearing impairments. Such attitudes build a barrier to acceptance by others and inclusion in the larger social community. Societal responses can create difficult and stressful situations for individuals with a hearing impairment, at times discouraging their further participation in social functions.

Although family members serve as a support group, their attitudes may also impede individuals' acceptance of their condition and subsequent rehabilitation. Family members may perceive a hearing loss as feigned or may attribute the difficulty to inattention. As a result, family members may become angry, ignore the individual, or exclude him or her from conversations rather than learning techniques that would enhance the individual's ability to maintain an active role in conversation. Family members who serve as interpreters for those with hearing impairments may, on the other hand, begin to resent their role, feeling somewhat stifled in social interactions.

Individuals who have been deaf since birth or early childhood may integrate well with the deaf community, where a common language is shared. Those who acquired their hearing impairment later in life, however, frequently do not join the deaf community and may feel more isolated, feeling that they fit neither into the deaf community nor into the hearing world.

Vocational Issues

Just as there are myths and stereotypes about hearing impairments in the social world, there are myths and stereotypes in the world of work. Employers and fellow workers may not understand hearing impairments and may be unaware of the special techniques available to enhance communication with the hearing-impaired individual.

In the work setting, an individual with a hearing impairment may need special assistive devices, communication aids, and signaling devices. The use of such devices is often dependent on the availability and expense of the purchase and installation of the special items. Equipment may be prioritized according to need if funds are limited. For example, a signaling device that may be crucial for the individual's safety may be considered vital, while equipment that would enhance the individual's performance may not receive as high a priority.

Because visual cues are so important to communication for individuals with hearing impairments, good lighting in the work place is a necessity. Many individuals with hearing impairments experience discomfort with loud noises; therefore, the noise level in the environment should be evaluated. In some instances, it may be necessary for the individual to wear ear protectors in order to prevent further hearing loss. Room acoustics must also be considered, because the reverberation of sound in an environment can interfere with hearing aid effectiveness.

Hearing aids can greatly enhance some individuals' performance in the work setting. They are intricate devices that are susceptible to damage from environmental factors, however. They are sensitive to extremes of temperature, especially extreme cold, and they require protection from perspiration in hot and humid environments.

Individuals with hearing impairments are a heterogeneous group and should be considered as such. Not only their special needs, but also their special talents and interests should be considered in helping them adjust to the work environment. With the use of assistive devices, many job opportunities that were not previously available to individuals with hearing impairments are now well within the range of possibilities.

BIBLIOGRAPHY

Barber, T.C., and Langfitt, D.E. *Teaching the Medical/Surgical Patient—Diagnostics and Procedures.* Bowie, Md.: Robert J. Brady Co., 1983.

Berkow, R., and Fletcher, A.J., eds. *The Merck Manual of Diagnosis and Therapy.* Rahway, N.J.: Merck Sharpe and Dohme Research Laboratories, 1987.

Brunner, L.S.; Emerson, C.P.; Ferguson, L.K.; and Suddarth, D.S. *Textbook of Medical-Surgical Nursing.* Philadelphia: W.B. Saunders Co., 1970.

Corbett, J.V. *Diagnostic Procedures in Nursing Practice.* Norwalk, Conn.: Appleton-Century-Crofts, 1982.

Corbett, J.V. *Laboratory Tests in Nursing Practice.* Norwalk, Conn.: Appleton-Century-Crofts, 1983.

Danek, M. "Rehabilitation Counseling with Deaf Clients." *Journal of Applied Rehabilitation Counseling* 12(1983):20–25.

Farrar, C.L.; Mangham, C.A.; and Kuprenas, S.V. "The Cochlear Prosthesis." *Postgraduate Medicine* 76(1984):73–76.

Fernandes, C.C., and Brandt, F.D. *Assistive Learning Devices: A Consumer-Oriented Summary.* Washington, D.C.: Gallaudet University.

Guyton, A.C. *Human Physiology and Mechanisms of Disease.* Philadelphia: W.B. Saunders Co., 1982.

Keele, C.A.; Neil, E.; and Joels, N. *Samson Wright's Applied Physiology.* New York: Oxford University Press, 1982.

Luckman, J., and Sorensen, K.C. *Medical-Surgical Nursing: A Psychophysiologic Approach.* Philadelphia: W.B. Saunders Co., 1987.

National Institute of Handicapped Research. "Vocational Rehabilitation with Hearing Impaired Clients." *Rehab Brief* 6(1983):1–4.

National Institute of Handicapped Research. "Assistive Listening Devices in Education and Vocational Rehabilitation." *Rehab Brief* 12(1990):1–4.

Nursing 87 Books. *Patient Teaching.* Springhouse, Pa.: Springhouse Corporation Book Division, 1987.

Ostby, S., and Thomas, K.R. "Deafness and Hearing Impairment: A Review and Proposal." *Journal of Applied Rehabilitation Counseling* 15(1984):7–11.

Rakel, R.E. *Conn's Current Therapy 1990.* Philadelphia: W.B. Saunders Co., 1990.

Riley, M.A.K. *Nursing Care of the Client with Ear, Nose, and Throat Disorders.* New York: Springer Publishing Co., 1987.

Rubin, W. "Noise-Induced Deafness." *Hospital Medicine* 23(1987):19–45.

Scheer, S.J., ed. *Medical Perspectives in Vocational Assessment of Impaired Workers.* Gaithersburg, Md.: Aspen Publishers, 1991.

Smith, D.W., and Hanley-Germain, C.P. *Care of the Adult Patient.* Philadelphia: J.B. Lippincott Co., 1975.

Stolov, W.C., and Clowers, M.R. *Handbook of Severe Disability.* Washington, D.C.: U.S. Department of Education, Rehabilitation Services Administration, 1981.

Vander, A.J.; Sherman, J.H.; and Luciano, D.S. *Human Physiology: The Mechanisms of Body Function.* New York: McGraw-Hill Book Co., 1985.

Wyngaarden, J.B., and Smith, J.H. *Cecil Textbook of Medicine.* Philadelphia: W.B. Saunders Co., 1988.

chapter 10

Visual Disorders

NORMAL STRUCTURE AND FUNCTION

The eyeballs are spherical organs encased in the orbital cavities of the skull. Muscles located on the top, bottom, and side of each eye enable it to rotate easily in different directions (Figure 10-1). The eyelid serves a protective function; through frequent blinking, it helps to keep the eye moist and prevent irritation. The **lacrimal glands**, which lie in the upper outer side of the eye behind the eye lid, secrete tears to keep the eyeball moist and help rid the eye of foreign material.

The **conjunctiva** is a sensitive membrane that lines the inner eyelid and covers the front part of the eye. In the front of the eye lies a transparent curved window called the cornea, which admits light and protects the inner eye from foreign particles and organisms. Although the cornea contains no blood vessels, it is richly supplied with nerve cells. Connected to the cornea is the **sclera**, or white part of the eye. The primary function of the sclera, a fibrous membrane, is to support and protect the eye. It completely covers the eyeball, except for the part that is covered by the cornea. Covering the exposed area of the sclera is the conjunctiva. Lying inside the sclera and also surrounding the eyeball is the **choroid coat**, which contains most of the blood vessels that nourish the eye.

The cornea covers both the iris and the pupil of the eye. The iris is the colored part of the eye. In the center of the iris is a round opening called the pupil, which admits light to the inner part of the eye. Smooth muscle fibers on either side of the pupil cause the pupil to contract or dilate, thereby automatically regulating the amount of light that enters the eye. In bright light, for example, the pupil contracts to reduce the amount of light admitted; in the dark, the pupil dilates to admit as much light as possible.

Between the cornea and the iris is a space **(the anterior chamber)** filled with a transparent fluid **(aqueous humor)** that nourishes the cornea and the lens. The

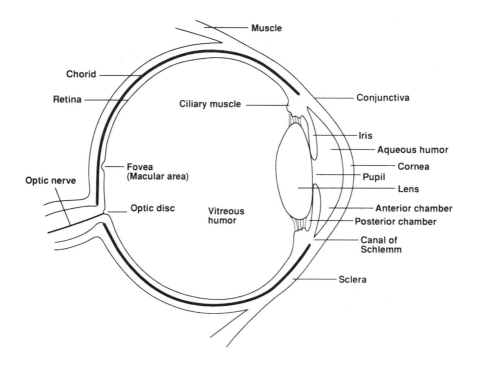

Figure 10-1 The Eye.

aqueous humor, which is produced by the **ciliary process** located directly behind the iris, escapes from the posterior chamber through the pupil into the anterior chamber. It then drains from the eye into lymph channels through a sievelike structure called the **canal of Schlemm**, which is located at the junction of the iris and the sclera. The balance between the amount of aqueous humor produced and the amount drained helps to maintain normal **intraocular pressure** (pressure within the eyeball).

Directly behind the iris is the **lens**, a small transparent disk that is enclosed in a transparent capsule. Attachments around the circumference of the lens **(ciliary muscle)** contract or expand, changing the shape of the lens from fat to thin or vice versa. The changing shape of the lens permits the eye to focus for near or far vision, a process called **accommodation**. Behind the lens is a larger cavity known as the **vitreous space**. This space is filled with a jellylike, translucent substance called the **vitreous humor**, which helps to maintain the form and shape of the eyeball.

At the very back of the eye, lying inside the choroid, is the innermost coat of the eye, the **retina**. It contains two layers, a pigmented layer that is fixed to the choroid and an inner layer that contains special light-sensitive cells and blood vessels. The special cells within the retina's inner layer are called **rods** and **cones**, and they receive visual stimuli. Rods contain a derivative of vitamin A, **rhodopsin**, which is highly light-sensitive and breaks down rapidly when exposed to light, causing a reaction that activates the rods. This chemical process, through which the eye adjusts so that the individual can see in the dark, is called **adaptation**. Rods are concerned primarily with night vision and peripheral vision.

Cones are involved primarily in daylight and color vision, and in the perception of sharp visual detail. The **macula** is a spot on the retina that contains most of the cones and is the area of clearest central vision. The center of the macula, the **fovea**, contains no rods and is the area where vision is clearest in good light.

The **optic nerve** enters the back of the eye at the **optic disc**, sometimes called the blind spot because it does not contain light-sensitive cells. The sensory cells of the retina receive light stimuli and transmit them to the optic nerve, which carries the impulses to the occipital lobe of the brain. Although each eye takes in a slightly different visual image **(binocular vision)**, the coordinated use of both eyes blends the two images into one and heightens perception of depth.

In sum, vision is made possible by the passage of light rays through the cornea, aqueous humor, lens, and vitreous humor until they finally center on the retina, where impulses are received, encoded, and transmitted to the optic nerve, which, in turn, transmits them to the brain for interpretation as sight.

DISORDERS OF VISION

Visual disorders cause a number of different types of disturbances in **visual acuity** (ability to process visual detail). In the extreme, they may cause **blindness** (total lack of light perception); in other instances, they may cause a variety of **visual impairments** (any deviation of normal vision). A visual impairment may affect the **central field of vision** so that the individual is able to see images in the periphery of the visual field, but not images in the center; on the other hand, a visual impairment may consist of **tunnel vision**, in which the individual is able to see images in the center of the visual field, but not in the periphery. At times, an impairment affects individuals' **night vision**, so that they have night blindness. In some cases, **binocular vision** (the coordinated use of both eyes to produce a single image) may be affected so that individuals have double vision **(diplopia)** or loss of sight in one eye **(amblyopia)**. Some conditions may affect color vision.

Because of the variations in the degree and the type of visual impairment that may affect function even though light perception has not been totally lost, blindness has been defined legally. In most instances, **legal blindness** is defined as

244 ASPECTS OF CHRONIC ILLNESS AND DISABILITY

(1) visual acuity not exceeding 20/200 or worse in the better eye with correcting lenses or (2) central field of vision limited to an angle of 20 degrees or less.

Refractive Errors

The refraction of the eye is the bending of light rays to converge on the retina. Changes in the cornea, aqueous humor, lens, or vitreous humor can alter the bending of light rays, however, causing **refractive errors**. Such errors make up the most common type of eye disorder. One type of refractive error, **myopia** (nearsightedness), results from elongation of the eyeball so that the light rays focus on a point in front of the retina. Individuals with this condition have good visual acuity for close objects, but difficulty seeing objects in the distance. The opposite type of refractive error is **hyperopia** (farsightedness), in which light rays focus on a point beyond the retina. With hyperopia, individuals usually have good visual acuity for objects in the distance, but have difficulty focusing on things at close range. Both myopia and hyperopia can occur at any age and are generally remedied easily with corrective lenses.

Astigmatism occurs when there is an irregularity in the shape of the cornea or lens that distorts the visual image. It can occur with or without myopia. Like other types of refractive errors, astigmatism is correctable with lenses that compensate for the error.

The lens and ciliary muscle lose their elasticity with age. **Presbyopia** is the loss of the ability of the lens to accommodate to near images. Lenses that compensate for both near and far vision **(bifocals)** are generally able to correct the errors.

Injuries to the Eyes

The most common type of eye injury is an injury to the cornea or conjunctiva caused by a foreign body in the eye. Even an apparently minor injury can become serious if, for example, a scratch or abrasion of the cornea becomes infected or causes scarring that impedes vision. At other times, a foreign object may penetrate the eye. Only a physician should remove a foreign body that has penetrated the eye. Chemical burns of the cornea and conjunctiva also threaten vision and should be treated immediately by flooding the eye with water. Blows to the head or the eye can damage the internal structures of the eye, causing hemorrhage, retinal damage, or other injury.

An injury to the eye necessitates a consultation with an **ophthalmologist** (a physician who specializes in diseases and treatment of the eye). The degree of visual loss that results from an eye injury is a function not only of the extent and type of injury, but also frequently the consequence of the delay or promptness of emergency treatment.

Inflammation and Infections of the Eye

The most common eye disease is **conjunctivitis** (inflammation of the conjunctiva), which may be caused by infectious organisms, allergy, or chemicals. Many types of conjunctivitis are the result of poor hygienic practices, such as inadequate hand washing. In most instances, conjunctivitis is easily treated, is self-limiting, and has no untoward effects. Some types of conjunctivitis, however, can cause serious damage and visual loss. **Gonococcal conjunctivitis** commonly causes ulceration of the cornea and subsequent blindness. **Trachoma** is a chronic infectious disease of the conjunctiva and cornea that, if untreated, results in blindness.

Keratitis is an inflammation of the cornea. Because of its rich nerve supply, inflammation or injury to the cornea can cause severe pain. The treatment of a corneal inflammation should be prompt in order to avoid the subsequent formation of scar tissue that can interfere with vision.

Glaucoma

In **glaucoma**, there is an increased intraocular pressure that impairs peripheral vision and, if untreated, results in blindness. Glaucoma occurs when the amount of aqueous humor being produced exceeds the amount flowing out of the eye. The disease may be compared to a sink into which water continues to flow, although debris has narrowed or completely blocked the drainage pipe; as a result, the water in the sink begins to accumulate.

The most common type of glaucoma, **chronic open-angle (simple glaucoma)**, occurs when the outflow of aqueous humor from the eye is reduced. Because the outflow no longer equals the inflow, the amount of aqueous humor builds, and pressure in the eye increases.

Open-angle glaucoma generally progresses slowly over many years, producing no symptoms until the optic nerve is sufficiently damaged to reduce the individual's visual acuity and central visual field. At this point, the damage is irreversible. Vision loss generally begins with the loss of peripheral (side) vision so that individuals can see only straight ahead, as if looking through a tunnel (tunnel vision). If untreated, the field of vision continues to narrow until all vision is lost. There is no cure for chronic open-angle glaucoma. If the disease is detected early, however, appropriate medical treatment can control it for many years.

Acute closed-angle glaucoma develops much more rapidly. Its symptoms include sudden severe pain, sharply decreased vision, nausea and vomiting, and rapid damage to the optic nerve with associated vision loss. Acute closed-angle glaucoma results from an abrupt blockage and obstruction of the canal of

Schlemm so that the aqueous humor rapidly accumulates in the anterior chambers of the eye. Although this type of glaucoma is much less common, it is a medical emergency that must be treated immediately to prevent blindness. It may be treated initially with medications, but surgical intervention is usually necessary.

In either type of glaucoma, early detection and treatment are critical in order to prevent irreversible damage to the optic nerve and subsequent blindness. Regardless of the type of glaucoma, lifetime medical supervision is required. Most people with glaucoma can lead normal, unrestricted lives without blindness if the condition is identified early and the medical regimen is followed as prescribed.

Cataract

A **cataract** is a clouding, or opacity, of the lens of the eye. Cataracts may be congenital, may result from injury, or may develop with the aging process. They can also be drug-induced, for example, by high levels of certain types of steroids. Although cataracts are generally bilateral, they may form at different rates in each eye. As the lenses become more opaque, vision gradually diminishes. If cataracts are the result of injury, such as from radiation or a foreign object striking the lens, loss of vision occurs more rapidly. Cataracts associated with aging progress more slowly over time. Because there is no way to return the lens to its normal transparency, treatment involves the removal of the lens and the replacement of lens function with an implant, with glasses, or with both.

Retinopathy

Any disease or disorder of the retina is a **retinopathy**. **Arteriosclerotic retinopathy** results in changes that occur in the vessels of the retina because of arteriosclerosis; **hypertensive retinopathy**, from changes that occur in the retina because of high blood pressure. Treatment of the primary underlying condition can control arteriosclerotic and hypertensive retinopathies (see Chapter 2).

The most common type of retinopathy—and the most common cause of blindness—is **diabetic retinopathy**, a complication of diabetes mellitus (see Chapter 5). This eye disease is characterized by a deterioration of the small blood vessels that nourish the retina. In the early stages, the capillaries of the retina become more permeable and, thus, more vulnerable to small hemorrhages. Although there may be no visual symptoms initially, a physician who examines the eye can identify early changes, consisting of swelling of the small retinal blood vessels and leakage of blood and fluids into the retina. As the disease progresses, exudates may collect around the vessels of the retina, causing a visual impairment. If exudates collect on the macula, vision may be blurred. For some individuals, the condition may progress no further.

Proliferative retinopathy is the most serious form of diabetic retinopathy. It is characterized by the uncontrolled formation in the retina of weak blood vessels that are prone to rupture, causing blindness if the ensuing scar tissue causes the retina to detach.

Although controlling diabetes mellitus itself is important and may, in some instances, help to retard the development of diabetic retinopathy, changes cannot be completely reversed once they have begun. Laser photocoagulation may significantly slow the destructive process, however.

Retinal Detachment

In a **detached retina**, the sensory layer of the retina becomes separated from the pigmented layer. This separation deprives the sensory layer of a blood supply. A detached retina may result from a sudden blow to the head, but it usually results from degenerative changes in the retina.

Symptoms may develop suddenly or slowly over time. Individuals may notice flashes of light or a loss of vision in different areas of the visual field, or they may experience a complete loss of vision in the affected eye. No pain accompanies the symptoms. Retinal detachment in one eye may indicate an increased risk of detachment in the other eye. Prompt diagnosis and surgical treatment are essential in order to prevent a permanent vision loss.

Retinitis Pigmentosa

A hereditary condition, **retinitis pigmentosa** involves the slowly progressive loss of peripheral vision. The first symptom is night blindness, which usually begins in late youth or early adulthood.

Often, the total bilateral loss of vision occurs by the age of 50. There is no cure or treatment for the condition; however, a number of assistive devices may be utilized to enhance function.

Macular Degeneration

The macula, the part of the eye needed for seeing fine detail and central vision, may degenerate in some individuals. **Macular degeneration** usually occurs after the age of 50, with no apparent cause. The painless loss of central visual acuity is usually slow, with visual distortion in one eye usually the first symptom. Macular degeneration does not result in complete blindness, but it destroys some or all of the sight in the center of the field of vision. There is no treatment or cure for macular degeneration, but the use of assistive devices may increase visual function. In a small percentage of individuals, laser surgery may produce some positive temporary results.

Other Disorders

Several other conditions, although they do not cause total blindness, may impede vision to some degree. **Nystagmus** is a condition in which the eye moves involuntarily even though the gaze is fixed in one direction.The movement may be in any direction. Nystagmus may be congenital, or it may develop later as a result of a neurological disease or other disorder. The condition may be unapparent to the individual, but more noticeable to others.

Because vision requires not only intact eye structures, but also intact nerve pathways and receptor areas of the brain to interpret nerve impulses as visual images, disorders of the central nervous system may affect visual capacity. Conditions such as multiple sclerosis or brain trauma (see Chapter 8) may both cause varying degrees of visual impairment.

Strabismus is a disorder in which the eyes cannot be directed to the same object or there is a deviation of one eye. It may result from unequal ocular muscle tone or from a neurological condition. Sometimes, it can be corrected by surgery, by lenses, by drugs, or by a combination of the three. **Suppression amblyopia** ("lazy eye") is a condition in which one eye does not develop good vision, usually because of strabismus. The condition must be diagnosed and treated early (age 2 to 3). If treated early by placing a patch over the eye, the eye responds well. If not treated early, poor vision persists for life.

DIAGNOSTIC PROCEDURES

Testing of Visual Acuity

A common test of visual acuity (the sharpness of an individual's vision) is Snellen's test. The chart used for the test contains a series of letters on nine lines of decreasing size. Lines are identified according to the distance from which they can be read by individuals with unimpaired vision. For example, the top line can be read at 200 feet and the last line at 20 feet by those individuals with normal visual acuity.

For the test, individuals view the Snellen chart at the equivalent of 20 feet and read the lines on the chart from the largest to the smallest. The results of the test are expressed as a fraction, the numerator denoting the equivalent distance from the chart at which the individual being tested views (20 feet) and the denominator denoting the distance from the chart at which a person with normal vision would be able to read the same line. Consequently, a visual acuity of 20/200 means that the individual being tested can see at 20 feet what a person with normal visual acuity could see at 200 feet; such a result indicates that the individual being tested has a visual impairment. A result of 20/10 indicates that the individual being tested has better than normal visual acuity.

Individuals may also be asked to view a chart through an instrument called a refractor. The physician then shines a light through the refractor onto the retina in order to estimate the eye's ability to focus on distant objects.

Testing of the Visual Field

An individual's **visual field** is defined as the size of the area that he or she can see without turning or moving the eyes. A **perimeter**, a curved device that the individual being tested looks into, is used to measure **peripheral vision** (side vision). A test object is systematically moved from outside the peripheral field of vision toward the center until the individual indicates that he or she is able to see the object. **Central vision** (vision in the center of the visual field) is tested with a tangent screen on which a test object is systematically moved across the screen. The individual's ability to see the object at certain points is then mapped.

Tonometry

In **tonometry**, the pressure within the eye is measured. The tonometer is placed directly on the cornea after the cornea has been anesthetized with drops of a local anesthetic. The tonometer indicates the amount of pressure within the eye, thus making it possible to detect glaucoma.

Gonioscopy

For **gonioscopy**, a special contact lens that contains a mirror is gently placed on the eye. The ophthalmologist uses the lens like the periscope of a submarine to examine structures inside the eye. The test is especially helpful in detecting glaucoma.

Ophthalmoscopic Examination

A direct **ophthalmoscopic examination** is a procedure used to examine the internal structures of the eye. It is performed with an instrument called an **ophthalmoscope** that is placed close to the eye. The ophthalmoscope contains a light that shines into the eye and magnifies the internal structures so that the physician can note any pathological changes.

The internal structures of the eye may also be observed with a **slit lamp**, a type of microscope that is placed in front of the eye of the individual being tested. The physician shines a finely focused slit of brilliant light onto the eye to magnify details of the cornea, iris, and lens. A slit lamp is especially useful in identifying foreign bodies in the eye, evaluating corneal ulcers, and diagnosing cataracts.

Fluorescein Angiography

The purpose of **fluorescein angiography** is to detect changes in the blood vessels of the retina. A fluorescein dye is either taken orally or injected into the blood stream. When the dye reaches the blood vessels of the eye, special ultraviolet lights enable the physician to photograph the vessels for later study. Any swelling or leakage of the vessels of the retina is apparent on the photograph.

TREATMENT

Eyeglasses and Contact Lenses

Corrective lenses may be in the form of eyeglasses or contact lenses. Because there are so many different types of eye disorders that interfere with visual acuity, corrective lenses must be prescribed individually. They are prescribed by an **ophthalmologist** (a physician who has specialized in the diagnosis and treatment of disorders of the eye) or an **optometrist** (an individual who does not have a medical degree, but is trained to measure refractive errors of the eye). The lenses are made by an **optician**, a technician who grinds and constructs the lens according to the prescribed specifications.

When visual acuity at several different distances must be corrected, bifocal or trifocal lenses may be prescribed. Individuals with **bifocal** lenses use the lower portion of the lens for near vision and the upper portion for far vision. **Trifocal** lenses have three different divisions: one for near vision, one for intermediate vision, and one for far vision.

There are several different types of contact lenses; however, the most common are hard and soft corneal lenses. Hard lenses cover the central area of the cornea and are generally more durable. Soft lenses cover the entire cornea and are generally more fragile. Regardless of the type, contact lenses must be individually prescribed and constructed. They are helpful for a variety of visual disorders, but they do not correct astigmatism.

There are usually no complications associated with wearing eyeglasses. Contact lenses, however, can damage the eye if they are not worn and cared for properly. Not all people can or should wear contact lenses. Overwearing of hard lenses can cause an abrasion to the cornea, which can lead to a corneal ulcer and subsequent loss of the eye. Individuals who do not use good hygienic practices when inserting the contact lens may develop an infection of the eye, in which case contact lenses should not be worn.

Medical Treatment

Eye drops, ointments, or oral medications may be used in the treatment of some diseases of the eye. For example, infections and inflammation of the eye may be treated with antibiotic eye drops or ointment, or in combination with oral antibiotics.

Chronic open-angle glaucoma may be controlled with eye drops alone or in combination with oral medication that reduces pressure in the eye, thus halting the progression of the disease. Other eye drops may be prescribed to decrease the production of aqueous humor. Acute closed-angle glaucoma results from the forward displacement of the iris that in turn narrows or obstructs the aqueous humor outflow. Eye drops called **miotics** constrict the pupil, thus enlarging the drainage passageway and facilitating the outflow of aqueous humor. Because eye drops are absorbed into the bloodstream, they may affect other body functions as well.

Oral medications for the treatment of glaucoma work by decreasing the production of aqueous humor. Like eye drops, these medications can affect other body functions. Consequently, individuals who use eye drops or oral medication for the treatment of glaucoma should be under continuing medical supervision, not only to monitor the condition itself, but also to identify any side-effects of the medication.

Medication for the treatment of glaucoma, whether eye drops or oral medication, must be used daily for the rest of the individual's life in order to control eye pressure and prevent further damage to vision.

Surgical Treatment

Photocoagulation

Frequently used for treating retinal tears, macular degeneration, or retinopathies, **photocoagulation** is a procedure in which an intense beam of light from a laser is used to coagulate or cauterize blood vessels of the retina. The laser beam passes through the lens of the eye and vitreous fluid without harming the structures. It then is directed to a very precisely defined area to destroy fragile vessels prone to hemorrhage, or diseased areas of the retina in which there may be additional proliferative vessel changes. Laser treatment is not painful, as there are no pain fibers in the retina, and it can be performed on an outpatient basis.

Iridotomy

In the treatment of acute closed-angle glaucoma, a small section of the iris may be removed so that the aqueous humor can flow freely from the posterior to the anterior chamber of the eye. This procedure, called an iridotomy, is often performed with a laser. It prevents further eye damage by relieving the built-up pressure. An iridotomy may also be performed prophylactically in the unaffected eye after an acute attack of glaucoma in the opposite eye.

Filtration Surgery

When medical treatment has not successfully controlled chronic open-angle glaucoma, filtration surgery may be necessary. The procedure relieves pressure in the eye by creating a passageway around the blocked canal of Schlemm through which aqueous humor usually drains. In some instances, the procedure eliminates the need for medication in treating the condition.

Scleral Buckling

In a surgical procedure used to treat retinal detachment, **scleral buckling** mechanically restores contact of the retina with the choroid. The area of the sclera that lies over the retinal defect is depressed with an implant so that the choroid and retina are pressed together.

Cataract Surgery

There are two major methods of cataract removal. One method, **extracapsular cataract extraction**, is a procedure in which the lens is removed, but the posterior portion of its capsule is left in position. An **intraocular lens** is generally inserted into the eye at the time of surgery. The second method, **intra-**

capsular cataract extraction, is a procedure in which the lens and its capsule are completely removed. Both types of surgeries are usually performed on an outpatient basis.

Any implanted lens has a fixed focal length so that vision is clear at only one distance. Thus, individuals who have undergone cataract surgery may continue to need corrective lenses, such as bifocals. Vision is poor without the lens.

Vitrectomy

In a **vitrectomy,** the vitreous humor is removed. This procedure may be performed when trauma has caused the vitreous humor to prolapse into the anterior chamber of the eye or if there is unresolved hemorrhage into the vitreous humor, as may occur in diabetic retinopathy. The vitreous humor is removed with a probe and replaced with a clear fluid.

Corneal Transplant (Keratoplasty)

Generally, a corneal transplantation is performed because the cornea is scarred; however, it may also be performed if the shape of the cornea is distorted. Donor eyes for corneal transplantations come from individuals who have recently died. During the surgical procedure, the opaque area of cornea from the recipient's eye is replaced with the clear donor cornea, which is sutured into place. Because the cornea has no blood vessels, the healing process is slow. Although a corneal transplant can restore vision, there is also the chance of graft rejection or the need for a second operation.

Assistive Devices and Low-Vision Aids

Technological advances have produced highly specialized adaptive equipment for use by persons with varying degrees of visual impairment. These **low-vision optical aids** can be classified into two basic categories: magnifiers for near vision and telescopes for far vision. In addition to conventional prescription corrective lenses, the types of optical aids available include head-borne microscopes, telescopes, simple magnifiers, field expanders, and electronic magnifiers. **Telescopic** reading lenses make it possible to increase the distance from the face to the working material, but they also decrease the size of the visual field. The **telemicroscope** combines a telescopic distance lens with a reading lens, which allows the individual a comfortable working distance, but also decreases the usual visual field.

Several electronic devices may be valuable low-vision aids. Using closed circuit television, an electronic device can magnify a printed page on a television screen for reading. This device provides a more normal field of vision, as well as a greater range of magnification than do optical systems. Additionally, these devices permit contrast reversal and place white lettering on a black background, thus filtering out the reflective white light for ease of reading. Finally, this equipment can also be placed over a typewriter or calculator.

Numerous computer software programs and adaptive devices can be used to enlarge printed materials or to convert print into synthetic speech output. These devices include large print computer monitors, programs that enlarge print size on the screen, printers that modify font size, synthetic speech software programs with external audio units, and typewriters equipped with synthetic speech output that interfaces with personal computer units. The speech packages allow for adjustments in the rate of speech and the tone of voice to meet the needs of the individual user. Additional devices, such as talking clocks and timers, writing guides, and talking books and audio cassettes, also help meet the communication needs of individuals with visual impairments.

One of the best known tactile aids is braille. Hard copy braille uses the familiar raised dot method, while soft copy braille is stored on electromagnetic tape and presented as patterns by a set of pins that represent a braille dot. Individuals place their fingers on display units through which the pins protrude. Another type of tactile aid is an electromechanical vibratory system. A small camera is passed over a line of print, and each printed letter is then displayed as a pattern of vibration that the individual can feel with the finger.

Mobility Aids

Various types of aids are available to help the visually impaired or blind individual move about in the environment more freely. **Guide dogs** not only increase the mobility of the individual who has a visual impairment, but also can provide protection. The individual and dog train together for a period of weeks to become an effective team.

The most common mobility aid is the **prescription cane**, which is usually made of aluminum or fiberglass. An orientation-and-mobility specialist prescribes the cane according to the individual's height, length of stride, and comfort. The individual moves the cane rhythmically in an arc in front of the body to ensure a safe space for the next step. Although this provides some protection, it does not account for objects above the waist that are in the individual's path. In an attempt to compensate for this type of obstacle, some canes have tone-emitting radar units that give a differential pitch for the direction and height of obstacles in front of the individual.

Orientation-and-Mobility Training

The goal of orientation-and-mobility training is to enable the individual with a visual impairment to achieve as much mobility as possible according to his or her capabilities and desires. Through individualized training, those with visual impairments learn to orient themselves to their environment by using auditory and tactual cues rather than visual cues. This involves such things as listening for the direction of traffic, arm and hand positioning for guidance along walls and railings, and systematic search techniques for dropped or lost objects.

FUNCTIONAL IMPLICATIONS

Psychological Issues

A visual impairment may be present at birth, or it may develop suddenly or slowly at any time in an individual's life. An individual's adjustment to visual impairment depends on many factors, including the degree of the visual loss and the age at which the individual becomes visually impaired. Those who are congenitally blind have not, for example, had the opportunity to learn concepts such as distance, depth, proportion, and color. Because of their lack of visual experiences in their environment, such as the observation of tasks or behaviors of others, they must learn by other means concepts that sighted individuals often take for granted. This adaptive learning of tasks then becomes a natural part of their developmental process so that the adjustment to visual limitations is incorporated into their self-perception and daily activities as a normal part of growing up.

Individuals who lose their vision later in life have the advantage of being able to draw on visual experiences in the environment as a frame of reference for physical concepts, but they may find it more difficult to accept their blindness than do those who have never had vision. Individuals who lose their vision later in life are required to make certain modifications of self-perception as a result of physical changes and subsequent restructuring of daily activities. Newly blind individuals may experience grief and despair over the loss of visual function, become extremely dependent, feel insecure in new situations, and perceive a marked loss of autonomy. Some may become reluctant to interact in social situations, possibly because of the awkwardness of some initial attempts at social interactions. The loss of control over standard methods of initiating conversations (e.g., eye contact and other nonverbal cues), the noted uncomfortableness or overhelpfulness of sighted persons, and often prolonged gaps in conversations may lead newly blind individuals to believe that they are being watched or ignored.

There are many aspects to the process of accommodation to blindness. Individuals with a visual loss must adjust their self-concept and personal goals to take into account the realistic limits imposed by their disability. They must develop adaptive skills and new capabilities, and must draw on personal resources to adjust to the disability.

The special needs of the legally blind and partially sighted are often overlooked, because these individuals do not fit into the category of either the blind or the sighted population. These individuals may exhibit high levels of anxiety as a result of this discrepancy. They may try to function as a sighted person, or their families and their peers may expect them to do so. In addition, they may be unsure about whether or when they will lose more of their residual vision. This insecurity may lead them to deny the disability altogether and to associate only with sighted persons in an attempt to be accepted by the mainstream of society. They may also refuse to use low-vision aids, such as a cane, for mobility; reject suitable orientation-and-mobility training; or even engage in activities such as illegal driving. The emphasis on self-care and independence for the visually impaired must be tempered with judgment and concern for the welfare of the individual, as well as for that of others. People often view the ability to drive as very important in the maintenance of independence, especially in the socialization process. This makes it extremely difficult for the individuals who are losing their vision to give up this activity. Furthermore, by its very nature, the gradual loss of vision creates a time period in which the decision to stop driving is particularly difficult.

Life Style Issues

Vision is crucial for many activities of daily living. Individuals with little or no vision must learn new techniques for carrying out the routine activities of self-care and mobility. They must orient themselves to their home environment so that they may move freely from room to room without risk of injury. Those with visual impairments should be informed of any physical changes to their immediate environment (e.g., movement of furniture). In addition, doors should be left completely open or closed, and these individuals should be informed so that they do not bump into a partially open door. These individuals must also learn techniques of locating chairs and seating themselves so as not to fall.

At first, tasks such as pouring water into a glass without spilling it, buttering bread, or cutting meat may seem insurmountable. Most blind people learn to prepare their meals and dine independently, however, once they have been oriented to the location of food, tableware, and cooking utensils. They can learn cooking through techniques such as the systematic placement of cooking equipment and utensils and special labeling on cans, frozen foods, oven dials, and other items.

Through training, individuals with visual impairments are gradually able to assume personal responsibility for self-care. Rehabilitation teachers provide in-home training in the skills of daily living. Activities such as bathing, combing the hair, shaving, applying makeup, and dressing in a coordinated fashion can all be performed independently through skills training and systematic organization and labeling of personal items.

Although individuals with a moderate to mild visual impairment may carry on much of their personal business with low-vision aids, those with a severe visual impairment or blindness may need someone else's help to read a bill, a check, an invoice, or a personal letter. Some individuals have difficulty in adjusting to this loss of privacy. In other instances, documents or forms must be translated into braille or read to the individual, perhaps reducing the efficiency of action or response to the document.

Outside the home, individuals with severe visual impairments can learn techniques of mobility in new environments with the use of a cane or guide dog. Through these techniques, blind persons are able to travel to work or to other destinations of their choice. They can also learn methods of carrying money so as to discriminate between bills, as well as ways to discriminate between different coins. The leisure activities that individuals with visual impairments can continue to enjoy include many outdoor activities, such as swimming, hiking, and fishing. With special adaptive procedures, even bicycling is still possible.

Although a visual loss does not affect sexual activity directly, the impact of the loss of vision on self-esteem may impinge on sexual activity. In addition, the severely visually impaired person does not see the facial expressions and other nonverbal communication that are an integral part of sexual relationships. Information about relationships that is normally developed through visual modeling may not be available to visually impaired individuals if they have been without sight since an early age. Consequently, it may be necessary to teach the appropriate social behaviors that are generally learned by observation to the visually impaired teen-ager or young adult.

Social Issues

Major obstacles to the effective functioning of visually impaired individuals in social environments are the social stereotyping and attitudes of sighted individuals toward the blind. Many view the blind as helpless and dependent. Others believe the myth that the blind develop extraordinary powers of hearing and touch to compensate for the loss of vision, rather than recognizing that blind individuals learn to make more effective use of their other senses in their effort to interpret their environment. The negative attitudes or stereotypical views held by friends, employers, and casual acquaintances can have a major impact on the visually impaired individual. Unfortunately, many blind individuals tend to conform to social expectations, thus limiting their own potential.

The inability of the visually impaired individual to see the social behavior of others may also affect social interactions. Much social interaction and communication is mediated by watching the actions and reactions of others through posture, touching, and other forms of nonverbal communication. The absence of these visual cues can place the visually impaired person at a disadvantage in a social setting, unless all concerned have developed increased awareness and sensitivity.

Although the attitudes of family members are important factors in an individual's adjustment to most disabilities, their attitudes appear to have an especially powerful influence on the adjustment of a visually impaired individual. The family's attitude during rehabilitation may determine the individual's motivation to learn and accept major changes in life style. Families who are overprotective or highly anxious, or who encourage dependent behaviors may prevent or impede rehabilitation. Families who foster positive attitudes and demonstrate their recognition of the essential worth of the visually impaired individuals, on the other hand, can be a major asset to rehabilitation.

Vocational Issues

The degree of the vocational impact of a visual disorder depends on the nature of the employment, the type of visual impairment, and the life stage at which the visual impairment occurs. Many individuals with partial vision are able to continue in their field of employment with special adaptive or low-vision aids. Others must learn new job skills. When visual loss is progressive, ongoing evaluation and planning for decreasing visual acuity should be part of the rehabilitation plan.

Not only on-the-job activity, but also the ability to get to and from work must be considered. If the individual is no longer able to drive, but no public transportation is available, suitable alternatives for transportation to and from work must be devised.

BIBLIOGRAPHY

Barber, T.C., and Langfitt, D.E. *Teaching the Medical/Surgical Patient—Diagnostics and Procedures.* Bowie, Md.: Robert J. Brady Co., 1983.

Berkow, R., and Fletcher, A.J., eds. *The Merck Manual of Diagnosis and Therapy.* Rahway, N.J.: Merck Sharpe and Dohme Research Laboratories, 1987.

Brunner, L.S.; Emerson, C.P.; Ferguson, L.K.; and Suddarth, D.S. *Textbook of Medical-Surgical Nursing.* Philadelphia: W.B. Saunders Co., 1970.

Corbett, J.V. *Diagnostic Procedures in Nursing Practice.* Norwalk, Conn.: Appleton-Century-Crofts, 1982.

Corbett, J.V. *Laboratory Tests in Nursing Practice.* Norwalk, Conn.: Appleton-Century-Crofts, 1983.

Elman, M.J. "Retinal Detachment." *Hospital Medicine* 25(1989):120–135.

Emerson, D.L. "Facing Loss of Vision: The Response of Adults to Visual Impairment." *Journal of Visual Impairment and Blindness* 75(1981):41–45.

Guyton, A.C. *Human Physiology and Mechanisms of Disease.* Philadelphia: W.B. Saunders Co., 1982.

Keele, C.A.; Neil, E.; and Joels, N. *Samson Wright's Applied Physiology.* New York: Oxford University Press, 1982.

Luckman, J., and Sorensen, K.C. *Medical-Surgical Nursing: A Psychophysiologic Approach.* Philadelphia: W.B. Saunders Co., 1987.

Moore, J.E. "Impact of Family Attitudes toward Blindness/Visual Impairment on the Rehabilitation Process." *Journal of Visual Impairment and Blindness* 78(1984):100–106.

National Institute of Handicapped Research. "Sensory Aids for Visually-Impaired Clients." *Rehab Brief* 5 (1982):1–4.

Nursing 87 Books. *Patient Teaching.* Springhouse, Pa.: Springhouse Corporation Book Division, 1987.

Overbury, O.; Grieg, D.; and West, M. "The Psychodynamics of Low Vision: A Preliminary Study." *Journal of Visual Impairment and Blindness* 76(1982):101–105.

Rakel, R.E. *Conn's Current Therapy 1990.* Philadelphia: W.B. Saunders Co., 1990.

Scheer, S.J., ed. *Medical Perspectives in Vocational Assessment of Impaired Workers.* Gaithersburg, Md.: Aspen Publishers, 1991.

Silerston, D. "A Guide to Caring for Low-Vision Patients." *Medical Times* 115(1987):59–64.

Smith, D.W., and Hanley-Germain, C.P. *Care of the Adult Patient.* Philadelphia: J.B. Lippincott Co., 1975.

Stolov, W.C., and Clowers, M.R. *Handbook of Severe Disability.* Washington, D.C.: U.S. Department of Education, Rehabilitation Services Administration, 1981.

Vander Kolk, C. "Rehabilitation Counseling with the Visually Impaired." *Journal of Applied Rehabilitation Counseling* 14(1983):13–19.

Vander, A.J.; Sherman, J.H.; and Luciano, D.S. *Human Physiology: The Mechanisms of Body Function.* New York: McGraw-Hill Book Co., 1985.

Wyngaarden, J.B., and Smith, J.H. *Cecil Textbook of Medicine.* Philadelphia: W.B. Saunders Co., 1988.

chapter 11

Dermatologic Disorders

NORMAL STRUCTURE AND FUNCTION

The skin is the largest organ of the body. It has a number of functions, such as protecting the body's inner structures from the environment, regulating body temperature, and acting as a major sensory organ.

The skin consists of two layers, the epidermis and the dermis (Figure 11-1). The outer layer **(epidermis)** protects the deeper tissues from drying, from invasion by organisms, and from trauma. The epidermis has several layers. The deepest layer of the epidermis constantly produces new cells, which are pushed to the surface of the skin; there they die, are shed, and are replaced by new cells. Cells called **melanocytes** contain the skin pigment **melanin**, which is responsible for skin color. For example, fair-skinned people produce less melanin than do dark-skinned people.

The inner layer of skin **(dermis)** lies beneath the epidermis. It contains blood vessels, nerves, and lymphatics, as well as various types of cells that promote wound healing. With the exception of the palms of the hands and the soles of the feet, there are hair follicles in the dermis throughout the body. In addition, the dermis contains the major sensory fibers that are responsible for distinguishing pain, touch, heat, and cold. **Sebaceous glands**, which produce an oily substance that protects the skin from excessive dryness, and **sweat glands**, which produce perspiration, are also located in the dermis. Water and electrolytes are eliminated through perspiration. When the environment is warm, the evaporation of perspiration cools the body. When the environment is cool, the constriction of superficial blood vessels conserves the warmth in the body.

Interfacing with the dermis at its lower level is a **subcutaneous** layer of fat, also called **adipose tissue**. This subcutaneous fat not only provides insulation for the body, but also gives shape and contour over bone.

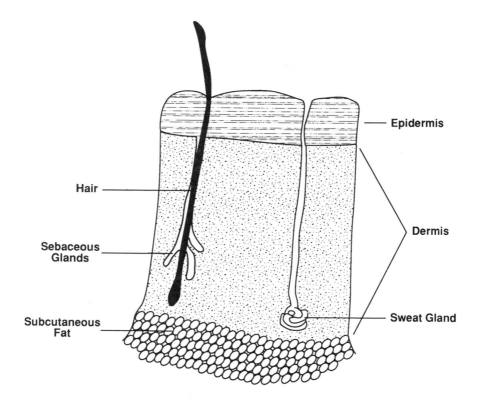

Figure 11-1 Section of Normal Skin.

DISORDERS OF THE SKIN

Because the skin is in constant contact with the environment, it is vulnerable to injury and irritation. It is also vulnerable to changes in the internal body environment, and may be the mirror of systemic conditions, such as lupus erythematosus (see Chapter 8). Emotional factors can also precipitate or contribute to disorders of the skin. Skin disorders may be localized or may involve the entire body; they may cause mild discomfort or severe pain and disfigurement.

Dermatitis

The general term **dermatitis** describes a superficial inflammation of the skin. The possible symptoms include redness **(erythema)**, swelling **(edema)**, itching

(pruritus), or rash (which may or may not include blisters). The term *eczema* is often used interchangeably with chronic dermatitis.

Contact dermatitis is a localized skin inflammation that results from contact with a specific substance. The symptoms occur at the site of contact. The substance may produce an allergic response as a result of a previous exposure, or the substance may be a primary irritant that causes a nonallergic skin reaction following exposure. Common causes of irritant contact dermatitis are chemicals, dyes, cosmetics, and industrial agents. Usually, only the skin that comes into contact with the substance is involved, so the area of skin affected is rather clearly demarcated. The symptoms generally disappear when contact with the offending agent is avoided.

Allergic Reactions

An **allergy** is a hypersensitivity to a specific substance or substances. Some individuals experience allergic reactions after exposure to certain substances that cause an immune response within the body. Their sensitization to the substance may take days or weeks, but, once the response has been established, the next contact with the substance produces allergic symptoms.

Allergic responses may be external or systemic. External allergic reactions consist of symptoms such as hives **(urticaria)**, redness, swelling, itching, or rash. Systemic allergic responses (e.g., allergic reactions to medication or certain foods) may include skin manifestations in addition to generalized body symptoms, some of which can seriously compromise respiratory function. The treatment of allergy is usually directed toward avoiding contact with the offending agent, toward reducing sensitivity to the substance if contact cannot be avoided, or toward reducing or eliminating the symptoms associated with the allergic response.

Psoriasis

A chronic, recurrent disease, **psoriasis** is characterized by patches of redness covered by unsightly scales. There are periods of remission and periods of exacerbation of varying frequency and duration. Itching may be mild or severe. Anxiety and stress can exacerbate the disease. Although the cause of psoriasis is unknown, there may be a familial tendency toward its development. Psoriasis does not affect the individual's general health, but the psychological and social stigma associated with an obvious unsightly skin disease may be debilitating. The prognosis depends on the extent and the severity of the disease. In general, the earlier the disease begins, the more severe the manifestations are. There is no cure for psoriasis. Treatment is directed toward controlling the symptoms.

Infections of the Skin

A number of organisms, including bacteria, fungi, parasites, or viruses, may infect the skin. Infection may be the primary cause of a skin disorder, or it may be a secondary condition associated with another skin disorder. The degree and length of disability associated with infections of the skin depend on the type and severity of the infection. Effective treatment requires the proper identification of the causative organisms and treatment appropriate to those particular organisms.

Herpes Zoster (Shingles)

Caused by the same virus that causes chickenpox, herpes zoster is an infection that affects the nerves of the central nervous system. The skin lesions that accompany the condition usually follow the course of a peripheral sensory nerve on the body. The symptoms often begin with fever, chills, and fatigue; later, blisters erupt along a nerve route, usually on the trunk of the body, although they may appear on other parts of the body. The pain associated with the skin lesions may be severe. Antiherpetic medication, administered either orally or intravenously, is often required. The disease usually has no residual effects, but the skin lesions may leave scars, which may be quite disfiguring if they involve a facial area. At times, some residual discomfort at the site of the skin lesion may remain after the lesions have subsided.

Skin Cancers

Cancer of the skin occurs more frequently than does cancer of any other organ. Because **basal cell carcinoma** is directly visible, it can be diagnosed earlier and, therefore, has a high cure rate. **Malignant melanoma**, a cancer that originates in the melanocytes, is a more dangerous type of skin cancer. Malignant melanomas are the most common fatal skin disorder, because they spread rapidly into deeper skin layers and metastasize.

Burns

Any tissue injury that results from direct heat, chemicals, radiation, or electrical current is a burn. The most common type of burns, **thermal burns**, are caused by fire, hot liquids, or direct contact with a hot surface. In addition to causing direct injury to the skin, thermal burns can cause severe damage to underlying structures if the heat has been intensive or if the exposure has been prolonged.

Chemical burns result from direct contact with strong acids or alkaline agents, gases (e.g., mustard gas), or other chemicals that cause tissue death. The extent of injury from chemical burns depends on the duration of the contact, the concentration or strength of the chemical, and the amount of tissue exposed to the chemical source. Some chemicals cause burns directly through the production of physiological changes in the tissue with which they come into contact, while other chemicals cause burns indirectly through the heat produced by their chemical reaction with the skin.

The degree of damage caused by a **radiation burn** depends on the dose of radiation received. Sources of radiation burns may include ultraviolet radiation, such as the sun, as well as ionizing radiation, such as nuclear materials and x-rays. Localized skin reactions to low doses of radiation may cause discomfort, but usually heal spontaneously. Larger doses of local radiation may damage underlying tissues and organs, however, requiring more extensive treatment.

Electrical burns result from direct contact with electrical current or lightening. Injuries from electrical burns range from sudden death due to cardiac arrest to local tissue damage. The effects of electricity on tissue depend on the current, the voltage, the type of current (e.g., direct or alternating), and the duration of contact. Because the entry point of the electric current may be relatively small, electrical burns may appear to have caused little external damage. However, there is usually extensive internal damage because the current travels through the body tissues. In addition to the interference with the electrical activity of the heart, which may cause cardiac arrest, electrical burns can injure nerves, blood vessels, and other major organs. Electrical burns are always full-thickness burns and are associated with severe postburn disabilities, which may include multiple amputations that the injury necessitated.

The degree of tissue damage caused by a burn varies with the source of the burn, but several other factors also affect burn severity. One such factor is the burn depth. Burn injuries may consist of only one burn depth, or there may be a combination of different burn depths. Burn depth is typically divided into three categories.

1. **superficial (first-degree) burn**: a burn that affects only the epidermis. The skin is reddened and painful, but no underlying structures are damaged.
2. **partial-thickness (second-degree) burn**: a burn that affects both the epidermis and dermis. Not only is the skin reddened and painful, but also blisters may erupt, providing a portal of entry for organisms that can cause infection at the burn site.
3. **full-thickness (third-degree) burn**: a burn that destroys the dermis and epidermis, as well as skin appendages, such as hair follicles, sebaceous

glands, and sweat glands. There is little pain, because nerve endings have been destroyed. Full-thickness burns cannot heal spontaneously and are more susceptible to infection.

When tissue damage extends to the underlying subcutaneous fat, muscle, or bone, the burn is sometimes referred to as a **fourth-degree burn**.

In addition to the source of the burn and the burn depth, the percentage of body surface affected determines the severity of the burn. A common method of calculating the amount of body surface injured is the "**Rule of Nines**," in which the body is graphically divided into areas that represent a different percentage of the total body surface (Figure 11-2). A more accurate method of estimating the total body surface burn is the **Lund and Browder method**. Since body proportions are different in children and adults, this method calculates the surface area of different body parts according to age. The chart lists various body sections and the percentage of body surface each section represents from one year of age to adult. Each burned area is thus given percentage points based on the age of the individual. Points are then added to estimate the total area of the body surface burned.

The location of the burn also affects burn severity. For example, those with burns to the upper body, especially the head and neck, may be prone to respiratory complications because of possible smoke inhalation, heat damage to the respiratory structures, or restriction of air passages owing to swelling caused by the injury. The points of contact and the pathway that the current followed through the body are important considerations in determining the severity of tissue damage caused by electrical burns.

The individual's age and medical history are also important. Individuals who are very young or very old are the most vulnerable to the effects and complications of burns. Preexisting debilitating systemic conditions, such as heart disease, diabetes, lung disease, or chronic abuse of drugs or alcohol, can further complicate recovery and severely affect the prognosis.

Severe burns disrupt the body's internal balance. Because of the tissue injury, plasma seeps from blood vessels into surrounding tissues, causing swelling and decreasing the amount of fluid in the general circulation. As a result, the body's general homeostasis is lost, which may affect all body systems. A second danger that affects the prognosis for individuals with burns is infection, especially for those with partial-thickness or full thickness burns.

Depending on the extent and location of the burn, individuals may experience a variety of disabilities following a burn. If the burn involved an extremity, contractures may occur, limiting joint motion. Severe burns of the extremities may sometimes necessitate amputation. Burns around the head and face may involve loss of vision or loss of nose, ears, or hair. Other causes of disfigurement may be **hypertrophic scars**, large ropelike configurations of scar tissue that

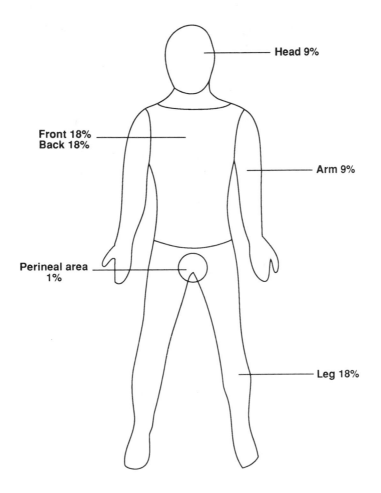

Figure 11-2 Rule of Nines.

form on the skin surface. Individuals with burns may experience severe **pruritus** (itching) for up to a year after the injury.

DIAGNOSTIC PROCEDURES

Biopsy

In a biopsy, a tissue specimen is removed for microscopic examination. A biopsy may be performed in order to diagnose a variety of conditions, including skin cancer and many other types of skin lesions. It is a relatively simple procedure that can be performed on an outpatient basis.

Scrapings, Cultures, and Smears

Scales of a skin lesion may be gently scraped from the surface of the skin and examined under a microscope. If there is an exudate, a sample of the exudate is removed with a swab and implanted in a culture medium. In other instances, the exudate is placed on a slide and examined immediately under the microscope; this procedure is known as a smear.

Patch Tests

In order to identify the substances that are responsible for allergic reactions, patch tests may be performed. Small amounts of various substances that are suspected of causing the reaction are applied to the skin, and the area is later examined for possible reactions.

Wood's Light Examination

Different types of skin infections can sometimes be identified by a Wood's light examination. The skin lesion is viewed in a darkened room under an ultraviolet light or black light (**Wood's light**). Lesions caused by different infecting organisms exhibit different colors, thus allowing the physician to identify fungal and bacterial skin infections.

TREATMENT

Medications

Many skin disorders are treated with **topical medications** (medications that are applied directly to the skin surface) in the form of lotions, creams, ointments, or powders. The type of medication chosen is dependent on the cause of the skin disorder. For example, **antifungals** are used for fungal infections, **antibiotics** or **antibacterials** for bacterial infections, and **antivirals** for viral infections. Topical **antipruritics** may be applied to reduce the discomfort due to itching. Topical **corticosteroids** are sometimes prescribed to reduce local inflammatory responses. Because topical medications can have side-effects, the prolonged use or overuse of medications such as corticosteroids should be avoided.

Some skin conditions may be treated with **systemic medication** (medications that are injected or taken orally to be carried throughout the body), such as antibiotics and corticosteroids. Although corticosteroids can produce dramatic improvement, they also have serious potential side-effects. Consequently, the use of corticosteroids requires careful monitoring by a physician (see Chapter 7).

Dressings and Therapeutic Baths or Soaks

The treatment of skin conditions in which there is excessive skin scaling or in which crusts have formed over lesions may include wet soaks or therapeutic baths to reduce the drying effects of air, relieve discomfort, or enhance the removal of scales and crusts so that healing may take place. In some instances, dressings are applied to skin lesions in order to protect the skin from injury and infection from the environment.

Light Treatment (Phototherapy)

Artificial light sources may be used for localized or generalized treatments of various skin conditions. Light therapies are frequently accompanied by therapeutic baths or soaks.

Burn Treatment

The type of treatment used for burns depends on the severity of the injury. Although individuals with minor burns and no complications may be treated at home, those with moderate or severe burns require hospitalization. Most individuals who have been moderately or severely burned are transferred to a hospital that has a specialized burn care unit.

During the acute phase, the treatment of moderate or severe burns is directed toward stabilizing the individual's general condition, restoring fluid balance, and preventing complications. The greater the surface area of the body burned and the greater the degree of the burn, the greater the risk of complications.

A major complication of burn injury is infection, which, unless controlled, can result in widespread infection throughout the body **(sepsis)**. Therefore, during the acute phase, the **eschar** (charred, dead tissue) must be removed **(débrided)** to reduce the risk of infection and to promote wound healing. If a large portion of the individual's body has been burned, débridement is usually performed. Débridement involves the clipping away of dead charred tissue in order to prevent growth of bacteria under the burn's surface. Débridement is a very stressful and painful procedure that is often performed on a daily basis until all **necrotic** (dead) tissue has been removed. In some instances, individuals may be taken to surgery for surgical débridement of dead tissue.

Because the severely burned individual is vulnerable to infection, the hospital environment must be relatively sterile. The individual may be placed in a room with a special air filtration system to screen out harmful organisms. All persons who provide care may wear caps, gowns, and masks to protect the individual from infection. During the acute phase of treatment, individuals undergo considerable stress not only because of the pain and discomfort associated with débridement, but also because of the social isolation that results from their restricted environment.

The nutritional needs of the individual with severe burns are great. In the early postburn period, individuals may lose up to 1 pound or more per day. Thus, a high caloric intake is essential to meet the increased energy requirements during the postburn period. In order to supply extra calories, it may be necessary to administer special fluids intravenously, as well as to provide a high-calorie diet.

Burn wounds are treated in different ways. At times, burns are treated with an exposure method in which no dressing, covering, or topical medication is applied to the wound. In these instances, strict sterile conditions are essential in order to prevent infection. In other instances, the wound may not be covered, but topical medication may be applied. In some cases, the burn wound is covered with dressings that are changed daily. The method of treatment depends on the type and extent of the burn wound, as well as on the general philosophy of the burn unit in which the individual is being treated.

Certain parts of the body require special care when burned. If the hands, arms, legs, or neck have been burned, special care is necessary to prevent the loss of function due to scarring or **contractures** (fixation of a joint in a position of nonfunction). In some cases, affected joints may be splinted in a position of function to prevent the formation of contractures. Facial burns not only can cause disfigurement, but also can damage the ears or eyes. Every effort must be made to prevent complications that could further interfere with function.

After the acute phase of treatment, which can last from several weeks to several months, grafting procedures usually begin. At times, **biological dressings** are used to cover a burn wound temporarily and prepare it for grafting. It is often necessary to change these biological dressings every several days. The types of biological dressings include

- **xenograft (heterograft)**: a graft taken from another species. **Porcine** (pig skin) grafts are often used for burn wounds.
- **homograft**: a graft taken from the same species, but not the same person. Homografts may be taken from a living donor or from a cadaver skin bank.
- **synthetic graft**: a graft that has been chemically manufactured.

When the burn wound appears healthy, an autograft is applied. An **autograft** is a section of the individual's own skin that has been removed from an uninvolved site. Depending on the size of the graft needed, the same donor site may be used repeatedly. A **split-thickness graft** is the epidermis and part of the dermis in which many little slits have been made to allow it to expand and cover a larger area. A **full-thickness graft**, which includes the epidermis and the dermis from the donor site, may be used for reconstruction.

The healing burn area may be compressed with elastic dressings to prevent or decrease the formation of hypertrophic scars. Special elasticized garments, such as gloves, vests, face masks, or neck garments, are available to be worn continually over the body part for a year or more to prevent this type of scar formation. The garments are customized to fit the specific body part involved.

If contractures have occurred as a result of the burn, physical therapy may be necessary to return mobility to a joint. When the measures are unsuccessful or if the contracture is severe, surgical intervention may be necessary.

Many individuals with severe burns require reconstructive or plastic surgery after the wound has healed, especially if there has been severe deformity or disfigurement. Such surgical interventions may be performed to reconstruct a body part, such as the nose or the ear, or to remove hypertrophic scar tissue. Many of these procedures take place over a number of years after the initial burn injury.

FUNCTIONAL IMPLICATIONS

Psychological Issues

The skin, exposed and readily observable, determines to a great extent an individual's appearance to others, and it is through personal appearance that others build an image about an individual. The individual, in turn, observes the reaction of others and incorporates it into his or her own self-image. Consequently, conditions that affect the skin can have a considerable impact on an individual's perception and attitudes.

Disease or injury that affects the face may be particularly devastating. More than any other body part, the face is tied to personal identity. Although other body parts can be covered by clothing, the face is left exposed so that disfigurement is readily observable. Our society places considerable emphasis on a clear, radiant appearance. When disease or injury mars this image, it is not surprising that the psychological impact on the affected individual is considerable.

Disease and injury of the skin may isolate an individual perhaps more than any other condition. Some people, because they associate skin diseases with uncleanliness and contagiousness, may avoid individuals with skin disorders even though these associations are unfounded. Because of the reactions of others, individuals with skin disease or injury may become very sensitive. Having experienced stares or other negative reactions, they may develop an accentuated state of awareness and assume that others are focusing totally on their appearance. They may become extremely self-conscious and withdraw from social contact.

The psychological impact of skin disease is multiplied for individuals who have experienced severe burns. The burn experience can be both physically and emotionally devastating. Individuals who have been scarred or disfigured by burns must make psychological and physiological adjustments not only to their disfigurement, but also to the immediate injury and to the long-term course of hospitalization and treatment. The suddenness of the injury itself produces a primary emotional stress. The impact is heightened by a variety of other situational factors, such as the separation from family, friends, and other sources of gratification; the experience of pain; the disruption of future life plans; and the threat to their sense of desirability and attractiveness to others.

The treatment of burns often involves isolation, pain, and multiple operations and treatment over an extended period of time. Depression frequently results from feelings of helplessness and grief over the losses experienced. Individuals in a burn unit are subjected to numerous painful treatments and procedures, as well as isolated from close human contact. They may feel that they have little power over what is done to them and for them, which can be frightening and frustrating. They may feel a loss of both personal and social satisfaction, as well as an alteration in their relationships with others.

Anxiety is also a common psychological response to burns. Individuals who have been burned may be apprehensive, realistically so, because of the painful procedures that they must endure. For some, the pain associated with the treatment procedures is a reminder of the initial injury, thus increasing anxiety and intensifying pain. Reactions may become generalized so that, even after the treatment period, individuals may continue to experience anxiety about unknown or unrecognized dangers.

Because burns are frequently associated with accidents, the circumstances sometimes lead to anger, guilt, regret, or resentment. If the accident was caused by the negligence or actions of others, the individuals who have been burned may experience considerable hostility and anger. If the accident was caused by their own actions or if others were also injured as a result, self-blame and guilt may intensify their reaction to the injury.

As these individuals begin to think about the future after the immediate burn treatment period, their psychological responses may be characterized by false hopes and magical optimism, particularly when skin grafting and reconstruction begin. They may have unrealistic expectations about the results of surgery or deny that there will be a permanent deformity. When the continuing disfigurement and/or limitations become apparent, they may again sink into a state of depression and withdrawal before gradually adjusting to their condition.

It is difficult psychologically for individuals who have been disfigured by burns to reenter the community. Individuals may test family and friends with unusual requests or with behaviors designed to get attention. Adjusting to the reactions of others, dealing with social stigma, and realistically accepting limitations are important psychological issues with which the individual with burns must deal.

Life Style Issues

The changes in life style that result from skin conditions are dependent on the severity of the condition and on the extent and circumstances of the disability. Skin conditions that result from exposure to or contact with certain substances within the environment make it necessary to avoid those substances. The discomfort associated with some skin conditions, such as itching, may affect daily activities to some degree. If special baths or dressings are required, these treatments must be provided for within the daily routine.

Acute skin conditions may be treated and prevented. Chronic skin conditions require ongoing treatment or intervention. Stress affects some skin conditions, and individuals with these conditions may need to learn ways to reduce stress in their environment or ways to alter their reaction to stress.

The life style issues that arise in relation to burns depend on the extent, nature, and location of the burn itself. For example, severe burns of the hands can result in contractures of the hands and fingers, necessitating the use of assistive devices for the activities of daily living. Burns to the face that result in loss of vision may also make it necessary to use adaptive devices (see Chapter 10).

Although conditions of the skin may not affect sexual function directly, society places considerable importance on physical attractiveness, especially when related to issues of sexuality. Consequently, skin disease or disfigurement, particularly of the face, as well as the reactions of others, may alter an individual's feelings of desirability. The anxiety or depression that accompanies skin conditions may further disrupt sexual function.

Social Issues

Visible disabilities provoke greater discrimination and social stigma than do invisible disabilities. Skin disorders, especially if they involve the face, evoke even more profound responses from others. People may feel uneasy in the presence of individuals with a disfigurement or deformity and uncertain what to do or say. In a social setting, individuals with deformity or disfigurement due to skin disease or injury may encounter staring, feelings of pity, or repulsion. These reactions may cause individuals with a skin condition to limit or avoid social activities or to restrict their social interactions with others.

Individuals who have been burned severely often require a series of reconstructive operations over several years. Thus, frequent hospitalizations interrupt their work and home activities. Relationships may be altered because of absences from the social environment necessitated by these repeated hospitalizations. The increased dependence and length of hospitalization due to burns can disrupt relationships within the family, as well as other social relationships.

Friends and family may be shocked at the sudden change in an individual's appearance after a burn injury. Depending on the circumstances of the accident, family members and friends may feel anger, guilt, or resentment, which can be manifest in a variety of ways. In an attempt to make sense of the tragedy and its aftermath, family members, friends, and co-workers may focus on the question of responsibility for the accident. Those who were present at the time of the injury may feel they should have done more or that they were to blame. Others may wonder why they escaped the same type of injury. These feelings may affect their reactions to the individual and their further social interactions with him or her.

Families may grieve for the loss of their image of the individual and for what might have been. Reactions may range from oversolicitude to emotional withdrawal. Concerns about financial considerations and altered social roles may cause additional family stress.

Vocational Issues

Most individuals with skin disorders continue in their regular mode of employment, although individuals whose skin condition is precipitated or exacerbated by exposure to substances in the work environment may require special considerations. In these instances, alterations in the work site or precautions in the performance of certain work-related activities may be necessary. If stress precipitates or exacerbates the skin condition, measures to decrease stress at the work site or to improve the individual's reaction to the stress should also be taken.

In some instances, it may be necessary to alter the work site. Because skin cancer appears to be related to exposure to the sun, those who work outside should take precautions to avoid excessive exposure, such as wearing protective clothing or sun shields. Those who have had skin cancer or who have a propensity toward it should take additional precautions to avoid direct exposure to the sun as much as possible.

The attitudes of employers and co-workers may create barriers to employment for individuals with skin conditions, especially when the condition alters their appearance considerably. Co-workers may fear contagiousness or may be uncomfortable because of the individual's appearance. In the case of burns, depending on the circumstances, guilt because of the injury may also affect the acceptance of the individual in the work place.

The ability of individuals who have been burned to return to their former occupations is dependent not only on the occupation itself, but also on the extent and location of the burn. Many individuals are able to return to employment within 6 months of injury. Those with severe burns that necessitate extensive reconstructive surgery may require intermittent hospitalizations for 1 to 2 years after the initial injury, however. The disruption to work activity associated with these hospitalizations should be considered before the individual returns to regular employment. Those who have other disabilities resulting from burns, such as the loss of a limb or the loss of vision, have the vocational limitations noted for those with the same disability due to other causes (see Chapters 7 and 10). Contractures as a result of burns may also limit mobility and, if the hands are involved, manual dexterity.

Individuals who must wear compression garments to prevent hypertrophic scarring may need to avoid extremely warm work environments because of the excessive warmth of the garment. Those who wear compression gloves also have decreased manual dexterity. A facial mask may be a cosmetic disability if dealing with the public is a requirement of the occupation. The degree to which cosmetic appearance due to the burn itself is a factor in employment depends on the individual, the occupation, and the employer.

Skin that has been grafted may be more sensitive than is normal skin. Consequently, grafts should not be exposed to extremes of temperature. In addition, there may not be as much fat insulation at burned areas as there is in healthy normal tissue, which affects the individual's ability to tolerate extremes of temperature. Extremely dry climates may exacerbate the itching that may be associated with the new skin growth of skin grafts, so a more humid environment may be desirable.

Other residual problems from burns may also affect the appropriateness of the work environment. For example, individuals who have experienced altered lung function as a result of smoke inhalation should avoid work settings in which there is air pollution or exposure to smoke and dust. Individuals with burns to the lower extremities may have difficulty in standing for prolonged periods and may need more sedentary employment.

BIBLIOGRAPHY

Barber, T.C., and Langfitt, D.E. *Teaching the Medical/Surgical Patient—Diagnostics and Procedures.* Bowie, MD: Robert J. Brady Co., 1983.

Berkow, R., and Fletcher, A.J., eds. *The Merck Manual of Diagnosis and Therapy.* Rahway, N.J.: Merck Sharpe and Dohme Research Laboratories, 1987.

Bernstein, N.R. *Emotional Care of the Burned and Disfigured.* Boston: Little, Brown & Co., 1976.

Brunner, L.S.; Emerson, C.P.; Ferguson, L.K.; and Suddarth, D.S. *Textbook of Medical-Surgical Nursing.* Philadelphia: W.B. Saunders Co., 1970.

Corbett, J.V. *Diagnostic Procedures in Nursing Practice.* Norwalk, Conn.: Appleton-Century-Crofts, 1982.

Corbett, J.V. *Laboratory Tests in Nursing Practice.* Norwalk, Conn.: Appleton-Century-Crofts, 1983.

Davidson, T.N.; Bowden, M.L.; Tholen, D.; James, M.H.; and Feller, I. "Social Support and Post-Burn Adjustment." *Archives of Physiology and Medical Rehabilitation* 62(1981):274–278.

Gelfand, J.A. "Burn Injuries: The Neglected Epidemic." *Drug Therapy* (October 1984):19–22.

Goldberg, R.T.; Bernstein, N.R.; and Crosby, R. "Vocational Development of Adolescents with Burn Injury." *Rehabilitation Counseling Bulletin* 18(1975):140–146.

Guyton, A.C. *Human Physiology and Mechanisms of Disease.* Philadelphia: W.B. Saunders Co., 1982.

Keele, C.A.; Neil, E.; and Joels, N. *Samson Wright's Applied Physiology.* New York: Oxford University Press, 1982.

Luckman, J., and Sorensen, K.C. *Medical-Surgical Nursing: A Psychophysiologic Approach.* Philadelphia: W.B. Saunders Co., 1987.

Nursing 87 Books. *Patient Teaching.* Springhouse, Pa.: Springhouse Corporation Book Division, 1987.

Punch, J.D.; Smith, D.J.; and Robson, M.C. "Hospital Care of Major Burns." *Postgraduate Medicine* 85(1989):205–215.

Rakel, R.E. *Conn's Current Therapy 1990.* Philadelphia: W.B. Saunders Co., 1990.

Robertson, K.E.; Cross, P.J.; and Terry, J.C. "Burn Care: The Crucial First Days." *American Journal of Nursing* 85(1985):30–47.

Scheer, S.J.,ed. *Medical Perspectives in Vocational Assessment of Impaired Workers.* Gaithersburg, Md.: Aspen Publishers, 1991.

Smith, D.W., and Hanley-Germain, C.P. *Care of the Adult Patient.* Philadelphia: J.B. Lippincott Co., 1975.

Stolov, W.C., and Clowers, M.R. *Handbook of Severe Disability.* Washington, D.C.: U.S. Department of Education, Rehabilitation Services Administration, 1981.

Vander, A.J.; Sherman, J.H.; and Luciano, D.S. *Human Physiology: The Mechanisms of Body Function.* New York: McGraw-Hill Book Co., 1985.

Wernick, R.L.; Jarmeko, M.E.; and Taylor, P.W. "Pain Management in Severely Burned Adults: A Test of Stress Inoculation." *Journal of Behavioral Medicine* 4(1981):103–109.

Wyngaarden, J.B., and Smith, J.H. *Cecil Textbook of Medicine.* Philadelphia: W.B. Saunders Co., 1988.

chapter 12

Cancers

NORMAL STRUCTURE AND FUNCTION OF THE CELL

The basic unit of all living things is the **cell**. The human body contains approximately 75 trillion cells. Although different types of cells perform different functions, all cells have certain basic characteristics in common. All cells require nutrition and oxygen in order to live, and almost all cells have the ability to reproduce. The reproduction of cells is a controlled process so that cells die and form at an approximately equal rate in adults, maintaining a balance in the number of cells present at any time.

The precise way in which cell growth and reproduction are regulated within the human body is unknown. Some cells, such as the cells that make up the layers of the skin or the lining of the intestine, grow and reproduce frequently. Other cells, such as those that make up the musculature of the gastrointestinal tract, may not reproduce for years. Cells that make up neurons, the functional unit of the nervous system, do not reproduce at all. Similarly little is known about the mechanism that controls the number of each specific cell type that is produced.

Different types of cells make up different parts of body tissue. Cells are named for their different characteristics. For example, **epithelial cells** are cells found in the skin, the lining of body organs (e.g., the lining of the intestine), and glandular tissue (e.g., the breast or prostate). Blood vessels, lymph vessels, and other lymph tissue are composed of **endothelial cells**. Different types of cells are also found in muscle, nerve, bone, and other tissues in the body.

Every cell contains **DNA** (genetic material that is the blueprint for all the body's structures). **Genes**, composed of DNA, carry hereditary information about all the characteristics of the organism. Although each cell contains all the genes for a particular organism, it uses only particular genes. This discrimination in the use of genes is the basis for different cell types. Genes determine the growth characteristics of cells, as well as when or whether the cells divide to form new cells. Before the cells can reproduce, however, the genes must reproduce themselves. After the genes reproduce, the cell divides, forming another cell identical to itself. It is through this systematic, organized reproduction of cells that continuity of life is maintained.

DEVELOPMENT OF CANCER

Cancer is not one disease, but many diseases. There are well over 100 types of cancers. They can arise from any type of cell and are classified according to the cell of origin.

Most frequently, the term *tumor* is assumed to be synonymous with cancer; however, not all tumors are cancerous. A **tumor,** also called a neoplasm, is a new and abnormal growth of cells that serves no useful function and may interfere with healthy tissue function. The reason for the proliferation of cells is often unknown. Tumors may be either **benign** (noncancerous) or **malignant** (cancerous). Although benign tumors may disturb body function by exerting pressure on surrounding tissues and, thus, preventing surrounding organs from obtaining a sufficient blood supply, they usually grow slowly, do not invade surrounding tissue, remain localized, and do not recur once removed. Generally, the cells in benign tumors closely resemble the normal cells in the tissue from which they multiplied.

Cancer develops when there has been an alteration **(mutation)** in the DNA within the normal cell. As a result, the control mechanism that regulates cell reproduction is lost. Because the reproduction of cancer cells is uncontrolled, they reproduce at a rate that exceeds the rate at which the normal cells in the tissue are dying. Some of the more virulent cancer cells are often described as **anaplastic**, meaning that their appearance takes on abnormal characteristics so that they are less differentiated than are the normal cells from which they are derived.

The original site of cancer cell reproduction is called the **primary site**, sometimes referred to as the **primary tumor**. Cancer cells do not remain confined to the original site, but extend and invade surrounding tissues as they reproduce. In addition, cancer cells are less adhesive than are normal cells. Selected cancer cells may break off from the original cluster, enter the bloodstream or the lymph system, and travel to other parts of the body, where they begin another abnormal pattern of reproduction. The movement of cancer cells from the original site to another part of the body is called **metastasis**. Cancer cell reproduction at this additional site is called a **secondary tumor**, meaning that metastasis has occurred and that the secondary tumor is not the original site of cancer growth.

Cancer cells compete with normal cells for nutrients. The reproduction of cancer cells is not well regulated, and some cancer cells reproduce at a more rapid rate than do normal cells. Eventually, available nutrients are taken from the normal cells in order to nourish the cancer cells.

Causes of Cancer

The exact cause of cancer is unknown. There are probably many causes, and it may be necessary for a variety of factors to be present in order for cancer to develop. Although specific causes are unknown, several factors are known to increase the risk of cancer.

- radiation
- some chemicals and pollutants
- smoking and tobacco use
- some viruses
- chronic physical irritation to a body part
- ultraviolet rays (sun)
- hereditary predisposition

The chemicals or other substances that are thought to cause cancer are called **carcinogens**. Some carcinogens may be present in the environment, but not readily evident. Individuals may be exposed to carcinogens within the environment or work place for a number of years before cancer develops. Some substances may not be carcinogenic in themselves, but may serve as co-carcinogens, promoting tumor formation in combination with other carcinogenic agents. Other factors, such as hormonal secretion, diet, and stress have been implicated as potential factors in the development of or propensity for cancer, but the specific mechanisms that contribute to this relationship are unknown.

Types of Cancer

Any type of cell in the body may be the source of cancer. Cancers are named for the type of tissue from which they originated. Some common types of cancers and the corresponding tissue from which they arise are

- **carcinoma**: cancer of the epithelial cells
- **sarcoma**: cancer of the bone, muscle, or other connective tissue
- **lymphoma**: cancer of the lymphatic system
- **leukemia**: cancer of blood cells or blood precursor cells
- **melanoma**: cancer of the pigment-producing cells, usually of the skin

Because the specific behavior of cancer cells depends on the type of cell from which they originated, there can be no generalizations made about cancer. Each type of cancer may progress at a different rate and may respond to different types of treatment in different ways. Consequently, the physician's classification of cancer is important in determining both treatment and prognosis.

Staging and Grading of Cancer

When cancer is diagnosed, it is important to determine not only the cancer type, but also the extent to which cancer cells have spread. This process is called **staging**. The most common system for staging today is the **TNM system**. The letter *T* stands for tumor; *N*, for node; and *M*, for metastasis. When there is no evidence of a primary tumor, the stage is defined as T0. If the cancer cells are present, but have not invaded the surrounding lymph nodes, the stage is defined as Tis (previously called **in situ**). As the tumor increases in size, it may be staged from T1 to T4, depending on the tumor size and involvement. When there is no lymph node involvement, the N staging is N0. If cancer cells extend beyond the initial tissue site and involve the lymph nodes in the surrounding area, however, the stage is N1, N2, or N3 (previously called **regional** involvement), depending on the degree of involvement and the abnormality of nodes. If the cancer cells remain at the original site, even though the surrounding tissues and lymph nodes are involved, the M staging is M0. When cancer cells have metastasized to another area of the body, however, staging is M1, M2, or M3, depending on the extent of the metastasis.

Histological studies and **grading** are laboratory procedures in which the type and structure of cancer cells are determined microscopically. A **pathologist** (a physician who specializes in the diagnosis of abnormal changes is tissues) examines the the cells under a microscope to determine their type and the extent to which they differ from their normal precursors. The histological type of cell and the grading of the cell are important in the determination of the treatment implemented and the prognosis. Individuals with tumor cells that are well **differentiated** (more similar to the cell of origin, with a more organized structure) may have a better prognosis, for example, than does an individual with tumor cells that are considered anaplastic (containing more abnormalities in structure).

DIAGNOSTIC PROCEDURES

In general, the earlier the diagnosis of cancer, the better the prognosis. Some cancers grow and invade surrounding tissue without causing physical symptoms. These cancers are called **occult malignancies**. Tests and procedures used to detect abnormalities before symptoms develop are called **cancer screening** procedures. When symptoms occur or when screening procedures have positive or suspicious results, additional diagnostic testing is necessary.

Radiographic Procedures (X-ray)

In addition to conventional roentgenography, computed axial tomography, magnetic resonance imaging, ultrasound, and, occasionally, arteriography may be helpful in identifying an abnormality in normal anatomical structure or the presence of a tumor. **Mammography** is a soft tissue radiographic examination of the breast that is frequently used as a screening procedure, as well as a diagnostic procedure, because it can reveal cancerous lesions before they can be detected by direct examination of the breast. Although these tests are important in identifying abnormalities, they rarely are used alone in the diagnosis of cancer. A positive diagnosis requires microscopic examination of the tumor cells (histological testing).

Diagnostic Surgery

In some instances, surgery may be done to confirm or rule out the presence of cancer. Depending on the size and location of the tumor, the surgical procedure may be relatively minor, such as the removal of an external wart or polyp, or a major intervention, such as an **exploratory laparotomy** (the surgical opening of the abdomen for the purpose of investigation).

Regardless of the type of diagnostic surgery performed, an accurate diagnosis of cancer can be made only after a microscopic examination of the tissue. For such an examination, a biopsy is performed to remove a small portion of tissue from the body. Biopsies may be done by inserting a needle into the tumor and removing some cells through the needle **(needle biopsy)**. Biopsies may also be done by making an incision and removing a portion of the tumor **(incisional biopsy)**. The type of biopsy done depends on the size and location of the tumor.

Cytology

The study of cells that have been scraped from tissue surrounding the area of interest is a cytological study. Perhaps the best known example of diagnostic cytology is the Papanicolaou smear (Pap smear). Cells from sputum specimens that have been coughed up from the lungs and other types of fluids may also be examined through diagnostic cytology.

Endoscopy

An **endoscopic examination** involves the insertion of a tubular device into a hollow organ or cavity in order to visualize the inside of the structure directly. The procedure may be done through a natural body opening or through a small incision. Examples of endoscopic examinations are bronchoscopy (see Chapter 3); sigmoidoscopy, gastroscopy, and esophagoscopy (see Chapter 6); and **laryngoscopy** (examination of the larynx or vocal cords). Endoscopy is also a method of obtaining a tissue sample from the internal structure for a histological examination.

Nuclear Medicine

In nuclear medicine, small amounts of radioactive materials are used for diagnostic procedures, and somewhat larger amounts are used for the treatment of disease. In the diagnosis of cancer, nuclear medicine procedures may be used for the detection and staging of cancers in the thyroid glands, liver, and bone. They may also be used to detect the presence of metastatic disease.

Laboratory Tests

Although laboratory tests per se may not be diagnostic of cancer, the results of laboratory tests may indicate impaired physiological function as a result of the cancer, such as the anemia or altered white blood cell count associated with leukemia. In some instances, laboratory tests are used for screening purposes. For example, both alpha-fetoprotein and carcinoembryonic antigen are normally found in embryonic and fetal tissues, but disappear after birth. In later life, however, tumors may produce these substances. Consequently, elevated levels of either in adults may be an indication of certain types of cancers, as well as of other diseases.

TREATMENT

Many factors are considered in determining which procedures are best for the treatment of a particular cancer. A major consideration is the type of cancer itself. Because different cancers grow at different rates, metastasize to different spots, and react differently to various forms of treatment, the histological *type* of cancer is a major determinant in treatment decisions. The *stage* of cancer is also considered. The extent to which cancer has invaded surrounding tissues and the presence of any *metastases* determine the aggressiveness, as well as the type, of treatment. The tumor location and its relationship to other vital organs determine the accessibility of the tumor for removal or treatment.

The goal of intervention also affects the type of treatment. Goals can include cure, extension of life or prevention of metastasis, and palliation. In terms of cancer treatment, **cure** is usually defined as no evidence of cancer for 5 years after treatment, indicating a normal life expectancy for the individual. Treatment for the prevention of metastasis, also called **adjuvant therapy**, is directed toward eliminating cancer that, although not detectable and not symptomatic, may be present and may cause a recurrence of disease. **Palliative therapy** is directed toward the relief of symptoms or complications of cancer, such as obstruction or severe pain, rather than toward cure.

Factors related to the individual with cancer must also be taken into consideration. Debilitation because of disease, the cancer itself, or age may compromise the individual's ability to withstand certain treatments. In some cases, the individual may feel that the benefits of some forms of cancer therapy are not worth the risks and side-effects; consequently, the individual may refuse the recommended treatment.

Cancer may be treated systemically or locally. Often, the treatment of cancer consists of a combination of the two. Cancer may be treated surgically, chemically **(chemotherapy)**, with radiation, or with other means—separately or in combination.

Surgical Procedures

Usually directed toward the local treatment of cancer, surgical procedures may be preventive, curative, palliative, or reconstructive. **Preventive surgery** may be performed when precancerous or suspicious lesions are found. For example, a mole or polyp that, although not malignant, has a high probability of becoming malignant in the future may be removed. **Curative surgery** is generally more extensive; it may involve not only the tumor, but also an organ or surrounding tissue. Depending on the size and location of the tumor, curative surgery can affect subsequent function only minimally, can impair function severely, or can cause permanent disfigurement. **Palliative surgery** is directed toward reducing the size or retarding the growth of the tumor, or relieving severe discomfort associated with the presence of the tumor. In all instances, the goal of palliative surgery is to prolong or increase the quality of life rather than to cure the disease. **Reconstructive surgery** is directed toward restoring maximal function or correcting disfigurement.

The surgical procedures used in the treatment of cancer may be considered simple or radical. **Simple** surgical procedures usually involve the removal of the tumor, while the surrounding structures and organs remain intact. **Radical** surgical procedures are more extensive; not only the tumor, but also some underlying tissue (e.g., muscle or organ) is removed. Radical surgery usually results in an alteration in function or appearance to some degree.

Chemotherapy

Chemical agents **(antineoplastic medications)** are used in the systemic treatment of cancer. These agents may be used alone or in conjunction with other forms of therapy, such as surgery and irradiation. This type of therapy, called chemotherapy, can be used for cure, prevention, or palliation. In general, chemotherapeutic agents affect the growth and reproduction of cancer cells.

There are a number of antineoplastic medications used in the treatment of cancer. Although these medications are different and may be administered differently, most affect rapidly dividing cells. Unfortunately, in addition to destroying and damaging cancer cells, these medications can also damage normal cells that grow rapidly, such as the cells of the hair follicles, skin, lining of the gastrointestinal tract, and bone marrow. As a result of the vulnerability of these cells, the toxic side-effects of chemotherapy may include hair loss **(alopecia)**, loss of appetite, nausea, vomiting, diarrhea, fatigue, and suppression of bone marrow function. The altered bone marrow function may interfere with the production of various components of blood; therefore, individuals undergoing chemotherapy may develop anemia, may bruise easily because of decreased blood clotting ability, and may be highly susceptible to infection because they have fewer white blood cells.

Chemotherapeutic agents may be given intravenously, intramuscularly, or orally; at times, they may be given intra-arterially, into a body cavity, and even topically. Treatment may be conducted on either an outpatient or an inpatient basis. The regimens vary with the agent and the disease. Some regimens are given daily; others are given for 1 day every 3 to 8 weeks. Some individuals may use a portable device that pumps small amounts of the chemotherapeutic agent constantly into a vein. In some instances, because the chemotherapeutic agent is administered in small doses over time, the toxic side-effects may be reduced. In other instances, high concentrations of chemotherapeutic agents may be injected directly into a body cavity, such as the bladder or the peritoneal cavity, in order to treat localized tumors. This type of treatment delivers maximal dosage of the medication to the tumor site and can also reduce systemic side-effects.

Not all individuals who receive chemotherapy experience side-effects. Those who do not have severe side-effects can, for the most part, continue their daily activities. No special precautions are necessary, with the exception of avoiding exposure to individuals with colds or flu because resistance may be lowered during chemotherapy.

Radiation Therapy

With **radiation therapy**, high-energy rays are used to damage cancer cells and prevent them from growing and reproducing. This technique may be used to cure cancer, to relieve symptoms, or to keep cancer under control.

Radiation therapy may be delivered externally or internally. During **external radiation therapy**, a machine beams high-energy rays to the cancer so that the maximum effect of radiation takes place in the tumor itself within the body. Even though the radiation penetrates the skin and underlying tissue, it does minimal damage to these structures. **Internal radiation therapy** involves inserting small amounts of radioactive material into the body. There are various types of internal radiation. With **intracavity therapy**, a radioactive substance is placed in a body cavity for a period of approximately 24 to 72 hours and is then removed; for example, a radioactive implant may be placed into the vagina for the treatment of cervical cancer. With **interstitial therapy**, a radioactive substance is placed into needles, beads, or seeds and implanted directly into the tumor. The interstitial implant may be removed after a specific period of time, or it may be left in place permanently, depending upon the half-life of the radioactive source.

Like chemotherapy, radiation therapy can affect the growth and reproduction of normal cells, resulting in potentially toxic side-effects. The number of normal cells exposed to the radiation, the dosage of radiation, the part of the body receiving radiation therapy, and individual variability determine the side-effects experienced. These side-effects may appear immediately or weeks or months after the radiation therapy was administered. Some individuals experience generalized symptoms similar to those of radiation sickness: nausea, vomiting, loss of appetite, fatigue, and headache. Other individuals may experience side-effects specific to the area irradiated, such as sore throat if the head or neck has been irradiated, or localized skin reactions, such as radiation burn. Like chemotherapy, radiation therapy may also cause bone marrow depression, resulting in anemia, lowered resistance to infection, and possible hemorrhage.

Other Forms of Cancer Therapy

A newer approach to the treatment of cancer is **immunotherapy**. The goal of immunotherapy is to strengthen the individual's own immune system so that it recognizes cancer cells as foreign objects and destroys them. Although currently not widely used, this form of therapy appears to show some promise for the future.

Some specific types of leukemia may be treated by **bone marrow transplantation**. This procedure is performed when the escalation of chemotherapy (marrow-toxic drugs) may result in a cure of the cancer, but the dosage would be le-thal to the individual's bone marrow. The goal of bone marrow transplantation is to provide healthy cells that can differentiate into blood cells to replace deficient or pathological cells. In preparation for bone marrow transplantation, individuals receive large doses of radiation and/or chemotherapy that eradicates any viable marrow. The preparatory treatment suppresses the immune system in order to reduce the incidence of graft rejection. Total body irradiation may produce reversible side-effects, but it may also result in sterility, which is not always reversible.

The most critical period is 2 to 4 weeks after the bone marrow transplantation. Because of the immunosuppression prior to surgery, individuals may have an in-creased susceptibility to infections. In addition, because immunosuppressive therapy drastically reduces the components in the blood that control bleeding, complications such as hemorrhage may result.

Common Cancers and Specific Treatments

The diagnostic procedure, treatment, and functional limitations associated with cancer differ with the anatomical site involved. In many instances, a combination of treatments, including surgery, chemotherapy, and irradiation, is used. In the treatment of cancer in its very early stages, surgery alone may be sufficient.

Cancer of the Gastrointestinal Tract

The treatment of cancer of the gastrointestinal tract or accessory organs often consists of the removal or major resection of the organs involved. Because the symptoms of cancers of the esophagus, stomach, liver, and pancreas frequently occur late in the disease, treatment may be directed toward palliation rather than cure.

The surgical treatment for cancer of the mouth may include the removal of the tumor, as well as the removal of the nearby lymph glands to determine whether the cancer has spread. If the cancer has spread to the neck or other tissues, more radical surgery may be indicated, resulting in facial deformity or disfigurement because of the amount of tissue removed. If the tongue has been partially re-moved, speech may be affected. Reconstructive surgery may be required later in order to minimize these effects.

The treatment of cancer of the large bowel (colon and rectum) usually involves both the surgical removal of the tumor and some resection of the colon itself. In many instances, the diseased part of the bowel can be removed and the two remaining ends joined together, enabling the individual to retain normal bowel function. When this is not possible, a colostomy may be performed (see Chapter 6).

Cancer of the Larynx

One of the most common cancers of the head and neck is cancer of the **larynx** (voice box). The larynx contains the vocal cords. The diagnostic procedures used to identify problems of the larynx often include a procedure called a **laryngoscopy**, in which a hollow tube is inserted into the larynx so that the physician can inspect the structures of the larynx and assess the function of the vocal cords.

Although the treatment of cancer of the larynx is dependent on a number of factors, it usually involves irradiation, surgery, or a combination of the two. For advanced cancer of the larynx, chemotherapy may also be indicated. If the tumor is discovered early, before there has been extensive involvement of the surrounding tissues, it may be necessary to remove only part of the larynx. This procedure is called a **subtotal (partial) laryngectomy**. Laser treatment, which destroys the tumor by intense light beams, may also be used to treat cancer of the larynx in its early stages. Both subtotal laryngectomy and laser treatment can preserve the capacity for normal speech, although they may affect voice quality to some degree.

When the cancer is more advanced, it may be necessary to remove the larynx completely. This procedure is called a **laryngectomy**. Usually, individuals who have undergone this type of surgery are unable to breathe or speak by normal mechanisms. After the larynx has been removed, the trachea is no longer connected either to the nasopharynx or to the nasal passages (see Chapter 3). The surgeon creates a permanent opening called a **tracheostomy** in the individual's neck and trachea, and the individual breathes through this opening rather than through the nose and mouth. Although able to eat and drink normally, the individual must breathe, cough, and sneeze through the tracheostomy.

After a laryngectomy, an individual must learn new techniques for speaking. One common technique is **esophageal speech**, which involves trapping air in the esophagus and gradually releasing it at the top of the esophagus to produce a pseudovoice. If the sounds produced by esophageal speech are too soft to be heard, a personal amplifier-speaker may be used to increase sound volume. For those individuals who are unable to master esophageal speech, there are alternatives. For example, in a special surgical procedure, a small plastic shunt may be placed between the trachea and esophagus so that closing the tracheostomy with the hand or fingers shunts air from the trachea to the esophagus, creating a pseudovoice. The plastic tube prevents food and liquid from entering the airway when the individual is eating.

An **artificial larynx** may also be used for speech. There are several types available; however, most are electronic, battery-operated devices that are held against the throat to produce sound. Although the artificial larynx is relatively easy to use, the speech produced has an electronic sound that some individuals find objectionable.

Individuals who have undergone a laryngectomy can carry out most activities of daily living normally. Because the opening leads directly into the trachea and lungs, individuals with a permanent tracheostomy should avoid activities such as swimming and water sports in which water could enter the opening, however. For cosmetic purposes, they may wear a scarf or other covering loosely around the neck; a covering also keeps dust and dirt out of the opening. Some individuals may notice a decreased ability to lift heavy objects, because they cannot close the tracheostomy to build up internal pressure as those who breathe normally can do by compressing their lips and holding their breath. Individuals who have had a total laryngectomy should always carry an identification card or wear a medical identification bracelet to inform emergency personnel that they are a total neck breather.

Only a few jobs may prove difficult for an individual after a laryngectomy. Those jobs that are performed in environments with extreme heat or cold, or those that would expose the individual to extreme dust or fumes should probably be avoided.

Cancer of the Lung

When used in the treatment of lung cancer, x-ray therapy is usually for palliation, rarely for cure. For individuals with small-cell cancer, chemotherapy is generally the treatment of choice. If surgical intervention is used for lung cancer, the primary aim is to remove the total tumor. The extent of the surgery depends on the cancer and its location in the lung. The removal of an entire lung is called a **pneumonectomy**; the removal of only one lobe of the lung is called a **lobectomy**. A **segmental resection** is the removal of a segment of the lung. After having a portion of the lung removed, individuals may need to limit their physical activity to some degree, depending on the amount of lung removed and the functional capacity remaining.

Cancer of the Musculoskeletal System

Musculoskeletal cancers frequently result in the amputation of an extremity (see Chapter 7). For some types of bone cancers, however, it may be possible to remove only a section of bone and to avoid amputating the whole extremity. In some instances, bone cancers may be reduced by chemotherapy and then controlled by radiotherapy.

Cancer of the Urinary System

Cancer can develop in any organ of the urinary system, but the most frequent site of cancer in the urinary tract is the bladder. Cancer of the bladder may be treated in a variety of ways, depending on the stage and type of cancer involved. A portion of the bladder or, at times, the total bladder may be surgically removed. The removal of a portion of the bladder may greatly diminish the capacity of the bladder. The removal of the whole bladder necessitates surgical reconstruction to provide a means for urinary drainage.

There are several means of urinary diversion. In some instances, the ureters are connected to the colon so that urine is excreted through the rectum; this procedure is called a **ureterosigmoidostomy**. Because urine mixes with the contents of the colon, bowel movements are liquid, and frequent evacuation of stool is necessary. Owing to the potential contamination of the urinary system by organisms of the colon, a major complication of this type of urinary diversion is chronic pyelonephritis (see Chapter 4).

In another procedure for urinary diversion, **cutaneous ureterostomy,** the ureters are brought through the abdomen to the outside of the body, where they drain directly into a bag attached to the outside of the abdomen. Still another urinary diversion procedure is called an **ileal conduit**, which involves removing a segment of small intestine (the ileum) and reconnecting the two remaining ends of bowel. Ureters are then connected to one end of the loop of small intestine that has been removed, and bringing the other end of the loop of small intestine to the outside of the abdomen to form an opening through which urine can drain. There is no voluntary control over the drainage of urine through the opening of either the cutaneous ureterostomy or the ileal conduit. A special bag called an **urostomy bag** is worn over the opening to collect urine.

Cancer of the kidney may necessitate removal of the kidney **(nephrectomy)**. When both kidneys are involved, a portion of one kidney may be left intact in order to maintain renal function. If both kidneys must be completely removed, the individual must be placed on regular dialysis (see Chapter 4). Although individuals who have undergone bilateral nephrectomy because of cancer are candidates for renal transplantation, they are usually maintained on dialysis for at least 1 year to observe for any cancer recurrence before a transplantation is attempted.

Cancer of the Brain or Spinal Cord

At times, a malignant tumor of the brain can be surgically removed and subsequently treated with chemotherapy and/or radiation therapy. If the tumor is small and has not invaded the surrounding tissue, the individual may be able to return to an active life. At other times, however, the tumor may be embedded in the brain to such an extent that surgery is not possible. In these instances, chemotherapy or radiation therapy alone may be instituted as a means of control or palliation. The degree of type of limitation that results from a malignant brain tumor depends on the type of cancer, its size, and its location within the brain.

Cancers develop less often in the spinal cord than in the brain. The symptoms of a spinal cord tumor may be similar to those experienced with a spinal cord injury, including paralysis. Spinal cord tumors are usually treated surgically, with irradiation and chemotherapy as adjunct therapies.

Lymphomas

Cancers of the lymphatic system are called **lymphomas**. The lymphatic system is a connection of lymph nodes and vessels in which a clear fluid called lymph circulates through the body. The lymphatic system acts to fight infection and contributes to the body's immune system.

There are two classifications of lymphomas: Hodgkin's disease or non-Hodgkin's lymphomas. **Hodgkin's disease** is a chronic, progressive disease in which abnormal cells gradually replace the normal elements within the lymph nodes. Hodgkin's disease is usually diagnosed through a biopsy of the lymph nodes. The treatment of Hodgkin's disease varies with the stage at which it is diagnosed. Early stages are usually treated with radiation therapy; later stages, with chemotherapeutic agents. When treated, Hodgkin's disease has a high rate of remission, and individuals with this condition have an excellent prognosis.

Non-Hodgkin's lymphomas occur more frequently than does Hodgkin's disease. They consist of a proliferation of lymphoid cells that usually disseminate throughout the body. The diagnosis is made through a histological study of tissue that has been removed. Like Hodgkin's disease, non-Hodgkin's lymphomas are usually treated with radiation therapy in the early stages, and chemotherapy in conjunction with radiation therapy in the later stages.

Multiple Myeloma

Multiple myeloma is a slowly progressive cancer, in which there is the uncontrolled reproduction of abnormal plasma cells leading to the destruction of the bone marrow, and extending into the bone. Bone marrow produces red blood cells, white blood cells, and platelets, which control blood clotting. As the bone marrow is destroyed, individuals with multiple myeloma may experience anemia, abnormal bleeding, and bone pain; often the first symptom, bone pain may be concentrated in the back.

Multiple myeloma occurs most frequently after the age of 40, with an increasing incidence after the age of 55. Diagnosis may be based on blood tests, radiologic examination of the skeletal system to identify bone destruction, or biopsy of the bone marrow itself. Chemotherapy and, at times, radiation therapy are the major forms of treatment. Because inactivity results in additional breakdown of bone, emphasis is placed on helping the individual remain active. The prognosis is dependent on the stage of the disease when diagnosed; however, multiple myeloma is not currently curable.

Leukemia

A cancer of the tissues in which blood is formed, **leukemia** is characterized by the proliferation of abnormal, immature white blood cells. Because the cells are immature, they cannot carry out their normal function of fighting infection. Leukemia can be classified as acute or chronic. In **acute leukemia**, many abnormal, immature white blood cells are released into the circulatory system. They crowd out normal blood cells, such as red cells and platelets, causing anemia and hemorrhage. **Chronic leukemia** involves the proliferation of other types of white blood cells that are more mature. Although chronic leukemia may progress more slowly, its symptoms are similar to those of acute leukemia. The type of leukemia depends on the particular type of white cell that is multiplying. Acute lymphoblastic leukemia is more common in children, chronic myelocytic leukemia occurs more frequently in young adulthood, and chronic lymphocytic leukemia occurs more often in or after middle age.

Leukemia is usually diagnosed through laboratory examination of the blood and biopsy of the bone marrow. Chemotherapy is the most common form of treatment, together with additional supportive therapy, such as blood transfusions and measures to prevent infections. In some instances, radiation therapy may also be used. As the disease progresses, individuals become more susceptible to infection, anemia, and hemorrhage.

Cancer of the Breast

As with other types of cancer, the time of the diagnosis of breast cancer is most predictive of prognosis and cure. The use of breast self-examination and mammography, described previously, can lead to early detection and, thus, permit early treatment. The primary treatment of breast cancer is based on the stage of the disease at the time of diagnosis. The treatment may be local, regional, and systemic. Local/regional control usually involves surgery.

Although the entire breast and its underlying tissue, including muscle and lymph nodes, were once commonly removed **(radical mastectomy)**, recent studies have suggested that modified procedures may, in many cases, be just as effective in preventing metastasis or improving survival. The appropriateness of using more conservative surgical techniques that preserve as much of the breast tissue as possible depends on the size and location of the tumor. These alternative surgical techniques may include (1) **lumpectomy**, in which the cancerous lesion itself and a small amount of surrounding breast tissue are removed, and (2) the removal of a quadrant of the breast, which is called a **partial** or **segmental mastectomy**. In many instances, regardless of the type of surgery, radiation therapy and chemotherapy are used as adjunct therapies.

Depending on the extent of surgery, the individual may experience some limitation in arm motion on the affected side. Individuals may engage in physical therapy or other exercises to gain mobility and range of motion gradually. **Lymphedema**, in which there is a swelling of the arm on the side of the mastectomy, may also occur, usually when the lymph nodes have been removed and the circulation of lymph fluid is slowed. There may also be an increased susceptibility to infection on the operative side.

The emotional impact of the loss of breast tissue varies from individual to individual. Not only are there concerns associated with the cancer itself, but also there are concerns regarding changes in appearance. Because of recent advances in plastic surgery, breast reconstruction may be an option for some individuals. The entire breast may be reconstructed (a procedure that may require two or more operations over several months time), or, if there is sufficient chest muscle and the skin remaining after the removal of the tumor is of good quality, an implant may be inserted in a pocket created under the chest muscle. When the amount of muscle and tissue remaining is insufficient for these types of breast reconstruction, other surgical procedures may be performed in which tissues from other parts of the body are used in the reconstruction of the breast.

When breast reconstruction is not an option or the individual chooses not to have such a procedure, a permanent breast form called a prosthesis may be used. Breast forms vary in weight and are matched to the size and contour of the remaining breast. Breast prostheses are sold in surgical supply stores, or they may be available in the lingerie departments of large department stores.

FUNCTIONAL IMPLICATIONS

Psychological Issues

Regardless of the type of cancer or the type of treatment, psychological issues arise in all individuals with cancer. Despite medical and treatment advances, the word *cancer* still holds a stigma for many individuals. They perceive cancer as a threat to their mortality and their future, no matter what the actual prognosis. They may fear the loss of relationships, independence, job, integrity of the body and its functions, as well as loss of life. The diagnosis of cancer may also be a symbol of vulnerability, loss of control, or helplessness. Even when the prognosis is good, the fear of recurrence lingers with many individuals. When disfigurement due to surgical procedures accompanies the diagnosis of cancer, adjustment to the altered self-image causes further stress and anxiety.

Reactions to the diagnosis of cancer vary according to the individual and often depend not only on the type and extent of the cancer, but also on the individual's own particular situation and coping skills. Many individuals with cancer are emotionally overwhelmed when they first learn their diagnosis. Their initial reactions may include depression, irritability, fear, withdrawal, anger and hostility, or denial. Over time, they may come to accept the condition and try to make whatever adaptations are necessary to proceed with life.

In some instances, individuals may minimize the seriousness of the illness in an attempt to assimilate its impact and to marshal their resources and coping skills to deal with the perceived threat. Clarifying ambiguity and uncertainty while permitting denial is at times a difficult balance for all concerned. Some individuals cope by finding a general purpose or meaning to the illness that establishes a framework for the events experienced. Other individuals gain a sense of control by seeking as much information as possible about their disease and treatment. Information can be an important tool in reducing anxiety, but it must be acquired at a rate that is manageable for the individual. As a result of increased cancer survival rates, the quality of the individual's life and involvement in treatment decisions has become a central issue.

Coping with cancer is an ongoing effort in which the individual reacts to the disease and its implications. Individuals may exhibit a wide spectrum of normal adaptive responses that may change over the course of the disease or over time.

Life Style Issues

The extent to which cancer affects an individual's everyday activities depends on the type and location of the cancer and its treatment. The side-effects of radiation therapy or chemotherapy, such as nausea, loss of appetite, or fatigue, may affect daily activities during treatment or for a short time after treatment. Certain surgical procedures for various types of cancer may also affect an individual's life style to some degree. For example, amputation, colostomy, and laryngectomy all require some adaptation of certain daily tasks.

The effects of cancer on sexuality are diverse. Some individuals experience no difficulty with sexual functioning. Others experience a decrease in sexual desire because of fatigue, pain, depression, or anxiety. Some forms of cancer and their treatment may have a direct impact on sexual activity; for example, surgery may directly affect the organs of sexual function. Surgery may also have indirect effects on sexual activity if it alters the individual's physical appearance, thus changing body image and self-esteem. Regardless of whether the disease directly or indirectly affects the individual's ability to engage in sexual intercourse, the need for closeness and demonstration of affection, such as hugging, touching, or kissing, is usually unchanged.

Social Issues

Despite public education about the new medical advances that render many cancers curable, the general public, and perhaps even the family and friends of the individual with cancer, may still hold the unfounded belief that cancer is a synonym for death. Such misconceptions may lead to the emotional withdrawal of friends and acquaintances in order to lessen the impact of loss before it occurs. Acquaintances may avoid the individual with cancer because the diagnosis reminds them of their own mortality and because it engenders unpleasant feelings. The physical changes that occur because of surgery or treatment may make them uncomfortable and may contribute to aversion and further avoidance of the individual. Others may have the mistaken notion that cancer is contagious and avoid close physical contact with the individual or shun the individual altogether.

Just as alienation may result from the diagnosis of cancer, so may overprotection and enforced dependency, both of which erode the individual's sense of self-esteem and control. Family and friends may feel the need to protect the individual, as well as themselves, from the realities of cancer. Family members may not share their feelings and concerns, creating tension within the family group. As a result, the impact of the condition and the associated emotions may be denied. The individual with cancer, in order to avoid alienation or rejection, may also conceal his or her true emotions.

The extent to which the cancer affects social activities depends not only on the attitudes and acceptance of the individuals involved, but also on physical factors, such as pain and fatigue. Medical considerations, including the time spent at the hospital and in treatment, may supersede social and family activities. Special provisions that encourage them to participate in social activities can decrease the disruption and the sense of conflict felt by these individuals and their families over time.

Vocational Issues

The economic implications of cancer can be great. Work takes on particular importance, not only from a financial standpoint, but also as a symbol of self-esteem, self-sufficiency, and an affirmation of life. As with other diseases and disabilities, the most significant barriers to employment after the diagnosis of cancer may be the attitudes of employers and fellow workers, who may have the same misperceptions about cancer that some other social groups have. Attitudes of hopelessness related to cancer diagnosis may be expressed in employers' reluctance to allow individuals with cancer to return to work, their unwillingness to make concessions for any associated limitations, or their rejection of special aspects of treatment. Employers may also express concern about the ability of these individuals to perform the same work-related tasks for which they had been responsible prior to diagnosis.

Vocational planning requires an awareness of the attitudes and prejudice that may exist in the work setting, as well as a specific knowledge about the condition and its treatment requirements, the individual's functional limitations, and demands of the work setting. Because of the variability of the limitations and prognoses with the type and location of cancer, the importance of short-term versus long-term planning should be considered. The variability of the limitations experienced and the prognosis for morbidity and life expectancy vary with the type and location of the cancer. Therefore, the type of plan, and whether short-term or long-term planning is most feasible, is dependent to a great extent on these factors. It is also necessary to understand the multidimensional impact of the diagnosis of cancer on the individual and the family. The degree to which the individual's former employment is still suitable is dependent on many variables and must be examined realistically in the context of the demands and implications of returning to the former work setting, as well as the individual's own particular strengths and limitations.

BIBLIOGRAPHY

Barber, T.C., and Langfitt, D.E. *Teaching the Medical/Surgial Patient—Diagnostics and Procedures.* Bowie, Md.: Robert J. Brady Co., 1983.

Berkow, R., and Fletcher, A.J., eds. *The Merck Manual of Diagnosis and Therapy.* Rahway, N.J.: Merck Sharpe and Dohme Research Laboratories, 1987.

Blumberg, B.; Flaherty, M.; and Lewis, J. *Coping with Cancer.* Bethesda, Md.: NIH Publication No. 890-2080, 1980.

Bruckstein, A.H. "Gastric Carcinoma—Battling a Stalwart Enemy." *Postgraduate Medicine* 85(1989):235–238.

Brunner, L.S.; Emerson, C.P.; Ferguson, L.K.; and Suddarth, D.S. *Textbook of Medical-Surgical Nursing.* Philadelphia: W.B. Saunders Co., 1970.

Canellos, G.P.; Portlock, C.S.; and Tucker, M.A. "Hodgkin's Disease: Current Outlook." *Patient Care* 23(1989):41–52.

Corbett, J.V. *Diagnostic Procedures in Nursing Practice.* Norwalk, Conn.: Appleton-Century-Crofts, 1982.

Corbett, J.V. *Laboratory Tests in Nursing Practice.* Norwalk, Conn.: Appleton-Century-Crofts, 1983.

Costanzi, J.J. "Malignant Melanoma—Why Early Diagnosis and Treatment Are Crucial." *Postgraduate Medicine* 84(1988):159–168.

Cummings, C.W.; Flint, P.; and Krause, C.J. "Neck Cancer: What's Optimal Therapy?" *Patient Care* 24(1990):44–61.

Farley, P.C., and McFaden, K.H. "Colorectal Cancer—Are Adjuvant Therapies Beneficial?" *Postgraduate Medicine* 84(1988):175–183.

Glatstein, E.; Jett, J.R.; and Scoggin, C.H. "Your Role in Lung Cancer Management." *Patient Care* 22(1988):56–72.

Gonsalves, L., and Covington, E. "Depression in Patients with Cancer: Management in the Primary Care Office." *Primary Care and Cancer* 10(1990):9–13.

Graydon, J.E. "Stress Points." *American Journal of Nursing* 84(1984):1124–1125.

Gump, F.E. "Options in the Treatment of Mammary Cancer." *Resident & Staff Physician* 34(1988):29–33.

Guyton, A.C. *Human Physiology and Mechanisms of Disease.* Philadelphia: W.B. Saunders Co., 1982.

Harper, A.P. "Mammography 1990: State of the Art." *Hospital Medicine* 26(1990):25–45.

Holland, J. *Understanding the Cancer Patient.* New York: American Cancer Society, 1980.

Keele, C.A.; Neil, E.; and Joels, N. *Samson Wright's Applied Physiology.* New York: Oxford University Press, 1982.

Knopf, K.T. "Breast Cancer—The Treatment Evolution." *American Journal of Nursing* 84(1984):1110–1120.

Konrad, H.R. "Carcinoma of the Larynx." *Hospital Medicine* (August 1984):165–180.

Lebow, J.; Maisiak, R.; Sanders, E.; Soong, S.; and Cain, M. "Rehabilitation Counseling Needs of Cancer Patients." *Rehabilitation Counseling Bulletin* 25(1982):231–234.

Luckman, J., and Sorensen, K.C. *Medical-Surgical Nursing: A Psychophysiologic Approach.* Philadelphia: W.B. Saunders Co., 1987.

Nail, L.; Jones, L.S.; Giuffre, M.; and Johnson, J.E. "Sensations after Mastectomy." *American Journal of Nursing* 84(1984): 1121–1124.

National Cancer Institute. *Breast Cancer: Understanding Treatment Options.* Bethesda,Md.: National Cancer Institute Publication, 1979.

National Cancer Institute. *Advanced Cancer: Living Each Day.* Bethesda,Md.: NIH Publication 85-856, 1985.

Nursing 87 Books. *Patient Teaching.* Springhouse, Pa.: Springhouse Corporation Book Division, 1987.

Nuscher, R.; Baltzer, L.; Repinec, D.A.; Almquist, G.; Barrett, J.E.; LaBombardi, S.; DeMao, J.D.; Diver, M.E.; Field, B.A.; Lee, M.C.; Mamora, J.; Pizo, B.; Sheehy, B.N.; Sullivan, M.; and Tierney, J. "Bone Marrow Transplantation." *American Journal of Nursing* (June 1984):764–772.

Onion, P. "Breast Cancer Prognosis with Pregnancy." *American Journal of Nursing* 84(1984):1126–1128.

Rakel, R.E. *Conn's Current Therapy 1990.* Philadelphia: W.B. Saunders Co., 1990.

Rivera, R.R. "Breast Cancer: Current Guidelines in Staging, Treatment, and Follow-Up." *Postgraduate Medicine* 84(1988):142–151.

Rosenthal, S.N., and Bennett, J.M., eds. *Practical Cancer Chemotherapy.* Garden City, N.Y.: Medical Examination Publishing Co., 1981.

Scheer, S.J., ed. *Medical Perspectives in Vocational Assessment of Impaired Workers.* Gaithersburg, Md.: Aspen Publishers, 1991.

Smith, D.W., and Hanley-Germain, C.P. *Care of the Adult Patient.* Philadelphia: J.B. Lippincott Co., 1975.

Stolov, W.C., and Clowers, M.R. *Handbook of Severe Disability.* Washington, D.C.: U.S. Department of Education, Rehabilitation Services Administration, 1981.

Stoudemire, A. "Medical and Psychological Support of the Patient on Chemotherapy." *Medical Aspects of Human Sexuality* 19(1985):88–102.

Vander, A.J.; Sherman, J.H.; and Luciano, D.S. *Human Physiology: The Mechanisms of Body Function.* New York: McGraw-Hill Book Co., 1985.

Vredevoe, D.I.; Derdiarian, A.; Sarna, L.P.; Friel, M.; and Shiplacoff, J.A. *Concepts of Oncology Nursing.* Englewood Cliffs, N.J.: Prentice-Hall, 1981.

Williams, C. *All about Cancer: A Practical Guide to Cancer Care.* New York: John Wiley & Sons, 1984.

Wyngaarden, J.B., and Smith, J.H. *Cecil Textbook of Medicine.* Philadelphia: W.B. Saunders Co., 1988.

chapter *13*

Disorders of the Blood and the Immune System

NORMAL STRUCTURE AND FUNCTION

Blood is a combination of different types of cells and liquid that circulates continuously through the body. The quantity of blood in the adult body remains constant under normal conditions. Blood has many important functions; for example, it

- carries oxygen and nutrients to the body tissues
- facilitates communication between the endocrine glands and other body organs by transporting hormones
- carries waste products from the tissues to the organs of excretion, such as the lungs and the kidneys
- protects the body from dangerous organisms
- promotes clotting to minimize excessive bleeding
- helps to regulate the body temperature

Several different types of cells make up the blood. Approximately two-fifths of the total blood volume is comprised of cells, which are formed by a process called **hemopoiesis** or **hematopoiesis**. The types of cells contained within the blood are red blood cells **(erythrocytes)**, white blood cells **(leukocytes)**, and platelets **(thrombocytes)**. More than 99 percent of the cells in blood are red blood cells. The number of circulating white blood cells under normal circumstances is minimal; when infection or other foreign stimuli are present, however, white blood cells proliferate so that there are large numbers of them circulating in the bloodstream. This condition is called **leukocytosis**. The number of platelets circulating in the blood normally does not change. If there should be a decrease in the number of platelets, however, the condition is called **thrombocytopenia**; an increase in the number of platelets is called **thrombocytosis**.

299

The liquid portion of the blood is a watery, colorless fluid called **plasma**. It contains no blood cells, but is essential for carrying blood cells and nutrients through the circulation, as well as for transporting wastes from the tissues. Approximately three-fifths of the total blood volume is plasma.

Normal Structure and Function of Red Blood Cells

Erythrocytes carry oxygen to the tissues. They are normally disk shaped, with a thin center and thicker edges. They are flexible, which allows them to adapt their shape to fit through blood vessels of differing sizes. **Hemoglobin** contains iron and is the pigment in red blood cells that gives them their characteristic color. Hemoglobin is important because it is the specific part of the red blood cell that carries oxygen.

Special cells in the bone marrow produce erythrocytes. Several vitamins, such as vitamin B_{12} and folic acid (which is part of the vitamin B complex), are necessary for the formation of erythrocytes. They are obtained from the diet. Iron, which is also obtained from the diet, is important for the formation of hemoglobin. Excess amounts of iron and vitamin B_{12} are stored in the liver.

New red blood cells are constantly being formed. Although most erythrocytes are released into the blood, some are taken up by the spleen to be stored for emergency use when the red blood cell count drops significantly below normal levels, such as during hemorrhage. Newly formed red blood cells enter the bloodstream before they are totally mature. At this stage, they are called **reticulocytes**. Within several days, the cells mature to become erythrocytes. The life cycle of erythrocytes is approximately 120 days. As the erythrocytes reach the end of their life cycle, they become more fragile and rupture. Some of the old erythrocytes are destroyed in the spleen. Special cells within the spleen and liver absorb the old erythrocytes, making room for more new cells.

A decrease in the quantity of oxygen supplied to the tissues results in an increase in the number of red blood cells produced. For example, at higher altitudes, where less oxygen is available in the air, the bone marrow reacts by producing more red blood cells even if there is an adequate number of red blood cells in the circulation.

Normal Structure and Function of White Blood Cells and Immunity

Although constantly bombarded by microorganisms or trauma that can result in infection, disease, or injury, the body has specific defenses to protect it against such invasions. The body's first line of defense against foreign material is called **nonspecific** or **innate immunity**. This type of immunity includes the protection provided by the skin, which acts as a barrier to organisms, and by the mucous membranes, gastric secretions, and tears, which contain special chemicals that destroy potentially harmful organisms. This type of immunity requires no previous exposure to the foreign substance nor recognition of any specific properties of the foreign material. When, despite external and chemical barriers, an organism or other foreign material gains entry into the body, an **inflammatory response** results. The main purpose of the inflammatory response is to bring cells called **phagocytes** to the area to destroy or inactivate the foreign substances so that the repair of tissue may begin.

Also important to the body's defense is the **lymphatic system**, which is a collection of lymph vessels, lymph nodes, and lymph ducts. The lymphatic system is separate from the general circulatory system and depends on muscle movement to circulate the lymph fluid within it. As a mechanism by which fluids surrounding cells in the body are able to move into the bloodstream, the lymphatic system is crucial to the body's defense against invading organisms and other foreign substances. **Lymph nodes** throughout the body mediate the lymphatic system's defensive activity by acting as filters. They also serve as temporary storage reservoirs for lymphocytes (white blood cells that fight infection) and, with appropriate stimulus, as manufacturers of lymphocytes.

Other organs and tissues important to the body's defense against the invasion of organisms or other foreign substances are the spleen, the thymus, and the bone marrow. Located in the upper left quadrant of the abdomen, the spleen is composed of spongelike tissue. In addition to producing blood cells and storing blood, it filters blood so that organisms or other substances can be removed from the circulation and destroyed. The **thymus**, which lies in the upper portion of the chest, is a lymphoid organ that produces a hormone important in controlling the of development of lymphocytes. Bone marrow also produces lymphocytes and, consequently, is also classified as a lymphoid organ.

White blood cells (leukocytes), formed in the bone marrow, have the predominant role in the body's defense system. Leukocytes take action when body tissues have been damaged or invaded by organisms or other foreign material, and any infection or invasion by foreign substances causes a dramatic increase in the number of white blood cells in the blood.

Leukocytes are divided into two different groups, **granulocytes** and **agranulocytes**. The types of leukocytes that are categorized as granulocytes are cells called **neutrophils, basophils**, and **eosinophils; lymphocytes** and **monocytes** are categorized as agranulocytes. Monocytes are precursors of two other types of cells called macrophages. Scavengers, **macrophages** ingest organisms (a process called **phagocytosis**) that the body has identified as foreign.

In addition to their phagocytosis activity, white blood cells fight infection through a process called **acquired immunity** (the ability of cells to recognize an organism to which there has been previous exposure and to neutralize or destroy the invading organism). **Lymphocytes**, which circulate throughout the bloodstream and the lymphatic system, are important to acquired immunity. The two major types of lymphocytes that are important to immunity are **B lymphocytes** and **T lymphocytes**. **B lymphocytes** migrate to lymphoid tissue, such as the lymph nodes and spleen. When they are exposed to a foreign substance **(antigen)**, they produce special substances called **antibodies** that, in turn, enter the bloodstream to lock with the antigen and destroy it. This type of immune response is called **humoral immunity**.

T lymphocytes are the regulators and controllers of the immune system. When T lymphocytes are exposed to an antigen, they become sensitized. Some T lymphocytes become **memory cells** so that, if the body is invaded by the specific organism again, it is "remembered" and the immune response is more intense. Some T lymphocytes directly attack the foreign invader. These cells are able to react with antigens that are inside cells and are inaccessible to antibodies. Some T lymphocytes, called **helper cells**, enhance B-lymphocyte activity and antibody production. Others, called **suppressor cells**, halt B-lymphocyte activity when appropriate antibody levels have been reached. Normally, helper cells outnumber suppressor cells 2:1.

Cells carry markers **(allogens)** to ensure that the body recognizes its own tissue as self and not foreign. When these allogens stimulate an immune response in which body cells are attacked as if they were foreign substances, individuals are said to have an **autoimmune response**. Examples of autoimmune diseases are **systemic lupus erythematosus** and **rheumatoid arthritis** (see Chapter 7).

A variety of conditions can alter the body's immune response and leave individuals more susceptible to disease. Because it is necessary to suppress the immune system of individuals who are about to receive an organ transplant in order to prevent rejection of the donor tissue, these individuals are more prone to infections. Individuals with certain types of cancers, such as lymphoma and leukemia, may become immunodeficient and develop serious infections. The overuse or abuse of narcotics or steroid drugs can also alter the immune response.

Normal Structure and Function of Platelets and Coagulation

The term *hemostasis* refers to a series of events that stops bleeding from damaged vessels. **Platelets** are involved in the important first step in preventing excessive bleeding after an injury. Formed by special cells in the bone marrow, platelets are the smallest of the cells in the blood. They are disk-shaped and contain no hemoglobin, but are concerned with the clotting of blood. When an injury occurs, the walls of the blood vessels contract, and platelets adhere to the site of the injury. They release a special substance that causes other platelets to collect at the site; thus, they "plug" injured blood vessels to stop the bleeding momentarily.

Platelets alone cannot stop the bleeding indefinitely. The formation of the plug activates **clotting factors** (coagulation factors from the liver, plasma, and other sources) so that a clot forms to control the bleeding. There are intrinsic and extrinsic blood clotting factors, most named by Roman numerals designated from I to XIII, in which different sets of substances play major roles. Vitamin K is necessary for the formation of some clotting factors. To prevent excessive clotting, other body mechanisms are also activated. For example, basophils (a type of white blood cell) are thought to have some role in stopping the coagulation process, once the bleeding is under control.

BLOOD DISORDERS

The term *blood dyscrasias* is used to describe a large group of disorders that affect the blood. Disorders of the blood or blood-forming organs may arise from a number of different sources; may be manifest in a number of different ways; and may involve abnormalities of erythrocytes, leukocytes, platelets, or clotting mechanisms. These disorders may be characterized by the overproduction of cells, the underproduction of cells, or defects in the clotting mechanism.

Anemia

In the conditions that fall under the general term *anemia*, there is a reduction in the amount of hemoglobin or the number of red blood cells. Rather than a disease itself, anemia is a symptom of various diseases. Anemias are sometimes classified by the size and color of the red blood cell. For example, healthy, normal-sized cells are called **normocytic**; normal cells that are of normal color are called **normochromic**. Anemias in which the red blood cells are larger than usual are called **macrocytic anemias**, while those with cells smaller than usual are called **microcytic anemias**. Anemias in which the color of the red blood cells is paler than usual are called **hypochromic anemias**.

Anemias may also be classified according to their causative mechanisms. For example, anemias may result from an excessive blood loss, from decreased or abnormal red blood cell formation, or from the destruction of red blood cells. **Aplastic anemia** (sometimes called **pancytopenia**) is caused by inadequate functioning of the bone marrow in manufacturing red blood cells. Aplastic anemia can occur spontaneously, or it can result from damage to the bone marrow through drugs, chemicals, or ionizing radiation.

The destruction of red blood cells is called **hemolysis**. Anemias caused by excessive and/or premature destruction of red blood cells are called **hemolytic anemias**. A variety of abnormal conditions can cause red blood cell destruction. Hemolytic anemia may occur in association with some infectious diseases or with certain inherited red blood cell disorders, or it may develop as a response to drugs or other foreign or toxic agents. Anemia results when the rate of destruction is greater than the ability of the body to produce red cells. The degree of anemia reflects the ability of the bone marrow to increase the production of red blood cells. The spleen usually becomes enlarged **(splenomegaly)** in chronic hemolytic conditions because of the need to remove an excessive number of damaged red cells.

Iron deficiency anemia, one of the most common types of anemia, is often caused by a deficiency of iron in the diet. It can also result from the body's failure to absorb iron, excessive or chronic blood loss, or increases in the body's iron requirements, however.

Pernicious anemia is a chronic condition caused by the inadequate secretion by the stomach of a substance **(intrinsic factor)** that is necessary for the intestine to absorb Vitamin B_{12}. The deficiency of vitamin B_{12} impairs the production and maturation of blood cells. Consequently, the body is unable to produce adequate numbers of red blood cells, resulting in anemia.

Regardless of the cause, anemias disrupt the transport of oxygen to tissues throughout the body. Severe anemia increases the workload of the heart. The common symptoms of anemia are pale skin **(pallor)**, weakness, fatigue, difficulty in breathing **(dyspnea)**, and fast heart rate **(tachycardia)**. Other possible symptoms of anemia include the inability to concentrate, irritability, and susceptibility to infection.

Treatment must be specific to the cause. If anemia is the result of blood loss, blood replacement through transfusion may be necessary. In other instances, dietary, vitamin, or iron supplements may be necessary.

Thalassemia (Cooley's Anemia, Mediterranean Anemia)

The **thalassemias** are inherited hemolytic anemias in which there is production of thin, fragile red blood cells and defective hemoglobin synthesis. As a result, the hemoglobin content of red blood cells is inadequate. In addition, there is often some interference with erythrocyte metabolism that causes the red blood cells to be deformed and decreases their survival time. Thus, the anemia associated with the thalassemias can result both from the increased destruction of red blood cells and from the impaired production of hemoglobin.

The thalassemias affect predominantly people of Mediterranean, African, or southern Asian ancestry. The symptoms are similar to those of other anemias. Treatment is mainly replacement therapy through transfusion.

Polycythemia

In **polycythemia**, there is an increase in the number of red blood cells, as well as in the concentration of hemoglobin, within the blood. There are several types of polycythemia. One type, **polycythemia vera**, is associated with an overproduction of both red and white blood cells. The cause of polycythemia vera is unknown. Because of the increased number of cells in the blood, individuals with this condition may experience hypertension, congestive heart failure, stroke, or heart attack (see Chapter 2), or they may experience a hemorrhage because the congestion in the blood vessels may cause the vessels to rupture.

Secondary polycythemia occurs in conjunction with another disease. When the body's demand for oxygen increases, the bone marrow produces additional red blood cells in order to meet the increased demand. Chronic obstructive pulmonary disease is a condition in which secondary polycythemia may occur (see Chapter 3). The treatment focuses on the underlying condition.

Individuals with conditions in which there has been a loss of plasma without a loss of red blood cells, such as burns, may develop a state similar to polycythemia. Although there is no actual increase in the number of red blood cells, the loss of fluid increases the proportion of red blood cells in the blood. In these cases, treatment involves fluid replacement to decrease the viscosity of the blood.

Agranulocytosis (Neutropenia)

Agranulocytosis is the marked reduction in the level of a specific type of leukocyte, called a neutrophil. The reduction in circulating neutrophils is called **neutropenia**. The most common cause of agranulocytosis is a toxic or hypersensitive reaction to drugs, chemicals, or ionizing radiation. Because white blood cells are important to fight infection, a reduction in the number of these cells increases an individual's susceptibility to infection. Agranulocytosis is a potentially serious condition and, without prompt treatment, can result in death. The treatment is directed toward removing the toxic agent responsible, as well as providing medications (e.g., antibiotics) to treat resulting infections.

Purpura

In **purpura**, small amounts of blood leak into various tissues of the body. It can be caused by damage to the blood vessels or by a deficiency in platelets.

Leukemia

The **leukemias** are caused by cancerous production of lymph cells or by cancerous production of white blood cells. The leukemias are discussed in greater detail in Chapter 12.

Hemophilia

Several inherited blood disorders make up the condition known as **hemophilia**, in which there is a deficiency in or absence of one of the clotting factors. As a result, individuals with hemophilia have a bleeding tendency. Although these individuals do not initially bleed faster, the normal clotting mechanism is disturbed so that the bleeding is prolonged or the oozing of blood may persist after injury. The disease is transmitted from mother to son. Women do not develop the disease, but they can inherit the trait and pass it to their sons. If a woman is a carrier, each of her sons has a 50 percent chance of developing hemophilia; each of her daughters has a 50 percent chance of becoming a carrier. None of the sons of a man with hemophilia will have hemophilia; however, all of his daughters will be carriers.

There are several different types of hemophilia, which are differentiated by the specific clotting factor that is deficient. The most common type is **hemophilia A**, also known as **classical hemophilia**, in which a protein in clotting Factor VIII is deficient. The next most common type is **hemophilia B**, also called **Christmas disease**, in which clotting Factor IX is defective. The rarest type of hemophilia is **von Willebrand's disease**, in which Factor VIII manifests platelet dysfunction.

The severity of hemophilia varies along a continuum from a tendency toward slow, prolonged, persistent bleeding to a tendency toward severe hemorrhage. The normal level of clotting factors ranges from 50 percent to 150 percent of a standard baseline figure. Individuals with a level of clotting factors between 6 percent and 30 percent of this figure are considered to have mild hemophilia. These individuals will probably experience abnormal bleeding only after major injuries or with minor surgery, such as a tooth extraction. Individuals with a level of clotting factors of 5 percent or below are considered to have moderate hemophilia; they may have prolonged bleeding after a relatively minor injury, such as a bump or a small cut.

Individuals with a level of clotting factors below 1 percent of the standard baseline figure are considered to have severe hemophilia. These individuals may have spontaneous hemorrhages into deep muscles and joints. Bleeding into the joint **(hemarthrosis)** is extremely painful. Knees and ankles are affected most frequently, although elbows may become involved later. Joint deformity and crippling may result from damage to the joint structure. Bleeding into the muscle, if severe, may exert pressure on nerves and cause a temporary sensory loss. If the hemorrhage damages muscle tissue, fibrous tissue may form, causing varying degrees of functional loss.

Hemophilia is not curable and requires treatment for bleeding problems throughout the individual's life. With proper care and treatment, however, individuals with hemophilia can manage their chronic disease, and their life expectancy approaches normal. To prevent damage from abnormal bleeding, significant blood loss, and chronic joint disease, all bleeding must be detected early and treated promptly.

Sickle Cell Anemia

A chronic, hereditary disorder that is most common in people of African or Mediterranean ancestry, sickle cell anemia is caused by a mutation in the structure of hemoglobin. Normal hemoglobin is called **hemoglobin A**. Individuals with sickle cell anemia have an abnormal hemoglobin called **hemoglobin S**. When hemoglobin S molecules interact with each other, they become stacked up, especially when the oxygen concentration in the blood is low. The red blood cells become deformed so that, instead of being disk-shaped, they assume the abnormal shape of a crescent or sickle. Owing to this distortion, the red blood cell becomes rigid and is unable to adapt its shape to fit through tiny blood vessels. The abnormal sickled cell becomes very fragile and is easily destroyed, which severely curtails its normal life span. As a result, the bone marrow drastically increases its production of erythrocytes in order to keep up with the rate of destruction. Because the rate of production cannot keep up with the rate of destruction, however, individuals with sickle cell disease can become severely anemic.

The sickled red blood cells thicken the blood and can obstruct the blood flow in small vessels. When they lodge in small blood vessels, blocking blood flow, the surrounding tissues do not receive sufficient oxygen. The diminished blood flow and the subsequent lack of oxygen causes severe pain. Such episodes are called sickle cell crisis. If the blood flow is severely diminished, the affected tissue may undergo **necrosis** (tissue death). Any part of the body, including organs, may be affected; the resulting damage may be mild to severe, depending on the degree and length of blockage. The specific causes of sickle cell crisis are unknown; however, it is known that certain factors, such as mental or physical stress, infection, or dehydration, may precipitate a crisis.

Individuals with sickle cell anemia have multiple bouts of sickle cell crisis during their life, leading to chronic organ damage. Although, as mentioned earlier, any organ may be affected, the kidney is a frequent site of damage. Recurrent insults to the kidney can lead to chronic renal disease (see Chapter 4). In some instances the spleen may become so damaged that it ceases to function. Because of the lowered resistance due to anemia, as well as the altered splenic function, serious infections may also become problems.

A variety of other disorders can result from sickle cell anemia. The chronic anemia causes the heart to pump faster in an attempt to supply additional oxygen to the tissues. This increased heart action can contribute to enlargement of the heart **(cardiomegaly)** and decreased cardiac efficiency. The decreased oxygen supply caused by the chronic anemia can also produce symptoms of fatigue and difficulty in breathing on exertion **(exertional dyspnea)**. If the lungs were damaged during a sickle cell crisis, scarring can affect lung function, producing symptoms similar to those of chronic obstructive pulmonary disease (see Chapter 3). The occlusion of blood flow during a sickle cell crisis can damage bones and joints, leading to pain, swelling, and limited mobility of the joints. Occlusion of vessels in the brain can cause a stroke (see Chapter 8).

The prognosis of individuals with sickle cell anemia is dependent on the individual and the degree of organ damage experienced. In the past, many individuals with sickle cell anemia did not live to adulthood, but many now reach mid-life and beyond, living productive lives. The prediction of outcome is individually determined.

Individuals who are carriers of the abnormal gene (called **sickle cell trait**) that causes the hemoglobin abnormality may pass the abnormal gene to their offspring. They do not themselves have sickle cell anemia and usually experience no symptoms, however. The offspring of an individual with sickle cell trait and an individual with normal genes have a 50 percent chance of being carriers of the abnormal gene. If both parents have the sickle cell trait, the chances with each pregnancy are one in four that the offspring will have sickle cell anemia. The children of one parent with sickle cell anemia and one with normal hemoglobin will all have sickle cell trait. If one parent has sickle cell trait and one has sickle cell anemia, there is a 50 percent chance with each pregnancy that the child will have sickle cell trait and a 50 percent chance that the child will have sickle cell anemia. When both parents have sickle cell anemia, so will all of their children.

HUMAN IMMUNODEFICIENCY VIRUS SPECTRUM (HIV INFECTION, AIDS)

Not all viruses are harmful to humans, although some viruses can cause disease. The diseases that result from viruses range from the common cold and common childhood illness to more serious diseases, such as polio myelitis and AIDS.

A virus can be defined as an organism that cannot grow or reproduce outside living cells. In order to survive, a virus must enter a living cell and use the reproductive capacity of that cell for its own replication. Consequently, when a virus enters a cell, it instructs the cell to reproduce the virus. Normally, the body recognizes viruses as foreign and activates the immune system to attack and destroy the offending agent. Of those viruses that are not destroyed, some remain inactive (dormant) for long periods without causing problems; however, they remain integrated within the genetic material of the cell, and they are capable of replicating when triggered to do so. The direct damage the virus does to the cell itself may vary from slight to total destruction. Some cells are able to reproduce after being damaged, but others, especially those of the nervous system, are not able to reproduce and, consequently, are not replaced after invasion by a virus.

The human immunodeficiency virus (HIV) destroys a subset of helper T cells and impairs their ability to recognize antigens. The virus reproduces within the T cell itself, producing additional HIV, which, in turn, invades other T cells. The normal 2:1 ratio of helper cells to suppressor cells becomes reversed. The increased number of suppressor cells severely limits normal B-cell function, and they fail to respond to new antigens. The normal immune response becomes dysfunctional.

The HIV spectrum (**AIDS**) is a disorder of the immune system in which HIV disrupts the body's defenses against even the least aggressive organism. Many organisms commonly found in the environment pose no threat under normal circumstances, because the functioning immune system resists them. When individuals have HIV infection, the immune system is no longer able to act as a defense, and there is no resistance to these organisms. Therefore, HIV infection is characterized by a number of rare infections. Death is not caused by the dysfunction of the immune system per se, but by complications of conditions that develop because of inadequate immune system function. Without resistance, individuals are left susceptible to disease and infections that, under normal circumstances, would not become full-blown. These diseases and infections are called **opportunistic**.

One common opportunistic infection associated with HIV infection is ***Pneumocystis carinii* pneumonia**, a parasitic infection of the lung. This condition is highly uncommon in healthy individuals, although it may be found in other immunocompromised individuals, such as in those who have cancer or those who have received immunosuppressants in association with organ transplantation. *Pneumocystis carinii* pneumonia is one of the most common manifestations of HIV infections. The symptoms usually begin with a dry cough and difficulty in breathing. Although some drugs are available to treat the disease, these drugs can have toxic side-effects that can further jeopardize the individual's condition.

Another type of opportunistic infection is **candidiasis** (yeast infection). The fungus *Candida* frequently invades the oral cavity of the HIV-infected individual, causing a superficial infection in the mouth and throat that is manifested by pain and white plaques. This condition, also known as oral thrush, may be the first clue that the individual is infected with HIV. Although it is uncomfortable and difficult to cure, infection with *Candida* is not likely to be fatal. Individuals with debilitating conditions other than HIV infections may also develop candidiasis.

In addition to opportunistic infections, an otherwise rare form of cancer called **Kaposi's sarcoma** is frequently associated with HIV infection; this is considered an opportunistic cancer. Kaposi's sarcoma is a form of cancer that causes pink, brown, or purplish blotches on the skin.

Nearly 40 percent of individuals with HIV infection develop neurological symptoms at some time during the course of the disease. Neurological symptoms may be mild, such as a headache, or more severe, such as aphasia, seizures, gait disturbances, visual disturbances, and incontinence. Individuals with HIV infections may also experience a type of dementia called **AIDS dementia complex**, which may include cognitive symptoms, such as poor concentration or forgetfulness; motor symptoms, such as loss of balance or clumsiness; and behavioral symptoms, such as apathy and social withdrawal. The precise mechanism by which HIV causes dementia is unknown.

The human immunodeficiency virus is found in the blood, as well as in body secretions such as sperm. Transmission can occur in a variety of ways. The virus can be transmitted through the infusion of infected blood or blood products or through sticks with infected needles. It can be transferred through anal, oral, or genital intercourse, or it can be transferred through contact with a cut or open wound on the skin. It can also be transmitted from a woman with HIV infection to her unborn child. There is no evidence to show that transmission can occur in any way other than direct blood to blood or sexual contact with an infected individual. The virus does not appear to be transmitted through coughing, sneezing, or through casual contact. Moreover, because all viruses require living tissue to survive and multiply, the virus dies quickly once outside the body.

Infections with HIV can be separated roughly into several stages, although there are no firm guidelines that distinguish the different phases. During the early or acute phase, symptoms may be subtle or nonexistent. Initially some individuals may experience mild flulike symptoms that subside, leaving the individual symptom-free. The virus is still transmissible to others, however. As the HIV infection progresses, the levels of the circulating virus increase. At the same time, there is a decline in the number of helper T cells of the immune system. Infected individuals may experience some or all of the following symptoms.

- weight loss of 10 or more pounds in less than 2 months for no apparent reason
- loss of appetite

- unexplained persistent fever
- drenching night sweats
- severe fatigue that is unrelated to exercise, stress, or drug use
- persistent diarrhea
- swollen lymph nodes (lymphadenopathy)

Early categorizations of the progression of HIV infections included an intermediate stage called AIDS-related complex (ARC), with the final stage of HIV infections being categorized as AIDS. There was disagreement about whether some of a combination of symptoms constituted ARC or whether the presence of these symptoms was merely the early stage of AIDS. Stages of HIV disease can now be characterized with greater precision. Although the terms ARC and AIDS continue to be used in discussions, classification established by the Centers for Disease Control, described below, more accurately reflect stages of HIV infection.

Group I   Stage of acute infection with presence of flulike symptoms
Group II   Stage of asymptomatic infection in which there are no outward signs and symptoms
Group III   Stage characterized by persistent, generalized **lymphadenopathy** (swelling of lymph nodes) for more than 3 months in the absence of other causes
Group IV   Stage characterized by presence of weight loss, diarrhea, opportunistic infections such as *Pneumocystis carinii* pneumonia, neurological symptoms, or secondary cancers such as Kaposi's sarcoma

During the last stage of the disease, the immune system is severely depleted and infections run rampant, showing resistance to standard therapy that would normally be used to treat them.

DIAGNOSTIC PROCEDURES

Standard Blood Tests

The diagnosis of many blood disorders is dependent on laboratory analyses of the blood itself. A **complete blood count** is used to evaluate a number of different components in the blood. Sometimes various components measured in a complete blood count may also be measured separately. The components of a complete blood count include

- **red blood cell count**: measurement of the total number of red blood cells in a cubic millimeter of blood.
- **white blood cell count**: measurement of the total number of white blood cells in a cubic millimeter of blood.
- **differential**: measurement of the proportion of each type of white blood cell (i.e., neutrophils, eosinophils, basophils, lymphocytes, monocytes) in a sample of 100 white blood cells.
- **hemoglobin**: evaluation of the amount of hemoglobin content of erythrocytes in 100 milliliters of blood.
- **hematocrit**: measurement of the percentage or proportion of red blood cells in the plasma. It is based on the assumption that the volume of plasma is normal.

Other types of blood tests that are used to measure specific components of blood are

- **reticulocyte count**: assessment of bone marrow function by measuring its production of immature red blood cells (reticulocytes)
- **platelet count**: measurement of the number of platelets in a cubic millimeter of blood
- **mean corpuscular volume** (MCV): calculation of the volume of a single red blood cell by dividing the hematocrit by the red blood cell count
- **mean corpuscular hemoglobin concentration**: calculation of the amount of hemoglobin in each red blood cell by dividing the hemoglobin concentration by the hematocrit

Bleeding Time

Bleeding time is a test that measures the length of time it takes for bleeding to stop after a small puncture wound. The test determines how quickly a platelet clot forms. An abnormal bleeding time would indicate a tendency toward prolonged bleeding such as that found in conditions in which there is an abnormally low number of platelets circulating in the blood.

Prothrombin Time (PT, Pro Time)

Prothrombin time is a blood test that measures the length of time that a blood sample takes to clot when certain chemicals are added to it in the laboratory.

Prothrombin time tests for very specific factors involved in clotting and may be used diagnostically to identify pathological clotting disorders, such as may be found with liver dysfunction or in the absence of vitamin K. The test may also be used to monitor the effectiveness of certain anticoagulant medications used in the treatment of conditions in which clot formation is or has been a problem. A prolongation of clotting time indicates that the individual may be prone to abnormal bleeding. If the test indicates that clotting time is reduced, there may be hypercoagulability of blood, contributing to the formation of blood clots.

Partial Thromboplastin Time (PTT)

The partial thromboplastin time is a blood test that is used to evaluate a special part of the clotting mechanism not evaluated by prothrombin time. Like prothrombin time, certain chemicals are added to a blood sample in the laboratory and the amount of time it takes a clot to form is measured. Prolongation of time in which it takes a clot to form is indicative of a bleeding disorder, such as that found in hemophilia. A prolongation of clot formation may also be found with the use of the anticoagulant heparin, which effects a specific part of the clotting mechanism that is not measured by the prothrombin time test.

Bone Marrow Aspiration

Bone marrow is removed by inserting a special needle into the marrow space of the bone and then aspirating a small sample. The bone marrow is then examined microscopically for various abnormalities in the number, size, and shape of the precursors of red blood cells, white blood cells, and platelets.

ELISA and Western Blot

Both the **ELISA** and **Western Blot** are blood tests that screen for HIV antibodies. If the initial screening with the ELISA test produces positive results, a second ELISA test is performed. If the result of the second test is negative, the test result is considered negative. If the result of the second test is positive, the Western Blot test is usually performed as a confirmatory test. If the result of the Western Blot test is positive, it is highly suggestive that the HIV antibody is present and that the individual has been exposed to HIV.

TREATMENT

General Treatment

For many disorders of the blood, treatment is directed at the symptoms and/or the underlying cause. If a blood disorder is caused by a toxic substance, the first line of treatment is to remove the offending agent. Anemias that are caused by deficiencies may be treated by supplementation or replacement therapy. For instance, iron deficiency anemia may be treated by the administration of oral or injectable iron preparations. Pernicious anemia may be treated with injections of vitamin B_{12}. When there is an overproduction of red blood cells, as in polycythemia, treatment may involve the removal of blood. **Venesection (phlebotomy)** is a procedure in which quantities of blood are removed in order to reduce the volume.

Part of the treatment for a number of blood disorders may be the transfusion of whole blood or a blood component, such as packed red blood cells, plasma, or platelets. Because blood is living tissue, a transfusion can be thought of as a form of transplantation, carrying the same risks of immune response as do other types of transplantation. For this reason, the exact matching of a number of factors in the blood between the donor and the recipient is crucial to prevent serious allergic reactions that could be fatal. In addition to the risk of such a reaction, there is a risk that a blood transfusion will transmit a disease, such as hepatitis or HIV. Careful screening of blood by blood banks has significantly reduced this risk, however.

Hemophilia

Because there is no cure for hemophilia, treatment is directed toward preventing any injury that could precipitate bleeding and toward controlling bleeding episodes when they do occur. The mainstay of treatment for hemophilia is the administration of **plasma** or **plasma concentrates** that contain the clotting factors in which the individual's blood is deficient. Because they have higher concentrations of clotting factors, plasma concentrates are given more frequently than is fresh plasma. The clotting factors are usually replaced through intravenous infusion. The amount and duration of the infusion depend on the individual's size, as well as on the severity of the bleeding problem. Treatment may be instituted prior to surgery to prevent excessive bleeding.

Early treatment of bleeding helps to prevent complications. Consequently, some individuals learn to administer clotting factor concentrates at home. They must be able to calculate the appropriate dose, mix, and administer the concentrate intravenously. Home therapy is appropriate for mild bleeding, but is not sufficient for more severe bleeding. Major bleeding requires medical evaluation.

There are possible complications associated with replacement therapy. As with all therapies that involve intravenous infusion, there is the chance of the transmission of disease, such as hepatitis and HIV. Needles and equipment should always be sterile and never shared. Although most blood products are now carefully screened for disease, individuals who received replacement therapy before 1985 may already have been exposed to HIV, which can be a persistent source of anxiety and concern. Individuals who receive blood products intravenously can also develop an allergic reaction to the infusion. Such reactions should be reported to a physician promptly.

Individuals with bleeding into a joint may require joint immobilization for several days in addition to replacement therapy. Joint pain may be treated with anti-inflammatory medications and analgesics. Medications that contain aspirin, should be avoided, however, because aspirin interferes with platelet function. Physical therapy or prescribed exercise carried out at home may be necessary to maintain the range of motion of affected joints. If the joints undergo severe degeneration, reconstructive orthopedic surgery, such as joint replacement, may also be necessary (see Chapter 7).

Individuals with hemophilia should always wear a Medic Alert identification bracelet or necklace to alert others to their condition in case of an emergency.

Sickle Cell Anemia

Like hemophilia, sickle cell anemia has no cure. Treatment is directed toward controlling its symptoms. Good nutrition is essential to combat anemia and to maintain the body's resistance to infection. The maintenance of adequate fluid intake is also important for individuals with sickle cell anemia, because adequate hydration can minimize the sickling of red blood cells and decrease the blood viscosity. The anemia associated with this condition sometimes necessitates transfusion therapy. Because of the propensity of those who have sickle cell anemia to develop infections, prophylactic antibiotics may be given on occasion.

Care should be taken to avoid any factors that precipitate a sickle cell crisis. Individuals in a sickle cell crisis often require hospitalization. During the crisis, treatment focuses on restoring fluids, if dehydration has occurred, and relieving the pain associated with the crisis, which usually requires the administration of narcotics. If another condition, such as an infection, has precipitated the crisis, treatment of that condition may also be instituted. Organ damage as a result of sickle cell anemia is treated in a similar fashion to chronic organ disease from other causes.

HIV Infections/AIDS

Currently, there is no means of restoring the damaged immunological function characteristic of HIV infections. Several drugs that interfere with the HIV's ability to reproduce, which, in turn, increases the immune system's effectiveness, are being tested. These drugs are in the experimental stages, however, and have potentially serious side-effects. One drug, Zidovudine **(Retrovir)**, formerly called **azidothymidine** or AZT, is currently in clinical use and has been found to both increase the survival period and improve the quality of life for individuals with HIV infection. It has serious side-effects, however, because its effect on the bone marrow leads to anemia and suppresses the formation of some types of white blood cells.

Much of the treatment for individuals with HIV infection is geared toward supportive care and the prevention of opportunistic infections. These individuals should have adequate rest, should engage in a program of moderate exercise, and should maintain adequate nutrition. As the condition progresses, it will be necessary to modify the exercise program and allow for more frequent rest periods in order to conserve energy.

As much as possible, individuals with HIV infection should attempt to prevent opportunistic infection. In addition to maintaining good health practices, they should avoid crowds and people with known infections such as colds and flu. If they develop symptoms of infection, they should consult a physician immediately. In the later stages of HIV infections, when opportunistic and/or neurological symptoms occur, treatment is directed toward the specific infection or symptom manifestation. It is not unusual for individuals with later stages of HIV to experience a number of hospitalizations for acute opportunistic infections.

Individuals with HIV infection should take precautions not to transmit the virus. They should fully understand the importance of practicing safe sex; of informing sexual partners of their condition prior to sexual activity; and of not sharing needles, razors, toothbrushes, or any other item that could be contaminated with blood.

FUNCTIONAL IMPLICATIONS

Psychological Issues

General Considerations

Disorders of the blood and immune system have a variety of psychological implications. The specific implications for a particular individual are dependent on the disorder. Some disorders may be controlled relatively easily, while others require constant vigilance. Although some disorders may be treated and, in some instances, cured, others require lifelong treatment and carry a more ominous prognosis.

Individuals with disorders of the blood and immune system generally have no visible reminders of their disability. Without external adaptive devices, such as wheelchairs, crutches, or canes, or any other signs of disability, these individuals may react by denying the seriousness of the illness and resisting medical directives. For example, individuals with hemophilia may engage in risk-taking behaviors, even though injury and subsequent bleeding could occur. Individuals with sickle cell anemia may engage in a flurry of activity, even though the associated stress and fatigue may precipitate a sickle cell crisis. Individuals with HIV infections may withhold their diagnosis from others with whom they engage in sexual activity, even though their behavior could put those others at risk.

Some disorders occur later in life, necessitating adjustment at the time the disability occurs. Disorders such as sickle cell anemia and hemophilia are lifelong disorders, however. Consequently, individuals with these disorders have had to cope with their condition in one way or another from childhood into adulthood. Most individuals with either sickle cell anemia or hemophilia experience frequent illness and medical care throughout their childhood and adolescence. Although these experiences can build confidence in their ability to cope with adversity, they can also have a negative impact on development. These individuals may carry the coping behaviors and attitudes learned in childhood into the adult years, where they continue to affect the individuals' perception of themselves, their condition, and their abilities. Depending on the constructiveness of the coping strategy used, such behaviors may be an asset or a hindrance.

Sickle cell anemia carries the additional stress of unpredictability. Although some of the factors that provoke a sickle cell crisis may be identifiable, the crises are often unpredictable and beyond the individual's control. Not only are the crises painful and debilitating, but there is also the potential for organ damage each time a crisis occurs. The lack of control over the frequency or severity of sickle cell crises can lead to feelings of hopelessness and depression.

The possibility of early death, a source of anxiety and depression for those with any disorder, is a reality for individuals with hemophilia and sickle cell anemia. Although hemophilia can be controlled to some degree, there is always the fear that an accident or traumatic event may occur in which bleeding may not be controlled. Individuals with sickle cell anemia are aware of the possibility that sudden death will occur as a result of a sickle cell crisis or complications. Individuals may cope with the threat of early death in a variety of ways, ranging from the adoption of a philosophical view toward life to passivity and withdrawal.

The way in which an individual copes with a lifelong disorder of the blood depends on a wide variety of factors, some of which relate to the coping mechanisms learned in childhood. An individual's reaction as an adult to the condition is dependent to some extent on how well his or her psychological adjustment was managed throughout development. Children who were encouraged to live as normal a life as possible, despite their condition, may exhibit a greater sense of self-esteem and autonomy as adults than do those who were kept in a dependent, overprotected state.

Special Considerations for Individuals with HIV Infections

Distress and preoccupation with illness and imminent death may characterize individuals with any fatal disorder. Individuals with HIV infection face an even more grim realization that, to date, no one with later stages of HIV has survived. Consequently, those who have tested HIV-positive are likely to experience considerable anxiety. In addition to the grave prognosis, there is much ambiguity associated with positive test results. It is impossible to predict when or how rapidly the infection will progress to the later stages. Living with the potential for progressing to the later stage and the uncertainty about the disease's progression often lead to additional stress and anxiety. These individuals may retreat from most of their former activities and may find it difficult to set goals for the future. They may put aside their personal aspirations and focus on the struggle to survive.

Individuals with HIV infection often bear the additional stress of the stigma and fear associated with the disease, both of which can lead to rejection and abandonment by others. Feelings of depression, despair, and hopelessness are common. These individuals may also experience considerable anger. There may be anger and resentment toward the societally imposed isolation that hampers HIV-infected individuals in their efforts to obtain the social support and, at times, even the medical care afforded to individuals with other life-threatening conditions. Individuals who have become infected with HIV through medical treatment, such as blood transfusions, may experience additional anger at contracting the disease as "innocent victims." Those infected through contact with others may direct their anger against the individual or individuals from whom they contracted the disease.

If the HIV infection is the result of their own past behavior or life style, infected individuals may also experience considerable guilt and self-incrimination. Guilt, self-blame, fear of abandonment, and fear of imminent painful death can lead to self-destructive behaviors, including attempted suicide. For individuals whose families and friends had not been aware of their life style, exposure may result in increased anxiety and fear of abandonment. In other instances, HIV-infected individuals may experience guilt because of the fear that they have been the source of contagion to others.

Life Style Issues

Different disorders of the blood and immune system affect the activities of daily living in varying degrees, depending on the associated symptoms. Symptoms of fatigue or difficulty in breathing with exertion may require individuals to pace their activities throughout the day to conserve energy. These individuals may need more frequent rest periods, or they may need to divide activities into smaller steps that they perform throughout the day rather than completing a task all at once.

Good health practices are important to everyone; however, because of the increased susceptibility to infection that is part of many blood disorders (especially HIV infections), individuals with such disorders should take extra care to have well-balanced diets and well-balanced regimens of rest and activity. Exercise is especially important to individuals with hemophilia. Regular, moderate exercise can build the muscles that protect joints and decrease the incidence of bleeding into the joints. Activities that carry a higher probability of injury, such as contact sports, should be avoided, however.

The degree to which individuals with disorders of the blood and immune system can maintain routine daily schedules depends on the specific condition, its progression, and complications. For the most part, individuals with hemophilia need not interrupt their daily schedules. The use of home self-infusion therapy has greatly reduce their incapacity by providing prompt and early treatment of spontaneous bleeding.

Individuals with sickle cell anemia can usually maintain their regular schedules; however, the onset of sickle cell crises is unpredictable and may necessitate hospitalization when they occur. In most instances, individuals with sickle cell anemia do not need to alter their activities, unless the activities appear to provoke a sickle cell crisis. Most activities, if performed in moderation, can be tolerated.

Individuals with HIV infection may need to balance periods of activity and rest in order to prevent overfatigue. A moderate, regular program of exercise can help individuals with HIV infection to maintain optimal emotional, as well as physical, health. As the condition progresses and stamina decreases, they will need to modify their activities. Individuals in the later stages of HIV infection often need assistance with everyday activities, including at first housekeeping chores and later extending to personal care.

Although neither hemophilia nor sickle cell anemia alters sexual function, both are inherited disorders, and individuals may wish to consider genetic counseling before deciding to have children. There is no direct effect on sexual function associated with HIV infection; however, because of the possibility of transmission of the virus to others, individuals with HIV infections should inform their sexual partners about their diagnosis prior to sexual contact and should engage only in safe sexual practices. When women with HIV infection become pregnant, the child may be born HIV-infected.

Social Issues

The social effects of blood disorders vary with the condition, the individual, and the particular circumstances. Fatigue and susceptibility to infection, characteristic of many blood disorders, may alter social functioning to some degree. The unpredictability of sickle cell crises can alter social functioning for individuals with sickle cell anemia, who may have to cancel or alter plans at the last minute if a crisis should occur. The role of stress as a precipitating factor in sickle cell crisis must also be considered. Although stress is frequently associated with negative events, stress can also be associated with positive events, such as a graduation celebration or a wedding.

Because many blood disorders have no readily observable outward cues and signs, and because their symptoms are often intermittent, others may not understand why individuals with such disorders must adhere to certain restrictions or why they are under continuing medical care. Owing to the fact that these individuals do not appear to be legitimately ill and, in many instances, have little physical impairment, they may receive less social support and understanding than do those individuals with more visible disabilities.

Conditions that are hereditary and those that occur in childhood can alter the socialization process necessary for social functioning in adulthood. Recurrent hospitalizations may affect a child's school performance and, consequently, his or her sense of industry and achievement. In addition, frequent school absences, hospitalizations, or the inability to engage in some activities may affect a child's interactions and relationships with peers, which, in turn, could affect the child's self-esteem and sense of self-worth. Some children, as a means of dealing with the stress inherent in their condition, may learn to use their condition to manipulate and control the behaviors of others. Each of these possible effects of childhood illness can determine an individual's ability to function in the social world as an adult.

The parents of a child with an inherited disorder, such as hemophilia or sickle cell anemia, may experience guilt, react with overprotectiveness, and foster a sense of dependency in the child. They may adopt a permissive or indulgent attitude toward their child. Rather than correcting the child when he or she misbehaves, the parents may allow the misbehaviors as a means to appease their own sense of guilt. They may also excuse the child from the normal responsibilities or the limits established for the child's siblings. Such parental reactions can impede the child's ability to function adequately as an adult in society.

The social effects of HIV infection are as varied as the symptoms associated with the condition. Individuals with HIV infection have a disease that many fear and perceive as shrouded in mystery, and many of the social implications of HIV infection are related to this fear and misunderstanding. Some segments of society believe that the illness is "deserved" because it has been associated with behavior that they consider unacceptable. Others avoid individuals with HIV infection because they fear contagion and are not aware of the actual modes of transmission. Such societal concepts can result in ostracism and discrimination against these individuals. They may find their activities at school, work, and social functions restricted or banned because of social prejudice. The social stigma attached to the condition may be particularly overwhelming and traumatic if family and friends also express such reactions. Individuals with HIV infection are often left with little social support at a time when they need it most. Support groups, although beneficial in many chronic diseases, are even more important for individuals with HIV infection.

In addition to the threatened loss of job, friends, family, and other means of social support, individuals with HIV infection may fear being shunned by hospital and medical personnel when they need care. Even when hospitalized, individuals with HIV infection often experience stigmatization, adding to the detrimental effects of the illness.

Vocational Issues

The cause and symptoms of an individual's blood disorder determine its vocational impact. If, for example, the condition has been caused in part by exposure to toxic substances within the environment, these hazards should be removed before the individual returns to the work place. If fatigue or dyspnea is a symptom of the disorder, as in those disorders characterized by anemia, it may be necessary to consider the physical demands of the job and the need for more frequent rest periods. When infection is a potential complication of the disorder, the individual should avoid exposure to factors and environments that may precipitate infection.

Individuals with sickle cell anemia must consider not only the physical demands of the job as related to stamina, but also the role that strenuous exertion has in precipitating sickle cell crises. Because sickle cell anemia is a lifelong disease, most individuals with this disorder learn over the years which type and how much activity they can usually tolerate. Despite the potential relationship of overexertion and sickle cell crisis, most individuals with sickle cell anemia are capable of performing moderate and, in some instances, even heavy work.

Individuals who have experienced specific organ or joint damage as a result of repeated sickle cell crises have many of the same limitations imposed on those who have similar conditions for other reasons. In addition, they should avoid extremes in temperature. Very hot weather places extra strain on the heart and predisposes to dehydration, which can precipitate a crisis. Very cold, damp environments can also precipitate a crisis. Consequently, it may be beneficial for individuals with sickle cell anemia to work in indoor environments.

The amount of stress in the work environment and its contribution to the development of sickle cell crisis is another factor that individuals with sickle cell anemia must consider. Not all individuals react to stress in the same way, nor do they always perceive stress in the same way. Consequently, the importance of stress must be determined on an individual basis. The degree to which absences due to sickle cell crises become a hindrance to work performance is dependent on the individual, the frequency, and the seriousness of the crises when they occur.

Improved medical technology and the availability of self-infused coagulation factors have greatly increased the ability of individuals with hemophilia to maintain employment in a variety of settings. Obviously they should avoid employment in which there is a direct threat of physical injury in most cases. Injuries that may be minimal by most standards can have serious implications for individuals with more severe forms of hemophilia. Joint damage and/or subsequent joint replacement due to complications of hemophilia may impose the same limitations as do joint disorders from other causes (see Chapter 7). For the most part, however, the vocational functioning of individuals with hemophilia is determined primarily by their abilities and interests.

For individuals with HIV infection, the most serious impediments to successful functioning in the work place are the fear, discrimination, and prejudice that they encounter. These individuals frequently fear that they will lose their jobs as a result of their diagnosis, regardless of their continued mental and physical ability to work. When they do maintain their employment, there are usually no special restrictions; however, because of the mode of transmission of the virus, they should avoid occupations in which their blood may contaminate the blood of others. Because infection can have such serious consequences for individuals with HIV infection, they should also avoid job situations in which they are likely to be exposed to infection. As the HIV infection progresses and individuals experience increasing fatigue, they may need to undertake less strenuous work or arrange for shorter work schedules or more frequent rest periods. In the later stages of the disease, mental changes may affect an individual's capacity to function in the work setting.

BIBLIOGRAPHY

Amin, N.M. "Zidovudine for Treating AIDS." *Postgraduate Medicine* 86(1989):195–207.

Baltimore, D., and Feinbert, M.B. "HIV Revealed—Toward a Natural History of the Infection." *New England Journal of Medicine* 321(1989):1673–1675.

Barber, T.C., and Langfitt, D.E. *Teaching the Medical/Surgical Patient—Diagnostics and Procedures.* Bowie, Md.: Robert J. Brady Co., 1983.

Berkow, R., and Fletcher, A.J., eds. *The Merck Manual of Diagnosis and Therapy.* Rahway, N.J.: Merck Sharpe and Dohme Research Laboratories, 1987.

Blendon, R.J., and Donelan, K. "Discrimination against People with AIDS." *New England Journal of Medicine* 319(1988):1022–1026.

Brogan, K.L., and Zell, S.C. "Hematologic Toxicity of Zidovudine in HIV-Infected Patients." *American Family Physician* 41(1990):1521–1526.

Brooke, G.L.; Safran, G.F.; Perlmutter, B.L.; Perez, J.A.; and Zatlin, G.S. "HIV Disease: A Review for the Family Physician. Part II. Secondary Infections, Malignancy and Experimental Therapy." *American Family Physician* 42(1990):1299–1308.

Brunner, L.S.; Emerson, C.P.; Ferguson, L.K.; and Suddarth, D.S. *Textbook of Medical-Surgical Nursing.* Philadelphia: W.B. Saunders Co., 1970.

Corbett, J.V. *Diagnostic Procedures in Nursing Practice.* Norwalk, Conn.: Appleton-Century-Crofts, 1982.

Corbett, J.V. *Laboratory Tests in Nursing Practice.* Norwalk, Conn.: Appleton-Century-Crofts, 1983.

Flaskerud, J.H. "AIDS: Psychological Aspects." *Health Values* 12(1988):44–52.

Gong, V., and Rudnick, N., eds. *AIDS: Facts and Issues.* New Brunswick, N.J: Rutgers University Press, 1986.

Greene, C.S., ed. *Handbook of Adult Primary Care.* New York: John Wiley & Sons, 1987.

Guyton, A.C. *Human Physiology and Mechanisms of Disease.* Philadelphia: W.B. Saunders Co., 1982.

Henry, K.; Thurn, J.; and Anderson, D. "Testing for Human Immunodeficiency Virus." *Postgraduate Medicine* 85(1989):293–309.

Institute of Medicine. National Academy of Sciences. *Mobilizing against AIDS: The Unfinished Story of a Virus.* Cambridge: Harvard University Press, 1986.

Keele, C.A.; Neil, E.; and Joels, N. *Samson Wright's Applied Physiology.* New York: Oxford University Press, 1982.

Levy, R.M.; Bredesen, D.E.; and Rosenblum, M.L. "Neurologic Complications of HIV Infection." *American Family Physician* 41(1990):517–534.

Luckman, J., and Sorensen, K.C. *Medical-Surgical Nursing: A Psychophysiologic Approach.* Philadelphia: W.B. Saunders Co., 1987.

McCabe, R.E. "Toxoplasmosis: Clinical Presentation and Diagnosis in Immunocompromised Patients." *Primary Care and Cancer* 10(1990):29–38.

Mills, J. "*Pneumocystis* Pneumonia in AIDS: Diagnosis and Treatment." *Modern Medicine* 55(1987):92–102.

Nursing 87 Books. *Patient Teaching.* Springhouse, Pa.: Springhouse Corporation Book Division, 1987.

Paauw, D.S., and O'Neill, J.F. "Human Immunodeficiency Virus and the Primary Care Physician." *Journal of Family Practice* 31(1990):646–650.

Rakel, R.E. *Conn's Current Therapy 1990*. Philadelphia: W.B. Saunders Co., 1990.

Rodgers, G.P.; Dover, G.J.; Noguchi, T.; Schechter, A.N.; and Nienhaus, A.W. "Hematologic Response of Patients with Sickle Cell Disease to Treatment with Hydroxyurea." *New England Journal of Medicine* 322(1990):1037–1045.

Rossitch, E.; Carrazana, E.J.; and Samuels, M.A. "Cerebral Toxoplasmosis in Patients with AIDS." *American Family Physician* 41(1990):867–872.

Runck, B. *Coping with AIDS—Psychological and Social Considerations in Helping People with HTLV-III Infection*. Washington, D.C.: U.S. Department of Health and Human Services, Alcohol, Drug Abuse, and Mental Health Administration, 1986.

Scheer, S.J.,ed. *Medical Perspectives in Vocational Assessment of Impaired Workers*. Gaithersburg, Md.: Aspen Publishers, 1991.

Schofferman, J., and Schoen, K. "AIDS-Dementia Syndrome." *Medical Aspects of Human Sexuality* (1987)58–69.

Scutchfield, F.D., and Benenson, A.S. "AIDS Update." *Postgraduate Medicine* 85(1989):289–304.

Smith, D.W., and Hanley-Germain, C.P. *Care of the Adult Patient*. Philadelphia: J.B. Lippincott Co., 1975.

Stolov, W.C., and Clowers, M.R. *Handbook of Severe Disability*. Washington, D.C.: U.S. Department of Education, Rehabilitation Services Administration, 1981.

U.S. Preventive Services Task Force. "Counseling To Prevent HIV Infection and Other Sexually Transmitted Disease." *American Family Physician* 41(1990):1179–1184.

Vander, A.J.; Sherman, J.H.; and Luciano, D.S. *Human Physiology: The Mechanisms of Body Function*. New York: McGraw-Hill Book Co., 1985.

Volberding, P.A. "Keeping Up-to-date with Zidovudine." *Patient Care* 24(1990):127–138.

Weisberg, L.A., and Ross, W. "AIDS Dementia Complex." *Postgraduate Medicine* 86(1989): 213–220.

Weiss, R., and Thier, S.O. "HIV Testing Is the Answer—What's the Question?" *New England Journal of Medicine* 319(1988):1010–1012.

Wong, H.; Allen, H.A.; and Moore, J. "AIDS: Dynamics and Rehabilitation Concerns." *Journal of Applied Rehabilitation Counseling* 19(1988):37–41.

Wormser, G.P., and Joline, C. "Would You Eat Cookies Prepared by an AIDS Patient? Survey Reveals Harmful Attitudes among Professionals." *Postgraduate Medicine* 86(1989):171–186.

Wyngaarden, J.B., and Smith, J.H. *Cecil Textbook of Medicine*. Philadelphia: W.B. Saunders Co., 1988.

chapter 14

Substance Use Disorders

Most cultures accept the social use of substances that alter mood or behavior (psychoactive substances) to some degree, although there is wide cultural variation regarding the type of substance considered acceptable and the amount of use considered appropriate. In many segments of our society, for example, the moderate use of alcohol for recreational purposes is condoned; in some other cultures, the use of alcohol for any purpose is condemned. In some cultures, the use of psychoactive substances for various rituals or ceremonies is widely accepted; in other cultures, however, the use of the same substance for any purpose is unacceptable or, in some cases, illegal. Although the use of substances in our society under appropriate conditions and circumstances is generally considered acceptable, the behavior is considered pathological when the use becomes injurious to health or disruptive to daily life.

Substance use disorders comprise the symptoms and maladaptive changes in behavior that occur as a result of the more or less regular use of psychoactive substances. These disorders may be classified either as abuse or as dependence. **Substance abuse** is the continued and repeated use of a substance, even though the individual knows that such use precipitates or exacerbates problems. **Substance dependence** is an impairment in the individual's ability to control the use of the substance so that the individual continues to use the substance despite adverse consequences. Dependence has different degrees of severity. The characteristics of dependence can include a physiological tolerance for the substance and the development of symptoms with varying degrees of severity should the substance be withdrawn.

As individuals increase the amount of the substance taken, their body metabolism, cells, and behavior adapt so that larger amounts of the substance are needed to produce the same effects. This occurrence is called **tolerance**. The degree of tolerance varies with the substance being used and with the individual. Those who are chronic substance users may be able to adapt their behavior so that they continue functioning at work, at home, or in social situations, even though they are under the influence of a substance. Although tolerance is not always an indication of dependence, tolerance is commonly observed in individuals with substance use disorders. Furthermore, individuals who have developed a tolerance for one substance frequently show a higher tolerance for related substances as well. This condition is known as **cross-tolerance**.

As the body adapts to the toxic effects of large concentrations of a substance, physical disturbances occur when the amount of the substance administered is decreased or suspended. Thus, the individual exhibits physical symptoms when the substance is absent from the body or when the dosage is decreased, a condition known as **withdrawal**. The exact symptoms of this process depend on the substance on which the individual is physically dependent.

Abuse and dependence may involve one or several substances, taken simultaneously or sequentially, and may involve substances that are licit, illicit, prescribed, or nonprescribed. Substance use disorders reflect a combination of biological, psychological, social, and environmental factors. The etiology and treatment of substance use disorders entail a complex interface among all these factors. No one factor explains the development of substance use disorders.

Just as all chronic illness and disability affect physical, social, psychological, and vocational aspects of individuals' lives, so do substance use disorders. Like other chronic, relapsing conditions, substance use disorders produce a variety of impairments. Therefore, the implications of these disorders must be evaluated in the context of the individual's specific situation. Substance abuse or dependence can occur alone or with one or more other physical or psychiatric disabilities. The effects of substance use combined with those of other disabilities can cause additional physical, psychological, and social complications, adding to the disabling effects of both.

SUBSTANCE USE AND CHRONIC ILLNESS/DISABILITY

When individuals have a dual diagnosis of substance use and chronic illness/disability, the treatment of both conditions becomes more complex. The individual may have developed the substance use disorder prior to the diagnosis of chronic illness or disability. In some instances, the substance use may have been responsible for the chronic illness or disability. For example, the chronic illness may have been precipitated by the long-term toxic effects of the substance on various body systems, or the disability may have resulted from a substance-related accident or traumatic injury.

Substance use disorders may develop after the diagnosis of chronic illness or disability as well. Some individuals may use substances to escape depression, boredom, frustration, or other associated problems. Social factors can also contribute to the development of substance abuse/dependence. The oppression, alienation, and social isolation experienced by some individuals with chronic illness or disability can increase their susceptibility to substance abuse/dependence as they attempt to gain acceptance and normalization through the recreational and social use of substance.

The coexistence of a substance use disorder with other illness or disability increases the individual's vulnerability to medical complications and often accentuates the symptoms of the chronic illness or disability. For example, the use of psychoactive substances may accentuate the problems with gait or balance sometimes associated with brain injury. Individuals with chronic illness or disability may have a variety of medications prescribed for the treatment of their condition that, when taken in combination with alcohol or other psychoactive substances, can cause untoward effects. In some instances, the ready accessibility of prescription medications for the treatment of medical needs, such as pain, makes it easier for individuals to begin to use the medication excessively. The incidence of substance use disorders in individuals with chronic illness and disability is not yet known. When a substance use disorder does coexist with physical or mental impairments, however, both the problems and the treatment become more complex.

ALCOHOL ABUSE AND DEPENDENCE

The effect of alcohol on the body, like the effect of any drug, depends on the interaction between properties of the specific pharmacologic agent and the characteristics of a specific individual. The medical complications of alcohol abuse result from the direct effects of alcohol (ethanol) on body tissues and from the adaptive responses of the body to excessive exposure to alcohol.

Alcohol is rapidly absorbed from the stomach and intestines into the bloodstream and is rapidly metabolized, making it a fast-acting drug. Because alcohol diffuses quickly into the water content of all body tissues, the blood concentration of alcohol is an accurate reflection of the concentration of alcohol in other body tissues. Some alcohol is eliminated through the kidneys and lungs, but most is metabolized by the liver. Although a moderate dose of alcohol normally clears from the blood in approximately 1 hour, only a fixed amount of alcohol can be metabolized at a time. When the rate of alcohol consumption exceeds the body's ability to metabolize it, alcohol accumulates in the bloodstream, elevating the blood alcohol concentration.

Intoxication

The level of intoxication is frequently determined by the alcohol concentration in the blood. The rate at which alcohol is absorbed into the bloodstream is dependent on the amount ingested, the presence or absence of food in the stomach, and the rate of gastric emptying. The concentration of alcohol in the blood is also dependent on body size. Blood alcohol levels are proportionately less in large individuals than small individuals, even though they consume equal amounts of alcohol under similar conditions.

Alcohol has a direct pharmacologic effect on the nervous system. It is a powerful central nervous system depressant. The intoxicating effects of alcohol correlate roughly with the alcohol concentrations in the blood, which, in turn, reflects the alcohol concentration in the brain. At low levels of intoxication (0.05 percent), alcohol may produce a sense of relaxation and well-being. As the concentration of alcohol increases (0.11 percent to 0.20 percent), neurological signs of **ataxia** (defective coordination of muscles, especially with voluntary movement) occur. Judgment may also be impaired. Continued elevation of blood alcohol concentrations (0.31 percent to 0.41 percent) can produce confusion, mild stupor, and ultimately coma. Blood alcohol levels of 0.51 percent usually lead to death from depression of the respiratory center of the brain.

Another effect in the spectrum of neurological disturbances associated with intensive alcohol intoxication is the occurrence of **blackouts**, periods of amnesia characterized by inability to remember events during the time of the blackout.

Withdrawal Syndromes

The consumption of large amounts of alcohol at frequent intervals for prolonged periods creates a state of physical dependence in which the cessation of intake or a reduction in the amount of alcohol ingested produces abnormal symptoms. The constellation of symptoms experienced in withdrawal syndromes varies in severity.

Early symptoms can begin within hours of the onset of withdrawal, but are usually the most pronounced within 12 to 48 hours. The symptoms consist of generalized tremor, nausea and vomiting, weakness, and sweating. Additional symptoms may include insomnia, agitation, and mild confusion. **Alcoholic hallucinosis**, consisting of auditory illusions and visual hallucinations, may also occur during withdrawal. Generalized seizures, sometimes called "rum fits" or **withdrawal convulsions**, may also be experienced.

The most severe form of alcohol withdrawal is **delirium tremens (DTs)**. Individuals with delirium tremens experience significant restlessness, gross disorientation and cognitive disruption, and elevation of temperature and pulse rate. Although delirium tremens can be fatal, the course is often self-limiting. The acute period of delirium tremens usually lasts from 2 to 10 days, but can be more prolonged if withdrawal is severe.

Withdrawal syndrome may be treated medically by the administration of a cross-tolerant drug, such as a sedative. Initially, sedatives are given in large doses to suppress the withdrawal symptoms; the dosage is then progressively tapered over 2 to 7 days. Tapering can consist of reducing the individual dose, increasing the interval between doses, or both. Because of wide variations in drug tolerance, treatment must be individualized.

Treatment

Alcohol dependence is a chronic, lifelong disorder. It requires long-term treatment that extends beyond the initial period of detoxification and generally involves a wide variety of services, including individual, group, and family therapy. In addition, self-help groups, such as Alcoholics Anonymous (AA) for alcohol-dependent individuals, and Alanon and Alateen for their families, are widely recommended. Typically, the goal of treatment is abstinence from alcohol and other mood-altering substances.

In some circumstances, drugs are used to discourage and inhibit the use of alcohol. One such drug, disulfiram **(Antabuse)**, interferes with the normal metabolism of alcohol. Consequently, individuals who ingest alcohol after taking Antabuse have severe gastrointestinal distress. Thus, the drug acts as a deterrent to alcohol intake.

ALCOHOL-RELATED ILLNESSES

The medical conditions that can result from chronic alcohol abuse are generally caused by dietary insufficiency, by the direct toxic effects of alcohol on body tissue, or both. These conditions can involve all organ systems. The prognosis of alcohol-related medical illness depends on the nature of the illness and its severity. Although some alcohol-related medical illnesses are reversible, almost no alcohol-related illness can be cured if the individual continues to abuse alcohol.

Nervous System

Korsakoff's Syndrome

Associated with an excessive intake of alcohol, chronic malnutrition, and a deficiency of the B vitamins (thiamine in particular), **Korsakoff's syndrome** is characterized by gross disturbances in forming new memories and recalling past memories. The use of **confabulation**, in which individuals make up experiences in order to fill memory gaps, is a common characteristic of those with Korsakoff's syndrome. In addition to abstinence, the treatment consists of the administration of thiamine. Some cognitive improvement is possible, but full recovery is unlikely. It may require several months before improvement is noticeable.

Wernicke's Encephalopathy (Wernicke's Disease)

Although Wernicke's encephalopathy can occur in other conditions, it is most commonly associated with chronic alcohol abuse. It is characterized by the sudden onset of confusion, double vision, and difficulty with balance. It often occurs in combination with Korsakoff's syndrome and, like Korsakoff's syndrome, is related to thiamine deficiency. The treatment consists of the replacement of thiamine. Early treatment is mandatory in order to prevent permanent deficits. Prompt treatment resolves many of the symptoms. When Korsakoff's syndrome accompanies Wernicke's encephalopathy, however, memory deficits remain.

Peripheral Neuropathy

Although there are many causes of peripheral neuropathy (see Chapter 8), a number of individuals who chronically abuse alcohol develop disorders of the peripheral nerves. Peripheral neuropathy associated with chronic alcohol abuse is thought to be the result of inadequate nutrition, specifically inadequate amounts of thiamine and the other B vitamins. The condition affects the extremities; symptoms include numbness, painful sensations, weakness, and muscle cramps. Burning pain of the feet may also occur. Good nutrition and the administration of supplemental B vitamins can bring about improvement, but the improvement may be slow.

Cardiovascular System

Cardiomyopathy

Alcoholic cardiomyopathy occurs after the long-term chronic use of alcohol and is the result of the direct toxic effects of alcohol on the heart muscle itself. The heart may become enlarged (**cardiomegaly**) and the heart muscle more fibrous. The heart's ability to pump effectively may be compromised so that symptoms of congestive heart failure, such as difficulty in breathing and swelling (see Chapter 2), may occur as the cardiac damage increases.

Beriberi Heart Disease

A deficiency in thiamine is thought to contribute to the development of beriberi heart disease. Individuals with the condition have a high cardiac output even at rest because of the dilation of the peripheral small blood vessels. Beriberi heart disease responds well to the administration of supplemental thiamine.

Alterations in Heart Rate and Rhythm

Alcohol can affect both the speed at which the heart beats and the rhythm that it maintains. The direct long-term effect on blood pressure is variable. Alcohol withdrawal can put a heavy load on the heart, sometimes compromising cardiac function so severely during detoxification that death can result. Consequently, detoxification should be conducted under careful medical supervision.

Alterations in Blood

Alcohol can have a direct and adverse effect on the development of red blood cells, white blood cells, and platelets, resulting in subsequent anemia, lower resistance to infection, and interference with blood clotting. One of the mechanisms by which alcohol affects blood cell formation is by interfering with the use of folic acid, a nutritional substance that bone marrow requires to manufacture healthy cells effectively. **Megaloblastic anemia** (presence of large abnormal red blood cells) with **leukopenia** (abnormal decrease in the number of white blood cells) and **thrombocytopenia** (abnormal decrease in the number of platelets) occurs frequently in individuals with a low folic acid intake. Treatment with the administration of supplemental folate, proper nutrition, and abstinence from alcohol can generally reverse these abnormalities.

Respiratory System

Alcohol has a direct toxic effect on lung tissue. In combination with cigarette smoking, this can lead to a higher incidence of chronic obstructive pulmonary disease (see Chapter 3) in individuals who chronically abuse alcohol. In addition, because the chronic abuse of alcohol affects some of the lungs' natural defenses, these individuals have a greater tendency to develop lung infections.

Musculoskeletal System

Regardless of the nutritional status, alcohol has a direct toxic effect on skeletal muscle. The result is the destruction of muscle fibers, leading to weakness, pain, tenderness, and swelling of affected muscles. **Myopathy** (disease of muscle) due to alcohol abuse may be acute or chronic. The more common form is chronic alcoholic myopathy which evolves over months to years. Pain may be less severe in chronic myopathy, although muscle cramps can occur. In addition, the muscles may **atrophy** and become weak. Most symptoms of myopathy improve with the cessation of the alcohol abuse, while continued alcohol abuse leads to continued deterioration. Excessive alcohol consumption can also contribute to **osteoporosis** (see Chapter 7), not only because calcium intake is insufficient, but also because alcohol interferes with the absorption of calcium from the intestine.

In addition to the direct effect on the musculoskeletal system, alcohol can also contribute to major injury. Individuals under the influence of alcohol may have decreased balance and coordination as well as demonstrate impaired judgment. As a result, the individual may experience injuries in falls, fires, or motor vehicle or pedestrian accidents.

Gastrointestinal System

It is possible for alcohol to affect almost every organ of the gastrointestinal tract. Individuals who consume alcohol excessively have an increased incidence of **cancer** of the throat and esophagus (see Chapter 12). Whether the increased incidence of cancer is due to direct contact of alcohol with the tissues, the presence of carcinogenic substances in some alcoholic beverages, or a combination of the two is unknown.

Despite the fact that alcohol is considered a **hepatotoxin** (substance that is harmful to the liver), individuals who chronically abuse alcohol differ widely in their susceptibility to liver disease. There is evidence to suggest, however, that women tend to be more susceptible to liver damage as a result of excessive alcohol consumption than are men.

Esophagitis and Gastritis

Esophagitis is an inflammation of the esophagus; **gastritis,** an inflammation of the stomach. Both can occur with the acute and chronic abuse of alcohol. The severity of these conditions depends on the individual. In some instances, the conditions produce only a mild discomfort, but in other instances, the irritation and inflammation produce ulcerations and bleeding. Treatment is directed toward reducing the inflammation. Obviously, abstinence from alcohol is a major treatment objective.

Esophageal Varices

Some individuals who abuse alcohol develop **esophageal varices**, "varicose" veins of the esophagus, a condition in which the veins become dilated and tortuous. Esophageal varices are usually a complication of cirrhosis and associated portal hypertension. They may cause no symptoms. If the varices become ulcerated due to irritation, however, or if there is increased strain from coughing or vomiting, the distended veins may rupture, causing serious hemorrhage.

The treatment is directed toward controlling the hemorrhage, usually through the insertion of a special tube (Sengstaken-Blakemore tube) into the esophagus. A balloon on the tube is then inflated to exert pressure against the bleeding vein. Because the esophagus needs rest in order to heal, other types of feeding may be instituted until the esophagus is healed (see Chapter 6).

Alcoholic Hepatitis

During alcohol metabolism, fat is deposited in the liver. When an individual consumes excessive amounts of alcohol, the accumulation of fat enlarges the liver, a condition called **fatty liver**. If the individual continues to consume alcohol, liver cells may die, causing the liver to become inflamed. This inflammatory condition, in which the liver is usually enlarged and painful, is known as **alcoholic hepatitis**. Abstinence from alcohol can reverse the effects of both fatty liver and alcoholic hepatitis. Individuals who continue to abuse alcohol, however, have a high chance of developing cirrhosis.

Cirrhosis

Although a number of chemicals or infections (e.g., hepatitis) can induce **cirrhosis**, a common cause is alcohol abuse. Cirrhosis involves a reaction of the liver to injury by **hepatotoxins**. When alcohol injures the liver repeatedly over a period of time, fibrous tissue replaces liver cells. Circulation within the liver becomes less efficient, resulting in obstructions and, thus, increasing pressure in the vessels.

All blood from the gastrointestinal tract, spleen, pancreas, and gallbladder is carried to the heart through the liver by the portal system. Because of the fibrous changes that occur in the liver with cirrhosis, there is increased pressure in the portal vein, a condition known as **portal hypertension**. The backflow of blood results in the enlargement of the spleen **(splenomegaly)**, the accumulation of fluid in the abdominal cavity **(ascites)**, and the development of esophageal varices.

Some individuals with cirrhosis experience no symptoms. Others experience weakness, nausea, loss of appetite **(anorexia)**, and **jaundice** (yellow discoloration of the skin and whites of the eyes due to the accumulation of bile pigments in the blood). The treatment of cirrhosis is largely symptomatic, but abstinence from alcohol is a necessity for survival. Individuals with cirrhotic changes in the liver have an increased risk of cancer of the liver, however. Those who continue to abuse alcohol despite cirrhotic changes in the liver or despite other complications have a significantly decreased survival rate.

Pancreatitis

A variety of conditions other than alcohol abuse may cause **pancreatitis** (inflammation of the pancreas). **Alcoholic pancreatitis**, however, is a form of pancreatitis that develops in susceptible individuals after chronic alcohol abuse. In this condition, the pancreatic ducts become obstructed. The enzymes that the pancreas normally secretes into the small intestine to aid in digestion become active while they are still in the pancreas. As a result, the pancreas essentially begins to digest itself, causing progressive degeneration with scarring and calcification of pancreatic tissues. Pancreatic function is often severely curtailed. (See Chapter 5 for a discussion of diabetes mellitus and Chapter 6 for a discussion of the digestive function of the pancreas.)

Chronic pancreatitis can lead to severe disability from pain, malabsorption of nutrients resulting in weight loss, and diabetes mellitus secondary to the destruction of the islets of Langerhans. The treatment of pancreatitis is directed toward halting the destruction of tissue and alleviating the symptoms. As with other conditions of the gastrointestinal tract, effective treatment requires the individual's abstinence from alcohol. If they no longer consume any alcohol, many individuals recover from alcoholic pancreatitis to live a normal life. If they continue to drink, however, the prognosis is generally poor.

Endocrine System and Reproduction

Excessive alcohol use has been found to lower the level of the male hormone testosterone, which, in turn, has been related to decreased libido and, in some instances, impotence. Excessive alcohol intake also increases the level of epinephrine and other hormones. As discussed previously, the destruction of the pancreas can lead to diabetes mellitus.

The toxic effects of alcohol on the developing fetus during pregnancy can result in a deformity of the infant called **fetal alcohol syndrome**. The amount of alcohol that the pregnant woman must consume before it causes injury to the fetus is unknown and appears to vary with the individual. Fetal alcohol syndrome is characterized by prenatal and postnatal growth retardation, **microcephaly** (abnormal smallness of the head), abnormalities of the nervous system, and facial disfiguration. Other congenital anomalies may include mental retardation, as well as musculoskeletal and cardiac abnormalities.

USE DISORDERS INVOLVING OTHER SUBSTANCES

Caffeine and Nicotine

Tolerance and dependence have been established for both caffeine and nicotine, although these substances are not commonly thought of as substances of abuse. Caffeine is commonly obtained from coffee or tea, but it may also be consumed in soft drinks, chocolate, and in many over-the-counter drugs. Caffeine produces mild stimulation of the central nervous system and cardiac muscle, increases gastric acid secretion, and has a diuretic effect. In some instances, caffeine has been implicated in high blood pressure. Caffeine can produce both psychological and physical dependence. Headaches that are not relieved by regular analgesics are a manifestation of withdrawal from caffeine. Although caffeine abuse in itself is not usually disabling, it may aggravate preexisting conditions, such as ulcer disease, hypertension, or cardiac arrhythmias. The availability of a large number of decaffeinated products makes it possible to decrease caffeine consumption, if necessary.

Nicotine can be a highly dependence-producing drug; the amount of dependence is proportional to the quantity of the drug used. Nicotine consumed through smoking, chewing, or snuffing tobacco is absorbed through the mucous membranes or surfaces of the lung. Taken into the body, nicotine produces initial stimulation, followed by sedation. The withdrawal effects include restlessness, irritability, and tension. The health consequences of tobacco use can be severe. Cancer of the lung or oral cavity and a variety of other lung diseases have been linked to tobacco use. In addition, tobacco use has been shown to aggravate other preexisting conditions, such as heart disease and hypertension. Although smoking was once socially acceptable, pressure from various groups and public awareness of the health hazards of smoking have resulted in sanctions on public smoking behavior. The treatment of nicotine dependence varies widely, ranging from the use of nicotine-containing gum to hypnosis to behavioral and group programs. The success of most programs to stop tobacco use is directly related to the smoker's motivation to stop.

Sedatives

Sedation implies calmness and tranquility. **Sedatives**, including alcohol, are classified according to the pharmacologic action they produce, namely depression of the central nervous system. If taken in higher doses to produce sleep, they are called **hypnotics**. Sedatives are sometimes also called **minor tranquilizers** or **anti-anxiety agents**. Whether they have been prescribed for treatment or whether they have been obtained illegally, sedatives may be associated with abuse, tolerance, and dependence.

Individuals commonly abuse sedatives in combination with alcohol, and they often abuse opiates and stimulants concurrently. Commonly abused sedatives are **barbiturates** (e.g., phenobarbital, secobarbital, and amobarbital sodium), **benzodiazepines** (e.g., chlordiazepoxide hydrochloride [Librium], diazepam [Valium], and chlorzepate dipotassium [Tranzene]), as well as other central nervous system depressants (e.g., methaqualone [Quaalude], meprobamate, and ethchlorvynol [Placidyl]).

Sudden withdrawal, especially from barbiturates, can result in acute psychosis and seizures. Benzodiazepine withdrawal often produces a hyperexcitable state that is opposite to the sedation normally produced by the drug. The therapeutic withdrawal from a sedative, like the therapeutic withdrawal from alcohol, usually involves the administration of a cross-tolerant drug to suppress the withdrawal symptoms and the gradual tapering of the dosage. The drug being withdrawn determines the length of time required for tapering. For some sedatives, 7 to 10 days is sufficient for detoxification. Longer acting drugs that have been used at high dosages may require 14 or more days for detoxification.

Opiates

Because opiates (narcotic drugs, such as morphine, meperidine [demerol], hydromorphone hydrochloride [dilaudid], oxycodone and aspirin [percodan], and codeine) are frequently prescribed for pain, addiction can occur through regular prescription use. In other instances, these medications are obtained illegally; a commonly used illegal opiate is heroin. In addition to producing pain relief, narcotics can also produce euphoria. At first, individuals may take illegal narcotics primarily for the feeling of euphoria. Eventually, as the dosage and/or frequency of drug administration increases, they need to continue to take the drug regularly in order to avoid the symptoms of physical withdrawal.

Not only does substance abuse lead to psychological, social, and vocational impairments, but also it may lead to criminal activity to obtain the drug or to obtain money for additional drugs. Furthermore, opiates are often injected, and the addition of adulterants to the substance or an unsterile technique of injection may produce medical complications.

Withdrawal symptoms vary in severity and duration, depending on the particular drug abused. Withdrawal from narcotics is generally not life-threatening; many symptoms are flulike, although symptoms may include anxiety, irritability, and restlessness. Methadone is a synthetically prepared narcotic used to provide medical assistance with withdrawal. The methadone dosage is gradually tapered over 7 to 10 days during the withdrawal period. Some individuals may be enrolled in a methadone maintenance program in which they do not undergo detoxification, but rather receive maintenance doses of methadone. The goal of such programs is first to help the individual to return to a socially rehabilitated state and then to help the individual achieve a drug-free state.

Stimulants

Acting directly on the central nervous system, stimulants create an increased state of arousal and speed up mental processes. Individuals may take stimulants for such effects as increased alertness and increased sense of well-being, increased confidence, reduction of fatigue, or decrease in appetite. **Amphetamines** (Benzedrine or Dexedrine), methylphenidate (Ritalin), cocaine, and caffeine are all stimulants. In addition to central nervous system effects, stimulants have generalized systemic effects, including an increase in heart rate, an increase in blood pressure, a rise in body temperature, and the constriction of peripheral blood vessels. Cocaine can also cause cardiac arrhythmias and increase the respiratory rate.

In recent years, **cocaine** has become one of the most widely abused stimulants. It may be taken orally, used intranasally (snorted), smoked, or injected intravenously. The technique of free basing cocaine, which gained popularity in the 1980s, involves heating a flammable solvent, such as petroleum or ethers. The process "frees" cocaine hydrochloride from its salts and adulterants, converting it to a form of cocaine that will vaporize. The free base cocaine can be inhaled or smoked, usually with a water pipe, for direct absorption through the alveoli in the lungs. The technique rapidly delivers high concentrations of cocaine to the brain and results in blood levels as high as those for self-injection. The technique used to convert the cocaine can cause additional disability, however, due to burns from fires started during the free basing process. The level of tolerance for cocaine rapidly increases, and the need for additional cocaine in order to function normally can rapidly lead to the use of crack.

Crack, a solid form of cocaine free base, is thought to be one of the most addictive substances yet encountered. Dependence is produced very rapidly. Crack is smoked rather than sniffed. Its concentrated form and its route of administration make its potency many times greater than that of cocaine alone. The euphoric effect produced by crack lasts only a matter of minutes, however, and is often followed by irritability, restlessness, and depression. The after-effects of crack can be so intense that the individual continues to smoke it, despite the obvious adverse consequences.

Individuals who use cocaine, especially at higher dosages, may use depressant drugs in order to counterbalance the stimulant effects. For example, alcohol and cocaine are commonly combined for this purpose. The simultaneous injection of cocaine and heroin **(speedballing)** is also common.

Aside from its psychological, social, and vocational consequences, cocaine use can have serious medical consequences. Free basing or smoking crack can lead to pulmonary complications. **Cocaine intoxication** produces neurological effects, such as confusion, anxiety, hyperexcitability, agitation, and violence. More serious neurological complications include stroke or seizures. Severe **hyperthermia** (increased body temperature), sometimes resulting in death, can also be a manifestation of cocaine intoxication. The cardiac effects of cocaine intoxication can include chest pain, **myocardial infarction** (heart attack), and, in some instances, sudden death in otherwise healthy individuals. The treatment of cocaine intoxication usually depends on the type of symptoms experienced.

Cocaine psychosis, another side-effect of cocaine use, is manifested by paranoia, panic, hallucinations, insomnia, and picking at the skin. The psychotic episode lasts from 24 to 36 hours. Individuals with this condition are usually hospitalized and treated with **antipsychotic** medication.

The substances added to adulterate cocaine in order to increase its weight, thereby increasing the profit on its sale, may cause additional medical complications. Problems can result either from the nature of the substance used to cut the cocaine or from the dosage taken. Such adulterants as talc or cornstarch can cause complications that range from inflammation to embolus. Procaine, PCP, or heroin, which also may be added to cocaine, may potentiate the effects. Because the user can never be certain of the potency of the cocaine, the effects are not always predictable.

The withdrawal syndrome from cocaine consists of a craving for more cocaine, depression, irritability, sleep disturbances, gastrointestinal disturbances, headaches, and, possibly, suicidal ideation. These symptoms usually begin within 48 hours after the cessation of cocaine use and last approximately 7 days to 6 weeks. Because it is not unusual for the individual who is cocaine-dependent to also be dependent on other drugs, a withdrawal reaction from other substances may be experienced as well.

Cannabis

When cannabis **(marijuana)** is smoked, the active compound **(THC)** that it contains produces euphoria, tranquility, dreamlike states, and sleepiness. Some individuals report enhanced perceptions of colors, tastes, and textures. The psychoactive responses to the drug depend to a great extent on the dose, the personality and the experience of the user, and the environment in which the drug is used. Often, users report a sense of the slowing of time and an impairment in their ability to learn new facts while they are under the influence of the drug. Some individuals experience adverse effects with cannabis use, such as anxiety, panic states, and psychosis.

Systemically, cannabis produces an increase in heart rate, dilation of the bronchioles, and dilation of the peripheral blood vessels. Because of the stimulatory effect on the heart, cannabis use may lead to cardiac complications in individuals with heart disease. Chronic smoking of cannabis produces inflammatory changes in the lungs that contribute to the development of chronic conditions, such as emphysema (see Chapter 3). Furthermore, the use of other drugs, including alcohol and tobacco, may compound the adverse effects of cannabis. The combination of tobacco and cannabis use is thought to increase the risk of development of lung cancer, for example.

Although cannabis may be ingested orally, this method of use may delay its effects for up to an hour, and the effects are less potent. **Hashish**, the concentrated form of THC, has considerably more potency than does cannabis; it is also smoked.

Some individuals use cannabis only on special occasions, but others become compulsively preoccupied with daily use. The degree to which cannabis can create a physical dependence has not been established: however, it is probably possible to develop a psychological dependence on cannabis

There is no specific medical treatment for cannabis abuse. When cannabis use severely hampers individual functioning, the treatment most often involves psychotherapeutic techniques directed at underlying problems. Because cannabis may be abused in combination with other drugs, the treatment may occasionally be multifocal in nature.

Hallucinogens

Sometimes called **psychedelics**, **hallucinogens** are drugs that, at some dosage, produce hallucinations or distortions in perceptions or thinking. Individuals under the influence of hallucinogens report an increased awareness of sensory input and a subjective feeling of enhanced mental activity. Common hallucinogens are **LSD**; **PCP (angel dust)**; **mescaline**; and **MDMA (ecstasy)**. These drugs are usually taken orally. Although the use of hallucinogens has declined in the last two decades, patterns of use vary widely; their use is now often concurrent with the use of other drugs.

One of the most powerful hallucinogens is LSD. Its effects vary with the individual, the dose, and the environment in which the drug is used. Generally, the effects develop within several hours and last up to 12 hours. Individuals may report heightened sensitivity and clarity, increased insights, a sense of time moving more slowly, and distortions of visual images. Some individuals experience adverse effects from LSD, however, such as a panic state with severe anxiety.

The physical consequences of hallucinogen abuse in and of themselves are not significant. The psychological consequences can be severe, however. The adverse effects of hallucinogens vary from acute psychosis to self-mutilation or suicide. Accidents can result from misjudgment or impairment. Some individuals experience "flashbacks" in which hallucinations reappear briefly even months after the last drug dose. An overdose of hallucinogens can result in exceedingly high body temperatures, seizures, and shock.

As there is no physical dependence from abuse of hallucinogens, there is no specific medical regimen for treatment. Adverse effects such as panic episodes are often best treated with a supportive environment and observation.

Inhalants

Substances that cause perceptible changes in brain function through inhalation are called **inhalants**. A wide variety of substances are abused in this way, often because they are readily accessible and inexpensive. For example, commonly used inhalants are airplane glue, typewriter correction fluid, marking pencils, industrial and household chemicals, gasoline, nitrites (poppers, snappers, or Rush), and nitrous oxide. Although individuals of all age groups practice inhalant abuse, it is especially prevalent among adolescents and pre-adolescents.

Although the effects of inhalants are brief, they can be serious, especially with prolonged or long-term use. The adverse effects of inhalants vary according to the type of substance inhaled. Organic solvents such as airplane glue can produce cardiac arrhythmias, bone marrow depression, damage to the kidney and liver, and, in some instances, death. The prolonged use of nitrites is thought to suppress the immune system, increasing the individual's susceptibility to infection. Nitrites are frequently used to enhance sexual pleasure; consequently, individuals who use nitrites in this way and are also exposed to the HIV virus may be at greater risk for developing HIV infection due to suppression of the immune system and subsequent increased vulnerability to infection. The chronic abuse of nitrous oxide can result in nerve damage, seizures, bone marrow changes, respiratory depression, or death. Because nitrous oxide distorts special senses, driving during intoxication is hazardous.

Even though the effects of inhalants are brief, their use can result in dependence. No specific medical treatment is usually indicated for inhalant abuse, but specific psychotherapeutic measures may be used to prevent relapse and to help the individual discontinue inhalant use.

DRUG RELATED ILLNESS

Many of the medical complications related to drug abuse result from unsterile injections or from adulterants rather than from the drug itself.

Dermatologic Complications

Abscess

Bacterial infection may cause pus to collect in the tissues, forming an abscess. In association with drug use, improper cleansing of the skin before injection or the use of an unsterile needle may lead to an abscess. The skin at the site becomes warm, red, swollen, and painful; there is a purulent discharge. The skin around the area frequently becomes **necrotic** (dies). If the abscess goes untreated, the individual may develop systemic symptoms of fever, loss of appetite, and fatigue. The infection may spread to the bloodstream, creating a generalized systemic infection **(bacteremia)**. The treatment of an abscess consists of draining the purulent material and débriding the area of dead tissue. **Antibiotics** are usually prescribed, especially if the individual demonstrates systemic symptoms.

Cellulitis

An acute inflammation of the tissues without necrosis (tissue death) is called cellulitis. When associated with intravenous drug abuse, cellulitis is caused by the invasion of a variety of organisms or by irritation of the tissues from the drug itself. The tissue becomes red and tender, and there may be **adenopathy** (swelling of lymph nodes). The treatment of cellulitis depends on the cause. Occasionally, cellulitis progresses to abscess formation.

Other Dermatologic Complications

Injections with unsterile needles or injections of drugs that have been contaminated by adulterants may leave **needle track scars**. The injections cause a mild inflammatory reaction and, with subsequent injections, produce scarring at the injection site.

The injection of a drug into an artery instead of a vein can cause an extreme reaction of intense pain, swelling, and coldness of an extremity. If not treated properly, gangrene that necessitates amputation can develop.

Cardiovascular Complications

In general, the cardiovascular complications that result from drug use are related to the use of unsterile injection techniques or to the contamination of the drug with adulterants. A common complication is **endocarditis**, which affects the valves of the heart and can lead to potentially serious consequences. (See Chapter 2.)

Some drugs have a direct toxic effect on the heart muscle or may directly affect heart rhythm. In some instances, inflammation of the veins **(thrombophlebitis)** may occur because of the toxic effects of the drug.

Pulmonary Complications

The intravenous injection of drugs to which adulterants such as talc, starch, or baking soda have been added may result in pulmonary complications. Because these substances do not dissolve, they circulate in the blood and may become lodged in lung tissue. The lodged particles cause an inflammatory reaction in the lungs, resulting in fibrosis of the lung tissue. If the fibrous changes are extensive, they affect the oxygen-exchanging ability of the lungs. Symptoms similar to those of emphysema may develop. The changes in lung elasticity can eventually result in pulmonary hypertension and subsequent heart failure. (See Chapter 3 for a discussion of the symptoms of emphysema and Chapter 2 for a discussion of pulmonary hypertension and heart failure.)

Lung infections or lung abscesses may occur if organisms localize in the lung after the unsterile injection of a substance. **Aspiration pneumonia**, an inflammation of the lung, may result from the inhalation of foreign substances or chemical irritants. The aspiration of gastric contents is also a common cause of aspiration pneumonia. Individuals who become unconscious because of a drug overdose may in their unconscious state vomit and subsequently inhale the vomitus; if they inhale a large quantity, the results can be fatal.

Individuals who abuse drugs, including alcohol, may also develop **tuberculosis** (see Chapter 3). Rather than being a direct result of the drug abuse itself, however, tuberculosis is probably the consequence of the general life style and living conditions of the individual who abuses drugs. Malnourishment, poor hygiene, and overcrowding all contribute to the development of the disease. In addition, because some drugs have an immunosuppressant effect, individuals who abuse these drugs may be more susceptible to the infection.

An overdose of narcotics or sedative/hypnotics can severely depress the respiratory center, causing the cessation of breathing and consequent death. Overdoses of narcotics have also been associated with the development of severe **pulmonary edema** (collection of fluid in the lungs), which, without treatment, can also result in death.

Gastrointestinal Complications

Because the liver acts as the detoxification center for the body, individuals who chronically abuse drugs may damage their liver. Some substances appear to be more directly harmful to the liver than others. Chronic, excessive abuse of solvents, for example, can cause liver **necrosis** (death). Other substances may cause such liver abnormalities as inflammation or fibrosis.

Hepatitis is a common complication of drug abuse. Hepatitis A may be related to the poor hygiene habits and poor environmental conditions that individuals who are chronic abusers of drugs often have. More commonly, hepatitis B (serum hepatitis) occurs as the result of unsterile or contaminated intravenous injections. (See Chapter 6 for a discussion of hepatitis A and hepatitis B.)

Neurological Complications

Seizures may result from an overdose of drugs or a hypersensitivity to adulterants. Seizures are especially prevalent after an overdose of amphetamines, heroin, or hallucinogens. In some instances, stroke may also accompany an overdose. The toxic effects of adulterants on the nervous system can lead to blindness and peripheral nerve damage.

Other Complications

The chronic use of some drugs may result in **nystagmus** (involuntary eye movement). The use of solvents can produce bone marrow changes and aplastic anemia. An overdose of drugs can result in **acute renal failure**, which can progress to permanent kidney damage (see Chapter 4). Individuals who abuse drugs also have a higher incidence of **venereal disease**, such as **gonorrhea** and **syphilis**, related to their general life style and sexual practices. One of the most serious and hazardous complications of drug use in the past few years has been infection with HIV (see Chapter 13), related to both intravenous drug use and unsafe sexual practices.

Drug abuse during pregnancy has serious implications for the offspring. Some fetal hazards are related to the life style of the mother, which results in poor prenatal care, poor nutrition, and a generally poor health status. The direct toxic effects of drugs on the developing fetus can include neurological and/or physical abnormalities, as well as the dangers of the withdrawal syndrome to the infant after birth.

DIAGNOSTIC PROCEDURES

The medical diagnosis of substance abuse/dependence is often delayed or overlooked, contributing to the continued disabling effects of the substance use, the development of medical complications, and the progression of dependence. Denial and resistance to acknowledging the problem are universal symptoms of substance abuse/dependence. Consequently, even if family members or associates have identified a substance use problem, the individual may deny the condition and refuse to seek treatment. When individuals with a substance use disorder enter medical settings, medical personnel may not recognize the signs and symptoms of substance abuse/dependence so that the disorder goes undiagnosed. In addition, because some medical personnel feel uncomfortable confronting individuals with a substance use disorder, they may avoid the diagnosis or treatment of the problem.

Medical personnel may gather data for the diagnosis of a substance use disorder from several sources. They should realize that the physical manifestations of substance abuse/dependence may include a variety of disorders and should ask questions about substance use practices in the examination of individuals with gastrointestinal disturbances, hypertension or heart disease, liver disease, neurological changes, or a history of traumatic injuries. Blood cell abnormalities, such as a decreased number of platelets or signs of bone marrow depression (see Chapter 13), or other indirect clinical laboratory signs, such as elevated levels of **serum gamma (glutamytransferase [GGI]**), an elevated red blood cell **mean corpuscular volume (MCV)**, or elevated levels of enzymes such as **SGOT** (serum glutamic oxaloacetic transaminase) and **SGPT** (serum glutamic pyruvic transaminase), may suggest problems with substance abuse. Increased concentrations of enzymes such as SGOT and SGPT can be associated with other conditions (e.g., myocardial infarction), however, even in the absence of substance abuse or dependence.

An investigation of subtle psychological or behavioral symptoms may also be important in the diagnosis of a substance use disorder. Depression, hyperactivity, sleep disturbances, anxiety, sexual problems, or personality changes are common manifestations of substance use disorders. In addition, the incidence of accidents and injury is often increased. The treatment of injuries sustained in accidents should include an investigation of potential substance use problems.

Direct testing for the presence of the substance in the body may involve breath analyzers and blood alcohol tests. Both tests serve as a measurement of intoxication, but they do not reveal the extent of abuse or dependence. Screening of blood or urine samples is also used to verify suspected substance use. As with any laboratory test, there is a possibility of false-negative or false-positive results. Newer screening methods are designed to be more sensitive and produce more accurate results. Two common methods of urine testing available in most laboratories are **thin-layer chromatography** and **gas chromatography**. Drug testing is valid, however, only if accomplished under strictly controlled conditions. Many individuals who abuse or are dependent on drugs are aware of a variety of methods to invalidate test results, such as substituting specimens from a drug-free individual for their own specimen.

The appropriate methods and times of drug screening are highly controversial. Routine screening for drugs without the individual's knowledge and consent evokes a variety of legal and ethical concerns.

TREATMENT

The first step in the treatment of substance use disorders is the acknowledgment of the problem. As mentioned previously, the denial by the individual and the reluctance of others, including medical personnel, to confront the problem once it is suspected are barriers to treatment.

Many individuals with substance use disorders eventually experience physical, social, or psychological crises that require hospitalization. The type of treatment received varies greatly from hospital to hospital and depends on the particular type of crisis experienced. Some hospitals provide treatment for substance use disorders solely on an outpatient basis. Others provide a combination of inpatient and outpatient treatment.

The treatment usually begins with detoxification, which may or may not involve hospitalization, depending on the individual, the specific substance, and the presence of additional complications. Detoxification is only an initial step in the treatment of substance use disorders, however. Ongoing therapy that includes a variety of rehabilitation strategies, such as psychotherapy, family therapy, and self-help programs (e.g., Alcoholics Anonymous or Narcotics Anonymous), is necessary to prevent relapse. There are several psychotherapeutic approaches to the treatment of substance abuse. The specific type of therapy used is often dependent on the facility in which the individual is being treated and the overall philosophy of those professionals who are conducting the treatment, but, in almost all instances, abstinence is a treatment goal.

In some instances, drugs are prescribed in the ongoing treatment of substance dependence. Antabuse and methadone, both of which were discussed earlier, are two drugs commonly used in the treatment of alcohol and narcotic dependence respectively. A newer drug, **Naltrexone**, may be used for opiate dependence. Taken several times a week, the drug blocks the effect of the opiates, thus decreasing the incidence of impulsive opiate use. The individual with a substance use disorder may also require ongoing medical treatment for any medical complications that have resulted from the substance use.

Because nutritional deficiencies frequently accompany substance use disorders, most detoxification centers and residential facilities provide nutrition therapy as a part of the treatment. Educational programs that stress the importance of nutrition, as well as other aspects of a healthy life style, are often incorporated into the general treatment program.

FUNCTIONAL IMPLICATIONS

Psychological Issues

The extent to which psychological disability is the direct result of a substance use disorder or the extent to which it is the cause of the disorder is not easily determined. Individuals with substance use disorders frequently have low self-esteem and experience depression. They may have feelings of inadequacy, loneliness, and isolation that lead to increased substance use. Influenced and controlled by the substance that they use, these individuals may rely on it rather than on their own resources. Doubt that they will be able to cope without the substance may erode their self-confidence and, consequently, their self-esteem even more.

Individuals who are psychologically dependent on a substance feel a need and longing for the substance; they become irritable, depressed, anxious, and resentful when the substance is not available. Individuals with a psychological craving for a substance may attribute their need to a personal flaw in their character or may consider their need as a negative reflection on themselves. Either interpretation further contributes to lowered self-esteem and self-deprecation. These individuals may use denial or rationalization as a form of self-protection and as a way to minimize substance use problems. They may deny that they have a problem with the substance or may rationalize their behavior by redefining their substance use so that it appears to be acceptable.

Some individuals become aggressive or perform violent acts when they are under the influence of certain substances. Those who are predisposed to this type of reaction may become involved in criminal acts, such as brawls, homicide, rape, or child abuse.

As the individual becomes increasingly dependent on the substance, the concept of living without it produces fear and dread. The individual interprets the removal of the substance as the removal of all joy and excitement from life. As with all types of perceived loss, the individual may experience grief and bereavement.

Recovery from a substance use disorder involves the restoration of self-esteem and confidence, as well as the willingness to accept responsibility for personal behavior. Individuals need assistance to accept the losses that they have experienced and to develop skills for coping in the future. Recovery is a continuing process that includes long-term vigilance and a continuing commitment to remain drug-free.

Life Style Issues

A substance use disorder affects every aspect of the individual's daily life. As dependence on the substance becomes more pronounced, the individual may lose interest in self-care; may show a decreased desire for food; and may have a variety of sleep disturbances, resulting in sleep deprivation. Daily activities may become focused on obtaining more of the substance. Activities that were once enjoyed may offer little joy or stimulate much interest.

Substance use frequently affects an individual's ability to drive. The poor driving performance often results in accidents or arrests that can lead to the loss of the individual's driver's license. Therefore, transportation may become a problem so that the individual must depend on others for his or her transportation needs.

Sexual dysfunction is common in individuals who are dependent on a substance. Women may experience decreased libido or may become promiscuous. Men may experience not only decreased libido, but also adverse effects on sexual performance, including impotence, a common side-effect of chronic alcohol abuse.

Individuals who are recovering from a substance use disorder may need to learn or relearn the components of a healthy life style, such as self-care, including hygiene and grooming; proper diet; and the importance of exercise. These aspects of daily living may be a vital part of an individual's rehabilitation.

Social Issues

The social effects of substance use disorders are widespread, touching on family relationships, relationships with friends and associates, and general functioning as a member of society. The individual's ability to function as a member of a social group may gradually deteriorate as the substance use increases. To some extent, social factors may determine the social implications of the substance use. For example, the availability of substances within a group or as part of a social event may determine whether or not the individual with a substance use disorder participates. The extent of the social tolerance of the individual's behavior when intoxicated may either curtail or enhance the substance use at first. As the individual becomes increasingly substance-dependent, however, the substance takes on an increasing importance; conversely, social contacts and activities take on a decreasing importance.

Individuals with a substance use disorder may be unable to function within their social network. Repeated, heavy use of the substance often leads to upheavals in relationships with their significant others. Social and family relationships are strained and, often, destroyed if an individual becomes abusive, violent, or engages in socially unacceptable behavior while under the influence of the substance. The individual's behavior often alienates others, leading to social isolation.

The individual's decreasing reliability in the performance of social roles and continued inability to maintain commitments cause those affected by the individual's deterioration in behavior to feel disappointed and angry. Others within the social environment may have to alter their own roles in order to incorporate the duties that the individual once fulfilled. This places additional burdens on all concerned and may eventually lead to resentment or even banishment of the individual from the group. Family members and associates may begin to withdraw from the individual emotionally. As the individual becomes increasingly more isolated, feelings of self-loathing, guilt, and shame may develop. Feeling rejected by family and associates, the individual may limit his or her social contacts to relationships with others who also focus on use of the substance.

The broader social consequences of substance use disorders may have legal and even criminal implications. There is a strong relationship between substance use disorders and a variety of accidents; motor vehicle accidents, for example, can lead to physical disability not only for the individual with the substance use disorder, but also for others. Thus, the loss of a driver's license, as well as more serious criminal charges, are potential effects of substance abuse/dependence. Furthermore, the individual who becomes dependent on illegal substances may engage in illegal activities in order to gain money for the purchase of additional drugs. Even if the individual does not face criminal charges, he or she can become focused on obtaining the drug rather than on functioning in a productive social role.

In some cases, family and social relationships can be salvaged in the recovery process. In other instances, however, the loss of these relationships is permanent. Depending on individual circumstances, therapeutic recovery may involve the development of new social roles and relationships or the reestablishment of old ones.

Vocational Issues

In the early stages of a substance use disorder, individuals may be concerned that the use of the substance will interfere with their work. If the substance use progresses to abuse or dependence, however, the concern may be reversed; the individuals may be concerned that their work will interfere with the use of the substance. The substance becomes ultimately important, thus drastically affecting work performance.

Although early identification of and intervention with the worker with a substance use disorder is most desirable, the problem may not be recognized until there is a progressive deterioration of work performance, increased absenteeism, or an increase in job-related accidents. The fear that they will lose their jobs if their employers become aware of these indicators may motivate individuals with a substance use disorder to seek treatment.

The ability of an individual to return to the former employment after treatment for substance abuse/dependence depends on the circumstances. In some instances, the stress and tension imposed by the job may be beyond the individual's stress tolerance and coping ability. It may be beneficial to find a less stressful work setting, especially in the early stages of recovery, until the individual's tolerance for stress gradually increases. Physical disability resulting from substance abuse/dependence must also be considered when evaluating vocational potential.

It is essential to identify past work problems, which may extend beyond issues of substance abuse/dependence. Some individuals may need to learn social skills, work-appropriate behaviors, or good hygiene or grooming practices; some need to improve their work skills. Individuals who began abusing substances at an early age may not have developed sufficient work skills or work history to obtain employment. These individuals particularly may require additional education or job training. If the individual returns to the same work setting that originally precipitated feelings of inadequacy, thus contributing to the substance abuse/dependence, the return to work may increase the risk of relapse. In some cases, learning new skills or coping strategies may enable the individual to return successfully to this work setting; in other instances, however, a new work environment may be necessary.

The loss of a driver's license because of a substance use disorder may make transportation to and from work more difficult. In addition, if driving a motor vehicle had been part of the former employment, job restructuring or job change may be necessary.

Some occupations require professional licensure. Therefore, the revocation of an individual's license as a result of a substance use disorder may limit the individual's ability to work in the former occupation. Many professional licensing boards have provisions for the reinstatement of licensure after documented rehabilitation. If the professional license is reinstated, there may be a probationary period in which the individual's work performance is closely observed and monitored.

Conviction of criminal charges, especially felony charges, may prohibit employment in some occupations. Although decisions may be made on a case-by-case basis, such charges and their impact on employment in different fields and in different locations must be considered.

As with most disabilities, the attitudes and concerns of employers must be addressed, especially since social stigma is usually attached to substance use disorders. Employers may require particular encouragement to reinstate or hire an individual who has been convicted of criminal charges. Knowing the potential for rejection by employers based on these attitudes, the recovering individual may be reluctant to share his or her complete history with employers or may become defensive when asked questions about substance use. The fear of rejection because of prejudice must be considered when the individual returns to work. With increasing awareness of substance abuse/dependence and with educational efforts directed toward employers, however, these individuals may encounter decreasing levels of prejudice.

Many individuals who are recovering from substance abuse and/or dependence return to their employment and lead full, productive lives. In all instances, however, abstinence is a prerequisite for continuing productivity. Ongoing long-term treatment or involvement with self-help groups may also be necessary in order to prevent relapse.

BIBLIOGRAPHY

American Psychiatric Association. *Diagnostic and Statistical Manual of Mental Disorders*. 3d ed., rev. Washington, D.C.: American Psychiatric Association, 1987.

Barber, T.C., and Langfitt, D.E. *Teaching the Medical/Surgical Patient—Diagnostics and Procedures*. Bowie, Md.: Robert J. Brady Co., 1983.

Berkow, R., and Fletcher, A.J., eds. *The Merck Manual of Diagnosis and Therapy*. Rahway, N.J.: Merck Sharpe and Dohme Research Laboratories, 1987.

Bigby, J.; Clark, W.D.; and May, H. "Diagnosing Early Treatable Alcoholism." *Patient Care* 24(1990):135–156.

Brunner, L.S.; Emerson, C.P.; Ferguson, L.K.; and Suddarth, D.S. *Textbook of Medical-Surgical Nursing*. Philadelphia: W.B. Saunders Co., 1970.

Charness, M.E.; Simon, R.P.; and Greenberg, D.A. "Ethanol and the Nervous System." *New England Journal of Medicine* 321(1989):442–454.

Cocroes, J.A.; Pottash, A.C.; Gold, M.S.; and Miller, N.S. "Sexual Dysfunction in Abusers of Cocaine and Alcohol." *Medical Times* 15(1987):103–109.

Cohen, S., and Gallant, D.M. *Diagnosis of Medical Complications of Alcohol and Drug Abuse*. Medical Monograph Series. Rockville, Md.: National Institute on Drug Abuse, 1982.

Corbett, J.V. *Laboratory Tests in Nursing Practice*. Norwalk, Conn.: Appleton-Century-Crofts, 1983.

Dennison, S.J., and White, C.F. "Cocaine Use and Associated Cardiovascular Risks." *Resident and Staff Physician* 36(1990):49–52.

Derlet, R.W. "Cocaine Intoxication." *Postgraduate Medicine* 86(1989):245–253.

Diamond, I. "Alcoholic Myopathy and Cardiomyopathy." *New England Journal of Medicine* 320(1989):458–460.

Dickson, E.R.; Koff, R.S.; Sabesin, S.M.; and Shaw, B.W., Jr. "Toxic Liver Disease: Alcohol? Drugs?" *Patient Care* 21(1987):153–163.

Digregorio, G.J. "Cocaine Update: Abuse and Therapy." *American Family Physician* 41(1990):247–250.

Garber, M.W., and Flaherty, D. "Cocaine and Sudden Death." *American Family Physician* 36(1987):227–230.

Gawin, F.H., and Ellinwood, E.H. "Cocaine and Other Stimulants—Actions, Abuse, and Treatment." *New England Journal of Medicine* 318(1988):1173–1182.

Gold, M.S. "Crack Abuse: Its Implications and Outcomes." *Medical Times* 115(1987):27–32.

Gordis, E. "Alcohol Withdrawal Syndrome." *Alcohol Alert* (1989):1–4.

Greer, B.G.; Roberts, R.; and Jenkins, W.M. "Substance Abuse among Clients with Other Primary Disabilities: Curricular Implication for Rehabilitation Education." *Rehabilitation Education* 4(1990):33–44.

Guyton, A.C. *Human Physiology and Mechanisms of Disease*. Philadelphia: W.B. Saunders Co., 1982.

Holister, L.E. *Drug Tolerance, Dependence and Abuse*. Kalamazoo, Mich.: Upjohn Co., 1985.

Keele, C.A.; Neil, E.; and Joels, N. *Samson Wright's Applied Physiology*. New York: Oxford University Press, 1982.

Klatsky, A.L. "Alcohol and Cardiovascular Disorders." *Primary Cardiology* 5(1979):86–89.

Klerman, G.L. "Treatment of Alcoholism." *New England Journal of Medicine* 320(1989):394–395.

Lawson, G.W.; Ellis, D.C.; and Rivers, P.C. *Essentials of Chemical Dependency Counseling*. Gaithersburg, Md.: Aspen Publishers, 1984.

Lawson, G.W.; Peterson, J.S.; and Lawson, A. *Alcoholism and the Family: A Guide to Treatment and Prevention*. Gaithersburg, Md.: Aspen Publishers, 1983.

Lindberg, M.D., and Oyler, R.A. "Wernicke's Encephalopathy." *American Family Physician* 41(1990):1205–1209.

Luckman, J., and Sorensen, K.C. *Medical-Surgical Nursing: A Psychophysiologic Approach*. Philadelphia: W.B. Saunders Co., 1987.

Miller, G.W. "The Cocaine Habit." *American Family Physician* 31(1985):173–176.

Miller, N.S., and Gold, M.S. "The Medical Diagnosis and Treatment of Alcohol Dependence." *Medical Times* 115(1987):109–126.

Miller, N.S., and Gold, M.S. "Identification and Treatment of Benzodiazepine Abuse." *American Family Physician* 40(1989):175–183.

Miller, N.S., and Gold, M.S. "Cocaine: Recognition of Abuse and Pharmacologic Responses." *Family Practice Recertification* 12(1990):86–98.

Mody, C.K.; Miller, B.L.; McIntyre, H.B.; Cobb, S.K.; and Goldberg, M.A. "Neurologic Complications of Cocaine Abuse." *Neurology* 38(1988):1189–1193.

Morali, G.A., and Blendis, L.M. "Treatment of Ascites and Its Complications." *Resident and Staff Physician* 36(1990):35–47.

Mullen, J., and Bracha, H.S. "Toxicology Screening—How To Assure Accurate Results." *Postgraduate Medicine* 84(1988):141–148.

National Institute on Alcohol Abuse and Alcoholism. "Alcohol and the Physically Impaired." *Alcohol, Health, and Research World* 13(1989):97–191.

Newman, R.G. "Methadone Treatment—Defining and Evaluating Success." *New England Journal of Medicine* 317(1987):447–450.

Nursing 87 Books. *Patient Teaching.* Springhouse, Pa.: Springhouse Corporation Book Division, 1987.

Pearsall, H.W., and Altesman, R.I. "Cocaine Abuse." *Hospital Medicine* 23(1987):126–139.

Pike, R.F. "Cocaine Withdrawal—An Effective Three-Drug Regimen." *Postgraduate Medicine* 85(1989):115–121.

Rakel, R.E. *Conn's Current Therapy.* Philadelphia: W.B. Saunders Co., 1990.

Sanders, J.M. "Identifying Substance Abuse in Adolescents." *Postgraduate Medicine* 84(1988):123–136.

Schnoll, S.H.; Daghestani, A.N.; and Hansen, T.R. "Cocaine Dependence." *Resident and Staff Physician* 30(1984):24–31.

Schwarz, R.H. "When To Suspect Inhalant Abuse." *Patient Care* 23(1989):39–64.

Simon, R.P. "Alcohol and Seizures." *New England Journal of Medicine* 319(1988):715–716.

Smith, D.W., and Hanley-Germain, C.P. *Care of the Adult Patient.* Philadelphia: J.B. Lippincott Co., 1975.

Stolov, W.C., and Clowers, M.R. *Handbook of Severe Disability.* Washington, D.C.: U.S. Department of Education, Rehabilitation Services Administration, 1981.

Urbano-Marquez, A.; Estruch, R.; Navarro-Lopez, F.; Grau, J.M.; Mont, L.; and Rubin, E. "The Effects of Alcoholism on Skeletal and Cardiac Muscle." *New England Journal of Medicine* 320(1989):409–415.

Vander, A.J.; Sherman, J.H.; and Luciano, D.S. *Human Physiology: The Mechanisms of Body Function.* New York: McGraw-Hill Book Co., 1985.

Wyngaarden, J.B., and Smith, J.H. *Cecil Textbook of Medicine.* Philadelphia: W.B. Saunders Co., 1988.

chapter *15*

Mental Disorders

Effective mental functioning depends on a variety of social and environmental factors, as well as on the efficient functioning of the structures within the brain. Mental disorders may be defined as those conditions that adversely affect perceptions, behavior, emotions, or cognition. As with physical disorders, the degree of disability experienced with mental disorders is variable.

Mental disorders are often more difficult to define and diagnose than are physical disorders; the causes of mental disorders are not always identifiable, and laboratory tests are not as readily available to confirm the diagnosis. In many cases, the experienced judgment of those professionals who are conducting the evaluation must be the primary basis for the diagnosis and the prediction of functional capacity. Moderating variables, such as the ethnic status, education, and/or socioeconomic status of both the client and the professional, may influence performance on evaluation and interpretation of the evaluation results.

Although there is no readily identifiable organic pathology associated with many mental disorders, mental symptoms often do occur with endocrine and neurological disorders (see Chapters 5 and 8). Newer advances in technology have also demonstrated that abnormalities in the brain and in the amount of neurotransmitters are present in various mental disorders. In addition, the treatment of mental disorders often involves altering the biochemical responses of the brain through the administration of medication. These facts suggest that there may be a biological basis for mental illness, even though demonstrable biological pathology has not yet been identified in all cases.

The symptoms of mental disorders vary widely, consisting of both behavioral manifestations and subjective feelings. Some mental disorders, such as **mental retardation** or **dementia**, are characterized by deficits in or loss of intellectual function. Some mental disorders, such as schizophrenia, are associated with loss of contact with reality **(psychosis)**, accompanied by hallucinations or delusions. Other mental disorders do not have the symptoms of psychoses, but are characterized by changes in mood that may cause distress or impair functioning, as in bipolar disorders. In still other mental disorders, intellectual function, sense of reality, or mood may be unimpaired, but symptoms are manifested by maladaptive behavior, as in personality disorders.

The disability experienced as a result of a mental disorder is greatly dependent on the degree to which the disorder interferes with the individual's function within the environment, the degree to which the individual's behavior disturbs others, and the degree to which the disorder causes subjective distress.

COMMON MENTAL DISORDERS

Mental Retardation

The term *mental retardation* describes conditions that occur before the age of 18 in which the individual's intellectual functioning is below average and adaptive behavior is deficient. Adaptive behavior encompasses the individual's social skills and performance in the social environment, including communication and management of the tasks of daily living. In most instances, adaptive behavior parallels intellectual capacity.

Although the exact cause of mental retardation cannot always be identified, a number of factors are known to be associated with mental retardation. Prenatal causes of mental retardation include maternal infections, exposure to toxic sources during fetal development, and compromise of the fetal blood supply. A variety of hereditary disorders may also result in mental retardation, such as metabolic disorders (e.g., **phenylketonuria** or **PKU**), chromosomal abnormalities, or some familial syndromes. Other specific conditions acquired in childhood, such as meningitis, or brain injury can also lead to mental retardation.

There are varying degrees of mental retardation. Classifications of mental retardation are generally labeled as mild, moderate, severe, or profound. They are expressed in relation to the **intelligence quotient (IQ)**, as shown in Table 15-1. For a particular individual, the degree of the retardation is classified according to evaluation and testing of the individual's intellectual performance and adaptive behavior. A variety of other factors, such as environment and stimulation, also help to determine intellectual functioning, however, so test results are not always absolute.

The individual's intellectual capacity, as well as other factors (e.g., availability of services and support), determines his or her level of functioning. In all instances, not only intellectual capacity, but also adaptive functioning must be considered. Generally, individuals in the mildly retarded group are considered capable of attaining intellectual function up to a sixth grade level; they may be

Table 15-1 Severity of Mental Retardation

Classification	IQ
Mild	50–70
Moderate	35–50
Severe	20–35
Profound	Below 20

Source: Diagnostic and Statistical Manual of Mental Disorders, 3rd. ed., revised, by the American Psychiatric Association, p. 32, 1987.

able to obtain employment and live independently or with minimal supervision. Individuals whose impairment is considered moderate often attain intellectual function at the second grade level, but may require more supervision in the activities of daily living. These individuals are usually capable of learning some vocational skills, although they may function best in a supervised work environment, such as a sheltered workshop or supported employment. Individuals whose intellectual impairment falls within the severe category of retardation generally have limited communication skills and poorly developed motor skills; they require close supervision for most tasks. Individuals with a profound mental impairment require close supervision and aid in most or all daily care.

In addition to their limited intellectual or adaptive capacity, mentally retarded individuals may have additional sensory or motor deficits that further affect their functional capacity. Any physical or behavioral problems must also be considered in determining the individual's ability to function within the environment.

Organic Mental Disorders

Some disturbances in brain function are caused by an identifiable organic factor. Organic mental disorders can occur at any age and can be caused by primary disease or injury to the brain itself, systemic disease, or by toxic substances (e.g., poisons, alcohol, or other drugs). More than one type of organic mental disorder may be present simultaneously. Abnormalities may be noted in psychological, cognitive, or behavioral function.

The diagnosis of organic mental disorders is usually based on a detailed history of symptoms, findings on physical and neurological evaluation, and clinical studies and laboratory studies. Neuropsychological assessments are also being used more frequently in the diagnosis of organic mental disorders.

Organic mental disorders can be acute or chronic. The symptoms of acute organic mental disorders are sudden in onset, as may be observed in an organic mental disorder caused by generalized infection or intoxication. The symptoms of chronic mental disorders generally occur more slowly and are characterized by the deterioration of cognitive processes over time, as occurs with arteriosclerosis or Alzheimer's disease. Organic mental disorders may be reversible or irreversible. If the underlying cause of the symptoms can be corrected and the brain has not been permanently damaged, the condition is said to be reversible. If the underlying cause cannot be corrected or treated or if the damage to the brain is permanent, however, the condition is irreversible.

Organic brain syndrome, a term sometimes used in association with organic mental disorders, refers to the constellation of symptoms exhibited with the condition rather than the cause. Two specific types of organic brain syndromes are delirium and dementia. **Delirium** often accompanies an acute disorder and may be reversible. It is characterized by difficulty in sustaining attention to external stimuli, difficulty in shifting attention to new stimuli, and difficulty in maintaining a coherent thought process. The symptoms of delirium include a clouded state of consciousness, confusion, or disorientation.

Dementia is a global deterioration of the intellectual abilities. The essential feature of dementia is the impairment of memory, although there are also impairments in other higher intellectual functions, such as the ability to abstract, judgment, and personality variables. Some dementias, such as those that occur with certain tumors, myxedema (see Chapter 5), or nutritional deficiencies, may be reversible. Other dementias, however, such as those that occur with Alzheimer's disease, are not reversible. **Alzheimer's disease** is a progressive, degenerative type of dementia. The onset is generally insidious, with gradual deterioration of cognitive function. Although it has commonly been thought of as a condition that occurs in older age groups, it may occur as early as middle life. Another irreversible dementia is that due to **multi-infarct dementia**, in which deficits result from small strokes in various locations of the brain.

Organic mental disorders affect a variety of cognitive abilities, such as memory, orientation, judgment, attention, and computational and organizational skills. There may also be associated psychomotor or language impairments, sleep disturbances, and other behavioral manifestations. Although some organic mental disorders remain stable, others are associated with progressive deterioration and decline of function.

Schizophrenia

Schizophrenic disorders encompass several types of symptoms, including disorders of thought, affect, perception, volition, sense of self, and behavior. The cause of schizophrenic disorders is unknown; however, there has been some evidence of physical or chemical disturbances in the brain of individuals with schizophrenic disorders. Moreover, there appears to be a familial tendency toward schizophrenia in some instances. The first episode of schizophrenia occurs most commonly in adolescence or young adulthood, but it may occur in later adult life.

The active form of schizophrenia is characterized by the presence of **psychosis** (loss of contact with reality). Prior to the appearance of the psychosis, the daily level of functioning usually deteriorates over several months. The decline in function may be marked by difficulty in concentrating or in expressing ideas logically. Individuals with this disorder may demonstrate emotional responses inappropriate to the situation, or they may display general apathy and indifference. **Delusions** (false beliefs) may also be present. These individuals may have bizarre ideas; for example, they may believe that their thoughts are being controlled or broadcast from outside sources. As a result of a **loosening of associations**, individuals with schizophrenia may have no logical progression of thought and may shift rapidly from one unrelated idea to the other. They may withdraw from involvement with the outside world, and have difficulty with self-initiated activity and decision making. Psychomotor activity may also be reduced. During the period of psychosis, these individuals may experience both visual and auditory hallucinations. They may hear voices or converse with someone who is not there; they may perceive that objects or persons are present when they are not.

There are several different types of schizophrenic disorders, which are differentiated by specific symptoms. The **disorganized type** (formerly called hebephrenic) is characterized by incoherence, loosening of associations, grossly disorganized behavior, and flat or inappropriate affect. In the **catatonic type**, psychomotor behavior can be either agitated or so retarded that the individual appears to be in a stupor. The **paranoid type** is characterized by persecutory or grandiose delusions that are often supported by the hallucinations experienced. Individuals with **undifferentiated schizophrenia** have prominent psychotic symptoms, but the symptoms do not fall into any specific category of schizophrenia. In the **residual type** of schizophrenia, the individual has experienced at least one schizophrenic episode in the past, but has no prominent psychotic symptoms currently; residual signs of the illness may remain, however.

The acute or active phase of the schizophrenia severely impairs personal and social functioning. During this phase, the individual may require supervision and direction in order to meet basic needs and in order to prevent self-injury. Depending on individual circumstances and the degree of available support, many individuals are able to function independently and obtain employment after the psychosis has been resolved. The degree of independent function possible depends on the success of the chemotherapeutic management of the disorder and the extent of the individual's insight into the disorder. Some individuals need continued assistance because of repeated exacerbations of symptoms, residual symptoms, or impairment.

Delusional Disorders (Paranoid Disorders)

The primary characteristic of delusional disorders is the presence of persistent delusions that cannot be attributed to another mental disorder. Delusional disorders may be categorized into different types depending on the predominant delusional theme present. For example, delusions may involve grandiosity in which individuals believe that they have special insights or talents that have not been recognized, or they believe they are being persecuted, conspired against, or cheated. In some instances, delusions may involve intense jealousy in which individuals believe, without cause, that their spouse or lover is being unfaithful. Although hallucinations may occur with delusional disorders, they are not a major feature.

Delusional disorders most commonly occur in middle life. Rarely does the disorder severely affect daily function; however, impairment of social, family, and occupational relationships is common.

Mood Disorders

Disturbances in mood can be subdivided into either **bipolar disorders** or **depressive disorders**. Most frequently, individuals begin experiencing symptoms of mood disorders in their 20s, but depressive disorders may be experienced as early as infancy. Hospitalization is frequently necessary during the acute phase of mood disorders because of the severity of the disturbance that the disorder creates in interpersonal and/or occupational functioning.

Bipolar Disorders

The occurrence of one or more episodes of mania, which may be accompanied by a depressive episode, characterizes bipolar disorders. These disorders may be classified as mixed, in which there are symptoms of both mania and depression; manic, in which there has been a manic episode without a depressive episode; or depressed, in which there has been a previous manic episode with a current or more recent depressive episode.

During **manic episodes**, mood becomes distinctly elevated and behavior hyperactive. Individuals in a manic episode appear flamboyant and overly enthusiastic, often engaging in excessive activity and needing little sleep. Speech becomes rapid, loud, and difficult to follow because of rapid changes from one unrelated topic to another. Manic episodes impair social and occupational functioning considerably. These individuals may be easily distracted, and their attention shifts rapidly from one activity to an unrelated activity with little provocation. They may have grandiose delusions in which they believe that they have special skills, knowledge, or relationships. The hallucinations that may occur during a manic episode often relate to their mood or delusions. Poor judgment during the manic phase may lead to catastrophic financial losses or illegal activities.

In contrast, a **depressive episode** is characterized by feelings of hopelessness and discouragement, loss of interest in activities previously found pleasurable, and decreased energy. Other symptoms, called vegetative signs, may consist of sleep disturbances (too much or too little), considerable change in weight (gain or loss), difficulty in concentrating, and, occasionally, suicide ideation.

Cyclothymia is a mood disorder characterized by symptoms similar to those of bipolar disorders. Because the symptoms are usually milder, cyclothymia causes less impairment in function than does a bipolar disorder. The distinction between bipolar disorders and cyclothymia is not clearly demarcated, and the diagnosis often depends on the judgment of the evaluator as to the severity of the episode. Because the condition is chronic, individuals with cyclothymia can experience symptoms for months or years.

Depressive Disorders

In depressive disorders, individuals have one or more depressive episodes like those in bipolar disorders, but they have no accompanying episodes of mania. Depressive disorders are classified as **major depression**. The degree of impairment due to major depression varies, although social and occupational activities are usually affected to some degree. With severe depression, the incapacitation can be so great that individuals are unable to attend to their own daily needs, such as basic hygiene and nutritional needs.

Dysthymia is a chronic condition characterized by symptoms similar to those experienced in major depression, but in a lesser degree. Although the symptoms are not so severe, the chronic nature of the condition may impair social and occupational functioning. The essential distinction between major depression and dysthymia is the severity and duration of the symptoms. Major depression generally has a more acute onset, while individuals with dysthymia may be in a depressed mood most of the time for months or years.

Anxiety Disorders

There are several different types of anxiety disorders. Their common features include not only anxiety but also increased arousal and avoidance of situations that the individual perceives as anxiety-provoking. Panic disorders, which usually occur in early adulthood, are characterized by **panic attacks,** episodes in which the individual has feelings of intense anxiety or terror, accompanied by a sense of impending doom. During a panic attack, the individual also experiences physical symptoms, such as shortness of breath, increased heart rate and palpitations, sweating, and, at times, nausea or other physical discomfort. Panic attacks are not triggered by a certain event and, at least initially, are unpredictable. The attacks usually last from a few minutes to a few hours. In themselves, they may be only mildly debilitating.

Panic attacks are sometimes accompanied by **agoraphobia**, the fear of being in a large open space. Because of the unpredictability of panic attacks, individuals with this anxiety disorder may be fearful of having an attack in a place where they would be unable to obtain help or escape, or where the symptoms of the panic attack would cause them embarrassment. Although not all individuals who have panic attacks experience agoraphobia, those who do may severely restrict their activity, hampering both their social functioning and their occupational functioning. They may refuse to venture outside their home alone, or they may be reluctant to travel by car, bus, or other common means of transportation.

The term **phobia** refers to fear and anxiety related to specific situations, persons, or objects. Several phobias can be classified as anxiety disorders. For example, **social phobia** is a phobic disorder in which the individual fears situations that may potentially result in ridicule or humiliation. Impairments that result from phobias may vary from mild to severe. A phobia may be more of a nuisance than a disability. On the other hand, a phobia may be so disabling that individuals are unable to function effectively in their day-to-day activities. For example, phobias can be debilitating if, as a result, individuals avoid particular objects or situations, or if, when exposed to the feared stimulus, they experience extreme anxiety.

Individuals with an **obsessive-compulsive disorder** have recurrent **obsessions** (persistent thoughts) or **compulsions** (persistent actions) that they are unable to control. For example, they may have recurrent thoughts of the death of a loved one, or they may have an irresistible urge to perform repetitively some behavior that seems purposeless, such as turning a light on and off three times before retiring for the night. Attempts by the individual to ignore the compulsions only increase anxiety, discomfort, and distress.

Post-traumatic stress disorder is an anxiety disorder that can develop after an individual has experienced or observed a traumatic or life-threatening event, such as violence, fire, natural disaster, or plane crash. The symptoms of the disorder may include persistent recollection of the event, sleep difficulties and recurrent nightmares, difficulty in concentrating, and a feeling of hypervigilance or increased arousal. The individual may lose interest in previously enjoyed activities or in important close relationships. The individual may also avoid stimuli that are associated with the event and may demonstrate little emotion or appear detached. The disorder, which may occur at any age, causes varying degrees of impairment.

Somatoform Disorders

In **somatoform disorders**, there are physical symptoms for which no organic cause can be found. Individuals with such a disorder do not consciously produce the symptoms, but truly experience them. A **conversion disorder** (hysterical neurosis, conversion type) is one type of somatoform disorder in which an individual loses physical function, often related to neurological function (e.g., paralysis, blindness, or numbness of a body part).

Hypochondriasis, another type of somatoform disorder, is characterized by a preoccupation with physical illness. Individuals with this disorder may fear or believe that they have a serious physical illness. In some instances, they perceive the symptoms of a coexisting disease or condition in an exaggerated way; for example, they may perceive a cough associated with a common cold as a sign of tuberculosis or lung cancer.

Somatoform pain disorder is a preoccupation with pain, although there is no organic cause for the pain. This type of pain disorder differs from malingering in that the individual does not consciously produce the symptoms of a somatoform pain disorder and actually experiences the pain reported. This disorder can be extremely incapacitating, often severely limiting social and work activities.

Dissociative Disorders

Conditions in which individuals experience an alteration in memory, consciousness, or identity for no organic reason are called dissociative disorders. **Psychogenic fugue** is a condition in which individuals leave their environment and assume a new identity without being able to recall their previous identity. **Psychogenic amnesia** is the inability to recall events that occurred within a certain period of time or the inability to recall information regarding one's own identity. **Multiple personality**, a disorder in which at least two personalities exist within the same individual and control the individual's behavior, is another type of dissociative disorder; it has been found to occur more commonly than was once believed.

Personality Disorders

Everyone has personality characteristics or traits. If these traits are maladaptive, they can interfere with function, especially during times of crisis. **Personal-**

ity disorders are inflexible or maladaptive behaviors, usually characteristic of long-term functioning, that impair interpersonal or occupational functioning or cause subjective distress. Sometimes personality disorders are identified in childhood. Individuals with personality disorders may have no insight into the role that their own behavior plays in creating problems within their environment. They may rationalize their actions, blaming others for their situation or misfortune without examining their own responsibility for the situation at hand. There are many types of personality disorders (e.g., **paranoid**, **antisocial**, and **borderline**), and they cause varying degrees of impairment.

When a personality disorder exists in combination with other mental disorders, the prognosis is more guarded, and the treatment and management of the personality disorder are more difficult. At times, these individuals may not have a full-blown personality disorder, but rather maladaptive personality traits that may interfere with the treatment or the diagnosis of the concomitant disorder.

Other Types of Disorders

Although not severely disabling, a variety of other types of mental disorders may interfere with effective functioning. **Factitious disorders** are conditions in which individuals voluntarily produce psychological or physical symptoms, feigning illness because of a seemingly compulsive need to assume the sick role. A factitious disorder differs from **malingering** (in which individuals also produce symptoms intentionally), in that the goal of a malingerer is usually obvious, such as a desire to receive an insurance settlement or to collect disability payments.

Individuals with an **adjustment disorder** overreact to a stressor; their reactions persist longer than would be expected in most cases. The symptoms of adjustment disorders vary, but can interfere with social and occupational functioning.

DIAGNOSTIC PROCEDURES

The diagnosis of mental disorders is often an art, as well as a science. It requires skill and experience on the part of those who are evaluating an individual's symptoms and interpreting the results of the various tests designed to measure psychological or intellectual function. Many professionals may be involved in the testing and evaluation; psychiatrists and clinical psychologists are frequently involved in the diagnosis of mental disorders. The diagnosis is usually based on information from a variety of different sources.

Diagnostic and Statistical Manual of Mental Disorders

The American Psychiatric Association developed the *Diagnostic and Statistical Manual of Mental Disorders* in an attempt to establish objective criteria for the diagnosis of mental disorders. In addition to providing specific criteria by which to diagnose mental disorders, it provides consistency among professionals in communicating about mental disorders. The use of the manual for diagnostic purposes requires specialized clinical training, as the criteria within the manual are meant to be guidelines and are not considered absolute. Professionals who work with individuals with mental disorders should be familiar with the manual; however, the responsibility for the diagnosis most frequently lies with psychiatrists, psychologists, and, in some states, social workers.

The first edition of the manual (*DSM-1*) was produced in 1952. Since then, the manual has undergone a series of revisions. Updated versions of the manual bear the number of the edition (e.g., *DSM-III-R*, or revision of the third updated version of the manual). A newer version of the manual, the *DSM IV*, is expected to be published soon.

Diagnostic Psychological Testing

Systematic samples of certain types of verbal, perceptual, intellectual, and motor behavior under standardized conditions can be obtained through psychological testing. The results of psychological tests provide only part of the information needed for the accurate diagnosis of a mental disorder. No single test is adequate to offer a definitive diagnosis in all situations. Often, because mental disorders affect a variety of functions, the use of several psychological tests that measure different functions is required. Psychological tests may be used to evaluate intelligence, personality, or behavior.

Intelligence Tests

The term *intelligence* is difficult to define. Theoretically, intelligence consists of a number of skills and abilities, some of which have no means of measurement. Intelligence is a combination of the individual's own unique mental structure and processes with the individual's cultural and educational experiences. Psychological science has developed a number of tests to define intelligence operationally for a variety of capacities. The most commonly used intelligence tests are the **Wechsler Intelligence Scale for Children-Revised (WISC-R)**, the **Wechsler Preschool and Primary Scale of Intelligence (WPPSI)**, the **Stanford Binet**, and the **Wechsler Adult Intelligence Scale-Revised (WAIS-R)**. The limitations of intelligence testing originate in the difficulty of tapping all aspects of intellectual ability, the effect of the individual's ability to take the test on results, the degree to which the test measures aptitude rather than prior learning and experience, and the impact of cultural variation on test results.

Much intelligence testing involves sampling an individual's intellectual capacity in a variety of different spheres. Many tests focus on the cognitive processes, including problem solving, adaptive thinking, and other aspects of performance. One way of classifying levels of intelligence is through a numerical value known as the **IQ**. There is considerable individual variability in abilities, however, and the results of intelligence tests, like results of other forms of psychological tests, must be evaluated within the context of the individual's cultural and environmental variables. Tests alone should not determine a definitive diagnosis.

Mental Status Examination and Assessment through Interview

The structured interview is one way in which the mental functioning of individuals with a suspected mental disorder may be assessed during the initial evaluation. The information obtained in this way may aid in determining the diagnosis, as well as in making plans for future treatment. Structured interviews provide information regarding the individual's orientation, form and content of thought, speech, affect, and degree of insight. Observations made throughout the interview of the individual's general appearance, behavior, and emotional state are also relevant.

The **mental status examination** is a specific type of structured interview used as a screening instrument in assessing intellectual impairment. Such an examination may be used to detect dementia or impaired intellectual function, as well as to determine to some degree the severity of the impairment. There are several mental status examinations of varying lengths. Although some mental status instruments are part of other instruments that measure functional status, a number of short screening instruments have been devised especially for the purpose of evaluating mental status. One widely used mental status test is the **Short Portable Mental Status Questionnaire (SPMSQ)**, which is used to assess orientation, personal history, remote memory, and calculation. Another short mental status examination is the **Mini-Mental State Examination**, which is used to assess orientation, memory, and attention, as well as the ability to write, name objects, copy a design, and follow verbal and written commands.

Personality Assessment

Personality may be assessed by either objective or projective means. Objective personality assessment instruments are structured, standardized tests for which clear and concise criteria have been established. These tests have undergone research and scientific scrutiny to establish their reliability and validity. Although, numerous objective personality tests are available, one of the most commonly used is the **Minnesota Multiphasic Personality Inventory (MMPI)**. The MMPI has a number of clinical scales that can be useful in the diagnosis of a variety of mental disorders, ranging from schizophrenia to depression, social introversion, and substance abuse.

Projective personality tests, such as the **Rorschach Inkblot Test** and the **Thematic Apperception Test**, also have criteria on which interpretations are based, but they are generally more subjective in nature. Projective testing usually consists of asking the individual to describe vague and ambiguous pictures. There are no right or wrong answers. The assumption is that the way in which the individual interprets the pictures is a reflection of his or her personality. Projective tests may be more time-consuming than are objective tests, and the professionals who administer them require more special training.

As with all other clinical data, the results of personality assessment tests are only part of the total information needed for an accurate diagnosis of a particular mental disorder. No matter what type of test is used, the accuracy of the results is dependent on the individual's honesty and care in answering test questions. If individuals answer questions in a socially desirable way rather than as an expression of their true feelings, the test results can be invalid.

Neuropsychological Testing

Standardized neuropsychological test batteries may be used to assess the major functional areas of the brain. These tests make it possible to assess a variety of cognitive, perceptual, and motor skills. Traditionally, neuropsychological testing has been used to identify or localize brain damage that has behavioral consequences; however, with the newer technological advances such as computed tomography and magnetic resonance imaging, this function is now not widely promoted.

Neuropsychological tests have become increasingly popular to rule out and/or monitor the progression of the symptoms of organic mental disorders. Because an individual's performance on neuropsychological tests changes with brain function, the test results provide a baseline against which future impairment of brain function can be measured, as well as information that can be incorporated into the diagnosis. There are a variety of comprehensive standard neuropsychological test batteries available for adults; two of the more widely recognized tests are the **Halstead-Reitan Battery** and the **Luria-Nebraska Neuropsychological Battery**.

Behavioral Assessment

Some methods of mental function assessment involve direct, systematic observation of the individual's behavior. Trained observers, family members, or even the individuals themselves may monitor and record the individual's behavior. The observation and measurement of behavior may take place in the individual's own environment or in a controlled environment. Behavioral assessment methods are being applied to an increasing number of disorders, as they offer not only information that can be used in diagnosis, but also a method of monitoring improvements in behavior once treatment has been initiated.

TREATMENT

The treatment of mental disorders is based on a comprehensive assessment of the individual's problems and needs. It is usually a collaborative effort that involves the individual, the family, and professionals from a variety of disciplines, such as psychiatrists, psychologists, social workers, nurses, and rehabilitation counselors. Treatment may be provided in a variety of settings, depending on the individual's particular mental disorder and specific needs. Levels of treatment range from the least restrictive, such as that provided in an outpatient setting, to the most restrictive, such as that provided in an institutional setting. Levels of treatment in between include intensive outpatient treatment, residential care, or halfway houses.

Acute episodes of mental disorders may be treated initially by attempts to alleviate the symptoms. Ongoing treatment is directed toward preventing the recurrence of symptoms and/or helping the individual attain maximal functional capacity. Many mental disorders require ongoing treatment or periodic evaluations of the effectiveness of the treatment prescribed. Some mental disorders, like many physical disorders, have periods of remission and periods of exacerbation; some require daily medication in order to control symptoms. In many instances, the individual's willingness and ability to adhere to the prescribed treatment can determine the success of treatment.

A variety of treatment modalities, including both nonpharmacologic and pharmacologic methods, may be used in the treatment of mental disorders. More intensive levels of care may include, in addition to psychotherapy and pharmacologic treatment, occupational therapy, art and music therapy, or recreational therapy. Often, different types of treatment are used simultaneously.

Nonpharmacologic Approaches to Treatment

Psychotherapy

In psychotherapy, a close relationship between the individual and the therapist is used as a therapeutic tool to explore and modify the individual's behavior in order to decrease his or her discomfort and/or to increase his or her satisfaction and productivity. There are several different types of psychotherapy, each having a different theoretical framework: **psychoanalysis, rational-emotive therapy, Gestalt therapy, reality therapy, behavior therapy,** and **transactional analysis.** Although therapists may use a specific theoretical framework predominantly in their treatment approach, many use a variety of therapeutic approaches, depending on which type seems most appropriate for a specific individual.

Psychotherapy may be conducted on an individual basis, in a group, with a family, or between marital partners. Depending on individual need, a combination of therapies may be included in the treatment plan. Individual therapy is directed toward effecting changes in the individual's behavior, while group therapy is directed toward helping the individual develop more satisfying modes of interaction with others. Group therapy may also be **educative,** in which the content is fixed and the goal of the group is to relay information, or **supportive,** in which group members receive and give mutual support and encouragement. Family therapy is directed toward improving the function of the family as an interdependent group. Marital therapy focuses on the marital relationship and the impact of both parties' behaviors on the relationship.

Behavioral Approaches

Behavior is a reflection of inner drives, traits, or patterns of thinking, as well as environmental influences. A number of treatments designed to help individuals modify their learned responses and learn new patterns of more adaptive behavior have been used in the treatment of mental disorders.

Several different forms of behavior therapy have been derived from different theoretical models, including the respondent (classical) model, instrumental (operant) model, observational model, or cognitive learning model. There are countless applications of behavioral approaches in the treatment of mental disorders. Behavior therapy may be used alone or in conjunction with other treatments.

Specialized Groups

Individuals with some types of mental disorders, as part of the disorder, may neglect their own needs of daily living, including personal hygiene, money management, or housing needs. Special groups (e.g., **activities of daily living groups**) may help individuals with these disorders learn the specific skills needed for day-to-day functioning.

Through **social skills training** groups, individuals learn to make specific responses to specific social situations, as well as to recognize relevant social cues and to determine appropriate action by using the cues. Social skills training may involve specific interventions, such as role modeling, feedback and reinforcement, and practice, in helping the individual to perform specified behaviors reliably and to generalize the behavior to other situations.

Individuals with some types of mental disorders may require ongoing supervision, and many require a period of transition from the inpatient to the outpatient setting. A variety of therapeutic living arrangements may be used to meet these needs, including **group homes**, **therapeutic communities**, and **transitional living centers**. **Day programs** provide a structured environment in which individuals may participate in the program during the day and return to the community setting at night. The goal of day programs is to facilitate the adjustment of these individuals to the community setting, to maintain their optimal level of functioning, and to prevent hospitalization.

Pharmacologic Approaches to Treatment

Antipsychotic Medications

The treatment of psychosis may require the use of **antipsychotic medications** (Appendix 15-A). The duration of treatment with antipsychotic medications is determined individually and is based on the individual's life situation and condition. Antipsychotic medications, sometimes called **neuroleptics** or **major tranquilizers**, do not cure psychosis, but rather control the symptoms. They may be prescribed for up to a year as a prophylactic measure after the psychosis is controlled. Medications for all individuals should be reviewed annually to evaluate the possibility of gradual discontinuation.

The first antipsychotic drug, chlorpromazine (Thorazine), was developed in the 1950s. Since that time, a number of other antipsychotic medications have been developed. Antipsychotic drugs are classified into different chemical groups. The drugs in each group have varying potency, and individual responses to any of the medications vary.

It is believed that the symptoms of psychosis may be due to excessive levels of the neurotransmitter *dopamine*. Consequently, it has been postulated that antipsychotic medications reduce symptoms by blocking the action or transmission of dopamine. Because of the blocking of dopamine activity, however, one of the side-effects of antipsychotic medications may be psychomotor symptoms similar to those seen in Parkinson's disease (see Chapter 8). These are called **extrapyramidal effects**, because the changes take place in the extrapyramidal tracts of the central nervous system. The possible extrapyramidal effects of antipsychotic medications include **dystonia**, characterized by severe contractions of the muscles of the jaw, neck, and eye so that the head is turned to one side and the eyes look upward; **akinesia**, characterized by decreased motor activity and apathy; and **akathisia**, characterized by extreme restlessness so that the individual cannot sit still or remain in one place for any length of time. The most severe extrapyramidal side-effect of antipsychotic medications is **tardive dyskinesia**, which consists of abnormal movements of the mouth, such as chewing motions or thrusting movements of the tongue. Tardive dyskinesia often indicates irreversible damage to the brain.

Antiparkinsonian medications, such as benztropine (Cogentin) and trihexphenidyl (Artane), are often prescribed along with antipsychotics in order to prevent these extrapyramidal side-effects. Tardive dyskinesia is best treated through prevention, as the occurrence of the symptom is frequently related to drug dosage. Individuals on antipsychotic medication need careful monitoring by a physician so that the early symptoms of tardive dyskinesia may be identified and the dosage of the medication adjusted to avoid permanent damage.

Individuals on antipsychotic medications may develop **photosensitivity**, which makes them more sensitive to the effects of the sun and predisposes them to sunburn. Some medications that have potent sedating effects may decrease alertness and produce drowsiness. These symptoms usually subside within 2 weeks after the individual begins to take the medication; if they persist, an alteration in medication may be necessary. These individuals may also experience **orthostatic hypotension**, in which their blood pressure drops when they move from a seated or prone position to a standing position, resulting in dizziness or lightheadedness. Individuals may complain of other uncomfortable side-effects, such as dry mouth, after beginning antipsychotic medications; these symptoms generally subside within 2 weeks, however. Men on antipsychotic medication may become impotent or unable to ejaculate. Reducing the dosage or changing the medication may alleviate this side-effect. Any medication change must be conducted under the direction of a physician, however.

Antidepressants

Individuals with a number of mental disorders in which depression is a symptom may be given antidepressants. Although the exact way in which antidepressants work has not been determined, they are classified according to their presumed mode of action. The most widely used antidepressants, **tricyclic antidepressants**, are thought to act by blocking the re-uptake of the neurotransmitters **norepinephrine** and **serotonin**, thus increasing their concentration. The levels of both of these neurotransmitters appear to be reduced in depression. **Monoamine oxidase (MAO) inhibitors**, less frequently used antidepressants, are thought to act by blocking the action of the enzyme monoamine oxidase, which usually breaks down norepinephrine and serotonin, so that the concentration of the neurotransmitters increases.

The type of depression and the symptoms experienced, as well as other individual factors, determine the type of antidepressant used. As with all medications, some side-effects may be experienced. Individuals on tricyclic antidepressants may experience symptoms such as orthostatic hypotension (described previously), dry mouth, or urinary retention. A more serious possible side-effect is the development of cardiac arrhythmias, which can result in myocardial infarction or, in the case of overdose, death.

The use of MAO inhibitors has been limited because of their potential side-effects; however, their use is gaining popularity. Individuals with chronic alcoholism or liver damage are not good candidates for treatment with MAO inhibitors. In addition, there are a number of dietary restrictions associated with their use, and the individuals who use these medications must follow these restrictions carefully in order to prevent potentially serious side-effects. Monoamine oxidase is essential for the metabolism of a substance called **tyramine**, which is present in a number of foods, including aged cheese, wine, beer, chocolate, coffee, and raisins. When individuals who are taking MAO inhibitors ingest tyramine-containing foods, they may experience a hypertensive crisis in which there is sudden and extreme elevation in blood pressure that could result in stroke.

Suicide is always a possibility with individuals who are depressed. The availability of antidepressant medication that could be used in a suicide attempt is a risk to be considered. The risk of attempted suicide may be higher at the beginning of the medication regimen, when the antidepressant begins to take effect and energy returns, but suicidal impulses are still present.

Although antidepressants are an important aspect of treatment for depressive disorders, psychotherapeutic modes of treatment should be used in combination with the pharmacologic approach.

Lithium for Bipolar Disorders

Lithium is an element that occurs naturally as a salt. It has been used in a number of ways for a number of conditions unrelated to mental disorders for more than 100 years. The use of lithium for the treatment of mental disorders in the United States began in the 1970s, and lithium is now widely used in bipolar disorders, both in the treatment of symptoms and in the prevention of recurring symptoms. In some instances, lithium has been used alone or in combination with antidepressants to treat depressive disorders. Because not all individuals respond to lithium in the same way, lithium use is decided on an individual basis.

The way in which lithium works is unclear. It may produce some side-effects, including endocrine effects (e.g., hyperthyroidism), muscle weakness, or weight gain. Other common side-effects include **polyuria** (excessive urination) and **polydipsia** (excessive thirst). Individuals who use lithium should have regular blood tests to measure levels of the medication in the blood and should be monitored by a physician on a regular basis.

Anti-Anxiety Medications

Formerly called **minor tranquilizers**, anti-anxiety medications are generally used for mental disorders in which anxiety is the predominant symptom. Common classifications of anti-anxiety medications are **benzodiazepines** (e.g., diazepam [Valium], oxazepam [Serax], or lorazepam [Ativan]), **barbiturates** (e.g., phenobarbital), or **antihistamines** (e.g., hydroxyzine [Vistaril or Atarax]). The major use of anti-anxiety medication is for time-limited, short-term treatment of anxiety. These medications should not be regarded as the mainstay or sole treatment of anxiety disorders, but rather should be used in combination with other types of treatment, such as psychotherapeutic approaches. Because many anti-anxiety agents also have the risk of abuse or physical dependence, their use should be carefully monitored. Side-effects can include drowsiness and sedation or motor difficulty.

Electroconvulsive Therapy

Before psychopharmacologic preparations were readily available, **electroconvulsive therapy (shock therapy)** was a major mode of treating some mental disorders. Its use has diminished with the advent of a variety of psychotherapeutic drugs, but some centers continue to use it in the treatment of some mental disorders, including depression. It may be especially useful when the long-term administration of medication is contraindicated. Although electroconvulsive therapy does not cure mental disorders, it can bring about a remission of symptoms. It may be used in conjunction with psychotherapeutic medications or alone.

FUNCTIONAL IMPLICATIONS

Psychological Issues

Individuals with mental disorders experience a wide range of symptoms that affect psychological and cognitive function. Although medication benefits many individuals enormously, it may not cure the disorder, but only control symptoms. Many of these individuals have a great many residual symptoms, deficits, and impairments. In addition, many are subject to periodic relapses with recurrence of symptoms.

Individuals with mental disorders may be particularly vulnerable to stress and may lack the ability to withstand pressure or to cope with the normal stresses of everyday life. They may have only a limited ability to solve problems or to engage in self-directed activity. Some individuals may become passive, apathetic, or oversubmissive as a direct result of repeated hospitalizations or of the condition itself.

The symptoms experienced vary with the disorder, causing varying degrees of impairment. Although fear and anger are normal emotional responses, these responses may be acutely disproportionate to the stimuli in some mental disorders. Some individuals' responses are covert, while others' responses are more pronounced. Some individuals manifest their condition through patterns of behavior rather than in emotional manifestations. Others experience subjective distress, such as an inner sense of weakness, jealousy, or anxiety, although function in most of their life is minimally disturbed.

Some mental disorders are characterized by the disorganization of mental capacities, which can affect the ability of an individual to function in an unstructured environment. Disorders of memory and perception can severely limit independent function. Individuals may fail to carry out age-appropriate role functions and have varying degrees of dependence on others.

The symptoms of the disorder may cause psychic stress and anxiety, further compounding the disabling component of the disorder. Individuals' own anguish over their impoverished life may be devastating. Their awareness of their own impaired function and the impact of their condition both on others and on their future may cause considerable pain and discomfort. In some instances, individuals with a mental disorder may be reluctant to seek appropriate help because of their fear of the stigma associated with psychological conditions that require professional help. In other instances, individuals may not be aware of their symptoms and the effect of their symptoms on function, also hindering appropriate treatment.

Life Style Issues

The degree to which mental disorders affect an individual's life style depends to a great extent on the nature of the disorder. Some mental disorders so severely impair the individual's ability to carry on the activities of daily living that constant supervision or hospitalization is necessary. In other instances, the individual may carry on these activities, but in an altered manner.

At times, the treatment itself requires life style changes. Individuals may need to rearrange their schedules so that they may attend therapy sessions. Some medications used in the treatment of mental disorders may require special life style considerations. For example, the use of MAO inhibitors in the treatment of depression requires careful monitoring of diet. Other medications have side-effects, such as drowsiness and sedation, that also affect daily function.

Either the condition or its treatment may alter sexual function. Individuals with a depressive disorder may lose interest in sexual activity, while individuals with a bipolar depression may have excessive sexual interests. The side-effects of some medications can alter sexual function as well. In addition, the subjective manifestations of lowered self-esteem and self-confidence may make it more difficult for individuals to form intimate relationships.

Social Issues

The impact of a mental disorder on social function also depends on the nature of the disorder. Individuals who experience mania as a part of their disorder may enjoy the euphoria and feel that it contributes to their social well-being. If, however, the individual manifests bizarre, abusive, or socially offensive behavior, family members or others within a social group may avoid the individual, leaving him or her socially isolated. Other mental disorders may lead to withdrawal.

The families of individuals with mental disorders may experience a variety of stresses engendered by the condition. These stresses may be caused by their objective problems in dealing with the individual and their condition, as well as by more subjective psychological distress. Mental disorders, especially those in which the individual needs close supervision or long-term care and treatment, may place financial hardships on the family as a result of medical bills, the individual's economic dependency, and special needs related to household functioning. In some instances, the demands of caregiving may require family members to curtail their social activities or alter their relationships with friends and acquaintances. The time commitments of caregiving may lead to neglect of other family members' needs, further disrupting the family as a unit.

Social barriers are frequently erected against individuals with a mental disorder and against their families. The social stigma may be the result of fear of the individual's behavior, ignorance about mental disorders, or feelings of inadequacy in interacting with those who have mental disorders. Regardless of the cause, the results can be a source of continuing stress for these individuals and their families as well as a barrier to social activity and interaction.

Vocational Issues

The ability of individuals with mental disorders to work depends on the type of disorder, the type of work in which they are involved, and the attitudes of those within the work setting. Although work is important to increase self-esteem for those with a number of disabilities, it can be an especially strong therapeutic tool for those with a mental disorder.

Not only the skills, aptitude, motivation, and objective symptoms of the individual with a mental disorder, but also the individual's ability to endure and cope with stress and to engage in active problem solving determine the individual's ability to work. Job restrictions may be related to job pressure or the ability to work with others, regardless of the individual's level of skill or physical and cognitive ability to perform work-related tasks.

Other considerations may relate to the individual's treatment. It may be necessary to arrange scheduled absences so that the individual can attend therapy sessions. Some medications used in treatment may produce side-effects, such as drowsiness or sedation, that could adversely affect work performances. In addition, the individual's level of compliance with the therapeutic regimen is especially important if failure to do so means possible relapse and recurrence of symptoms.

The individual's reaction to the work environment, including noise and distractions should be taken into account, as should the individual's level of personal responsibility and ability for self-direction and decision making. Some individuals may need a more structured work environment; in some instances, a workshop environment may be preferable. Some individuals' expectations of work or assessment of their own capabilities may be unrealistic. Unless these unrealistic notions are identified and dealt with before they enter or reenter the work setting, discouragement, disappointment, or even relapse may occur.

Supported employment may be successful for a number of individuals with mental disorders. In supported employment, individuals work in integrated settings with monitoring, support, and follow-up provided on a regular basis. Supported employment provides permanent jobs that are based on the individual's skills and abilities. This model is useful for individuals with intellectual disabilities, as well as other types of mental disorders.

Social skills, aptitude, and the ability to work are not necessarily concurrent in individuals with mental disorders. Employment for each individual must be considered in the context of the individual's particular symptoms and feelings, and the nature of the work environment. The role that social stigma plays in individuals' perceptions of their own condition and their willingness to accept and follow up with treatment are crucial aspects in the total rehabilitation of individuals with mental disorders.

BIBLIOGRAPHY

American Psychiatric Association. *Diagnostic and Statistical Manual of Mental Disorders.* 3rd ed., rev. Washington, D.C.: American Psychiatric Association, 1987.

Baroff, G.S. *Mental Retardation: Nature, Cause, and Management.* Washington, D.C.: Hemisphere Publishing Corp., 1986.

Berheim, K.F. "Psychologists and Families with the Severely Mentally Ill." *American Psychologist* 44(1989):561–564.

Boza, R.A.; Milanes, F.J.; and Hanna, S.G. "Memory Dysfunction." *Resident and Staff Physician* 36(1990):23–28.

Cancro, R.; Falloon, I.R.H.; and Guze S.B. "Zeroing in on Schizophrenia." *Patient Care* 18(1984): 66–94.

Corsini, R.J. *Current Psychotherapies*. Ihasca, Ill.: F.E. Peacock Publishers, 1979.

Dilsaver, S.C. "The Mental Status Examination." *American Family Physician* 41(1990): 1489–1495.

Donlon, P.T., and Rockwell, D.A. *Psychiatric Disorders: Diagnosis and Treatment*. Bowie, Md.: Robert J. Brady Co., 1982.

Finlayson, R. "Recognition and Management of Dysthymic Disorder." *American Family Physician* 40(1989):229–238.

Gold, P.W.; Goodwin, F.K.; and Chrousos, G.P. "Clinical and Biochemical Manifestations of Depression—Relation to the Neurobiology of Stress." *New England Journal of Medicine* 319(1988):413–420.

Goldstein, G., and Hersen, M., eds. *Handbook of Psychological Assessment*. New York: Pergamon Press, 1984.

Greene, R.L. *The MMPI: An Interpretive Manual*. Orlando, Fla.: Grune & Stratton, 1980.

Greist, J.; Papoport, J.L.; and Rasmussen, S.A. "Spotting the Obsessive-Compulsive." *Patient Care* 24(1990):47–73.

Grossman, H.J. *Classification in Mental Retardation*. Washington, D.C.: American Association on Mental Deficiency, 1983.

Kavan, M.G.; Pace, T.M.; Ponterotto, J.G.; and Barone, E.J. "Screening for Depression: Use of Patient Questionnaires." *American Family Physician*. 41(1990):897–903.

Lancaster, J. *Adult Psychiatric Nursing*. Garden City, N.Y.: Medical Examination Publishing Co., 1980.

Lawson, G.W., and Cooperrider, C.A. *Clinical Psychopharmacology: A Practical Reference for Nonmedical Psychotherapists*. Gaithersburg, Md.: Aspen Publishers, 1988.

Lefley, H.P. "Family Burden and Family Stigma in Major Mental Illness." *American Psychologist* 44(1989):556–560.

Lego, S., ed. *The American Handbook of Psychiatric Nursing*. Philadelphia: J.B. Lippincott Co., 1984.

Levensen, J.A. *Basic Psychopharmacology*. New York: Springer Publishing Co., 1981.

National Institute of Handicapped Research. "People with Chronic Schizophrenia: Their Rehabilitation Outlook." *Rehab Brief* 6(1983):1–4.

National Institute on Disability and Rehabilitation Research. "New Strategies in Psychiatric Rehabilitation." *Rehab Brief* 12(1989):1–4.

Rakel, R.E. *Conn's Current Therapy 1990*. Philadelphia: W.B. Saunders Co., 1990.

Scheer, S.J., ed. *Medical Perspectives in Vocational Assessment of Impaired Workers*. Gaithersburg, Md.: Aspen Publishers, 1991.

Schvehla, T.J.; Faust, L.J.; Herjanic, M.; and Muniz, C.E. "Lithium Therapy for Affective Disorders." *American Family Physician* 36(1987):169–175.

Silver, F.W., and Ruckle, J.L. "Depression—Management Techniques in Primary Care." *Postgraduate Medicine* 86(1989):359–366.

Stolov, W.C., and Clowers, M.R. *Handbook of Severe Disability*. Washington, D.C.: U.S. Department of Education, Rehabilitation Services Administration, 1981.

Young, J.T. "Controlling Side Effects of Antipsychotic Drugs. Part 2: Extrapyramidal Symptoms." *Family Practice Recertification* 9(1987):97–105.

Appendix 15-A

Common Antipsychotic Medications

Group	Generic Name	Trade Name
Phenothiazines		
Aliphatics	Chlorpromazine	Thorazine
	Triflupromazine	Vesprin
Piperidines	Thioridazine	Mellaril
	Mesoridazine	Serentil
Piperazines	Fluphenazine hydrochloride	Prolixin Hydrochloride
	Fluphenazine enanthate	Prolixin Enanthate
	Fluphenazine decanoate	Prolixin Decanoate
	Perphenazine	Trilafon
	Trifluoperazine	Stelazine
Butyrophenones	Haloperidol	Haldol
Thioxanthenes	Thiothixene	Navane
	Chlorprothixene	Taractan
Dibenzoxazepines	Loxapine	Loxitane
Dihydroindolones	Molindone	Moban

Source: Reprinted from *Clinical Psychopharmacology: A Practial Reference for Nonmedical Psychotherapists* by G.W. Lawson and C.A. Cooperrider, p. 74, Aspen Publishers Inc., © 1988.

Glossary of Medical Terms

abduction movement of a body part away from the midline of the body

accommodation change in the shape of the lens to help the eye to focus for near or far vision

active exercise individual's independent performance of a specified exercise regimen under the direction or supervision of the physical therapist

adaptation chemical process in which the eye adjusts to see in the dark

adduction movement of a body part toward the midline of the body

agnosia inability to interpret sounds or visual images, or to distinguish objects by touch

akinesia complete or partial absence of movement

allergy hypersensitivity to a specific substance or substances from previous exposure

alopecia hair loss

anaplastic term to describe cancer cells that take on abnormal characteristics, making them less differentiated than the normal cells from which they are derived

anasarca generalized edema

anastomosis procedure to remove or resect the diseased portion of the intestine and surgically connect the two remaining ends of intestine

aneurysm blood-filled sac formed by a dilation of the walls of an artery or vein

ankylosis stiffness

anomia inability to name objects or remember names

anorexia appetite loss

anosognosia one-sided neglect (e.g., condition in which individuals are unable to see objects on either the right or the left of the central field of vision)

anoxia lack of oxygen

anuria condition in which the kidney is unable to excrete urine

aphasia inability to recognize, manipulate, and/or express words or ideas (e.g., as a result of traumatic brain injury)

apraxia loss of ability to organize and sequence specific muscle movements in order to perform a task

arrhythmia abnormality of the heart rhythm

arthritis joint inflammation

articulation joint

ascites retention of fluid in the abdominal cavity

astigmatism distortion of the visual image due to an irregularity in the shape of the cornea or lens

ataxia impairment of muscle coordination

atelectasis collapse of the lung

atrophy shrinkage

aura warning (flash of light or other unusual sensation) prior to a seizure

bacteremia presence of bacteria in the bloodstream

benign noncancerous tumor

biopsy removal of a small portion of tissue from the body so that it may be examined microscopically (e.g., needle biopsy)

blindness total loss of light perception

bradycardia low heart beat

bradykinesia extreme slowness of movement

calculi renal stones

cancer cellular tumor; not one disease, but a broad term used to describe many diseases

carcinogens chemicals or other substances that are thought to cause cancer

carcinoma cancer of the epithelial cells

cardiomegaly enlargement of the heart

chorea jerky involuntary movements

cimetidine *See* histamine H_2 (receptor antagonist), Glossary of Medications

circumduction circular movement

clonic pertaining to jerky movement of muscle

coma state of unconsciousness

concussion mild to moderate head injury in which there is a loss of consciousness, varying from a few minutes to 24 hours after the injury

contracture deformity in which there is a permanent contraction of a muscle, resulting in the immobility of a joint

contusion soft tissue injury resulting from a blunt, diffuse blow in which the skin is not broken, nor are bones broken, but local hemorrhage occurs with associated bruising and damage to deep soft tissue under the skin

creatinine waste product eliminated by the kidney

cystitis inflammation of the bladder

cytology study of cells

deafness inability to discriminate conversational speech through the ear
débride remove dead tissue
decibels (dB) sound intensity or loudness
decubitus ulcers pressure sores
dementia mental deterioration
dialysis artificial means to replace for kidney function
diastole phase of heart activity when the heart is relaxed and the chambers are
    filling
diplopia double vision
dislocation displacement or separation of a bone from its normal joint position
distal farthest from the center body
dorsiflexion backward movement
dysarthria impairment in the coordination and accuracy of the movement of
    the lips, tongue, or other parts of the speech mechanism
dysgraphia impaired writing ability
dyskinesia abnormal involuntary movements
dyslexia inability to understand written words
dyspepsia indigestion
dysphagia difficulty in swallowing
dyspnea difficulty in breathing
dysuria painful urination

ecchymosis purplish discoloration at the site of injury due to bleeding under the
    skin
edema presence of abnormally large amounts of fluid in tissue spaces
edematous swollen
electrolytes electrically charged particles that are important to many of the
    body's internal functions (e.g., sodium and potassium)
embolus foreign particle or blood clot that travels in the bloodstream until it
    lodges in a blood vessel too small to allow its passage
epidural pertaining to the space between the dura and the skull
erythema redness
eschar dead tissue resulting from burns
eversion outward-turning movement
exacerbation time period when symptoms become worse
exophthalmos abnormal protrusion of the eyeball
expiration expulsion of air from the lungs
extension straightening movement

fistula opening between two tubular structures
flexion bending movement

glucosuria glucose in the urine
goiter swelling of the neck due to enlargement of the thyroid gland
grading system used to describe the structure of cancer cells

hearing impairment any degree and type of hearing disorder
hemarthrosis bleeding in the joint
hematemesis vomiting of blood
hematoma sac filled with accumulated blood
hematuria blood in the urine
hemiplegia paralysis on one side of the body
hemolysis destruction of red blood cells
hemopoiesis process by which blood cells are formed
hemoptysis blood-streaked sputum
hemostasis cessation of bleeding from damaged vessels
hernia (rupture) protrusion of an organ through the tissues in which it is
  normally contained
hertz (Hz) sound frequency or pitch
histology study of the structure of tissue
homeostasis maintenance of an internal chemical balance within the body
hypercapnia buildup of carbon dioxide
hyperglycemia accumulation of large amounts of glucose in the blood
hyperopia farsightedness
hyperproliferation overgrowth of renal cells due to a tumor
hypertrophy enlargement
hypoxemia decreased level of oxygen in the blood

immunosuppression suppression of the immune system
in situ state in which cancer cells are present, but remain localized (i.e., they
  have not invaded the surrounding lymph nodes)
incontinence loss of control of bladder or bowel
infarction death of tissue due to lack of blood supply
inspiration inhalation of air into the lungs
intermittent claudication aching, cramping, or fatigue of muscles in the legs
  when walking
inversion inward-turning movement
ischemia inadequate blood supply

jaundice yellowish appearance of the skin and whites of the eyes due to an excess level of bilirubin in the blood

ketoacidosis condition caused by an excessive level of ketones in the blood,
  which increases the acidity of the blood to toxic levels

ketone metabolic product of fat metabolism
ketosis buildup of ketone bodies in the blood
kyphosis (hump back) permanent postural deformity of the back

laceration injury involving a tear or cut in the skin and underlying tissues
language set of symbols combined in a certain way to convey concepts, ideas, and emotions
laparotomy surgical incision into the abdomen
legal blindness central visual acuity not exceeding 20/200 in the better eye with correcting lenses or central field of vision limited to an angle of no greater than 20 degrees
leukemia cancer of the tissues in which blood is formed
leukocytosis white blood cell proliferation
lordosis swayback
lymphadenopathy swollen lymph nodes
lymphedema swelling of the arm on the side of a mastectomy
lymphoma cancer of the lymphatic system

malignancy cancer
malignant cancerous
melanoma cancer of the pigment-producing cells
melena passage of dark tarry bowel movements
metastasis movement of cancer cells from their orginal site to another part of the body
micrographia reduction in handwriting size
mutation alteration or change of the DNA within the normal cell
myopia nearsightedness

necrosis tissue death
necrotic dead
neoplasm new and abnormal growth of cells that serve no useful function and may interfere with healthy tissue function
nephrosis general term used to describe conditions, other than direct infection of the kidney itself, that damage the kidney
neuropathy general term to describe functional disturbances or changes in the peripheral nervous system
nocturnal dyspnea difficulty in breathing while lying down at night
nystagmus involuntary eye movement

occult hidden
oliguria decreased production of urine

ophthalmologist physician who specializes in conditions and treatment of the eye

orthosis any mechanical device applied to the body to control motion of the joints and to control force or weight distribution on a body part

orthotist individual who constructs the orthosis to meet individual need

otolaryngologist physician who specializes in disorders of the ear and related structures

pallor pale-appearing skin

palpitations awareness of beating of the heart

pancreatitis inflammation of the pancreas

paraparesis incomplete paralysis below injury of the spinal cord

paresthesia sensation of numbness or tingling of some part of the body

passive exercise exercise of a body part by a therapist or by a mechanical device

pathologist physician who specializes in the diagnosis of abnormal changes in tissues

percussion manual tapping or vibration of the chest or other body cavity

perfusion blood supply to an organ

phlebotomy removal of quantities of blood to reduce plasma volume

polydipsia excessive and constant thirst

polyuria excessive urination

presbycusis hearing loss due to aging

presbyopia loss of the ability of the lens to accommodate to near and far images

pronation downward-turning movement

prosthesis fabricated substitute for a missing part for activities, occupation, and cosmetic needs

prosthetist individual who specializes in making prosthetic devices

proteinuria protein in the urine

pruritus itching of the skin

purulent pertaining to pus-containing material

radial deviation lateral movement of the hand inward toward the body

radiologist physician who specializes in radiographic procedures

recruitment hearing impairment characterized by an abnormal increase in the perception of loudness

remission period of weeks to years when symptoms subside

retinopathy disease or disorder of the retina

sarcoma cancers of the bone, muscle, or other connective tissue

scoliosis lateral curvature of the spine

sepsis widespread infection throughout the body
septicemia presence of toxins in the blood
speech verbal expression of language concepts
splenomegaly enlargement of the spleen
sprain injury to a ligament and its attachment site because of overstress
staging system to describe the extent to which cancer cells have spread
stasis stagnation of urine
stenosis narrowing of a vessel or tube
strabismus disorder in which the eyes cannot be directed to the same object or one eye deviates from the central tract
strain injury to the tendons and muscles due to overstretching or overuse
subdural pertaining to the space beneath the dura
subluxation dislocation when bone is not totally separated from the joint
supination upward-turning movement
syncope fainting, and visual or speech difficulties
systole contraction phase of the heart's work

tachycardia fast heart beat
tamponade pathological compression of a part
tetany involuntary contraction of the muscles
thrombocytopenia decrease in platelet number
thrombocytosis increase in platelet number
thrombus blood clot
tinnitus ringing in the ears
tonic rigid
tophi deposits of crystals in the joints
traction therapeutic method in which a mechanical or manual pull is used to restore or maintain the alignment of bones or to relieve pain and muscle spasm
tumor new and abnormal growth of cells that serve no useful function and may interfere with healthy tissue function

ulnar deviation lateral movement of the hand away from the body
urea waste product eliminated by the kidney
uremia buildup of waste products (e.g., urea and creatinine) in the blood
urticaria allergic response in which hives appear in skin

venesection removal of quantities of blood to reduce plasma volume
ventilation process by which gases are transported between the atmosphere and the alveoli
vertigo dizziness
visual impairment any deviation of normal vision

Glossary of Medications

antacid medication that counteracts excessive acidity

anti-arrhythmic medication to stabilize the rhythm of the heart

antibiotic/antibacterial medication for skin disorders caused by bacteria

anticholinergic medication that inhibits the action of the involuntary nervous system

anticoagulant medication that reduces the coagulability of blood and clot formation

anticonvulsant (anti-epileptic) medication that may effectively control seizures.

antidiarrheic medication given to prevent diarrhea

anti-emetic medication that prevents nausea and vomiting

antifungal medication for skin disorders caused by fungus

antihypertensive medication to lower blood pressure

antimicrobial (sulfonamide) medication that inhibits the growth of microorganisms

antineoplastic medication chemical agent used for systemic treatment of cancer

antipruritic topical medication to reduce discomfort due to itching

antithrombotic agent medication that decreases clotting

antithyroid medication drug that blocks thyroid hormone production

antiviral medication for skin disorders caused by viruses

azidothymidine (AZT) drug in clinical use found to prolong the survival period of AIDS patients

bronchodilator medication that helps to open the airways to permit air to pass more freely in and out of lungs

cardiotonic medication   medication that changes heart rhythm and rate, and generally strengthens the heart

cathartic and laxative   medication given for constipation

cholinergic   medication that stimulates the effect of the parasympathetic nervous system

corticosteroid   medication that can produce dramatic short-term anti-inflammatory effects

digestant   medication given when there is an enzyme deficiency in the gastrointestinal tract

digitalis preparation   medication that increases the pumping action of the heart muscle

diuretic   medication that helps rid the body of excess fluid

expectorant   oral medication that makes mucus thinner and easier to cough up

histamine H$_2$ (receptor antagonist)   new class of pharmacologic agents that blocks cells in the stomach lining from producing acid (e.g., Cimetidine)

hypoglycemic agent   oral medication that lowers blood sugar

immunosuppressant   medication that blocks the body's natural response to foreign substances

L-dopa   drug given to decrease the symptoms of Parkinson's disease

muscle relaxant (antispasmotic)   medication to reduce abnormal movement

nitroglycerine   medication that dilates the coronary arteries, enabling the heart muscle to receive more oxygen

nonsteroidal anti-inflammatory drugs (NSAIDs)   medications that reduce pain and inflammation

salicylate   aspirin

steroid   hormonal preparation that helps to reduce swelling

sulfasalazine (sulfonamide)   medication frequently prescribed in the treatment of inflammatory bowel disease to prevent or to control infections that occur because of the susceptibility of the inflamed bowel to infection

synthroid   synthetic thyroid preparation

Index

Note: Page numbers in *italics* indicate figures, tables, and exhibits.

C

Respiratory system
    alcohol-related illnesses and, 331
    anatomy and function of, 47 49, *48*
    disorders of. *See* Respiratory disorders
    lung cancer, treatment of, 288
Resting tremor, in Parkinson's disease, 193
Reticulocytes, 300
Retina, *242,* 242–243
    detached, 247
Retinitis pigmentosa, 247
Retinopathy, 246–247
    as complication of diabetes mellitus, 99
Retrograde pyelography, in renal and
    urinary tract disorders evaluation, 78–79
Retrovir, 316
Retruitment, hearing loss leading to, 222
Rheumatic disease, of the heart, 32
Rheumatoid arthritis, 141–142
    autoimmune response and, 302
    treatment of, 164–165
Rheumatoid factor test, in musculoskeletal
    evaluation, 157
Right ventricular failure, in COPD, 52
Roentgenography
    of chest and chest cavity. *See* Chest
        roentgenography
    of kidney, ureters, and bladder (KUB), 78
    of musculoskeletal system, 155
    of skull and spine, 200
Role, potential threats to, 2
Rorschach Inkblot Test, 365
"Rule of Nines," 266, *267*
Rupture. *See* Hernia
Ruptured disc, 145–146, *146*

S

Salicylates
    for musculoskeletal and connective
        tissue disorders, 161
    for rheumatoid arthritis, 164
    for systemic lupus erythematosus,
        165
Scanning speech, as multiple sclerosis
    symptom, 192

Scarring
    from drug injections, 341
    following burns. 266–267, 270
Schizophrenia
    active form of, 357
    phases of, 357–358
    symptoms and causes of, 356–357
    types of, 357
Schlemm, canal of. *See* Canal of Schlemm
School-aged child, developmental stages
    in, 12–13
Sciatica, 146–147
Scleral buckling, 252
Scoliosis, 147
    following amputation, 153–154
Scrapings, in skin disorder evaluation, 268
Secondary parkinsonianism, 193
Secretions, clearance in respiratory
    disorders, 58–59
Sedatives, use of, 335–336
Segmental resection, in lung cancer, 288
Seizures. *See* Epilepsy
Self-concept
    body image in, 3
    negative, 3
Sensorineural hearing impairment, 221
Septicemia, as hemodialysis complication, 86
Serum creatinine determination, in renal
    and urinary tract evaluation, 78
Serum thyroxine test, 100
Sexuality, 16
    and sexual fuction. *See* Life style
Sexually transmittted disease, drug use and,
    343
Shaking palsy. *See* Parkinson's disease
Shingles, 264
Shock therapy, 371
Short Portable Mental Status Questionnaire
    (SPMSQ), 364
Shortness of breath. *See* Dyspnea
Sickle cell anemia
    blood flow affected by, 307
    carriers of, 308
    disease course, 307–308
    disorders resulting from, 308